The Gospels in Anglish

© 2010 Julian Montinaro. All rights reserved
ISBN 978-0-557-83132-6

Alderlong thanks to the beshaper of
ednewenglish.tripod.com from whence the mosthood
of the wordbook comes, and without whom this
undertaking would have been much harder

Foreword

Is not 'aftertale' better sounding and more transparent in its etymology than 'epilogue,' and is 'lawcraft' not more homely and English-sounding than 'jurisprudence,' and 'wordbook' clearer than 'dictionary,' and 'manslaughter' more image-evoking and powerful than 'homicide.' Fordo (destroy), forsend (dismiss), forespeak (predict), winterwone (hibernate), elderdom (supremacy), owndom (property), speechlore (linguistics), starcraft (astronomy), withfare (escape), withlead (abduct), and the list goes on.

English is often obscured by our use of Latin and Greek words. So often a word newly met cannot be understood from its parts, and one must have recourse to a wordbook to find its meaning. 'Consanguinity,' for example. What on earth could that possibly mean? says every English speaker upon first encountering it. We recognize that it is made up of several parts, the 'con-,' like in 'confess,' 'concede,' 'conceive,' and the '-ity' we recognize. We know the -ity' makes the word a noun (or how about a thingword), but the 'Con' and the 'sanguin' we do not the meaning of unless we are familiar with a latin language. So, how then are we to deduce its meaning? Truth be told, we simply cannot, not without the help of a dictionary, our beloved wordbook. This is a rather unfortunate thing, for what is the value of words if they are not understood? Perhaps we should be more like the Germans, or any other Germanic speaking folk for that matter, and use more fully our native English morphemes— wordbits that English speakers can understand with the accursed dictionary that makes learning our tongue so detached, and so cold and intellectual. That way we could talk to virtually any English speaker about abstract topics, and use words like 'samebloodedness' instead of 'consanguinity' to express them. One could even speak to a five year old about samebloodedness and be understood. But how lofty and pretentious one seems when one uses words like consanguinity. Consanguinity— "bah, please, English, speak thine own tongue." Does 'con' not mean 'same,' does 'sanguin' not mean 'blood', and is 'ity' not alike unto 'ness?' And do they not all three— 'same,' 'blood,' and 'ness,' have as their sustenance the very depths and core of the soul of English? Do they not subsist on the flesh and blood of Englishness, and take it up into themselves, heralding the glory of its lifeblood and provider with every utterance of themselves that cometh forth out of the tongues of English speaker?

And the same goes for 'assume,' translated from its Latin parts into 'take on;' and 'presume' into 'foretake,' and 'deduce' into 'lead off,' and 'anatomy' into 'bodylore,' 'dermatology' into 'skinlore,' 'biology' into 'lifelore,' 'aerology' onto 'skylore,' 'transcribe' into 'yondwrite' and 'compare' into 'aliken.' In almost all cases the Anglish word simply makes more sense, the meaning of the word can be seen in its parts, without knowledge of Latin, without dictionary that shows etymology, for its parts are English indeed. This makes English more transparent, and for the aesthetically inclined, more beautiful, as it connects structure (English structure) to meaning

Not in all cases though, is the Anglish word gotten by a simple translation of the Latin word. Sometimes this produces words that simply don't capture the desired meaning. 'Defeat' translated morpheme by morpheme is 'undo,' and though having a similar figurative meaning as 'defeat,' it is perhaps not good enough. Anglish then is forced to innovate, using native English words and morphemes, mixing and combining them. 'Netherlay,' a cognate of the German 'niederlagen,' perhaps works better for 'destroy' than does 'undo,' or how about the more colloquial sounding 'to down under,' as in "The Spartans downed the enemy under."

Sometimes Anglish becomes simply about choosing native, or Germanic words over their French equivalents whenever mightly (another cognate from Germanic tongues— like the German 'm glich') — choosing 'motherly' instead of 'maternal,' 'earthly' instead of 'terrestrial,' 'water' instead of 'aqua,' at least using these native English words often enough to ensure they don't meet the same fate as the sorry lot of our many lost and forsaken Anglo-Saxon words.

Still other times Anglish looks to English's birth-giver, Old English, and uses Old English words that did not make it into modern English. This is sometimes done out of necessity, as neither translation of foreign morphemes into English morphemes, nor coining seems to work. Often times though OE words are resurrected simply because Anglish looks upon them with great regret and sorrow— so many lovely words of English spirit left to perish in history— the shame of it is to intense not to bring some back to life.

Though if you are not convinced of the above-mentioned reasons for Anglish, one reason for it still stands— its being an academic pursuit that explores the Germanic side of English, and of its Germanic potential; and that plays with the idea of what English would be like had history taken another route.

It is for the purpose of exploring what English would be like without its many foreign words, and for the purpose of making Anglish more widely known, in the hope that it might gain foothold among English speakers and writers, that I have wrought this work. I chose to translate the gospels, forwhy of the widespread familiarity with the gospels, and forwhy of its great linguistic importance. The bible is an important tool in linguistics and language comparison. The Our Father for example is widely known as being used to this end. The gospels are set over from the Authourized King James Version, mostly out of whim, thought it is rather appropriate that I should translate from this version, as its being highly Latinate makes the difference between it and its Anglish translation starker, thus allowing the translation's Anglishness to be shown more fully.

The Anglish words found in these four gospels are in large part resurrections of Old English words left behind. They get there proposed modern forms by having had applied to them the phonological and orthographical changes English went through to get to its now-time form. The words in their original Old English form can be found in Clark Hall's *A Concise Anglo-Saxon Dictionary University of Toronto Press; 4th edition edition (April 1 1984)*— the best Old English wordbook I know of. The rest are either archaic words or words coined from Saxon roots. Most of these words, as well as many more words not found in these gospels, can be found in the word-hoard found at the end of the four gospels.

And lastly, lest I be called a hypocrite, I must give reason for my use of so many foreign words in this foreword. It is essential that the foreword be understood, as it gives information about the contents of the work. I do not wish to hinder understanding of it for those who read it. The foreword therefore, had to be written in Standard English. But do not fret, there's plenty of Anglish in these the four Gospels, for the one who careth enough to read them.

Bible, King James Version

Matthew

Matt.1

[1] The book of the strind of Jesus Christ, the son of David, the son of Abraham.
[2] Abraham begat Isaac; and Isaac begat Jacob; and Jacob begat Judas and his brethren;
[3] And Judas begat Phares and Zara of Thamar; and Phares begat Esrom; and Esrom begat Aram;
[4] And Aram begat Aminadab; and Aminadab begat Naasson; and Naasson begat Salmon;
[5] And Salmon begat Booz of Rachab; and Booz begat Obed of Ruth; and Obed begat Jesse;
[6] And Jesse begat David the king; and David the king begat Solomon of her that had been the wife of Urias;
[7] And Solomon begat Roboam; and Roboam begat Abia; and Abia begat Asa;
[8] And Asa begat Josaphat; and Josaphat begat Joram; and Joram begat Ozias;
[9] And Ozias begat Joatham; and Joatham begat Achaz; and Achaz begat Ezekias;
[10] And Ezekias begat Manasses; and Manasses begat Amon; and Amon begat Josias;
[11] And Josias begat Jechonias and his brethren, about the time they were carried away to Babylon:
[12] And after they were brought to Babylon, Jechonias begat Salathiel; and Salathiel begat Zorobabel;
[13] And Zorobabel begat Abiud; and Abiud begat Eliakim; and Eliakim begat Azor;
[14] And Azor begat Sadoc; and Sadoc begat Achim; and Achim begat Eliud;
[15] And Eliud begat Eleazar; and Eleazar begat Matthan; and Matthan begat Jacob;
[16] And Jacob begat Joseph the husband of Mary, of whom was born Jesus, who is called Christ.
[17] So all the strinds from Abraham to David are fourteen strinds; and from David until the carrying away into Babylon are fourteen strinds; and from the carrying away into Babylon unto Christ are fourteen strinds.
[18] Now the birth of Jesus Christ was on this wise: When as his mother Mary was betrothed to Joseph, before they came together, she was found with child of the Holy Ghost.
[19] Then Joseph her husband, being a rightful man, and not willing to make her a folkish bisen, was minded to put her away in dern.
[20] But while he thought on these things, behold, the woulderghost of the Lord trod up unto him in a dream, saying, Joseph, thou son of David, fear not to take unto thee Mary thy wife: for that which is ataken in her is of the Holy Ghost.
[21] And she shall bring forth a son, and thou shalt call his name JESUS: for he shall redd his theed from their sins.
[22] Now all this was done, that it might be fulfilled which was spoken of the Lord by the forequeether, saying,
[23] Behold, a maiden shall be with child, and shall bring forth a son, and they shall call his name Emmanuel, which being awended is, God with us.
[24] Then Joseph being raised from sleep did as the woulderghost of the Lord had bidden him, and took unto him his wife:
[25] And knew her not till she had brought forth her firstborn son: and he called his name JESUS.

Matt.2

[1] Now when Jesus was born in Bethlehem of Judaea in the days of Herod the king, behold, there came wise men from the east to Jerusalem,
[2] Saying, Where is he that is born King of the Jews? for we have seen his tungle in the east, and are come to worship him.
[3] When Herod the king had heard these things, he was dreeved, and all Jerusalem with him.
[4] And when he had gathered all the alderpriests and scribes of the theed together, he fraigned of them where Christ should be born.
[5] And they said unto him, In Bethlehem of Judaea: for thus it is written by the forequeether,
[6] And thou Bethlehem, in the land of Juda, art not the least among the athelings of Juda: for out of thee shall

come a Awieldend, that shall rule my theed Israel.
[7] Then Herod, when he had in dern called the wise men, asked workfastly of them what time the tungle trod up.
[8] And he sent them to Bethlehem, and said, Go and seek workfastly the young child; and when ye have found him, bring me word again, that I may come and worship him also.
[9] When they had heard the king, they wote; and, lo, the tungle, which they saw in the east, went before them, till it came and stood over where the young child was.
[10] When they saw the tungle, they agleed with outest great mirth.
[11] And when they were come into the house, they saw the young child with Mary his mother, and fell down, and worshipped him: and when they had opened their mathem, they laid before him gifts; gold, and frankstoor, and myrrh.
[12] And being warned of God in a dream that they should not edwharve to Herod, they wote into their own folkdom another way.
[13] And when they were witen, behold, the woulderghost of the Lord trod up to Joseph in a dream, saying, Arise, and take the young child and his mother, and flee into Egypt, and be thou there until I bring thee word: for Herod will seek the young child to forswithe him.
[14] When he arose, he took the young child and his mother by night, and wote into Egypt:
[15] And was there until the death of Herod: that it might be fulfilled which was spoken of the Lord by the forequeether, saying, Out of Egypt have I called my son.
[16] Then Herod, when he saw that he was bismered of the wise men, was outestly wroth, and sent forth, and slew all the children that were in Bethlehem, and in all the coasts thereof, from two years old and under, by to the time which he had dofastly fraigned of the wise men.
[17] Then was fulfilled that which was spoken by Jeremy the forequeether, saying,
[18] In Rama was there a rord heard, cwithing, and weeping, and great mourning, Rachel weeping for her children, and would not be frovered, forwhy they are not.
[19] But when Herod was dead, behold, a woulderghost of the Lord trod up in a dream to Joseph in Egypt,
[20] Saying, Arise, and take the young child and his mother, and go into the land of Israel: for they are dead which sought the young child's life.
[21] And he arose, and took the young child and his mother, and came into the land of Israel.
[22] But when he heard that Archelaus did reign in Judaea in the room of his father Herod, he was afraid to go thither: notwithstanding, being warned of God in a dream, he whorve aside into the stows of Galilee:
[23] And he came and dwelt in a chester called Nazareth: that it might be fulfilled which was spoken by the forequeethers, He shall be called a Nazarene.

Matt.3

[1] In those days came John the Forwasher, preaching in the wilderness of Judaea,
[2] And saying, Berue ye: for the kingdom of heaven is at hand.
[3] For this is he that was spoken of by the forequeether Esaias, saying, The steven of one shouting out in the wilderness, Prepare ye the way of the Lord, make his paths straight.
[4] And the same John had his clothing of camel's hair, and a leathern girdle about his loins; and his meat was locusts and wild honey.
[5] Then went out to him Jerusalem, and all Judaea, and all the steaddeal imb about Jordan,
[6] And were forwashed of him in Jordan, adetting their sins.
[7] But when he saw many of the Pharisees and Sadducees come to his forwashing, he said unto them, O strinds of vipers, who hath warned you to flee from the wrath to come?
[8] Bring forth therefore ovet meet for berueance:
[9] And think not to say within yourselves, We have Abraham to our father: for I say unto you, that God is able of these stones to raise up children unto Abraham.
[10] And now also the axe is laid unto the root of the trees: therefore every tree which bringeth not forth good ovet is hewn down, and cast into the fire.
[11] I indeed forwash you with water unto berueance: but he that cometh after me is mightier than I, whose shoes I am not worthy to bear: he shall forwash you with the Holy Ghost, and with fire:
[12] Whose fan is in his hand, and he will throughly acleanse his floor, and gather his wheat into the garner; but he will burn up the chaff with unquenchable fire.
[13] Then cometh Jesus from Galilee to Jordan unto John, to be forwashed by him.
[14] But John forbad him, saying, I have need to be forwashed by thee, and comest thou to me?
[15] And Jesus answering said unto him, thraw it to be so now: for thus it becometh us to fulfil all rightsomeness. Then he thrawed him.
[16] And Jesus, when he was forwashed, went up straightway out of the water: and, lo, the heavens were opened unto him, and he saw the Ferth of God stighing down like a dove, and lighting upon him:

[17] And lo a rord from heaven, saying, This is my beloved Son, in whom I am well becweemed.

Matt.4

[1] Then was Jesus led up of the Ferth into the wilderness to be forlead of the devil.
[2] And when he had fasted forty days and forty nights, he was afterward an hungred.
[3] And when the forleader came to him, he said, If thou be the Son of God, bebid that these stones be made bread.
[4] But he answered and said, It is written, Man shall not live by bread alone, but by every word that cometh out of the mouth of God.
[5] Then the devil taketh him up into the holy chester, and setteth him on a peak of the worshipstead,
[6] And saith unto him, If thou be the Son of God, cast thyself down: for it is written, He shall give his woulderghosts care for thee: and in their hands they shall bear thee up, lest at any time thou dash thy foot against a stone.
[7] Jesus said unto him, It is written again, Thou shalt not forlead the Lord thy God.
[8] Again, the devil taketh him up into an outestly high barrow, and sheweth him all the kingdoms of the world, and the woulder of them;
[9] And saith unto him, All these things will I give thee, if thou wilt fall down and worship me.
[10] Then saith Jesus unto him, Get thee hence, Hellwarden: for it is written, Thou shalt worship the Lord thy God, and him only shalt thou serve.
[11] Then the devil leaveth him, and, behold, woulderghosts came and acared unto him.
[12] Now when Jesus had heard that John was cast into haftlingstow, he wote into Galilee;
[13] And leaving Nazareth, he came and woned in Capernaum, which is upon the sea coast, in the borders of Zabulon and Nephthalim:
[14] That it might be fulfilled which was spoken by Esaias the forequeether, saying,
[15] The land of Zabulon, and the land of Nephthalim, by the way of the sea, beyond Jordan, Galilee of the Gentiles;
[16] The theed which sat in darkness saw great light; and to them which sat in the stead and shadow of death light is sprung up.
[17] From that time Jesus began to preach, and to say, Berue: for the kingdom of heaven is at hand.
[18] And Jesus, walking by the sea of Galilee, saw two brethren, Simon called Peter, and Andrew his brother, casting a net into the sea: for they were fishers.
[19] And he saith unto them, Follow me, and I will make you fishers of men.
[20] And they straightway left their nets, and followed him.
[21] And going on from thence, he saw other two brethren, James the son of Zebedee, and John his brother, in a ship with Zebedee their father, mending their nets; and he called them.
[22] And they forthwith left the ship and their father, and followed him.
[23] And Jesus went about all Galilee, teaching in their worshipsteads, and preaching the gospel of the kingdom, and healing all kind of sickness and all manner of cothe among the theed.
[24] And his fame went throughout all Syria: and they brought unto him all sick theed that were taken with sundry cothes and sousels, and those which were throughtaken with devils, and those which were lunatick, and those that had the palsy; and he healed them.
[25] And there followed him great droves of theed from Galilee, and from Decapolis, and from Jerusalem, and from Judaea, and from beyond Jordan.

Matt.5

[1] And seeing the droves, he went up into a barrow: and when he was set, his loreknights came unto him:
[2] And he opened his mouth, and taught them, saying,
[3] Blessed are the arm in ferth: for theirs is the kingdom of heaven.
[4] Blessed are they that mourn: for they shall be frovered.
[5] Blessed are the meek: for they shall erve the earth.
[6] Blessed are they which do hunger and thirst after rightsomeness: for they shall be filled.
[7] Blessed are the ruthful: for they shall underfang ruth.
[8] Blessed are the siver in heart: for they shall see God.
[9] Blessed are the frithmakers: for they shall be called the children of God.
[10] Blessed are they which are dretched for rightsomeness' sake: for theirs is the kingdom of heaven.
[11] Blessed are ye, when men shall slight you, and dretch you, and shall say all kinds of evil against you unsoothly, for my sake.
[12] Aglee, and be outestly glad: for great is your edlean in heaven: for so dretched they the forequeethers which were before you.
[13] Ye are the salt of the earth: but if the salt have lost his smack, wherewith shall it be salted? it is thenceforth good for nothing, but to be cast out, and to be trodden under foot of men.
[14] Ye are the light of the world. A chester that is set

on an hill cannot be hid.
[15] Neither do men light a candle, and put it under a bushel, but on a candlestick; and it giveth light unto all that are in the house.
[16] Let your light so shine before men, that they may see your good works, and woulderen your Father which is in heaven.
[17] Think not that I am come to fordo the law, or the forequeethers: I am not come to fordo, but to fulfil.
[18] For in sooth I say unto you, Till heaven and earth wend off, one jot or one tittle shall in no wise wend off from the law, till all be fulfilled.
[19] Whosoever therefore shall break one of these least bodewords, and shall teach men so, he shall be called the least in the kingdom of heaven: but whosoever shall do and teach them, the same shall be called great in the kingdom of heaven.
[20] For I say unto you, That unless your rightsomeness shall outgo the rightsomeness of the scribes and Pharisees, ye shall in no case tred into the kingdom of heaven.
[21] Ye have heard that it was said by them of old time, Thou shalt not kill; and whosoever shall kill shall be in peril of the deeming:
[22] But I say unto you, That whosoever is angry with his brother without grounds shall be in danger of the deemword: and whosoever shall say to his brother, Raca, shall be in danger of the rownwitmoot: but whosoever shall say, Thou fool, shall be in danger of hell fire.
[23] Therefore if thou bring thy gift to the altar, and there munst that thy brother hath ought against thee;
[24] Leave there thy gift before the altar, and go thy way; first be asmoothed to thy brother, and then come and give thy gift.
[25] Thweer with thine foe quickly, whiles thou art in the way with him; lest at any time the foe bring thee before the deemer, and the deemer bring thee to the lawswinkers, and thou be cast into hafltingstow.
[26] Soothly I say unto thee, Thou shalt by no means come out thence, till thou hast paid the uttermost farthing.
[27] Ye have heard that it was said by them of old time, Thou shalt not bego forlying:
[28] But I say unto you, That whosoever looketh on a woman to lust after her hath begone dernlyership with her already in his heart.
[29] And if thy right eye abellow thee, pluck it out, and cast it from thee: for it is notesome for thee that one of thy limbs should swelt, and not that thy whole body should be cast into hell.
[30] And if thy right hand slight thee, cut if off, and cast it from thee: for it is winsome for thee that one of thy bodydeals should swelt, and not that thy whole body should be cast into hell.

[31] It hath been said, Whosoever shall put away his wife, let him give her a writing of wedcleave:
[32] But I say unto you, That whosoever shall put away his wife, unless for the grounds of dernlyership, abringeth her to forlie: and whosoever shall wed her that is wedcloven begoeth dernlyership.
[33] Again, ye have heard that it hath been said by them of old time, Thou shalt not forswear thyself, but shalt frem unto the Lord thine oaths:
[34] But I say unto you, Swear not at all; neither by heaven; for it is God's throne:
[35] Nor by the earth; for it is his footstool: neither by Jerusalem; for it is the chester of the great King.
[36] Neither shalt thou swear by thy head, forwhy thou canst not make one hair white or black.
[37] But let your outsay be, Yea, yea; Nay, nay: for whatsoever is more than these cometh of evil.
[38] Ye have heard that it hath been said, An eye for an eye, and a tooth for a tooth:
[39] But I say unto you, That ye withlay not evil: but whosoever shall smite thee on thy right cheek, wharve to him the other also.
[40] And if any man will sue thee at the law, and take away thy coat, let him have thy cloke also.
[41] And whosoever shall thrave thee to go a mile, go with him twain.
[42] Give to him that asketh thee, and from him that would borrow of thee wharve not thou away.
[43] Ye have heard that it hath been said, Thou shalt love thy neighbour, and hate thine foe.
[44] But I say unto you, Love your foes, bless them that curse you, do good to them that hate you, and abid for them which spirtefully use you, and dretch you;
[45] That ye may be the children of your Father which is in heaven: for he maketh his sun to rise on the evil and on the good, and sendeth rain on the upright and on the unuprightt.
[46] For if ye love them which love you, what edlean have ye? do not even the tollners the same?
[47] And if ye salute your brethren only, what do ye more than others? do not even the tollners so?
[48] Be ye therefore fullcomely, even as your Father which is in heaven is fullcomely.

Matt.6

[1] Take heed that ye do not your alms before men, to be seen of them: otherwise ye have no edlean of your Father which is in heaven.
[2] Therefore when thou doest thine alms, do not sound a trumpet before thee, as the leasers do in the worshipsteads and in the streets, that they may have woulder of men. Soothly I say unto you, They have their edlean.

[3] But when thou doest alms, let not thy left hand know what thy right hand doeth:
[4] That thine alms may be in dern: and thy Father which seeth in dern himself shall edlean thee openly.
[5] And when thou abidest, thou shalt not be as the leasers are: for they love to abid standing in the worshipsteads and in the corners of the streets, that they may be seen of men. Truly I say unto you, They have their edlean.
[6] But thou, when thou abidest, treddest into thy closet, and when thou hast shut thy door, abid to thy Father which is in dern; and thy Father which seeth in dern shall edlean thee openly.
[7] But when ye abid, use not vain edledgings, as the heathen do: for they think that they shall be heard for their much speaking.
[8] Be not ye therefore like unto them: for your Father knoweth what things ye have need of, before ye ask him.
[9] After this way therefore abid ye: Our Father which art in heaven, Hallowed be thy name.
[10] Thy kingdom come. Thy will be done in earth, as it is in heaven.
[11] Give us this day our daily bread.
[12] And forgive us our sins, as we forgive those who have sinned against us.
[13] And lead us not into forleading, but spare us from evil: For thine is the kingdom, and the thrith, and the woulder, for ever. Amen.
[14] For if ye forgive men their guilts, your heavenly Father will also forgive you:
[15] But if ye forgive not men their guilts, neither will your Father forgive your guilts.
[16] Moreover when ye fast, be not, as the leasers, of a sad neb: for they misshaped their anlits, that they may outsee unto men to fast. Soothly I say unto you, They have their edlean.
[17] But thou, when thou fastest, asmear thine head, and wash thy anlit;
[18] That thou outsee not unto men to fast, but unto thy Father which is in secret: and thy Father, which seeth in dern, shall edlean thee openly.
[19] Lay not up for yourselves mathems upon earth, where moth and rust doth sully, and where thieves break through and steal:
[20] But lay up for yourselves mathems in heaven, where neither moth nor rust doth brosen, and where thieves do not break through nor steal:
[21] For where your mathem is, there will your heart be also.
[22] The light of the body is the eye: if therefore thine eye be onele, thy whole body shall be full of light.
[23] But if thine eye be evil, thy whole body shall be full of darkness. If therefore the light that is in thee be darkness, how great is that darkness!

[24] No man can theen two harrs: for either he will hate the one, and love the other; or else he will hold to the one, and scorn the other. Ye cannot theen God and mammon.
[25] Therefore I say unto you, Take no thought for your life, what ye shall eat, or what ye shall drink; nor yet for your body, what ye shall put on. Is not the life more than meat, and the body than clothing?
[26] Behold the fowls of the air: for they sow not, neither do they reap, nor gather into barns; yet your heavenly Father feedeth them. Are ye not much better than they?
[27] Which of you by taking thought can add one cubit unto his height?
[28] And why take ye thought for clthing? Hidge the lilies of the field, how they grow; they toil not, neither do they spin:
[29] And yet I say unto you, That even Solomon in all his woulder was not dighted like one of these.
[30] Wherefore, if God so clothe the grass of the field, which to day is, and to morrow is cast into the oven, shall he not much more clothe you, O ye of little faith?
[31] Therefore take no thought, saying, What shall we eat? or, What shall we drink? or, Wherewithal shall we be clothed?
[32] (For after all these things do the Gentiles seek:) for your heavenly Father knoweth that ye have need of all these things.
[33] But seek ye first the kingdom of God, and his rightsomeness; and all these things shall be added unto you.
[34] Take therefore no thought for the morrow: for the morrow shall take thought for the things of itself. Enoughsome unto the day is the evil thereof.

Matt.7

[1] Deem not, that ye be not deemed.
[2] For with what deeming ye deem, ye shall be deemed: and with what mete ye mete, it shall be meted to you again.
[3] And why beholdest thou the mote that is in thy brother's eye, but hidgest not the beam that is in thine own eye?
[4] Or how wilt thou say to thy brother, Let me pull out the mote out of thine eye; and, behold, a beam is in thine own eye?
[5] Thou leaser, first cast out the beam out of thine own eye; and then shalt thou see clearly to cast out the mote out of thy brother's eye.
[6] Give not that which is holy unto the dogs, neither cast ye your pearls before swine, lest they trample them under their feet, and wharve again and rend you.
[7] Ask, and it shall be given you; seek, and ye shall

find; knock, and it shall be opened unto you:
[8] For every one that asketh thidgeth; and he that seeketh findeth; and to him that knocketh it shall be opened.
[9] Or what man is there of you, whom if his son ask bread, will he give him a stone?
[10] Or if he ask a fish, will he give him an nadder?
[11] If ye then, being evil, know how to give good gifts unto your children, how much more shall your Father which is in heaven give good things to them that ask him?
[12] Therefore all things whatsoever ye would that men should do to you, do ye even so to them: for this is the law and the forequeethers.
[13] Tread in ye in at the strait gate: for wide is the gate, and broad is the way, that leadeth to neecing, and many there be which go in thereat:
[14] Forwhy strait is the gate, and narrow is the way, which leadeth unto life, and few there be that find it.
[15] Beware of unsooth forequeethers, which come to you in sheep's clothing, but inwardly they are ravening wolves.
[16] Ye shall know them by their ovet. Do men gather grapes of thorns, or figs of thistles?
[17] Even so every good tree bringeth forth good wassom; but a corrupt tree bringeth forth evil wassom.
[18] A good tree cannot bring forth evil wassom, neither can a sullied tree bring forth good wassom.
[19] Every tree that bringeth not forth good ovet is hewn down, and cast into the fire.
[20] Wherefore by their wassom ye shall know them.
[21] Not every one that saith unto me, Lord, Lord, shall go into the kingdom of heaven; but he that doeth the will of my Father which is in heaven.
[22] Many will say to me in that day, Lord, Lord, have we not forequothe in thy name? and in thy name have cast out devils? and in thy name done many wonderful works?
[23] And then will I say forth unto them, I never knew you: wite from me, ye that work unrightdom.
[24] Therefore whosoever heareth these sayings of mine, and doeth them, I will liken him unto a wise man, which built his house upon a stone:
[25] And the rain stighed, and the floods came, and the winds blew, and beat upon that house; and it fell not: for it was founded upon a stone.
[26] And every one that heareth these sayings of mine, and doeth them not, shall be likened unto a foolish man, which built his house upon the sand:
[27] And the rain stighed down, and the floods came, and the winds blew, and beat upon that house; and it fell: and great was the fall of it.
[28] And it came to be, when Jesus had ended these sayings, the theed were amazed at his loreword:

[29] For he taught them as one having alderdom, and not as the scribes.

Matt.8

[1] When he was come down from the barrow, great droves followed him.
[2] And, behold, there came a leper and worshipped him, saying, Lord, if thou wilt, thou canst make me clean.
[3] And Jesus put forth his hand, and rone him, saying, I will; be thou clean. And forthwith his leprosy was cleansed.
[4] And Jesus saith unto him, See thou tell no man; but go thy way, shew thyself to the priest, and give the gift that Moses bebade, for a witness unto them.
[5] And when Jesus was gone into Capernaum, there came unto him a hundredman, beseeching him,
[6] And saying, Lord, my thane lieth at home sick of the palsy, heafly sousled.
[7] And Jesus saith unto him, I will come and heal him.
[8] The hundredman answered and said, Lord, I am not worthy that thou shouldest come under my roof: but speak the word only, and my thane shall be healed.
[9] For I am a man under alderdom, having heregomes under me: and I say to this man, Go, and he goeth; and to another, Come, and he cometh; and to my thane, Do this, and he doeth it.
[10] When Jesus heard it, he awondered, and said to them that followed, Truly I say unto you, I have not found so great faith, no, not in Israel.
[11] And I say unto you, That many shall come from the east and west, and shall sit down with Abraham, and Isaac, and Jacob, in the kingdom of heaven.
[12] But the children of the kingdom shall be cast out into outer darkness: there shall be weeping and gnashing of teeth.
[13] And Jesus said unto the hundredman, Go thy way; and as thou hast believed, so be it done unto thee. And his thane was healed in the selfsame stound.
[14] And when Jesus was come into Peter's house, he saw his wife's mother laid, and sick of a fever.
[15] And he remmed her hand, and the fever left her: and she arose, and acared unto them.
[16] When the even was come, they brought unto him many that were throughtaken with devils: and he cast out the ferths with his word, and healed all that were sick:
[17] That it might be fulfilled which was spoken by Esaias the forequeether, saying, Himself took our cothes, and bare our sicknesses.
[18] Now when Jesus saw great drights about him, he gave bodeword to wite unto the other side.
[19] And a somel scribe came, and said unto him, Harr,

I will follow thee whithersoever thou goest.

[20] And Jesus saith unto him, The foxes have holes, and the birds of the air have nests; but the Son of man hath not where to lay his head.

[21] And another of his loreknights said unto him, Lord, thraw me first to go and bury my father.

[22] But Jesus said unto him, Follow me; and let the dead bury their dead.

[23] And when he was goed into a ship, his loreknights followed him.

[24] And, behold, there arose a great tempest in the sea, insomuch that the ship was overthatched with the waves: but he was asleep.

[25] And his loreknights came to him, and awoke him, saying, Lord, nerr us: we forfare.

[26] And he saith unto them, Why are ye fearful, O ye of little faith? Then he arose, and threaped the winds and the sea; and there was a great stillness.

[27] But the men awondered, saying, What kind of man is this, that even the winds and the sea hearsome him!

[28] And when he was come to the other side into the folkdom of the Gergesenes, there met him two throughtaken with devils, coming out of the tombs, outestly grame, so that no man might wend by that way.

[29] And, behold, they yawled out, saying, What have we to do with thee, Jesus, thou Son of God? art thou come hither to sousel us before the time?

[30] And there was a good way off from them an herd of many swine feeding.

[31] So the devils besought him, saying, If thou cast us out, dree us to go away into the herd of swine.

[32] And he said unto them, Go. And when they were come out, they went into the herd of swine: and, behold, the whole herd of swine ran hastly down a steep stow into the sea, and swelted in the waters.

[33] And they that kept them fled, and went their ways into the chester, and told every thing, and what was befallen to the throughtaken of the devils.

[34] And, behold, the whole chester came out to meet Jesus: and when they saw him, they besought him that he would wote out of their coasts.

Matt.9

[1] And he trod into a ship, and fore over, and came into his own chester.

[2] And, behold, they brought to him a man sick of the palsy, lying on a bed: and Jesus seeing their faith said unto the sick of the palsy; Son, be of good cheer; thy sins be forgiven thee.

[3] And, behold, certain of the scribes said within themselves, This man evilsaketh.

[4] And Jesus knowing their thoughts said, Wherefore think ye evil in your hearts?

[5] For whether is easier, to say, Thy sins be forgiven thee; or to say, Arise, and walk?

[6] But that ye may know that the Son of man hath thrith on earth to forgive sins, (then saith he to the sick of the palsy,) Arise, take up thy bed, and go unto thine house.

[7] And he arose, and wote to his house.

[8] But when the drights saw it, they awondered, and woulderened God, which had given such wold unto men.

[9] And as Jesus wended forth from thence, he saw a man, named Matthew, sitting at the tollsettle: and he saith unto him, Follow me. And he arose, and followed him.

[10] And it came to be, as Jesus sat at meat in the house, behold, many tollners and sinners came and sat down with him and his loreknights.

[11] And when the Pharisees saw it, they said unto his loreknights, Why eateth your Harr with tollners and sinners?

[12] But when Jesus heard that, he said unto them, They that be whole need not a leechcrafter, but they that are sick.

[13] But go ye and learn what that meaneth, I will have ruth, and not bloot: for I am not come to call the rightsome, but sinners to berueing.

[14] Then came to him the loreknights of John, saying, Why do we and the Pharisees fast oft, but thy loreknights fast not?

[15] And Jesus said unto them, Can the children of the bridechamber mourn, as long as the bridegroom is with them? but the days will come, when the bridegroom shall be taken from them, and then shall they fast.

[16] No man putteth a piece of new cloth unto an old clothing, for that which is put in to fill it up taketh from the clothing, and the rent is made worse.

[17] Neither do men put new wine into old bottles: else the bottles break, and the wine runneth out, and the bottles swelt: but they put new wine into new bottles, and both are aspared.

[18] While he spake these things unto them, behold, there came a somel woldend, and worshipped him, saying, My daughter is even now dead: but come and lay thy hand upon her, and she shall live.

[19] And Jesus arose, and followed him, and so did his loreknights.

[20] And, behold, a woman, which was cothed with an issue of blood twelve years, came behind him, and remmed the hem of his clothing:

[21] For she said within herself, If I may but remm his clothing, I shall be whole.

[22] But Jesus whorve him imb, and when he saw her, he said, Daughter, be of good frover; thy faith hath

made thee whole. And the woman was made whole from that stound.

[23] And when Jesus came into the woldend's house, and saw the minstrels and the folk making a noise wooth,

[24] He said unto them, Give stead: for the maid is not dead, but sleepeth. And they laughed him to scorn.

[25] But when the folk were put forth, he went in, and took her by the hand, and the maid arose.

[26] And the fame hereof went abroad into all that land.

[27] And when Jesus wone thence, two blind men followed him, crying, and saying, Thou Son of David, have ruth on us.

[28] And when he was come into the house, the blind men came to him: and Jesus saith unto them, Believe ye that I am able to do this? They said unto him, Yea, Lord.

[29] Then rone he their eyes, saying, By to your faith be it unto you.

[30] And their eyes were opened; and Jesus straitly bade them, saying, See that no man know it.

[31] But they, when they were witten, spread abroad his fame in all that folkdom.

[32] As they went out, behold, they brought to him a dumb man throughtaken with a devil.

[33] And when the devil was cast out, the dumb spake: and the drights awondered, queething, It was never so seen in Israel.

[34] But the Pharisees said, He casteth out devils through the atheling of the devils.

[35] And Jesus went about all the chesters and towns, teaching in their worshipsteads, and preaching the gospel of the kingdom, and healing every sickness and every cothe among the theed.

[36] But when he saw the drights, he was bewayed with evensorrow on them, forwhy they fainted, and were scattered abroad, as sheep having no shepherd.

[37] Then saith he unto his loreknights, The harvest truly is plentiful, but the swinkers are few;

[38] Abid ye therefore the Lord of the harvest, that he will send forth swinkers into his harvest.

Matt.10

[1] And when he had called unto him his twelve loreknights, he gave them wold against unclean ferths, to cast them out, and to heal all manner of sickness and all kind of cothe.

[2] Now the names of the twelve loreknights are these; The first, Simon, who is called Peter, and Andrew his brother; James the son of Zebedee, and John his brother;

[3] Philip, and Bartholomew; Thomas, and Matthew the tollner; James the son of Alphaeus, and Lebbaeus, whose overname was Thaddaeus;

[4] Simon the Canaanite, and Judas Iscariot, who also forread him.

[5] These twelve Jesus sent forth, and bebade them, saying, Go not into the way of the Gentiles, and into any chester of the Samaritans go ye not:

[6] But go rather to the lost sheep of the house of Israel.

[7] And as ye go, preach, saying, The kingdom of heaven is at hand.

[8] Heal the sick, cleanse the lepers, raise the dead, cast out devils: freely ye have thidged, freely give.

[9] See on neither gold, nor silver, nor brass in your purses,

[10] Nor scrip for your sith, neither two coats, neither shoes, nor yet staves: for the workman is worthy of his meat.

[11] And into whatsoever chester or town ye shall go, fraign who in it is worthy; and there abide till ye go thence.

[12] And when ye come into an house, salute it.

[13] And if the house be worthy, let your frith come upon it: but if it be not worthy, let your frith edwharve to you.

[14] And whosoever shall not thidge you, nor hear your words, when ye wite out of that house or chester, shake off the dust of your feet.

[15] Soothly I say unto you, It shall be more brookable for the land of Sodom and Gomorrha in the day of deeming, than for that chester.

[16] Behold, I send you forth as sheep in the midst of wolves: be ye therefore wise as nadders, and harmless as doves.

[17] But beware of men: for they will give you up to the rownwitmoot, and they will scourge you in their worshipsteads;

[18] And ye shall be brought before awielders and kings for my sake, for a witness against them and the Gentiles.

[19] But when they atake you up, take no thought how or what ye shall speak: for it shall be given you in that same stound what ye shall speak.

[20] For it is not ye that speak, but the Seva of your Father which speaketh in you.

[21] And the brother shall atake up the brother to death, and the father the child: and the children shall rise up against their akennend, and have them to be put to death.

[22] And ye shall be hated of all men for my name's sake: but he that tholeth to the end shall be redded.

[23] But when they dretch you in this chester, flee ye into another: for soothly I say unto you, Ye shall not have gone over the chesters of Israel, till the Son of man be come.

[24] The loreknight is not above his harr, nor the thane above his lord.
[25] It is enough for the loreknight that he be as his harr, and the thane as his lord. If they have called the harr of the house Beelzebub, how much more shall they call them of his household?
[26] Fear them not therefore: for there is nothing decked, that shall not be swettled; and hid, that shall not be known.
[27] What I tell you in darkness, that speak ye in light: and what ye hear in the ear, that preach ye upon the housetops.
[28] And fear not them which kill the body, but are not able to kill the soul: but rather fear him which is able to aspill both soul and body in hell.
[29] Are not two sparrows sold for a farthing? and one of them shall not fall on the ground without your Father.
[30] But the very hairs of your head are all arimed.
[31] Fear ye not therefore, ye are of more value than many sparrows.
[32] Whosoever therefore shall adett me before men, him will I adett also before my Father which is in heaven.
[33] But whosoever shall andsake me before men, him will I also andsake before my Father which is in heaven.
[34] Think not that I am come to send frith on earth: I came not to send frith, but a meech.
[35] For I am come to set a man at witherdom against his father, and the daughter against her mother, and the daughter in law against her mother in law.
[36] And a man's foes shall be they of his own household.
[37] He that loveth father or mother more than me is not worthy of me: and he that loveth son or daughter more than me is not worthy of me.
[38] And he that taketh not his cross, and followeth after me, is not worthy of me.
[39] He that findeth his life shall lose it: and he that loseth his life for my sake shall find it.
[40] He that thidgeth you thidgeth me, and he that thidgeth me thidgeth him that sent me.
[41] He that thidgeth a forequeether in the name of a forequeether shall thidge a forequeether's edlean; and he that thidgeth a rightsome man in the name of a rightsome man shall thidge a rightsome man's edlean.
[42] And whosoever shall give to drink unto one of these little ones a cup of cold water only in the name of a loreknight, soothly I say unto you, he shall in no wise lose his edlean.

Matt.11

[1] And it came to be, when Jesus had made an end of bebiding his twelve loreknights, he wote thence to teach and to preach in their chesters.
[2] Now when John had heard in the witern the works of Christ, he sent two of his loreknights,
[3] And said unto him, Art thou he that should come, or do we look for another?
[4] Jesus answered and said unto them, Go and shew John again those things which ye do hear and see:
[5] The blind thidge their sight, and the lame walk, the lepers are cleansed, and the deaf hear, the dead are raised up, and the poor have the gospel preached to them.
[6] And blessed is he, whosoever shall not be abellowed in me.
[7] And as they wote, Jesus began to say unto the drights about John, What went ye out into the wilderness to see? A reed shaken with the wind?
[8] But what went ye out for to see? A man clothed in soft clothing? behold, they that wear soft clothing are in kings' houses.
[9] But what went ye out for to see? A forequeether? yea, I say unto you, and more than a forequeether.
[10] For this is he, of whom it is written, Behold, I send my herald before thy anlit, which shall yark thy way before thee.
[11] Soothly I say unto you, Among them that are born of women there hath not risen a greater than John the Forwasher: notwithstanding he that is least in the kingdom of heaven is greater than he.
[12] And from the days of John the Forwasher until now the kingdom of heaven dreeth hastness, and the hast neednim.
[13] For all the forequeethers and the law forequothe until John.
[14] And if ye will thidge it, this is Elias, which was for to come.
[15] He that hath ears to hear, let him hear.
[16] But whereunto shall I liken this strind? It is like unto children sitting in the buystow, and calling unto their fellows,
[17] And saying, We have piped unto you, and ye have not danced; we have mourned unto you, and ye have not cwithen.
[18] For John came neither eating nor drinking, and they say, He hath a devil.
[19] The Son of man came eating and drinking, and they say, Behold a man overettle, and a winebibber, a friend of tollners and sinners. But wisdom is rightsomed of her children.
[20] Then began he to upbraid the chesters wherein most of his mighty works were done, forwhy they berueed not:
[21] Woe unto thee, Chorazin! woe unto thee, Bethsaida! for if the mighty works, which were done in

you, had been done in Tyre and Sidon, they would have berueed long ago in sackcloth and ashes.
[22] But I say unto you, It shall be more tolerable for Tyre and Sidon at the day of deeming, than for you.
[23] And thou, Capernaum, which art exalted unto heaven, shalt be brought down to hell: for if the mighty works, which have been done in thee, had been done in Sodom, it would have bliven until this day.
[24] But I say unto you, That it shall be more brookable for the land of Sodom in the day of deeming, than for thee.
[25] At that time Jesus answered and said, I thank thee, O Father, Lord of heaven and earth, forwhy thou hast hid these things from the wise and snotter, and hast abared them unto babes.
[26] Even so, Father: for so it thencheth good in thy sight.
[27] All things are brought unto me of my Father: and no man knoweth the Son, but the Father; neither knoweth any man the Father, save the Son, and he to whomsoever the Son will swettle him.
[28] Come unto me, all ye that swink and are heavy laden, and I will give you rest.
[29] Take my yoke upon you, and learn of me; for I am meek and lowly in heart: and ye shall find rest unto your souls.
[30] For my yoke is easy, and my burden is light.

Matt.12

[1] At that time Jesus went on the sabbath day through the corn; and his loreknights were an hungred, and began to pluck the ears of corn, and to eat.
[2] But when the Pharisees saw it, they said unto him, Behold, thy loreknights do that which is not lawful to do upon the sabbath day.
[3] But he said unto them, Have ye not read what David did, when he was an hungred, and they that were with him;
[4] How he goed into the house of God, and did eat the shewbread, which was not lawful for him to eat, neither for them which were with him, but only for the priests?
[5] Or have ye not read in the law, how that on the sabbath days the priests in the worshipstead besully the sabbath, and are teelless?
[6] But I say unto you, That in this stead is one greater than the worshipstead.
[7] But if ye had known what this meaneth, I will have ruth, and not bloot, ye would not have fordeemed the guiltless.
[8] For the Son of man is Lord even of the sabbath day.
[9] And when he was wote thence, he went into their worshipstead:

[10] And, behold, there was a man which had his hand withered. And they asked him, saying, Is it lawful to heal on the sabbath days? that they might accuse him.
[11] And he said unto them, What man shall there be among you, that shall have one sheep, and if it fall into a pit on the sabbath day, will he not lay hold on it, and lift it out?
[12] How much then is a man better than a sheep? Wherefore it is lawful to do well on the sabbath days.
[13] Then saith he to the man, Stretch forth thine hand. And he stretched it forth; and it was edstatheled whole, like as the other.
[14] Then the Pharisees went out, and held a deemoot against him, how they might thrash him through.
[15] But when Jesus knew it, he withdrew himself from thence: and great drights followed him, and he healed them all;
[16] And bade them that they should not make him known:
[17] That it might be fulfilled which was spoken by Esaias the forequeether, saying,
[18] Behold my thane, whom I have chosen; my beloved, in whom my soul is well pleased: I will put my ferth upon him, and he shall shew deeming to the Gentiles.
[19] He shall not strive, nor cry; neither shall any man hear his steven in the streets.
[20] A bruised reed shall he not break, and smoking flax shall he not quench, till he send forth deeming unto sigor.
[21] And in his name shall the Gentiles trust.
[22] Then was brought unto him one throughtaken with a devil, blind, and dumb: and he healed him, insomuch that the blind and dumb both spake and saw.
[23] And all the theed were amazed, and said, Is not this the son of David?
[24] But when the Pharisees heard it, they said, This fellow doth not cast out devils, but by Beelzebub the atheling of the devils.
[25] And Jesus knew their thoughts, and said unto them, Every kingdom todealt against itself is brought to forwasting; and every chester or house todealt against itself shall not stand:
[26] And if Hellward cast out Hellward, he is todealt against himself; how shall then his kingdom stand?
[27] And if I by Beelzebub cast out devils, by whom do your children cast them out? therefore they shall be your deems.
[28] But if I cast out devils by the Ferth of God, then the kingdom of God is come unto you.
[29] Or else how can one go into a strong man's house, and spoil his goods, unless he first bind the strong man? and then he will spoil his house.
[30] He that is not with me is against me; and he that gathereth not with me scattereth abroad.

[31] Wherefore I say unto you, All manner of sin and evilsaking shall be forgiven unto men: but the evilsaking against the Holy Ghost shall not be forgiven unto men.
[32] And whosoever speaketh a word against the Son of man, it shall be forgiven him: but whosoever speaketh against the Holy Ghost, it shall not be forgiven him, neither in this world, neither in the world to come.
[33] Either make the tree good, and his ovet good; or else make the tree brosen, and his ovet sullied: for the tree is known by his wassom.
[34] O strind of vipers, how can ye, being evil, speak good things? for out of the fullsomeness of the heart the mouth speaketh.
[35] A good man out of the good mathem of the heart bringeth forth good things: and an evil man out of the evil mathem bringeth forth evil things.
[36] But I say unto you, That every idle word that men shall speak, they shall give ground thereof in the day of deeming.
[37] For by thy words thou shalt be rightsomed, and by thy words thou shalt be fordeemed.
[38] Then some of the scribes and of the Pharisees answered, saying, Harr, we would see a tocken from thee.
[39] But he answered and said unto them, An evil and forlying strind seeketh after a token; and there shall no token be given to it, but the tocken of the forequeether Jonas:
[40] For as Jonas was three days and three nights in the whale's belly; so shall the Son of man be three days and three nights in the heart of the earth.
[41] The men of Nineveh shall rise in deeming with this strind, and shall fordeem it: forwhy they berueed at the preaching of Jonas; and, behold, a greater than Jonas is here.
[42] The queen of the south shall rise up in the deeming with this strind, and shall fordeem it: for she came from the uttermost parts of the earth to hear the wisdom of Solomon; and, behold, a greater than Solomon is here.
[43] When the unclean ferth is gone out of a man, he walketh through dry steads, seeking rest, and findeth none.
[44] Then he saith, I will rewharve into my house from whence I came out; and when he is come, he findeth it empty, swept, and garnished.
[45] Then goeth he, and taketh with himself seven other ferths more wicked than himself, and they go in and dwell there: and the last state of that man is worse than the first. Even so shall it be also unto this wicked strind.
[46] While he yet talked to the theed, behold, his mother and his brethren stood without, wish to speak with him.
[47] Then one said unto him, Behold, thy mother and thy brethren stand without, wishing to speak with thee.
[48] But he answered and said unto him that told him, Who is my mother? and who are my brethren?
[49] And he stretched forth his hand toward his loreknights, and said, Behold my mother and my brethren!
[50] For whosoever shall do the will of my Father which is in heaven, the same is my brother, and sister, and mother.

Matt.13

[1] The same day went Jesus out of the house, and sat by the seaside.
[2] And great drights were gathered together unto him, so that he went into a ship, and sat; and the whole dright stood on the shore.
[3] And he spake many things unto them in likeningtales, saying, Behold, a sower went forth to sow;
[4] And when he sowed, some seeds fell by the way side, and the fowls came and glendered them up:
[5] Some fell upon stony steads, where they had not much earth: and forthwith they sprung up, forwhy they had no deepness of earth:
[6] And when the sun was up, they were scorched; and forwhy they had no root, they withered away.
[7] And some fell among thorns; and the thorns sprung up, and choked them:
[8] But other fell into good ground, and brought forth ovet, some an hundredfold, some sixtyfold, some thirtyfold.
[9] Who hath ears to hear, let him hear.
[10] And the loreknights came, and said unto him, Why speakest thou unto them in likeningtales?
[11] He answered and said unto them, Forwhy it is given unto you to know the rawns of the kingdom of heaven, but to them it is not given.
[12] For whosoever hath, to him shall be given, and he shall have more fullsomeness: but whosoever hath not, from him shall be taken away even that he hath.
[13] Therefore speak I to them in likeningtales: forwhy they seeing see not; and hearing they hear not, neither do they understand.
[14] And in them is fulfilled the forequeething of Esaias, which saith, By hearing ye shall hear, and shall not understand; and seeing ye shall see, and shall not onget:
[15] For this theed's heart is waxed gross, and their ears are dull of hearing, and their eyes they have closed; lest at any time they should see with their eyes, and hear with their ears, and should understand with

their heart, and should be overwended, and I should heal them.

[16] But blessed are your eyes, for they see: and your ears, for they hear.

[17] For soothly I say unto you, That many forequeethers and rightsome men have longed to see those things which ye see, and have not seen them; and to hear those things which ye hear, and have not heard them.

[18] Hear ye therefore the likeningtale of the sower.

[19] When any one heareth the word of the kingdom, and understandeth it not, then cometh the wicked one, and fangeth away that which was sown in his heart. This is he which thidged seed by the way side.

[20] But he that thidged the seed into stony steads, the same is he that heareth the word, and anon with mirth thidgeth it;

[21] Yet hath he not root in himself, but dureth for a while: for when derst or dretching ariseth forwhy of the word, by and by he is abellowed.

[22] He also that thidged seed among the thorns is he that heareth the word; and the care of this world, and the swikefulness of riches, choke the word, and he becometh unwassomful.

[23] But he that thidged seed into the good ground is he that heareth the word, and understandeth it; which also beareth ovet, and bringeth forth, some an hundredfold, some sixty, some thirty.

[24] Another likeningtale put he forth unto them, saying, The kingdom of heaven is likened unto a man which sowed good seed in his field:

[25] But while men slept, his foe came and sowed tares among the wheat, and went his way.

[26] But when the blade was sprung up, and brought forth ovet, then trod up the tares also.

[27] So the thanes of the householder came and said unto him, Sir, didst not thou sow good seed in thy field? from whence then hath it tares?

[28] He said unto them, An foe hath done this. The thanes said unto him, Wilt thou then that we go and gather them up?

[29] But he said, Nay; lest while ye gather up the tares, ye root up also the wheat with them.

[30] Let both grow together until the harvest: and in the time of harvest I will say to the reapers, Gather ye together first the tares, and bind them in bundles to burn them: but gather the wheat into my barn.

[31] Another likeningtale put he forth unto them, saying, The kingdom of heaven is like to a grain of mutungled seed, which a man took, and sowed in his field:

[32] Which indeed is the least of all seeds: but when it is grown, it is the greatest among herbs, and wertheth a tree, so that the birds of the air come and lodge in the boughs thereof.

[33] Another likeningtale spake he unto them; The kingdom of heaven is like unto leaven, which a woman took, and hid in three batches of meal, till the whole was leavened.

[34] All these things spake Jesus unto the dright in likeningtales; and without a likeningtale spake he not unto them:

[35] That it might be fulfilled which was spoken by the forequeether, saying, I will open my mouth in likeningtales; I will utter things which have been kept dern from the fromth of the world.

[36] Then Jesus sent the drights away, and went into the house: and his loreknights came unto him, saying, Akithe unto us the likeningtale of the tares of the field.

[37] He answered and said unto them, He that soweth the good seed is the Son of man;

[38] The field is the world; the good seed are the children of the kingdom; but the tares are the children of the wicked one;

[39] The foe that sowed them is the devil; the harvest is the end of the world; and the reapers are the woulderghosts.

[40] As therefore the tares are gathered and burned in the fire; so shall it be in the end of this world.

[41] The Son of man shall send forth his woulderghosts, and they shall gather out of his kingdom all things that abellow, and them which do unrightdom;

[42] And shall cast them into a furnace of fire: there shall be wailing and gnashing of teeth.

[43] Then shall the rightsome shine forth as the sun in the kingdom of their Father. Who hath ears to hear, let him hear.

[44] Again, the kingdom of heaven is like unto mathem hid in a field; the which when a man hath found, he hideth, and for joy thereof goeth and selleth all that he hath, and buyeth that field.

[45] Again, the kingdom of heaven is like unto a merchant man, seeking goodly pearls:

[46] Who, when he had found one pearl of great price, went and sold all that he had, and bought it.

[47] Again, the kingdom of heaven is like unto a net, that was cast into the sea, and gathered of every kind:

[48] Which, when it was full, they drew to shore, and sat down, and gathered the good into vessels, but cast the bad away.

[49] So shall it be at the end of the world: the woulderghosts shall come forth, and sever the wicked from among the rightful,

[50] And shall cast them into the furnace of fire: there shall be wailing and gnashing of teeth.

[51] Jesus saith unto them, Have ye understood all these things? They say unto him, Yea, Lord.

[52] Then said he unto them, Therefore every scribe which is learned unto the kingdom of heaven is like

unto a man that is an householder, which bringeth forth out of his mathem things new and old.

[53] And it came to be, that when Jesus had beended these likeningtales, he wote thence.

[54] And when he was come into his own land, he taught them in their worshipstead, insomuch that they were amazed, and said, Whence hath this man this wisdom, and these mighty works?

[55] Is not this the woodworker's son? is not his mother called Mary? and his brethren, James, and Joses, and Simon, and Judas?

[56] And his sisters, are they not all with us? Whence then hath this man all these things?

[57] And they were abellowed in him. But Jesus said unto them, A forequeether is not without meath, besides in his own land, and in his own house.

[58] And he did not many mighty works there forwhy of their unbelief.

Matt.14

[1] At that time Herod the tetrarch heard of the fame of Jesus,

[2] And said unto his thanes, This is John the Forwasher; he is risen from the dead; and therefore mighty works do shew forth themselves in him.

[3] For Herod had laid hold on John, and bound him, and put him in prison for Herodias' sake, his brother Philip's wife.

[4] For John said unto him, It is not lawful for thee to have her.

[5] And when he would have put him to death, he feared the dright, forwhy they counted him as a forequeether.

[6] But when Herod's birthday was kept, the daughter of Herodias danced before them, and pleased Herod.

[7] Whereupon he hoted with an oath to give her whatsoever she would ask.

[8] And she, being before bebade by her mother, said, Give me here John Forwasher's head in a platter.

[9] And the king was sorry: nevertheless for the oath's sake, and them which sat with him at meat, he bebade it to be given her.

[10] And he sent, and beheaded John in the witern.

[11] And his head was brought in a platter, and given to the damsel: and she brought it to her mother.

[12] And his loreknights came, and took up the body, and buried it, and went and told Jesus.

[13] When Jesus heard of it, he wote thence by ship into a throughdry stead away: and when the theed had heard thereof, they followed him on foot out of the chesters.

[14] And Jesus went forth, and saw a great dright, and was reered with evensorrow toward them, and he healed their sick.

[15] And when it was evening, his loreknights came to him, saying, This is a throughdry stead, and the time is now gone; send the dright away, that they may go into the towns, and buy themselves food.

[16] But Jesus said unto them, They need not wite; give ye them to eat.

[17] And they say unto him, We have here but five loaves, and two fishes.

[18] He said, Bring them hither to me.

[19] And he bebade the dright to sit down on the grass, and took the five loaves, and the two fishes, and looking up to heaven, he blessed, and brake, and gave the loaves to his loreknights, and the loreknights to the dright.

[20] And they did all eat, and were filled: and they took up of the breaklings that remained twelve baskets full.

[21] And they that had eaten were about five thousand men, beside women and children.

[22] And straightway Jesus bade his loreknights to get into a ship, and to go before him unto the other side, while he sent the drights away.

[23] And when he had sent the drights away, he went up into a barrow away to abid: and when the evening was come, he was there alone.

[24] But the ship was now in the midst of the sea, tossed with waves: for the wind was contrary.

[25] And in the fourth watch of the night Jesus went unto them, walking on the sea.

[26] And when the loreknights saw him walking on the sea, they were troubled, saying, It is a ferth; and they yarmed out for fear.

[27] But straightway Jesus spake unto them, saying, Be of good cheer; it is I; be not afraid.

[28] And Peter answered him and said, Lord, if it be thou, bid me come unto thee on the water.

[29] And he said, Come. And when Peter was come down out of the ship, he walked on the water, to go to Jesus.

[30] But when he saw the wind boisterous, he was afraid; and beginning to sink, he yarmed, saying, Lord, save me.

[31] And immediately Jesus stretched forth his hand, and caught him, and said unto him, O thou of little faith, wherefore didst thou doubt?

[32] And when they were come into the ship, the wind ceased.

[33] Then they that were in the ship came and worshipped him, saying, Of a truth thou art the Son of God.

[34] And when they were gone over, they came into the land of Gennesaret.

[35] And when the men of that stead had knowledge of him, they sent out into all that land round about, and

brought unto him all that were cothed;
[36] And besought him that they might only rine the hem of his garment: and as many as rone were made fullfremmedly whole.

Matt.15

[1] Then came to Jesus scribes and Pharisees, which were of Jerusalem, saying,
[2] Why do thy loreknights wrong the alderthews of the elders? for they wash not their hands when they eat bread.
[3] But he answered and said unto them, Why do ye also wrong the bodeword of God by your alderthew?
[4] For God bebade, saying, Meathe thy father and mother: and, He that curseth father or mother, let him die the death.
[5] But ye say, Whosoever shall say to his father or his mother, It is a gift, by whatsoever thou mightest be notesomed by me;
[6] And meathe not his father or his mother, he shall be free. Thus have ye made the bodeword of God of none effect by your alderthew.
[7] Ye leasers, well did Esaias forequeethe of you, saying,
[8] This theed draweth nigh unto me with their mouth, and meatheth me with their lips; but their heart is far from me.
[9] But in vain they do worship me, teaching for doctrines the bodewords of men.
[10] And he called the dright, and said unto them, Hear, and understand:
[11] Not that which goeth into the mouth broseneth a man; but that which cometh out of the mouth, this broseneth a man.
[12] Then came his loreknights, and said unto him, Knowest thou that the Pharisees were abellowed, after they heard this saying?
[13] But he answered and said, Every plant, which my heavenly Father hath not planted, shall be rooted up.
[14] Let them alone: they be blind leaders of the blind. And if the blind lead the blind, both shall fall into the ditch.
[15] Then answered Peter and said unto him, Akithe unto us this likeningtale.
[16] And Jesus said, Are ye also yet without understanding?
[17] Do not ye yet understand, that whatsoever goeth in at the mouth goeth into the belly, and is cast out into the draught?
[18] But those things which cometh out of the mouth come forth from the heart; and they brosen the man.
[19] For out of the heart cometh evil thoughts, murders, dernlyership, woughbysleep, thefts, unsooth witness, evilsaking:
[20] These are the things which brosen a man: but to eat with unwashen hands broseneth not a man.
[21] Then Jesus went thence, and wote into the coasts of Tyre and Sidon.
[22] And, behold, a woman of Canaan came out of the same coasts, and yarmed unto him, saying, Have ruth on me, O Lord, thou Son of David; my daughter is aisely swenched with a devil.
[23] But he answered her not a word. And his loreknights came and besought him, saying, Send her away; for she yarmeth after us.
[24] But he answered and said, I am not sent but unto the lost sheep of the house of Israel.
[25] Then came she and worshipped him, saying, Lord, help me.
[26] But he answered and said, It is not meet to take the children's bread, and to cast it to dogs.
[27] And she said, Truth, Lord: yet the dogs eat of the crumbs which fall from their harrs' table.
[28] Then Jesus answered and said unto her, O woman, great is thy faith: be it unto thee even as thou wilt. And her daughter was made whole from that very stound.
[29] And Jesus wote from thence, and came nigh unto the sea of Galilee; and went up into a barrow, and sat down there.
[30] And great drights came unto him, having with them those that were crippled, blind, dumb, lame, and many others, and cast them down at Jesus' feet; and he healed them:
[31] Insomuch that the dright wondered, when they saw the dumb to speak, the crippled to be whole, the lame to walk, and the blind to see: and they woulderened the God of Israel.
[32] Then Jesus called his loreknights unto him, and said, I have armheartness on the dright, forwhy they go on with me now three days, and have nothing to eat: and I will not send them away fasting, lest they faint in the way.
[33] And his loreknights say unto him, Whence should we have so much bread in the wilderness, as to fill so great a dright?
[34] And Jesus saith unto them, How many loaves have ye? And they said, Seven, and a few little fishes.
[35] And he bebade the dright to sit down on the ground.
[36] And he took the seven loaves and the fishes, and gave thanks, and brake them, and gave to his loreknights, and the loreknights to the dright.
[37] And they did all eat, and were filled: and they took up of the broken meat that was left seven baskets full.
[38] And they that did eat were four thousand men, beside women and children.

[39] And he sent away the dright, and took ship, and came into the coasts of Magdala,

Matt.16

[1] The Pharisees also with the Sadducees came, and costened him that he would shew them a tocken from heaven.
[2] He answered and said unto them, When it is evening, ye say, It will be fair weather: for the sky is red.
[3] And in the morning, It will be foul weather to day: for the sky is red and lowring. O ye leasers, ye can discern the anlit of the sky; but can ye not discern the tockens of the times?
[4] A wicked and adulterous strind seeketh after a tocken; and there shall no tocken be given unto it, but the tocken of the forequeether Jonas. And he left them, and wote.
[5] And when his loreknights were come to the other side, they had forgotten to take bread.
[6] Then Jesus said unto them, Take heed and beware of the leaven of the Pharisees and of the Sadducees.
[7] And they reasoned among themselves, saying, It is forwhy we have taken no bread.
[8] Which when Jesus ongot, he said unto them, O ye of little faith, why reason ye among yourselves, forwhy ye have brought no bread?
[9] Do ye not yet understand, neither muned the five loaves of the five thousand, and how many baskets ye took up?
[10] Neither the seven loaves of the four thousand, and how many baskets ye took up?
[11] How is it that ye do not understand that I spake it not to you concerning bread, that ye should beware of the leaven of the Pharisees and of the Sadducees?
[12] Then understood they how that he bade them not beware of the leaven of bread, but of the doctrine of the Pharisees and of the Sadducees.
[13] When Jesus came into the coasts of Caesarea Philippi, he asked his loreknights, saying, Whom do men say that I the Son of man am?
[14] And they said, Some say that thou art John the Forwasher: some, Elias; and others, Jeremias, or one of the forequeethers.
[15] He saith unto them, But whom say ye that I am?
[16] And Simon Peter answered and said, Thou art the Christ, the Son of the living God.
[17] And Jesus answered and said unto him, Blessed art thou, Simon Barjona: for flesh and blood hath not revealed it unto thee, but my Father which is in heaven.
[18] And I say also unto thee, That thou art Peter, and upon this rock I will build my church; and the gates of hell shall not prevail against it.
[19] And I will give unto thee the keys of the kingdom of heaven: and whatsoever thou shalt bind on earth shall be bound in heaven: and whatsoever thou shalt loose on earth shall be loosed in heaven.
[20] Then bebade he his loreknights that they should tell no man that he was Jesus the Christ.
[21] From that time forth began Jesus to shew unto his loreknights, how that he must go unto Jerusalem, and thraw many things of the elders and alderpriests and scribes, and be killed, and be raised again the third day.
[22] Then Peter took him, and began to scold him, saying, Be it far from thee, Lord: this shall not be unto thee.
[23] But he wharveed, and said unto Peter, Get thee behind me, Hellward: thou art a shild unto me: for thou adearest not the things that be of God, but those that be of men.
[24] Then said Jesus unto his loreknights, If any man will come after me, let him andsake himself, and take up his cross, and follow me.
[25] For whosoever will save his life shall lose it: and whosoever will lose his life for my sake shall find it.
[26] For what is a man notesomed, if he shall gain the whole world, and lose his own soul? or what shall a man give in wrixle for his soul?
[27] For the Son of man shall come in the woulder of his Father with his woulderghosts; and then he shall edlean every man according to his works.
[28] Soothly I say unto you, There be some standing here, which shall not taste of death, till they see the Son of man coming in his kingdom.

Matt.17

[1] And after six days Jesus taketh Peter, James, and John his brother, and bringeth them up into an high barrow away,
[2] And was yondshapen before them: and his anlit did shine as the sun, and his clothing was white as the light.
[3] And, behold, there appeared unto them Moses and Elias talking with him.
[4] Then answered Peter, and said unto Jesus, Lord, it is good for us to be here: if thou wilt, let us make here three tields; one for thee, and one for Moses, and one for Elias.
[5] While he yet spake, behold, a bright cloud overshadowed them: and behold a steven out of the cloud, which said, This is my beloved Son, in whom I am well pleased; hear ye him.
[6] And when the loreknights heard it, they fell on their anlit, and were sore afraid.
[7] And Jesus came and rone them, and said, Arise,

and be not afraid.
[8] And when they had lifted up their eyes, they saw no man, save Jesus only.
[9] And as they came down from the barrow, Jesus bebade them, saying, Tell the asighting to no man, until the Son of man be risen again from the dead.
[10] And his loreknights asked him, saying, Why then say the scribes that Elias must first come?
[11] And Jesus answered and said unto them, Elias truly shall first come, and edstathel all things.
[12] But I say unto you, That Elias is come already, and they knew him not, but have done unto him whatsoever they listed. Likewise shall also the Son of man thraw of them.
[13] Then the loreknights understood that he spake unto them of John the Forwasher.
[14] And when they were come to the dright, there came to him a certain man, kneeling down to him, and saying,
[15] Lord, have ruth on my son: for he is woed, and sore dretched: for ofttimes he falleth into the fire, and oft into the water.
[16] And I brought him to thy loreknights, and they could not heal him.
[17] Then Jesus answered and said, O faithless and wough strind, how long shall I be with you? how long shall I thraw you? bring him hither to me.
[18] And Jesus scolded the devil; and he wote out of him: and the child was heald from that very stound.
[19] Then came the loreknights to Jesus, and said, Why could not we cast him out?
[20] And Jesus said unto them, Forwhy of your unbelief: for soothly I say unto you, If ye have faith as a grain of mutungled seed, ye shall say unto this barrow, Go hence to yonder stead; and it shall go; and nothing shall be unmightly unto you.
[21] Howbeit this kind goeth not out but by ibead and fasting.
[22] And while they abode in Galilee, Jesus said unto them, The Son of man shall be forread into the hands of men:
[23] And they shall kill him, and the third day he shall be raised again. And they were outestly sorry.
[24] And when they were come to Capernaum, they that thidged gavel money came to Peter, and said, Doth not your harr pay gavel?
[25] He saith, Yes. And when he was come into the house, Jesus prevented him, saying, What thinkest thou, Simon? of whom do the kings of the earth take thew or gavel? of their own children, or of strangers?
[26] Peter saith unto him, Of strangers. Jesus saith unto him, Then are the children free.
[27] Notwithstanding, lest we should abellow them, go thou to the sea, and cast an hook, and take up the fish that first cometh up; and when thou hast opened his mouth, thou shalt find a piece of money: that take, and give unto them for me and thee.

Matt.18

[1] At the same time came the loreknights unto Jesus, saying, Who is the greatest in the kingdom of heaven?
[2] And Jesus called a little child unto him, and set him in the midst of them,
[3] And said, Soothly I say unto you, Unless ye be forwended, and become as little children, ye shall not go into the kingdom of heaven.
[4] Whosoever therefore shall lower himself as this little child, the same is greatest in the kingdom of heaven.
[5] And whoso shall thidge one such little child in my name thidgeth me.
[6] But whoso shall abellow one of these little ones which believe in me, it were better for him that a millstone were hanged about his neck, and that he were drowned in the depth of the sea.
[7] Woe unto the world forwhy of hurt done to inwits! for it must needs be that hurts come; but woe to that man by whom the hurt cometh!
[8] Wherefore if thy hand or thy foot abellow thee, cut them off, and cast them from thee: it is better for thee to go into life halt or crippled, rather than having two hands or two feet to be cast into everlasting fire.
[9] And if thine eye abellow thee, pluck it out, and cast it from thee: it is better for thee to go into life with one eye, rather than having two eyes to be cast into hell fire.
[10] Take heed that ye forhow not one of these little ones; for I say unto you, That in heaven their woulderghosts do always behold the anlit of my Father which is in heaven.
[11] For the Son of man is come to save that which was lost.
[12] How think ye? if a man have an hundred sheep, and one of them be gone astray, doth he not leave the ninety and nine, and goeth into the barrows, and seeketh that which is gone astray?
[13] And if so be that he find it, soothly I say unto you, he agleeth more of that sheep, than of the ninety and nine which went not astray.
[14] Even so it is not the will of your Father which is in heaven, that one of these little ones should swelt.
[15] Moreover if thy brother shall sin against thee, go and tell him his guilt between thee and him alone: if he shall hear thee, thou hast agot thy brother.
[16] But if he will not hear thee, then take with thee one or two more, that in the mouth of two or three witnesses every word may be established.
[17] And if he shall neglect to hear them, tell it unto

the church: but if he neglect to hear the church, let him be unto thee as an heathen man and a tollner.

[18] Soothly I say unto you, Whatsoever ye shall bind on earth shall be bound in heaven: and whatsoever ye shall loose on earth shall be loosed in heaven.

[19] Again I say unto you, That if two of you shall agree on earth on any thing that they shall ask, it shall be done for them of my Father which is in heaven.

[20] For where two or three are gathered together in my name, there am I in the midst of them.

[21] Then came Peter to him, and said, Lord, how oft shall my brother sin against me, and I forgive him? till seven times?

[22] Jesus saith unto him, I say not unto thee, Until seven times: but, Until seventy times seven.

[23] Therefore is the kingdom of heaven likened unto a somel king, which would take rime of his thanes.

[24] And when he had begun to reckon, one was brought unto him, which owed him ten thousand talents.

[25] But forasmuch as he had not to pay, his lord bebade him to be sold, and his wife, and children, and all that he had, and payment to be made.

[26] The thane therefore fell down, and worshipped him, saying, Lord, have patience with me, and I will pay thee all.

[27] Then the lord of that thane was stirred with evensorrow, and loosed him, and forgave him the owing.

[28] But the same thane went out, and found one of his fellowthanes, which owed him an hundred pence: and he laid hands on him, and took him by the throat, saying, Pay me that thou owest.

[29] And his fellowthane fell down at his feet, and besought him, saying, Have patience with me, and I will pay thee all.

[30] And he would not: but went and cast him into prison, till he should pay the owing.

[31] So when his fellowthanes saw what was done, they were very sorry, and came and told unto their lord all that was done.

[32] Then his lord, after that he had called him, said unto him, O thou wicked thane, I forgave thee all that owing, forwhy thou besought me:

[33] Shouldest not thou also have had togetherache on thy fellowthane, even as I had togetherache on thee?

[34] And his lord was wroth, and gave him over to the souselers, till he should pay all that was due unto him.

[35] So likewise shall my heavenly Father do also unto you, if ye from your hearts forgive not every one his brother their sins.

Matt.19

[1] And it came to be, that when Jesus had beended these sayings, he wote from Galilee, and came into the coasts of Judaea beyond Jordan;

[2] And great drights followed him; and he healed them there.

[3] The Pharisees also came unto him, costening him, and saying unto him, Is it lawful for a man to put away his wife for all grounds?

[4] And he answered and said unto them, Have ye not read, that he which made them at the beginning made them man and woman,

[5] And said, For this whyth shall a man leave father and mother, and shall cling to his wife: and they twain shall be one flesh?

[6] Wherefore they are no more twain, but one flesh. What therefore God hath fayed together, let not man put asunder.

[7] They say unto him, Why did Moses then bebid to give a writing of wedlockcleave, and to put her away?

[8] He saith unto them, Moses forwhy of the hardness of your hearts thrawed you to put away your wives: but from the beginning it was not so.

[9] And I say unto you, Whosoever shall put away his wife, unless it be for forlying, and shall ewen another, begoeth forlying: and whoso wedeth her which is put away doth bego forlying.

[10] His loreknights say unto him, If the case of the man be so with his wife, it is not good to ewen.

[11] But he said unto them, All men cannot thidge this saying, save they to whom it is given.

[12] For there are some orpintles, which were so born from their mother's womb: and there are some orpintles, which were made orpintles of men: and there be orpintles, which have made themselves orpintles for the kingdom of heaven's sake. He that is able to thidge it, let him thidge it.

[13] Then were there brought unto him little children, that he should put his hands on them, and abid: and the loreknights scolded them.

[14] But Jesus said, Thraw little children, and forbid them not, to come unto me: for of such is the kingdom of heaven.

[15] And he laid his hands on them, and wote thence.

[16] And, behold, one came and said unto him, Good Harr, what good thing shall I do, that I may have alderlong life?

[17] And he said unto him, Why callest thou me good? there is none good but one, that is, God: but if thou wilt go into life, keep the bodewords.

[18] He saith unto him, Which? Jesus said, Thou shalt do no murder, Thou shalt not bego dernlyership, Thou shalt not steal, Thou shalt not bear unsooth witness,

[19] Ore thy father and thy mother: and, Thou shalt love thy neighbour as thyself.

[20] The young man saith unto him, All these things

have I kept from my youth up: what lack I yet?
[21] Jesus said unto him, If thou wilt be fullfremmed, go and sell that thou hast, and give to the poor, and thou shalt have mathem in heaven: and come and follow me.
[22] But when the young man heard that saying, he went away yomerful: for he had great belongings.
[23] Then said Jesus unto his loreknights, Soothly I say unto you, That a rich man shall hardly go into the kingdom of heaven.
[24] And again I say unto you, It is easier for a camel to go through the eye of a needle, than for a rich man to go into the kingdom of God.
[25] When his loreknights heard it, they were outestly amazed, saying, Who then can be saved?
[26] But Jesus beheld them, and said unto them, With men this is unacomingly; but with God all things are acomingly.
[27] Then answered Peter and said unto him, Behold, we have forsaken all, and followed thee; what shall we have therefore?
[28] And Jesus said unto them, Soothly I say unto you, That ye which have followed me, in the edstatheling when the Son of man shall sit in the throne of his thrum, ye also shall sit upon twelve thrones, deeming the twelve tribes of Israel.
[29] And every one that hath forsaken houses, or brethren, or sisters, or father, or mother, or wife, or children, or lands, for my name's sake, shall thidge an hundredfold, and shall erve everlasting life.
[30] But many that are first shall be last; and the last shall be first.

Matt.20

[1] For the kingdom of heaven is like unto a man that is an householder, which went out early in the morning to hire swinkers into his vineyard.
[2] And when he had agreed with the swinkers for a penny a day, he sent them into his vineyard.
[3] And he went out about the third stound, and saw others standing idle in the marketstead,
[4] And said unto them; Go ye also into the vineyard, and whatsoever is right I will give you. And they went their way.
[5] Again he went out about the sixth and ninth stound, and did likewise.
[6] And about the eleventh stound he went out, and found others standing idle, and saith unto them, Why stand ye here all the day idle?
[7] They say unto him, Forwhy no man hath hired us. He saith unto them, Go ye also into the vineyard; and whatsoever is right, that shall ye thidge.
[8] So when even was come, the lord of the vineyard saith unto his steward, Call the swinkers, and give them their hire, beginning from the last unto the first.
[9] And when they came that were hired about the eleventh stound, they thidged every man a penny.
[10] But when the first came, they weend that they should have thidged more; and they likewise thidged every man a penny.
[11] And when they had thidged it, they murmured against the goodman of the house,
[12] Saying, These last have wrought but one stound, and thou hast made them sameworthed unto us, which have borne the burden and heat of the day.
[13] But he answered one of them, and said, Friend, I do thee no wrong: didst not thou thweer with me for a penny?
[14] Take that thine is, and go thy way: I will give unto this last, even as unto thee.
[15] Is it not lawful for me to do what I will with mine own? Is thine eye evil, forwhy I am good?
[16] So the last shall be first, and the first last: for many be called, but few chosen.
[17] And Jesus going up to Jerusalem took the twelve loreknights afar, and said unto them,
[18] Behold, we go up to Jerusalem; and the Son of man shall be forreded unto the alderpriests and unto the scribes, and they shall fordeem him to death,
[19] And shall bring him before the Gentiles to bismer, and to scourge, and to roodfasten him: and the third day he shall rise again.
[20] Then came to him the mother of Zebedee's children with her sons, worshipping him, and wishing a somel thing of him.
[21] And he said unto her, What wilt thou? She saith unto him, Grant that these my two sons may sit, the one on thy right hand, and the other on the left, in thy kingdom.
[22] But Jesus answered and said, Ye know not what ye ask. Are ye able to drink of the cup that I shall drink of, and to be forwashed with the forwashing that I am forwashed with? They say unto him, We are able.
[23] And he saith unto them, Ye shall drink indeed of my cup, and be forwashed with the forwashing that I am forwashed with: but to sit on my right hand, and on my left, is not mine to give, but it shall be given to them for whom it is yarked of my Father.
[24] And when the ten heard it, they were bewayed with unfairnessanger against the two brethren.
[25] But Jesus called them unto him, and said, Ye know that the athelings of the Gentiles wield wold over them, and they that are great wield alderdom upon them.
[26] But it shall not be so among you: but whosoever will be great among you, let him be your acarer;
[27] And whosoever will be head among you, let him be your thane:

[28] Even as the Son of man came not to be acared unto, but to acarer, and to give his life as a boughtling for many.
[29] And as they wote from Jericho, a great dright followed him.
[30] And, behold, two blind men sitting by the way side, when they heard that Jesus wended by, yarmed out, saying, Have ruth on us, O Lord, thou Son of David.
[31] And the dright scorned them, forwhy they should hold their frith: but they yarmed the more, saying, Have ruth on us, O Lord, thou Son of David.
[32] And Jesus stood still, and called them, and said, What will ye that I shall do unto you?
[33] They say unto him, Lord, that our eyes may be opened.
[34] So Jesus had evensorrow on them, and remmed their eyes: and forthwith their eyes thidged sight, and they followed him.

Matt.21

[1] And when they drew nigh unto Jerusalem, and were come to Bethphage, unto the barrow of Olives, then sent Jesus two loreknights,
[2] Saying unto them, Go into the town over against you, and straightway ye shall find an ass tied, and a colt with her: loose them, and bring them unto me.
[3] And if any man say ought unto you, ye shall say, The Lord hath need of them; and straightway he will send them.
[4] All this was done, that it might be fulfilled which was spoken by the forequeether, saying,
[5] Tell ye the daughter of Sion, Behold, thy King cometh unto thee, meek, and sitting upon an ass, and a colt the foal of an ass.
[6] And the loreknights went, and did as Jesus bebade them,
[7] And brought the ass, and the colt, and put on them their clothes, and they set him thereon.
[8] And a very great dright spread their clothes in the way; others cut down branches from the trees, and strawed them in the way.
[9] And the drights that went before, and that followed, yarmed, saying, Hosanna to the Son of David: Blessed is he that cometh in the name of the Lord; Hosanna in the highest.
[10] And when he was come into Jerusalem, all the chester was aquetched, saying, Who is this?
[11] And the dright said, This is Jesus the forequeether of Nazareth of Galilee.
[12] And Jesus went into the worshipstead of God, and cast out all them that sold and bought in the worshipstead, and overthrew the tables of the moneyawenders, and the seats of them that sold doves,
[13] And said unto them, It is written, My house shall be called the house of ibead; but ye have made it a den of thieves.
[14] And the blind and the lame came to him in the worshipstead; and he healed them.
[15] And when the alderpriests and scribes saw the wonderful things that he did, and the children crying in the worshipstead, and saying, Hosanna to the Son of David; they were sore andcweemed,
[16] And said unto him, Hearest thou what these say? And Jesus saith unto them, Yea; have ye never read, Out of the mouth of babes and sucklings thou hast fullcome praise?
[17] And he left them, and went out of the chester into Bethany; and he woned there.
[18] Now in the morning as he edwhorve into the chester, he hungered.
[19] And when he saw a fig tree in the way, he came to it, and found nothing thereon, but leaves only, and said unto it, Let no ovet grow on thee henceforward for ever. And then fast the fig tree withered away.
[20] And when the loreknights saw it, they awondered, saying, How soon is the fig tree withered away!
[21] Jesus answered and said unto them, Soothly I say unto you, If ye have faith, and twight not, ye shall not only do this which is done to the fig tree, but also if ye shall say unto this barrow, Be thou bewayed, and be thou cast into the sea; it shall be done.
[22] And all things, whatsoever ye shall ask in ibead, believing, ye shall thidge.
[23] And when he was come into the worshipstead, the alderpriests and the elders of the theed came unto him as he was teaching, and said, By what alderdom doest thou these things? and who gave thee this alderdom?
[24] And Jesus answered and said unto them, I also will ask you one thing, which if ye tell me, I in like wise will tell you by what alderdom I do these things.
[25] The forwashing of John, whence was it? from heaven, or of men? And they hidged with themselves, saying, If we shall say, From heaven; he will say unto us, Why did ye not then believe him?
[26] But if we shall say, Of men; we fear the theed; for all hold John as a forequeether.
[27] And they answered Jesus, and said, We cannot tell. And he said unto them, Neither tell I you by what alderdom I do these things.
[28] But what think ye? A certain man had two sons; and he came to the first, and said, Son, go work to day in my vineyard.
[29] He answered and said, I will not: but afterward he berueed, and went.
[30] And he came to the twoth, and said likewise. And he answered and said, I go, sir: and went not.
[31] Whether of them twain did the will of his father?

They say unto him, The first. Jesus saith unto them, Soothly I say unto you, That the tollners and the harlots go into the kingdom of God before you.

[32] For John came unto you in the way of rightsomeness, and ye believed him not: but the tollners and the harlots believed him: and ye, when ye had seen it, berueed not afterward, that ye might believe him.

[33] Hear another likeningtale: There was a somel householder, which planted a vineyard, and hedged it round about, and digged a winethrism in it, and built a tower, and let it out to husbandmen, and went into a far land:

[34] And when the time of the ovet drew near, he sent his thanes to the husbandmen, that they might thidge the ovets of it.

[35] And the husbandmen took his thanes, and beat one, and killed another, and stoned another.

[36] Again, he sent other thanes more than the first: and they did unto them likewise.

[37] But last of all he sent unto them his son, saying, They will ore my son.

[38] But when the husbandmen saw the son, they said among themselves, This is the heir; come, let us kill him, and let us seize on his erve.

[39] And they caught him, and cast him out of the vineyard, and slew him.

[40] When the lord therefore of the vineyard cometh, what will he do unto those husbandmen?

[41] They say unto him, He will gnornfully forswithe those wicked men, and will let out his vineyard unto other husbandmen, which shall give him the ovets in their yeartides.

[42] Jesus saith unto them, Did ye never read in the writ, The stone which the builders withchose, the same is become the head of the corner: this is the Lord's doing, and it is wondersome in our eyes?

[43] Therefore say I unto you, The kingdom of God shall be taken from you, and given to a folkdom bringing forth the ovets thereof.

[44] And whosoever shall fall on this stone shall be broken: but on whomsoever it shall fall, it will grind him to powder.

[45] And when the alderprisests and Pharisees had heard his likeningtales, they ongot that he spake of them.

[46] But when they sought to lay hands on him, they feared the dright, forwhy they took him for a forequeether.

Matt.22

[1] And Jesus answered and spake unto them again by likeningtales, and said,

[2] The kingdom of heaven is like unto a certain king, which made a wedding for his son,

[3] And sent forth his thanes to call them that were bidden to the wedding: and they would not come.

[4] Again, he sent forth other thanes, saying, Tell them which are bidden, Behold, I have yarked my dinner: my oxen and my fatlings are killed, and all things are ready: come unto the wedding.

[5] But they made light of it, and went their ways, one to his thorp, another to his sellstuff:

[6] And the gome took his thanes, and bade them spitefully, and slew them.

[7] But when the king heard thereof, he was wroth: and he sent forth his heres, and fordid those murderers, and burned up their chester.

[8] Then saith he to his thanes, The wedding is ready, but they which were bidden were not worthy.

[9] Go ye therefore into the highways, and as many as ye shall find, bid to the wedding.

[10] So those thanes went out into the highways, and gathered together all as many as they found, both bad and good: and the wedding was sided with guests.

[11] And when the king came in to see the guests, he saw there a man which had not on a wedding clothing:

[12] And he saith unto him, Friend, how camest thou in hither not having a wedding clothing? And he was speechless.

[13] Then said the king to the thanes, Bind him hand and foot, and take him away, and cast him into outer darkness; there shall be weeping and gnashing of teeth.

[14] For many are called, but few are chosen.

[15] Then went the Pharisees, and took thoughting how they might bemaze him in his talk.

[16] And they sent out unto him their loreknights with the Herodians, saying, Harr, we know that thou art true, and teachest the way of God in truth, neither carest thou for any man: for thou hidgest not the gome of men.

[17] Tell us therefore, What thinkest thou? Is it lawful to give gavel unto Caesar, or not?

[18] But Jesus freeded their wickedness, and said, Why costen ye me, ye leasers?

[19] Shew me the gavel money. And they brought unto him a penny.

[20] And he saith unto them, Whose is this alikeness and overwriting?

[21] They say unto him, Caesar's. Then saith he unto them, Give therefore unto Caesar the things which are Caesar's; and unto God the things that are God's.

[22] When they had heard these words, they awonered, and left him, and went their way.

[23] The same day came to him the Sadducees, which say that there is no arist, and asked him,

[24] Saying, Harr, Moses said, If a man die, having no children, his brother shall heam his wife, and raise up

seed unto his brother.

[25] Now there were with us seven brethren: and the first, when he had wed a wife, acwelled, and, having no unsoundness, left his wife unto his brother:

[26] Likewise the second also, and the third, unto the seventh.

[27] And last of all the woman died also.

[28] Therefore in the arist whose wife shall she be of the seven? for they all had her.

[29] Jesus answered and said unto them, Ye do err, not knowing the writ, nor the wold of God.

[30] For in the arist they neither wed, nor are given in wedlock, but are as the woulderghosts of God in heaven.

[31] But as for the arist of the dead, have ye not read that which was spoken unto you by God, saying,

[32] I am the God of Abraham, and the God of Isaac, and the God of Jacob? God is not the God of the dead, but of the living.

[33] And when the dright heard this, they were awondered at his bodeword.

[34] But when the Pharisees had heard that he had put the Sadducees to swie, they were gathered together.

[35] Then one of them, which was a lawyer, asked him a fraign, costening him, and saying,

[36] Harr, which is the great bodeword in the law?

[37] Jesus said unto him, Thou shalt love the Lord thy God with all thy heart, and with all thy soul, and with all thy mind.

[38] This is the first and great bodeword.

[39] And the twoth is like unto it, Thou shalt love thy neighbour as thyself.

[40] On these two bodewords hang all the law and the forequeethers.

[41] While the Pharisees were gathered together, Jesus asked them,

[42] Saying, What think ye of Christ? whose son is he? They say unto him, The Son of David.

[43] He saith unto them, How then doth David in ferth call him Lord, saying,

[44] The LORD said unto my Lord, Sit thou on my right hand, till I make thine fiends thy footstool?

[45] If David then call him Lord, how is he his son?

[46] And no man was able to answer him a word, neither durst any man from that day forth ask him any more fraigns.

Matt.23

[1] Then spake Jesus to the dright, and to his loreknights,

[2] Saying, The scribes and the Pharisees sit in Moses' seat:

[3] All therefore whatsoever they bid you alook, that alook and do; but do not ye after their works: for they say, and do not.

[4] For they bind heavy burdens and heafly to be borne, and lay them on men's shoulders; but they themselves will not aquetch them with one of their fingers.

[5] But all their works they do for to be seen of men: they make broad their writfolders, and bigen the borders of their clothes,

[6] And love the uppermost rooms at simbletides, and the head seats in the worshipsteads,

[7] And greetings in the sellstead, and to be called of men, Rabbi, Rabbi.

[8] But be not ye called Rabbi: for one is your Harr, even Christ; and all ye are brethren.

[9] And call no man your father upon the earth: for one is your Father, which is in heaven.

[10] Neither be ye called harrs: for one is your Harr, even Christ.

[11] But he that is greatest among you shall be your thane.

[12] And whosoever shall reem himself shall be alowered; and he that shall lower himself shall be reemed.

[13] But woe unto you, scribes and Pharisees, leasers! for ye shut up the kingdom of heaven against men: for ye neither go in yourselves, neither thole ye them that are going to go in.

[14] Woe unto you, scribes and Pharisees, leasers! for ye glender widows' houses, and for upshow make long ibead: therefore ye shall thidge the greater hellwitred.

[15] Woe unto you, scribes and Pharisees, leasers! for ye fare through sea and land to make one forwended, and when he is made, ye make him twofold more the child of hell than yourselves.

[16] Woe unto you, blind waywitter, which say, Whosoever shall swear by the worshipstead, it is nothing; but whosoever shall swear by the gold of the worshipstead, he is a sinner!

[17] Ye fools and blind: for whether is greater, the gold, or the worshipstead that halloweth the gold?

[18] And, Whosoever shall swear by the altar, it is nothing; but whosoever sweareth by the gift that is upon it, he is guilty.

[19] Ye fools and blind: for whether is greater, the gift, or the altar that halloweth the gift?

[20] Whoso therefore shall swear by the altar, sweareth by it, and by all things thereon.

[21] And whoso shall swear by the worshipstead, sweareth by it, and by him that dwelleth therein.

[22] And he that shall swear by heaven, sweareth by the throne of God, and by him that sitteth thereon.

[23] Woe unto you, scribes and Pharisees, leasers! for ye pay tithe of mint and anise and cummin, and have left out the weightier matters of the law, deeming, ruth,

and faith: these ought ye to have done, and not to leave the other undone.
[24] Ye blind guides, which strain at a gnat, and swallow a camel.
[25] Woe unto you, scribes and Pharisees, leasers! for ye make clean the outside of the cup and of the platter, but within they are full of greed and overmuch.
[26] Thou blind Pharisee, cleanse first that which is within the cup and platter, that the outside of them may be clean also.
[27] Woe unto you, scribes and Pharisees, leasers! for ye are like unto whited lichrests, which indeed outsee litty outward, but are within full of dead men's bones, and of all uncleanness.
[28] Even so ye also outwardly thench rightsome unto men, but within ye are full of leaserhood and unrightdom.
[29] Woe unto you, scribes and Pharisees, leasers! forwhy ye build the tombs of the forequeethers, and sid the lichrests of the rightsome,
[30] And say, If we had been in the days of our fathers, we would not have been dealtakers with them in the blood of the forequeethers.
[31] Wherefore ye be witnesses unto yourselves, that ye are the children of them which killed the forequeethers.
[32] Fill ye up then the meath of your fathers.
[33] Ye nadders, ye strind of nadders, how can ye withfare the hellwitred of hell?
[34] Wherefore, behold, I send unto you forequeethers, and wise men, and scribes: and some of them ye shall kill and roodfasten; and some of them shall ye scourge in your worshipsteads, and dretch them from chester to chester:
[35] That upon you may come all the rightsome blood shed upon the earth, from the blood of rightsome Abel unto the blood of Zacharias son of Barachias, whom ye slew between the worshipstead and the altar.
[36] Soothly I say unto you, All these things shall come upon this strind.
[37] O Jerusalem, Jerusalem, thou that killest the forequeethers, and stonest them which are sent unto thee, how often would I have gathered thy children together, even as a hen gathereth her chickens under her wings, and ye would not!
[38] Behold, your house is left unto you forwasted.
[39] For I say unto you, Ye shall not see me henceforth, till ye shall say, Blessed is he that cometh in the name of the Lord.

Matt.24

[1] And Jesus went out, and wote from the worshipstead: and his loreknights came to him for to shew him the buildings of the worshipstead.
[2] And Jesus said unto them, See ye not all these things? soothly I say unto you, There shall not be left here one stone upon another, that shall not be thrown down.
[3] And as he sat upon the barrow of Olives, the loreknights came unto him dernly, saying, Tell us, when shall these things be? and what shall be the tocken of thy coming, and of the end of the world?
[4] And Jesus answered and said unto them, Take heed that no man swike you.
[5] For many shall come in my name, saying, I am Christ; and shall swike many.
[6] And ye shall hear of gouths and imbsays of gouths: see that ye be not filled with derf: for all these things must come to be, but the end is not yet.
[7] For folkdopm shall rise against folkdom, and kingdom against kingdom: and there shall be hungers, and smittles, and earthquakes, in sundry steads.
[8] All these are the beginning of sorrows.
[9] Then shall they bring you up to be brocked, and shall kill you: and ye shall be hated of all folkdom for my name's sake.
[10] And then shall many be abellowed, and shall forread one another, and shall hate one another.
[11] And many unsooth forequeethers shall rise, and shall swike many.
[12] And forwhy unrightdom shall abound, the love of many shall wax cold.
[13] But he that shall thole unto the end, the same shall be saved.
[14] And this gospel of the kingdom shall be preached in all the world for a witness unto all folkdoms; and then shall the end come.
[15] When ye therefore shall see the grir of forwastedness, spoken of by Daniel the forequeether, stand in the holy stead, (whoso readeth, let him understand:)
[16] Then let them which be in Judaea flee into the barrow:
[17] Let him which is on the housetop not come down to take any thing out of his house:
[18] Neither let him which is in the field wharve back to take his clothes.
[19] And woe unto them that are with child, and to them that give suck in those days!
[20] But abid ye that your flight be not in the winter, neither on the sabbath day:
[21] For then shall be great derst, such as was not since the beginning of the world to this time, no, nor ever shall be.
[22] And unless those days should be shortened, there should no flesh be nerred: but for the chosen's sake those days shall be shortened.
[23] Then if any man shall say unto you, Lo, here is

Christ, or there; believe it not.
[24] For there shall arise unsooth Christs, and unsooth forequeethers, and shall shew great tockens and wonders; insomuch that, if it were acomingly, they shall swike the very adler.
[25] Behold, I have told you before.
[26] Wherefore if they shall say unto you, Behold, he is in the throughdry-stead; go not forth: behold, he is in the dern rooms; believe it not.
[27] For as the lightning cometh out of the east, and shineth even unto the west; so shall also the coming of the Son of man be.
[28] For wheresoever the lich is, there will the eagles be gathered together.
[29] Forthwith after the derst of those days shall the sun be darkened, and the moon shall not give her light, and the tungles shall fall from heaven, and the wolds of the heavens shall be shaken:
[30] And then shall tred up the token of the Son of man in heaven: and then shall all the maiths of the earth mourn, and they shall see the Son of man coming in the clouds of heaven with wold and great thrum.
[31] And he shall send his woulderghosts with a great sound of a trumpet, and they shall gather together his chosen from the four winds, from one end of heaven to the other.
[32] Now learn a likeningtale of the fig tree; When his branch is yet tender, and putteth forth leaves, ye know that summer is nigh:
[33] So likewise ye, when ye shall see all these things, know that it is near, even at the doors.
[34] Soothly I say unto you, This strind shall not wend away, till all these things be fulfilled.
[35] Heaven and earth shall wend away, but my words shall not wend away.
[36] But of that day and stound knoweth no man, no, not the woulderghosts of heaven, but my Father only.
[37] But as the days of Noe were, so shall also the coming of the Son of man be.
[38] For as in the days that were before the flood they were eating and drinking, bewedding and giving in wedlock, until the day that Noe goed into the ark,
[39] And knew not until the flood came, and took them all away; so shall also the coming of the Son of man be.
[40] Then shall two be in the field; the one shall be taken, and the other left.
[41] Two women shall be grinding at the mill; the one shall be taken, and the other left.
[42] Watch therefore: for ye know not what stound your Lord doth come.
[43] But know this, that if the goodman of the house had known in what watch the thief would come, he would have watched, and would not have dreed his house to be broken up.
[44] Therefore be ye also ready: for in such an stound as ye think not the Son of man cometh.
[45] Who then is a faithful and wise thane, whom his lord hath made woldend over his household, to give them meat in due time?
[46] Blessed is that thane, whom his lord when he cometh shall find so doing.
[47] Soothly I say unto you, That he shall make him woldend over all his goods.
[48] But and if that evil thane shall say in his heart, My lord eldeth his coming;
[49] And shall begin to smite his fellow thanes, and to eat and drink with the drunken;
[50] The lord of that thane shall come in a day when he looketh not for him, and in an stound that he is not aware of,
[51] And shall cut him asunder, and give to him his deal with the leasers: there shall be weeping and gnashing of teeth.

Matt.25

[1] Then shall the kingdom of heaven be likened unto ten maidens, which took their lamps, and went forth to meet the bridegroom.
[2] And five of them were wise, and five were unwitly.
[3] They that were foolish took their lamps, and took no oil with them:
[4] But the wise took oil in their vessels with their lamps.
[5] While the bridegroom tarried, they all slumbered and slept.
[6] And at midnight there was a yarm made, Behold, the bridegroom cometh; go ye out to meet him.
[7] Then all those maiths arose, and trimmed their lamps.
[8] And the foolish said unto the wise, Give us of your oil; for our lamps are gone out.
[9] But the wise answered, saying, Not so; lest there be not enough for us and you: but go ye rather to them that sell, and buy for yourselves.
[10] And while they went to buy, the bridegroom came; and they that were ready went in with him to the wedding: and the door was shut.
[11] Afterward came also the other maidens, saying, Lord, Lord, open to us.
[12] But he answered and said, Soothly I say unto you, I know you not.
[13] Watch therefore, for ye know neither the day nor the stound wherein the Son of man cometh.
[14] For the kingdom of heaven is as a man faring into a far land, who called his own thanes, and gave unto them his goods.
[15] And unto one he gave five talents, to another two,

and to another one; to every man by his canhood; and straightway took his sith.
[16] Then he that had thidged the five talents went and traded with the same, and made them other five talents.
[17] And likewise he that had thidged two, he also agot other two.
[18] But he that had thidged one went and digged in the earth, and hid his lord's money.
[19] After a long time the lord of those thanes cometh, and reckoneth with them.
[20] And so he that had thidged five talents came and brought other five talents, saying, Lord, thou gavest unto me five talents: behold, I have agot beside them five talents more.
[21] His lord said unto him, Well done, thou good and truthfast thane: thou hast been faithful over a few things, I will make thee woldend over many things: go thou into the mirth of thy lord.
[22] He also that had thidged two talents came and said, Lord, thou gavest unto me two talents: behold, I have agot two other talents beside them.
[23] His lord said unto him, Well done, good and faithful thane; thou hast been faithful over a few things, I will make thee woldend over many things: go thou into the joy of thy lord.
[24] Then he which had thidged the one talent came and said, Lord, I knew thee that thou art an hard man, reaping where thou hast not sown, and gathering where thou hast not strawed:
[25] And I was afraid, and went and hid thy talent in the earth: lo, there thou hast that is thine.
[26] His lord answered and said unto him, Thou wicked and slothful thane, thou knewest that I reap where I sowed not, and gather where I have not strawed:
[27] Thou oughtest therefore to have put my money to the wrixlers, and then at my coming I should have thidged mine own with usury.
[28] Take therefore the talent from him, and give it unto him which hath ten talents.
[29] For unto every one that hath shall be given, and he shall have fullsomeness: but from him that hath not shall be taken away even that which he hath.
[30] And cast ye the unnotesome thane into outer darkness: there shall be weeping and gnashing of teeth.
[31] When the Son of man shall come in his woulder, and all the holy woulderghosts with him, then shall he sit upon the throne of his woulder:
[32] And before him shall be gathered all folkdoms: and he shall side them out one from another, as a shepherd todealeth his sheep from the goats:
[33] And he shall set the sheep on his right hand, but the goats on the left.
[34] Then shall the King say unto them on his right hand, Come, ye blessed of my Father, erve the kingdom yarked for you from the fromth of the world:
[35] For I was an hungred, and ye gave me meat: I was thirsty, and ye gave me drink: I was a comeling, and ye took me in:
[36] Naked, and ye clothed me: I was sick, and ye neased me: I was in witern, and ye came unto me.
[37] Then shall the rightsome answer him, saying, Lord, when saw we thee an hungred, and fed thee? or thirsty, and gave thee drink?
[38] When saw we thee a comeling, and took thee in? or naked, and clothed thee?
[39] Or when saw we thee sick, or in witern, and came unto thee?
[40] And the King shall answer and say unto them, Soothly I say unto you, Inasmuch as ye have done it unto one of the least of these my brethren, ye have done it unto me.
[41] Then shall he say also unto them on the left hand, Wite from me, ye cursed, into everlasting fire, yarked for the devil and his woulderghosts:
[42] For I was an hungred, and ye gave me no meat: I was thirsty, and ye gave me no drink:
[43] I was a comeling, and ye took me not in: naked, and ye clothed me not: sick, and in witern, and ye neased me not.
[44] Then shall they also answer him, saying, Lord, when saw we thee an hungred, or athirst, or a comeling, or naked, or sick, or in witern, and did not acare unto thee?
[45] Then shall he answer them, saying, Soothly I say unto you, Inasmuch as ye did it not to one of the least of these, ye did it not to me.
[46] And these shall go away into everlasting witered: but the rightsome into life alderlong.

Matt.26

[1] And it came to be, when Jesus had beended all these sayings, he said unto his loreknights,
[2] Ye know that after two days is the simbletide of the eaastersimble, and the Son of man is forread to be roodfastened.
[3] Then gathered together the alderpriests, and the scribes, and the elders of the theed, unto the thronestead of the high priest, who was called Caiaphas,
[4] And sought up that they might take Jesus by underwebishness, and kill him.
[5] But they said, Not on the simbletide day, lest there be an uproar among the theed.
[6] Now when Jesus was in Bethany, in the house of Simon the leper,
[7] There came unto him a woman having an alabaster box of very worthful smearls , and poured it on his

head, as he sat at meat.

[8] But when his loreknights saw it, they had unfairnessanger, saying, To what end is this waste?

[9] For this smealrs might have been sold for much, and given to the arm.

[10] When Jesus understood it, he said unto them, Why trouble ye the woman? for she hath wrought a good work upon me.

[11] For ye have the poor always with you; but me ye have not always.

[12] For in that she hath poured this smearls on my body, she did it for my burial.

[13] Soothly I say unto you, Wheresoever this gospel shall be preached in the whole world, there shall also this, that this woman hath done, be told for a min of her.

[14] Then one of the twelve, called Judas Iscariot, went unto the alderpriests,

[15] And said unto them, What will ye give me, and I will give him over unto you? And they dealt with him for thirty pieces of silver.

[16] And from that time he sought tideliness to forread him.

[17] Now the first day of the simbletide of unleavened bread the loreknights came to Jesus, saying unto him, Where wilt thou that we yark for thee to eat the eaastersimble?

[18] And he said, Go into the chester to such a man, and say unto him, The Harr saith, My time is at hand; I will keep the eaastersimble at thy house with my loreknights.

[19] And the loreknights did as Jesus had bade them; and they made ready the eaastersimble.

[20] Now when the even was come, he sat down with the twelve.

[21] And as they did eat, he said, Soothly I say unto you, that one of you shall forread me.

[22] And they were outesty sorrowful, and began every one of them to say unto him, Lord, is it I?

[23] And he answered and said, He that dippeth his hand with me in the dish, the same shall forread me.

[24] The Son of man goeth as it is written of him: but woe unto that man by whom the Son of man is forread! it had been good for that man if he had not been born.

[25] Then Judas, which forread him, answered and said, Harr, is it I? He said unto him, Thou hast said.

[26] And as they were eating, Jesus took bread, and blessed it, and brake it, and gave it to the loreknights, and said, Take, eat; this is my body.

[27] And he took the cup, and gave thanks, and gave it to them, saying, Drink ye all of it;

[28] For this is my blood of the new kitheness, which is shed for many for the eftgiving of sins.

[29] But I say unto you, I will not drink henceforth of this ovet of the vine, until that day when I drink it new with you in my Father's kingdom.

[30] And when they had sung an hymn, they went out into the barrow of Olives.

[31] Then saith Jesus unto them, All ye shall be abellowed forwhy of me this night: for it is written, I will smite the shepherd, and the sheep of the flock shall be scattered abroad.

[32] But after I am risen again, I will go before you into Galilee.

[33] Peter answered and said unto him, Though all men shall be abellowed forwhy of thee, yet will I never be abellowed.

[34] Jesus said unto him, Soothly I say unto thee, That this night, before the cock crow, thou shalt andsake me thrice.

[35] Peter said unto him, Though I should die with thee, yet will I not andsake thee. Likewise also said all the loreknights.

[36] Then cometh Jesus with them unto a stead called Gethsemane, and saith unto the loreknights, Sit ye here, while I go and abid yonder.

[37] And he took with him Peter and the two sons of Zebedee, and began to be sorrowful and very heavy.

[38] Then saith he unto them, My soul is outestly sorrowful, even unto death: tarry ye here, and watch with me.

[39] And he went a little further, and fell on his anlit, and abade, saying, O my Father, if it be acomingly, let this cup wend from me: nevertheless not as I will, but as thou wilt.

[40] And he cometh unto the loreknights, and findeth them asleep, and saith unto Peter, What, could ye not watch with me one stound?

[41] Watch and abid, that ye go not into costening: the ferth indeed is willing, but the flesh is weak.

[42] He went away again the twoth time, and abade, saying, O my Father, if this cup may not wend away from me, unless I drink it, thy will be done.

[43] And he came and found them asleep again: for their eyes were heavy.

[44] And he left them, and went away again, and abade the third time, saying the same words.

[45] Then cometh he to his loreknights, and saith unto them, Sleep on now, and take your rest: behold, the stound is at hand, and the Son of man is forread into the hands of sinners.

[46] Rise, let us be going: behold, he is at hand that doth forread me.

[47] And while he yet spake, lo, Judas, one of the twelve, came, and with him a great dright with swords and staves, from the alderpriests and elders of the theed.

[48] Now he that forread him gave them a tocken, saying, Whomsoever I shall kiss, that same is he: hold him fast.

[49] And forthwith he came to Jesus, and said, Hail, harr; and kissed him.
[50] And Jesus said unto him, Friend, wherefore art thou come? Then came they, and laid hands on Jesus, and took him.
[51] And, behold, one of them which were with Jesus stretched out his hand, and drew his sword, and struck a thane of the high priest's, and smote off his ear.
[52] Then said Jesus unto him, Put up again thy sword into his stead: for all they that take the sword shall swelt with the sword.
[53] Thinkest thou that I cannot now abid to my Father, and he shall soon give me more than twelve legions of woulderghosts?
[54] But how then shall the writ be fulfilled, that thus it must be?
[55] In that same stound said Jesus to the drights, Are ye come out as against a thief with swords and staves for to take me? I sat daily with you teaching in the worshipstead, and ye laid no hold on me.
[56] But all this was done, that the writ of the forequeethers might be fulfilled. Then all the loreknights forsook him, and fled.
[57] And they that had laid hold on Jesus led him away to Caiaphas the high priest, where the scribes and the elders were gathered.
[58] But Peter followed him afar off unto the high priest's thronestead, and went in, and sat with the thanes, to see the end.
[59] Now the alderprisests, and elders, and all the rownwitmoot, sought unsooth witness against Jesus, to put him to death;
[60] But found none: yea, though many unsooth witnesses came, yet found they none. At the last came two unsooth witnesses,
[61] And said, This fellow said, I am able to fordo the worshipstead of God, and to build it in three days.
[62] And the high priest arose, and said unto him, Answerest thou nothing? what is it which these witness against thee?
[63] But Jesus held his frith. And the high priest answered and said unto him, I hote thee by the living God, that thou tell us whether thou be the Christ, the Son of God.
[64] Jesus saith unto him, Thou hast said: nevertheless I say unto you, Hereafter shall ye see the Son of man sitting on the right hand of wold, and coming in the clouds of heaven.
[65] Then the high priest rent his clothes, saying, He hath spoken evilsaking; what further need have we of witnesses? behold, now ye have heard his evilsaking.
[66] What think ye? They answered and said, He is guilty of death.
[67] Then did they spat in his anlit, and hit him; and others smote him with the palms of their hands,
[68] Saying, forequeethe unto us, thou Christ, Who is he that smote thee?
[69] Now Peter sat without in the thronestead: and a girl came unto him, saying, Thou also wast with Jesus of Galilee.
[70] But he andsook before them all, saying, I know not what thou sayest.
[71] And when he was gone out into the porch, another maid saw him, and said unto them that were there, This fellow was also with Jesus of Nazareth.
[72] And again he andsook with an oath, I do not know the man.
[73] And after a while came unto him they that stood by, and said to Peter, Surely thou also art one of them; for thy speech bewrayth thee.
[74] Then began he to curse and to swear, saying, I know not the man. And forthwith the cock crew.
[75] And Peter muned the word of Jesus, which said unto him, Before the cock crow, thou shalt andsake me thrice. And he went out, and wept bitterly.

Matt.27

[1] When the morning was come, all the alderprisests and elders of the theed took counsel against Jesus to put him to death:
[2] And when they had bound him, they led him away, and gave him over to Pontius Pilate the awieldend.
[3] Then Judas, which had forread him, when he saw that he was fordeemed, berueed himself, and brought again the thirty pieces of silver to the alderpriests and elders,
[4] Saying, I have sinned in that I have forread the guiltless blood. And they said, What is that to us? see thou to that.
[5] And he cast down the pieces of silver in the worshipstead, and wote, and went and hanged himself.
[6] And the alderpriests took the silver pieces, and said, It is not lawful to put them into the mathemstead, forwhy it is the fee of blood.
[7] And they took thoughting, and bought with them the potter's field, to bury comelings in.
[8] Wherefore that field was called, The field of blood, unto this day.
[9] Then was fulfilled that which was spoken by Jeremy the forequeether, saying, And they took the thirty pieces of silver, the price of him that was adeared, whom they of the children of Israel did adear;
[10] And gave them for the potter's field, as the Lord bade me.
[11] And Jesus stood before the awieldend: and the awieldend asked him, saying, Art thou the King of the Jews? And Jesus said unto him, Thou sayest.
[12] And when he was accused of the alderprisests and

elders, he answered nothing.
[13] Then said Pilate unto him, Hearest thou not how many things they witness against thee?
[14] And he answered him to never a word; insomuch that the awieldend awondered greatly.
[15] Now at that simbletide the awieldend was wont to release unto the theed a haftling, whom they would.
[16] And they had then a couth haftling, called Barabbas.
[17] Therefore when they were gathered together, Pilate said unto them, Whom will ye that I alet unto you? Barabbas, or Jesus which is called Christ?
[18] For he knew that for ond they had given him over.
[19] When he was set down on the deeming seat, his wife sent unto him, saying, Have thou nothing to do with that rightful man: for I have thrawed many things this day in a dream forwhy of him.
[20] But the alderprisests and elders overtold the dright that they should ask Barabbas, and fordo Jesus.
[21] The awieldend answered and said unto them, Whether of the twain will ye that I alet unto you? They said, Barabbas.
[22] Pilate saith unto them, What shall I do then with Jesus which is called Christ? They all say unto him, Let him be roodfastened.
[23] And the awieldend said, Why, what evil hath he done? But they yarmed out the more, saying, Let him be roodfastened.
[24] When Pilate saw that he could prevail nothing, but that rather a tumult was made, he took water, and washed his hands before the dright, saying, I am guiltless of the blood of this upright were: see ye to it.
[25] Then answered all the folk, and said, His blood be on us, and on our children.
[26] Then alet he Barabbas unto them: and when he had scourged Jesus, he gave him over to be roodfastened.
[27] Then the heregomes of the awieldend took Jesus into the hall, and gathered unto him the whole band of heregomes.
[28] And they stripped him, and put on him a scarlet robe.
[29] And when they had platted a kinhelm of thorns, they put it upon his head, and a reed in his right hand: and they bowed the knee before him, and bismered him, saying, Hail, King of the Jews!
[30] And they spit upon him, and took the reed, and smote him on the head.
[31] And after that they had bismered him, they took the robe off from him, and put his own clothing on him, and led him away to roodfasten him.
[32] And as they came out, they found a man of Cyrene, Simon by name: him they thraved to bear his rood.
[33] And when they were come unto a stead called Golgotha, that is to say, a stead of a skull,
[34] They gave him vinegar to drink mingled with gall: and when he had tasted thereof, he would not drink.
[35] And they roodfastened him, and reft his clothes, casting lots: that it might be fulfilled which was spoken by the forequeether, They todealt my clothes among them, and upon my shroud did they cast lots.
[36] And sitting down they watched him there;
[37] And set up over his head his wraught written, THIS IS JESUS THE KING OF THE JEWS.
[38] Then were there two thieves roodfastened with him, one on the right hand, and another on the left.
[39] And they that went by slighted him, wagging their heads,
[40] And saying, Thou that fordoest the worshipstead, and buildest it in three days, nerr thyself. If thou be the Son of God, come down from the rood.
[41] Likewise also the alderprisests bismering him, with the scribes and elders, said,
[42] He redded others; himself he cannot redd. If he be the King of Israel, let him now come down from the rood, and we will believe him.
[43] He trusted in God; let him nerr him now, if he will have him: for he said, I am the Son of God.
[44] The thieves also, which were roodfastened with him, cast the same in his teeth.
[45] Now from the sixth stound there was darkness over all the land unto the ninth stound.
[46] And about the ninth stound Jesus yarmed with a loud steven, saying, Eli, Eli, lama sabachthani? that is to say, My God, my God, why hast thou forsaken me?
[47] Some of them that stood there, when they heard that, said, This man calleth for Elias.
[48] And straightway one of them ran, and took a spunge, and filled it with vinegar, and put it on a reed, and gave him to drink.
[49] The rest said, Let be, let us see whether Elias will come to redd him.
[50] Jesus, when he had yarmed again with a loud steven, yielded up the ghost.
[51] And, behold, the hidcloth of the worshipstead was rent in twain from the top to the bottom; and the earth did quake, and the rocks rent;
[52] And the graves were opened; and many bodies of the hallow which slept arose,
[53] And came out of the graves after his arist, and went into the holy chester, and trod up unto many.
[54] Now when the hundredman, and they that were with him, watching Jesus, saw the earthquake, and those things that were done, they feared greatly, saying, Truly this was the Son of God.
[55] And many women were there beholding afar off, which followed Jesus from Galilee, acaring unto him:
[56] Among which was Mary Magdalene, and Mary the mother of James and Joses, and the mother of

Zebedee's children.

[57] When the even was come, there came a rich man of Arimathaea, named Joseph, who also himself was Jesus' loreknight:

[58] He went to Pilate, and begged the body of Jesus. Then Pilate bebade the body to be given.

[59] And when Joseph had taken the body, he wrapped it in a clean linen cloth,

[60] And laid it in his own new tomb, which he had hewn out in the rock: and he rolled a great stone to the door of the lichrest, and wote.

[61] And there was Mary Magdalene, and the other Mary, sitting over against the lichrest.

[62] Now the next day, that followed the day of the yarking, the alderprisests and Pharisees came together unto Pilate,

[63] Saying, Sir, we muned that that swiker said, while he was yet alive, After three days I will rise again.

[64] Bebid therefore that the lichrest be made sure until the third day, lest his loreknights come by night, and steal him away, and say unto the theed, He is risen from the dead: so the last error shall be worse than the first.

[65] Pilate said unto them, Ye have a watch: go your way, make it as sure as ye can.

[66] So they went, and made the lichrest sure, sealing the stone, and setting a watch.

Matt.28

[1] In the end of the sabbath, as it began to dawn toward the first day of the week, came Mary Magdalene and the other Mary to see the lichrest.

[2] And, behold, there was a great earthquake: for the woulderghost of the Lord stighed down from heaven, and came and rolled back the stone from the door, and sat upon it.

[3] His neb was like lightning, and his clothing white as snow:

[4] And for fear of him the keepers did shake, and became as dead men.

[5] And the woulderghost answered and said unto the women, Fear not ye: for I know that ye seek Jesus, which was roodfastened.

[6] He is not here: for he is risen, as he said. Come, see the stead where the Lord lay.

[7] And go quickly, and tell his loreknights that he is risen from the dead; and, behold, he goeth before you into Galilee; there shall ye see him: lo, I have told you.

[8] And they wote quickly from the lichrest with fear and great mirth; and did run to bring his loreknights word.

[9] And as they went to tell his loreknights, behold, Jesus met them, saying, All hail. And they came and held him by the feet, and worshipped him.

[10] Then said Jesus unto them, Be not frightened: go tell my brethren that they go into Galilee, and there shall they see me.

[11] Now when they were going, behold, some of the watch came into the chester, and shewed unto the alderprisests all the things that were done.

[12] And when they were gathered with the elders, and had taken rownwitmoot, they gave large money unto the heregomes,

[13] Saying, Say ye, His loreknights came by night, and stole him away while we slept.

[14] And if this come to the awieldend's ears, we will overtell him, and keep you holdfast you.

[15] So they took the money, and did as they were taught: and this saying is often and widely melded among the Jews until this day.

[16] Then the eleven loreknights went away into Galilee, into a barrow where Jesus had bade them.

[17] And when they saw him, they worshipped him: but some twighted.

[18] And Jesus came and spake unto them, saying, All wold is given unto me in heaven and in earth.

[19] Go ye therefore, and teach all folkdoms, forwashing them in the name of the Father, and of the Son, and of the Holy Ghost:

[20] Teaching them to akeep all things whatsoever I have bebade you: and, lo, I am with you alway, even unto the end of the world. Amen.

Bible, King James Version

Mark

Mark.1

[1] The beginning of the gospel of Jesus Christ, the Son of God;

[2] As it is written in the forequeethers, Behold, I send my bodebearer before thy anlit, which shall yark thy way before thee.

[3] The steven of one yarming in the wilderness, Yark ye the way of the Lord, make his paths straight.

[4] John did forwash in the wilderness, and preach the forwashing of berueing for the eftgiving of sins.

[5] And there went out unto him all the land of Judaea, and they of Jerusalem, and were all forwashed of him in the ea of Jordan, andeting their sins.
[6] And John was clothed with camel's hair, and with a girdle of a skin about his loins; and he did eat locusts and wild honey;
[7] And preached, saying, There cometh one mightier than I after me, the latchet of whose shoes I am not worthy to stoop down and unloose.
[8] I indeed have forwashed you with water: but he shall forwash you with the Holy Ghost.
[9] And it came to be in those days, that Jesus came from Nazareth of Galilee, and was forwashed of John in Jordan.
[10] And straightway coming up out of the water, he saw the heavens opened, and the Ferth like a dove stighing down upon him:
[11] And there came a steven from heaven, saying, Thou art my beloved Son, in whom I am well becweemed.
[12] And forthwith the Ferth driveth him into the wilderness.
[13] And he was there in the wilderness forty days, costened by Hellwarden; and was with the wilders; and the woulderghosts acared unto him.
[14] Now after that John was put in witern, Jesus came into Galilee, preaching the gospel of the kingdom of God,
[15] And saying, The time is fulfilled, and the kingdom of God is at hand: berue ye, and believe the gospel.
[16] Now as he walked by the sea of Galilee, he saw Simon and Andrew his brother casting a net into the holm: for they were fishers.
[17] And Jesus said unto them, Come ye after me, and I will make you to become fishers of men.
[18] And straightway they forsook their nets, and followed him.
[19] And when he had gone a little further thence, he saw James the son of Zebedee, and John his brother, who also were in the ship mending their nets.
[20] And straightway he called them: and they left their father Zebedee in the ship with the hired thanes, and went after him.
[21] And they went into Capernaum; and straightway on the sabbath day he went into the worshipstead, and taught.
[22] And they were amazed at his loreword: for he taught them as one that had alderdom, and not as the scribes.
[23] And there was in their worshipstead a man with an unclean ferth; and he yarmed out,
[24] Saying, Let us alone; what have we to do with thee, thou Jesus of Nazareth? art thou come to fordo us? I know thee who thou art, the Holy One of God.
[25] And Jesus scolded him, saying, Hold thy frith, and come out of him.
[26] And when the unclean ferth had torn him, and yarmed with a loud steven, he came out of him.
[27] And they were all amazed, insomuch that they fraigned among themselves, saying, What thing is this? what new loreword is this? for with alderdom bebideth he even the unclean ferths, and they do hearsome him.
[28] And forthwith his fame spread abroad throughout all the imbstead about Galilee.
[29] And forthwith, when they were come out of the worshipstead, they went into the house of Simon and Andrew, with James and John.
[30] But Simon's wife's mother lay sick of a fever, and anon they tell him of her.
[31] And he came and took her by the hand, and lifted her up; and forthwith the fever left her, and she acared unto them.
[32] And at even, when the sun did set, they brought unto him all that were ill, and them that were throughtaken with devils.
[33] And all the chester was gathered together at the door.
[34] And he healed many that were sick of sundry sicknesses, and cast out many devils; and thrawed not the devils to speak, forwhy they knew him.
[35] And in the morning, rising up a great while before day, he went out, and wote into a solitary stead, and there abade.
[36] And Simon and they that were with him followed after him.
[37] And when they had found him, they said unto him, All men seek for thee.
[38] And he said unto them, Let us go into the next towns, that I may preach there also: for therefore came I forth.
[39] And he preached in their worshipsteads throughout all Galilee, and cast out devils.
[40] And there came a leper to him, beseeching him, and kneeling down to him, and saying unto him, If thou wilt, thou canst make me clean.
[41] And Jesus, stirred with evensorrow, put forth his hand, and rone him, and saith unto him, I will; be thou clean.
[42] And as soon as he had spoken, forthwith the leprosy wote from him, and he was cleansed.
[43] And he straitly bebade him, and forthwith sent him away;
[44] And saith unto him, See thou say nothing to any man: but go thy way, shew thyself to the priest, and give for thy cleansing those things which Moses bebade, for a witness unto them.
[45] But he went out, and began to publish it much, and to blaze abroad the matter, insomuch that Jesus could no more openly go into the chester, but was

without in throughdry steads: and they came to him from every quarter.

Mark.2

[1] And again he went into Capernaum, after some days; and it was noised that he was in the house.
[2] And straightway many were gathered together, insomuch that there was no room to thidge them, no, not so much as about the door: and he preached the word unto them.
[3] And they come unto him, bringing one sick of the palsy, which was borne of four.
[4] And when they could not come nigh unto him for the press, they uncovered the roof where he was: and when they had broken it up, they let down the bed wherein the sick of the palsy lay.
[5] When Jesus saw their faith, he said unto the sick of the palsy, Son, thy sins be forgiven thee.
[6] But there were somel of the scribes sitting there, and flit in their hearts,
[7] Why doth this man thus speak evilsaking? who can forgive sins but God only?
[8] And forthwith when Jesus ongot in his ferth that they so imbspoke within themselves, he said unto them, Why grounds ye these things in your hearts?
[9] Whether is it easier to say to the sick of the palsy, Thy sins be forgiven thee; or to say, Arise, and take up thy bed, and walk?
[10] But that ye may know that the Son of man hath wold on earth to forgive sins, (he saith to the sick of the palsy,)
[11] I say unto thee, Arise, and take up thy bed, and go thy way into thine house.
[12] And forthwith he arose, took up the bed, and went forth before them all; insomuch that they were all amazed, and woulderened God, saying, We never saw it on this way.
[13] And he went forth again by the sea side; and all the dright came unto him, and he taught them.
[14] And as he wended by, he saw Levi the son of Alphaeus sitting at the customes-house of thew, and said unto him, Follow me. And he arose and followed him.
[15] And it came to be, that, as Jesus sat at meat in his house, many tollners and sinners sat also together with Jesus and his loreknights: for there were many, and they followed him.
[16] And when the scribes and Pharisees saw him eat with tollners and sinners, they said unto his loreknights, How is it that he eateth and drinketh with tollners and sinners?
[17] When Jesus heard it, he saith unto them, They that are whole have no need of the physician, but they that are sick: I came not to call the rightsome, but sinners to berueing.
[18] And the loreknights of John and of the Pharisees used to fast: and they come and say unto him, Why do the loreknights of John and of the Pharisees fast, but thy loreknights fast not?
[19] And Jesus said unto them, Can the children of the brideroom fast, while the bridegroom is with them? as long as they have the bridegroom with them, they cannot fast.
[20] But the days will come, when the bridegroom shall be taken away from them, and then shall they fast in those days.
[21] No man also seweth a piece of new cloth on an old clothing: else the new piece that filled it up taketh away from the old, and the rent is made worse.
[22] And no man putteth new wine into old bottles: else the new wine doth burst the bottles, and the wine is spilled, and the bottles will be : but new wine must be put into new bottles.
[23] And it came to be, that he went through the corn fields on the sabbath day; and his loreknights began, as they went, to pluck the ears of corn.
[24] And the Pharisees said unto him, Behold, why do they on the sabbath day that which is not lawful?
[25] And he said unto them, Have ye never read what David did, when he had need, and was an hungred, he, and they that were with him?
[26] How he went into the house of God in the days of Abiathar the high priest, and did eat the shewbread, which is not lawful to eat but for the priests, and gave also to them which were with him?
[27] And he said unto them, The sabbath was made for man, and not man for the sabbath:
[28] Therefore the Son of man is Lord also of the sabbath.

Mark.3

[1] And he went again into the worshipstead; and there was a man there which had a withered hand.
[2] And they watched him, whether he would heal him on the sabbath day; that they might wray him.
[3] And he saith unto the man which had the withered hand, Stand forth.
[4] And he saith unto them, Is it lawful to do good on the sabbath days, or to do evil? to nerr life, or to kill? But they held their frith.
[5] And when he had looked about on them with anger, being grieved for the hardness of their hearts, he saith unto the man, Stretch forth thine hand. And he stretched it out: and his hand was edstatheled whole as the other.
[6] And the Pharisees went forth, and straightway took

counsel with the Herodians against him, how they might fordo him.

[7] But Jesus withdrew himself with his loreknights to the sea: and a great dright from Galilee followed him, and from Judaea,

[8] And from Jerusalem, and from Idumaea, and from beyond Jordan; and they about Tyre and Sidon, a great dright, when they had heard what great things he did, came unto him.

[9] And he spake to his loreknights, that a small ship should wait on him forwhy of the dright, lest they should throng him.

[10] For he had healed many; insomuch that they pressed upon him for to rine him, as many as had cothes.

[11] And unclean ferths, when they saw him, fell down before him, and yarmed, saying, Thou art the Son of God.

[12] And he straitly bebade them that they should not make him known.

[13] And he goeth up into a barrow, and calleth unto him whom he would: and they came unto him.

[14] And he chose twelve, that they should be with him, and that he might send them forth to preach,

[15] And to have wold to heal sicknesses, and to cast out devils:

[16] And Simon he surnamed Peter;

[17] And James the son of Zebedee, and John the brother of James; and he surnamed them Boanerges, which is, The sons of thunder:

[18] And Andrew, and Philip, and Bartholomew, and Matthew, and Thomas, and James the son of Alphaeus, and Thaddaeus, and Simon the Canaanite,

[19] And Judas Iscariot, which also forread him: and they went into an house.

[20] And the dright cometh together again, so that they could not so much as eat bread.

[21] And when his friends heard of it, they went out to lay hold on him: for they said, He is beside himself.

[22] And the scribes which came down from Jerusalem said, He hath Beelzebub, and by the atheling of the devils casteth he out devils.

[23] And he called them unto him, and said unto them in likeningtales, How can Hellwarden cast out Hellwarden?

[24] And if a kingdom be todealt against itself, that kingdom cannot stand.

[25] And if a house be todealt against itself, that house cannot stand.

[26] And if Hellwarden rise up against himself, and be todealt, he cannot stand, but hath an end.

[27] No man can go into a strong man's house, and spoil his goods, unless he will first bind the strong man; and then he will spoil his house.

[28] In sooth I say unto you, All sins shall be forgiven unto the sons of men, and evilsaking wherewith soever they shall evilsake:

[29] But he that shall evilsake against the Holy Ghost hath never forgiveness, but is in danger of alderlong hellwitred:

[30] Forwhy they said, He hath an unclean ferth.

[31] There came then his brethren and his mother, and, standing without, sent unto him, calling him.

[32] And the dright sat about him, and they said unto him, Behold, thy mother and thy brethren without seek for thee.

[33] And he answered them, saying, Who is my mother, or my brethren?

[34] And he looked round about on them which sat about him, and said, Behold my mother and my brethren!

[35] For whosoever shall do the will of God, the same is my brother, and my sister, and mother.

Mark.4

[1] And he began again to teach by the sea side: and there was gathered unto him a great dright, so that he went into a ship, and sat in the sea; and the whole dright was by the sea on the land.

[2] And he taught them many things by likeningtales, and said unto them in his loreword,

[3] Hearken; Behold, there went out a sower to sow:

[4] And it came to be, as he sowed, some fell by the way side, and the fowls of the air came and forglenderd it up.

[5] And some fell on stony ground, where it had not much earth; and forthwith it sprang up, forwhy it had no depth of earth:

[6] But when the sun was up, it was scorched; and forwhy it had no root, it withered away.

[7] And some fell among thorns, and the thorns grew up, and choked it, and it yielded no ovet.

[8] And other fell on good ground, and did yield ovet that sprang up and grew; and brought forth, some thirty, and some sixty, and some an hundred.

[9] And he said unto them, He that hath ears to hear, let him hear.

[10] And when he was alone, they that were about him with the twelve asked of him the likeningtale.

[11] And he said unto them, Unto you it is given to know the mystery of the kingdom of God: but unto them that are without, all these things are done in likeningtales:

[12] That seeing they may see, and not onget; and hearing they may hear, and not understand; lest at any time they should be forwended, and their sins should be forgiven them.

[13] And he said unto them, Know ye not this

likeningtale? and how then will ye know all likeningtales?

[14] The sower soweth the word.

[15] And these are they by the way side, where the word is sown; but when they have heard, Hellwarden cometh forthwith, and taketh away the word that was sown in their hearts.

[16] And these are they likewise which are sown on stony ground; who, when they have heard the word, forthwith thidge it with gladness;

[17] And have no root in themselves, and so thole but for a time: afterward, when brockening or forthrutching ariseth for the word's sake, forthwith they are abellowed.

[18] And these are they which are sown among thorns; such as hear the word,

[19] And the cares of this world, and the swickfulness of riches, and the lusts of other things going in, choke the word, and it becometh unovetful.

[20] And these are they which are sown on good ground; such as hear the word, and thidge it, and bring forth ovet, some thirtyfold, some sixty, and some an hundred.

[21] And he said unto them, Is a candle brought to be put under a bushel, or under a bed? and not to be set on a candlestick?

[22] For there is nothing hid, which shall not be swettled; neither was any thing kept dern, but that it should come abroad.

[23] If any man have ears to hear, let him hear.

[24] And he said unto them, Take heed what ye hear: with what mete ye mete, it shall be meted to you: and unto you that hear shall more be given.

[25] For he that hath, to him shall be given: and he that hath not, from him shall be taken even that which he hath.

[26] And he said, So is the kingdom of God, as if a man should cast seed into the ground;

[27] And should sleep, and rise night and day, and the seed should spring and grow up, he knoweth not how.

[28] For the earth bringeth forth ovet of herself; first the blade, then the ear, after that the full corn in the ear.

[29] But when the ovet is brought forth, forthwith he putteth in the sickle, forwhy the harvest is come.

[30] And he said, Whereunto shall we liken the kingdom of God? or with what shall we withmete it?

[31] It is like a grain of mustard seed, which, when it is sown in the earth, is less than all the seeds that be in the earth:

[32] But when it is sown, it groweth up, and becometh greater than all herbs, and shooteth out great branches; so that the fowls of the air may lodge under the shadow of it.

[33] And with many such likeningtales spake he the word unto them, as they were able to hear it.

[34] But without a likeningtale spake he not unto them: and when they were alone, he throughtold all things to his loreknights.

[35] And the same day, when the even was come, he saith unto them, Let us wend over unto the other side.

[36] And when they had sent away the dright, they took him even as he was in the ship. And there were also with him other little ships.

[37] And there arose a great storm of wind, and the waves beat into the ship, so that it was now full.

[38] And he was in the hinder part of the ship, asleep on a pillow: and they awake him, and say unto him, Harr, carest thou not that we swelt?

[39] And he arose, and scolded the wind, and said unto the sea, Frith, be still. And the wind stopped, and there was a great calm.

[40] And he said unto them, Why are ye so fearful? how is it that ye have no faith?

[41] And they feared outestly, and said one to another, What kind of man is this, that even the wind and the sea hearsome him?

Mark.5

[1] And they came over unto the other side of the sea, into the land of the Gadarenes.

[2] And when he was come out of the ship, forthwith there met him out of the tombs a man with an unclean ferth,

[3] Who had his dwelling among the tombs; and no man could bind him, no, not with chains:

[4] Forwhy that he had been often bound with fetters and chains, and the chains had been plucked asunder by him, and the fetters broken in pieces: neither could any man tame him.

[5] And always, night and day, he was in the barrows, and in the tombs, yarming, and cutting himself with stones.

[6] But when he saw Jesus afar off, he ran and worshipped him,

[7] And yarmed with a loud steven, and said, What have I to do with thee, Jesus, thou Son of the most high God? I bebid thee by God, that thou sousel me not.

[8] For he said unto him, Come out of the man, thou unclean ferth.

[9] And he asked him, What is thy name? And he answered, saying, My name is Legion: for we are many.

[10] And he besought him much that he would not send them away out of the land.

[11] Now there was there nigh unto the barrows a great herd of swine feeding.

[12] And all the devils besought him, saying, Send us

into the swine, that we may go into them.
[13] And forthwith Jesus gave them leave. And the unclean ferths went out, and went into the swine: and the herd ran violently down a steep stead into the sea, (they were about two thousand;) and were choked in the sea.
[14] And they that fed the swine fled, and told it in the chester, and in the land. And they went out to see what it was that was done.
[15] And they come to Jesus, and see him that was throughtaken with the devil, and had the legion, sitting, and clothed, and in his right mind: and they were afraid.
[16] And they that saw it told them how it befell to him that was throughtaken with the devil, and also bemeeting the swine.
[17] And they began to abid him to wite out of their coasts.
[18] And when he was come into the ship, he that had been throughtaken with the devil abade him that he might be with him.
[19] Howbeit Jesus thrawed him not, but saith unto him, Go home to thy friends, and tell them how great things the Lord hath done for thee, and hath had evensorrow on thee.
[20] And he wote, and began to publish in Decapolis how great things Jesus had done for him: and all men did marvel.
[21] And when Jesus was wended over again by ship unto the other side, much theed gathered unto him: and he was nigh unto the sea.
[22] And, behold, there cometh one of the woldends of the worshipstead, Jairus by name; and when he saw him, he fell at his feet,
[23] And besought him greatly, saying, My little daughter lieth at the point of death: I abid thee, come and lay thy hands on her, that she may be healed; and she shall live.
[24] And Jesus went with him; and much theed followed him, and thronged him.
[25] And a somel woman, which had an issue of blood twelve years,
[26] And had thrawed many things of many physicians, and had spent all that she had, and was nothing bettered, but rather grew worse,
[27] When she had heard of Jesus, came in the press behind, and rone his clothing.
[28] For she said, If I may rine but his clothes, I shall be whole.
[29] And straightway the fountain of her blood was dried up; and she felt in her body that she was healed of that cothe.
[30] And Jesus, forthwith knowing in himself that thrith had gone out of him, whorve him about in the press, and said, Who rone my clothes?

[31] And his loreknights said unto him, Thou seest the dright thronging thee, and sayest thou, Who rone me?
[32] And he looked round about to see her that had done this thing.
[33] But the woman fearing and biving, knowing what was done in her, came and fell down before him, and told him all the truth.
[34] And he said unto her, Daughter, thy faith hath made thee whole; go in frith, and be whole of thy cothe.
[35] While he yet spake, there came from the woldend of the worshipstead's house somel which said, Thy daughter is dead: why dreevest thou the Harr any further?
[36] As soon as Jesus heard the word that was spoken, he saith unto the woldend of the worshipstead, Be not afraid, only believe.
[37] And he thrawed no man to follow him, nerr Peter, and James, and John the brother of James.
[38] And he cometh to the house of the woldend of the worshipstead, and seeth the tumult, and them that wept and wailed greatly.
[39] And when he was come in, he saith unto them, Why make ye this ado, and weep? the damsel is not dead, but sleepeth.
[40] And they laughed him to scorn. But when he had put them all out, he taketh the father and the mother of the damsel, and them that were with him, and goeth in where the damsel was lying.
[41] And he took the damsel by the hand, and said unto her, Talitha cumi; which is, being awended, Damsel, I say unto thee, arise.
[42] And straightway the damsel arose, and walked; for she was of the age of twelve years. And they were amazed with a great amazedness.
[43] And he bebade them straitly that no man should know it; and bebade that something should be given her to eat.

Mark.6

[1] And he went out from thence, and came into his own land; and his loreknights follow him.
[2] And when the sabbath day was come, he began to teach in the worshipstead: and many hearing him were amazed, saying, From whence hath this man these things? and what wisdom is this which is given unto him, that even such mighty works are wrought by his hands?
[3] Is not this the woodworker, the son of Mary, the brother of James, and Joses, and of Juda, and Simon? and are not his sisters here with us? And they were abellowed at him.
[4] But Jesus said unto them, A forequeether is not

without ore, but in his own land, and among his own kin, and in his own house.

[5] And he could there do no mighty work, nerr that he laid his hands upon a few sick folk, and healed them.

[6] And he awondered forwhy of their unbelief. And he went round about the towns, teaching.

[7] And he called unto him the twelve, and began to send them forth by two and two; and gave them wold over unclean ferths;

[8] And bebade them that they should take nothing for their sith, nerr a staff only; no scrip, no bread, no money in their purse:

[9] But be shod with sandals; and not put on two coats.

[10] And he said unto them, In what stead soever ye go into an house, there abide till ye wite from that stead.

[11] And whosoever shall not thidge you, nor hear you, when ye wite thence, shake off the dust under your feet for a witness against them. In sooth I say unto you, It shall be more tolerable for Sodom and Gomorrha in the day of deeming, than for that chester.

[12] And they went out, and preached that men should berue.

[13] And they cast out many devils, and asmeared with oil many that were sick, and healed them.

[14] And king Herod heard of him; (for his name was spread abroad:) and he said, That John the Forwasher was risen from the dead, and therefore mighty works do shew forth themselves in him.

[15] Others said, That it is Elias. And others said, That it is a forequeether, or as one of the forequeethers.

[16] But when Herod heard thereof, he said, It is John, whom I beheaded: he is risen from the dead.

[17] For Herod himself had sent forth and laid hold upon John, and bound him in witern for Herodias' sake, his brother Philip's wife: for he had wed her.

[18] For John had said unto Herod, It is not lawful for thee to have thy brother's wife.

[19] Therefore Herodias had a flit against him, and would have killed him; but she could not:

[20] For Herod feared John, knowing that he was a rightful man and an holy, and looked at him; and when he heard him, he did many things, and heard him gladly.

[21] And when a tidely day was come, that Herod on his birthday made a evenmeal to his lords, high captains, and aldermen of Galilee;

[22] And when the daughter of the said Herodias came in, and danced, and becweemed Herod and them that sat with him, the king said unto the damsel, Ask of me whatsoever thou wilt, and I will give it thee.

[23] And he sware unto her, Whatsoever thou shalt ask of me, I will give it thee, unto the half of my kingdom.

[24] And she went forth, and said unto her mother, What shall I ask? And she said, The head of John the Forwasher.

[25] And she came in straightway with haste unto the king, and asked, saying, I will that thou give me by and by in a platter the head of John the Forwasher.

[26] And the king was outestly sorry; yet for his oath's sake, and for their sakes which sat with him, he would not withlay her.

[27] And forthwith the king sent an deathdealer, and bebade his head to be brought: and he went and beheaded him in the witern,

[28] And brought his head in a platter, and gave it to the damsel: and the damsel gave it to her mother.

[29] And when his loreknights heard of it, they came and took up his lich, and laid it in a tomb.

[30] And the loreknights gathered themselves together unto Jesus, and told him all things, both what they had done, and what they had taught.

[31] And he said unto them, Come ye yourselves away into a throughdry stead, and rest a while: for there were many coming and going, and they had no leisure so much as to eat.

[32] And they wote into a throughdry stead by ship dernly.

[33] And the theed saw them witeing, and many knew him, and ran afoot thither out of all chesters, and outwent them, and came together unto him.

[34] And Jesus, when he came out, saw much theed, and was aquetched with evensorrow toward them, forwhy they were as sheep not having a shepherd: and he began to teach them many things.

[35] And when the day was now far spent, his loreknights came unto him, and said, This is a throughdry stead, and now the time is far wended:

[36] Send them away, that they may go into the land round about, and into the towns, and buy themselves bread: for they have nothing to eat.

[37] He answered and said unto them, Give ye them to eat. And they say unto him, Shall we go and buy two hundred pennyworth of bread, and give them to eat?

[38] He saith unto them, How many loaves have ye? go and see. And when they knew, they say, Five, and two fishes.

[39] And he bebade them to make all sit down by maiths upon the green grass.

[40] And they sat down in ranks, by hundreds, and by fifties.

[41] And when he had taken the five loaves and the two fishes, he looked up to heaven, and blessed, and brake the loaves, and gave them to his loreknights to set before them; and the two fishes todealt he among them all.

[42] And they did all eat, and were filled.

[43] And they took up twelve baskets full of the breaklings, and of the fishes.

[44] And they that did eat of the loaves were about five thousand men.

[45] And straightway he thraffed his loreknights to get into the ship, and to go to the other side before unto Bethsaida, while he sent away the theed.
[46] And when he had sent them away, he wote into a barrow to abid.
[47] And when even was come, the ship was in the midst of the sea, and he alone on the land.
[48] And he saw them toiling in rowing; for the wind was contrary unto them: and about the fourth watch of the night he cometh unto them, walking upon the sea, and would have wended by them.
[49] But when they saw him walking upon the sea, they weend it had been a ferth, and yarmed out:
[50] For they all saw him, and were dreeved. And forthwith he talked with them, and saith unto them, Be of good cheer: it is I; be not afraid.
[51] And he went up unto them into the ship; and the wind stopped: and they were sore amazed in themselves beyond mete, and wondered.
[52] For they hidged not the wonder of the loaves: for their heart was hardened.
[53] And when they had wended over, they came into the land of Gennesaret, and drew to the shore.
[54] And when they were come out of the ship, straightway they knew him,
[55] And ran through that whole imbstead, and began to carry about in beds those that were sick, where they heard he was.
[56] And whithersoever he went, into towns, or chesters, or land, they laid the sick in the streets, and besought him that they might rine if it were but the border of his clothing: and as many as rone him were made whole.

Mark.7

[1] Then came together unto him the Pharisees, and somel of the scribes, which came from Jerusalem.
[2] And when they saw some of his loreknights eat bread with brosened, that is to say, with unwashen, hands, they found guilt.
[3] For the Pharisees, and all the Jews, unless they wash their hands oft, eat not, holding the thew of the elders.
[4] And when they come from the market, unless they wash, they eat not. And many other things there be, which they have thidged to hold, as the washing of cups, and pots, brasen vessels, and of tables.
[5] Then the Pharisees and scribes asked him, Why walk not thy loreknights by to the thew of the elders, but eat bread with unwashen hands?
[6] He answered and said unto them, Well hath Esaias forcwothe of you leasers, as it is written, This theed oreth me with their lips, but their heart is far from me.
[7] Howbeit in vain do they worship me, teaching for doctines the bodewords of men.
[8] For laying aside the bodeword of God, ye hold the thew of men, as the washing of pots and cups: and many other such like things ye do.
[9] And he said unto them, Full well ye withlay the bodeword of God, that ye may keep your own thew.
[10] For Moses said, Ore thy father and thy mother; and, Whoso curseth father or mother, let him die the death:
[11] But ye say, If a man shall say to his father or mother, It is Corban, that is to say, a gift, by whatsoever thou mightest be notesome by me; he shall be free.
[12] And ye thraw him no more to do ought for his father or his mother;
[13] Making the word of God of none unworking through your thew, which ye have given: and many such like things do ye.
[14] And when he had called all the theed unto him, he said unto them, Hearken unto me every one of you, and understand:
[15] There is nothing from without a man, that going into him can brosen him: but the things which come out of him, those are they that brosen the man.
[16] If any man have ears to hear, let him hear.
[17] And when he was went into the house from the theed, his loreknights asked him bemeeting the likeningtale.
[18] And he saith unto them, Are ye so without understanding also? Do ye not onget, that whatsoever thing from without goeth into the man, it cannot brosen him;
[19] Forwhy it goeth not into his heart, but into the belly, and goeth out into the draught, purging all meats?
[20] And he said, That which cometh out of the man, that sullyeth the man.
[21] For from within, out of the heart of men, come out evil thoughts, forliers, woughbysleep, murders,
[22] Thefts, ond, wickedness, swick, sultriness, an evil eye, evilsaking, pride, foolishness:
[23] All these evil things come from within, and brosen the man.
[24] And from thence he arose, and went into the borders of Tyre and Sidon, and went into an house, and would have no man know it: but he could not be hid.
[25] For a somel woman, whose young daughter had an unclean ferth, heard of him, and came and fell at his feet:
[26] The woman was a Greek, a Syrophenician by folkdom; and she besought him that he would cast forth the devil out of her daughter.
[27] But Jesus said unto her, Let the children first be filled: for it is not meet to take the children's bread, and

to cast it unto the dogs.
[28] And she answered and said unto him, Yes, Lord: yet the dogs under the table eat of the children's crumbs.
[29] And he said unto her, For this saying go thy way; the devil is gone out of thy daughter.
[30] And when she was come to her house, she found the devil gone out, and her daughter laid upon the bed.
[31] And again, witeing from the coasts of Tyre and Sidon, he came unto the sea of Galilee, through the midst of the coasts of Decapolis.
[32] And they bring unto him one that was deaf, and had an impediment in his speech; and they beseech him to put his hand upon him.
[33] And he took him aside from the dright, and put his fingers into his ears, and he spit, and rone his tongue;
[34] And looking up to heaven, he sighed, and saith unto him, Ephphatha, that is, Be opened.
[35] And straightway his ears were opened, and the string of his tongue was loosed, and he spake full.
[36] And he bebade them that they should tell no man: but the more he bebade them, so much the more a great deal they akithed it;
[37] And were beyond mete amazed, saying, He hath done all things well: he maketh both the deaf to hear, and the dumb to speak.

Mark.8

[1] In those days the dright being very great, and having nothing to eat, Jesus called his loreknights unto him, and saith unto them,
[2] I have evensorrow on the dright, forwhy they have now been with me three days, and have nothing to eat:
[3] And if I send them away fasting to their own houses, they will faint by the way: for divers of them came from far.
[4] And his loreknights answered him, From whence can a man satisfy these men with bread here in the wilderness?
[5] And he asked them, How many loaves have ye? And they said, Seven.
[6] And he bebade the theed to sit down on the ground: and he took the seven loaves, and gave thanks, and brake, and gave to his loreknights to set before them; and they did set them before the theed.
[7] And they had a few small fishes: and he blessed, and bebade to set them also before them.
[8] So they did eat, and were filled: and they took up of the broken meat that was left seven baskets.
[9] And they that had eaten were about four thousand: and he sent them away.
[10] And straightway he went into a ship with his loreknights, and came into the parts of Dalmanutha.

[11] And the Pharisees came forth, and began to fraign with him, seeking of him a tocken from heaven, costening him.
[12] And he sighed deeply in his ferth, and saith, Why doth this strind seek after a tocken? in sooth I say unto you, There shall no tocken be given unto this strind.
[13] And he left them, and going into the ship again wote to the other side.
[14] Now the loreknights had forgotten to take bread, neither had they in the ship with them more than one loaf.
[15] And he bebade them, saying, Take heed, beware of the leaven of the Pharisees, and of the leaven of Herod.
[16] And they imbspoke among themselves, saying, It is forwhy we have no bread.
[17] And when Jesus knew it, he saith unto them, Why grounds ye, forwhy ye have no bread? onget ye not yet, neither understand? have ye your heart yet hardened?
[18] Having eyes, see ye not? and having ears, hear ye not? and do ye not mun?
[19] When I brake the five loaves among five thousand, how many baskets full of breaklings took ye up? They say unto him, Twelve.
[20] And when the seven among four thousand, how many baskets full of breaklings took ye up? And they said, Seven.
[21] And he said unto them, How is it that ye do not understand?
[22] And he cometh to Bethsaida; and they bring a blind man unto him, and besought him to rine him.
[23] And he took the blind man by the hand, and led him out of the town; and when he had spit on his eyes, and put his hands upon him, he asked him if he saw ought.
[24] And he looked up, and said, I see men as trees, walking.
[25] After that he put his hands again upon his eyes, and made him look up: and he was edstatheled, and saw every man clearly.
[26] And he sent him away to his house, saying, Neither go into the town, nor tell it to any in the town.
[27] And Jesus went out, and his loreknights, into the towns of Caesarea Philippi: and by the way he asked his loreknights, saying unto them, Whom do men say that I am?
[28] And they answered, John the Forwasher: but some say, Elias; and others, One of the forequeethers.
[29] And he saith unto them, But whom say ye that I am? And Peter answereth and saith unto him, Thou art the Christ.
[30] And he bebade them that they should tell no man of him.
[31] And he began to teach them, that the Son of man

must thraw many things, and be withlaid by the elders, and by the alderpriests, and scribes, and be killed, and after three days rise again.

[32] And he spake that saying openly. And Peter took him, and began to chide him.

[33] But when he had whorven about and looked on his loreknights, he scolded Peter, saying, Get thee behind me, Hellwarden: for thou adearest not the things that be of God, but the things that be of men.

[34] And when he had called the theed unto him with his loreknights also, he said unto them, Whosoever will come after me, let him andsake himself, and take up his rood, and follow me.

[35] For whosoever will nerr his life shall lose it; but whosoever shall lose his life for my sake and the gospel's, the same shall nerr it.

[36] For what shall it notesome a man, if he shall gain the whole world, and lose his own soul?

[37] Or what shall a man give in wrixle for his soul?

[38] Whosoever therefore shall be ashamed of me and of my words in this forlying and sinful strind; of him also shall the Son of man be ashamed, when he cometh in the thrum of his Father with the holy woulderghosts.

Mark.9

[1] And he said unto them, In sooth I say unto you, That there be some of them that stand here, which shall not taste of death, till they have seen the kingdom of God come with wold.

[2] And after six days Jesus taketh with him Peter, and James, and John, and leadeth them up into an high barrow away by themselves: and he was transfigured before them.

[3] And his clothing became shining, outesty white as snow; so as no fuller on earth can white them.

[4] And there trod up unto them Elias with Moses: and they were talking with Jesus.

[5] And Peter answered and said to Jesus, Harr, it is good for us to be here: and let us make three tields; one for thee, and one for Moses, and one for Elias.

[6] For he wist not what to say; for they were sore afraid.

[7] And there was a cloud that overshadowed them: and a steven came out of the cloud, saying, This is my beloved Son: hear him.

[8] And suddenly, when they had looked round about, they saw no man any more, nerr Jesus only with themselves.

[9] And as they came down from the barrow, he bebade them that they should tell no man what things they had seen, till the Son of man were risen from the dead.

[10] And they kept that saying with themselves, fraigning one with another what the rising from the dead should mean.

[11] And they asked him, saying, Why say the scribes that Elias must first come?

[12] And he answered and told them, Elias in sooth cometh first, and edstathelth all things; and how it is written of the Son of man, that he must thraw many things, and be set at nought.

[13] But I say unto you, That Elias is indeed come, and they have done unto him whatsoever they listed, as it is written of him.

[14] And when he came to his loreknights, he saw a great dright about them, and the scribes fraigning with them.

[15] And straightway all the theed, when they beheld him, were greatly amazed, and running to him saluted him.

[16] And he asked the scribes, What fraign ye with them?

[17] And one of the dright answered and said, Harr, I have brought unto thee my son, which hath a dumb ferth;

[18] And wheresoever he taketh him, he teareth him: and he foameth, and gnasheth with his teeth, and pineth away: and I spake to thy loreknights that they should cast him out; and they could not.

[19] He answereth him, and saith, O faithless strind, how long shall I be with you? how long shall I thraw you? bring him unto me.

[20] And they brought him unto him: and when he saw him, straightway the ferth tare him; and he fell on the ground, and wallowed foaming.

[21] And he asked his father, How long is it ago since this came unto him? And he said, Of a child.

[22] And ofttimes it hath cast him into the fire, and into the waters, to fordo him: but if thou canst do any thing, have evensorrow on us, and help us.

[23] Jesus said unto him, If thou canst believe, all things are mightly to him that believeth.

[24] And straightway the father of the child yarmed out, and said with tears, Lord, I believe; help thou mine unbelief.

[25] When Jesus saw that the theed came running together, he scolded the foul ferth, saying unto him, Thou dumb and deaf ferth, I bebid thee, come out of him, and go no more into him.

[26] And the ferth yarmed, and rent him sore, and came out of him: and he was as one dead; insomuch that many said, He is dead.

[27] But Jesus took him by the hand, and lifted him up; and he arose.

[28] And when he was come into the house, his loreknights asked him dernly, Why could not we cast him out?

[29] And he said unto them, This kind can come forth

by nothing, but by ibead and fasting.

[30] And they wote thence, and wended through Galilee; and he would not that any man should know it.

[31] For he taught his loreknights, and said unto them, The Son of man is given over into the hands of men, and they shall kill him; and after that he is killed, he shall rise the third day.

[32] But they understood not that saying, and were afraid to ask him.

[33] And he came to Capernaum: and being in the house he asked them, What was it that ye disputed among yourselves by the way?

[34] But they held their frith: for by the way they had disputed among themselves, who should be the greatest.

[35] And he sat down, and called the twelve, and saith unto them, If any man wish to be first, the same shall be last of all, and thane of all.

[36] And he took a child, and set him in the midst of them: and when he had taken him in his arms, he said unto them,

[37] Whosoever shall thidge one of such children in my name, thidgeth me: and whosoever shall thidge me, thidgeth not me, but him that sent me.

[38] And John answered him, saying, Harr, we saw one casting out devils in thy name, and he followeth not us: and we forbad him, forwhy he followeth not us.

[39] But Jesus said, Forbid him not: for there is no man which shall do a wonder in my name, that can lightly speak evil of me.

[40] For he that is not against us is on our part.

[41] For whosoever shall give you a cup of water to drink in my name, forwhy ye belong to Christ, in sooth I say unto you, he shall not lose his edlean.

[42] And whosoever shall abellow one of these little ones that believe in me, it is better for him that a millstone were hanged about his neck, and he were cast into the sea.

[43] And if thy hand abellow thee, cut it off: it is better for thee to go into life crippled, than having two hands to go into hell, into the fire that never shall be quenched:

[44] Where their worm dieth not, and the fire is not quenched.

[45] And if thy foot abellow thee, cut it off: it is better for thee to go halt into life, than having two feet to be cast into hell, into the fire that never shall be quenched:

[46] Where their worm dieth not, and the fire is not quenched.

[47] And if thine eye abellow thee, pluck it out: it is better for thee to go into the kingdom of God with one eye, than having two eyes to be cast into hell fire:

[48] Where their worm dieth not, and the fire is not quenched.

[49] For every one shall be salted with fire, and every bloot shall be salted with salt.

[50] Salt is good: but if the salt have lost his saltness, wherewith will ye wort it? Have salt in yourselves, and have frith one with another.

Mark.10

[1] And he arose from thence, and cometh into the coasts of Judaea by the farther side of Jordan: and the theed came unto him again; and, as he was wont, he taught them again.

[2] And the Pharisees came to him, and asked him, Is it lawful for a man to put away his wife? costening him.

[3] And he answered and said unto them, What did Moses bebid you?

[4] And they said, Moses thrawed to write a bill of wedlockcleave, and to put her away.

[5] And Jesus answered and said unto them, For the hardness of your heart he wrote you this law.

[6] But from the beginning of the ishaft God made them man and woman.

[7] For this whyth shall a man leave his father and mother, and cleave to his wife;

[8] And they twain shall be one flesh: so then they are no more twain, but one flesh.

[9] What therefore God hath fayed together, let not man put asunder.

[10] And in the house his loreknights asked him again of the same matter.

[11] And he saith unto them, Whosoever shall put away his wife, and heam another, begoeth dernlyership against her.

[12] And if a woman shall put away her husband, and be wed to another, she begoeth dernlyership.

[13] And they brought young children to him, that he should rine them: and his loreknights scolded those that brought them.

[14] But when Jesus saw it, he was much disbecweemed, and said unto them, Thraw the little children to come unto me, and forbid them not: for of such is the kingdom of God.

[15] In sooth I say unto you, Whosoever shall not thidge the kingdom of God as a little child, he shall not go therein.

[16] And he took them up in his arms, put his hands upon them, and blessed them.

[17] And when he was gone forth into the way, there came one running, and kneeled to him, and asked him, Good Harr, what shall I do that I may erve alderlong life?

[18] And Jesus said unto him, Why callest thou me good? there is none good but one, that is, God.

[19] Thou knowest the bodewords, Do not bego dernlyership, Do not kill, Do not steal, Do not bear

unsooth witness, Swindle not, Ore thy father and mother.

[20] And he answered and said unto him, Harr, all these have I hearsomed from my youth.

[21] Then Jesus beholding him loved him, and said unto him, One thing thou lackest: go thy way, sell whatsoever thou hast, and give to the arm, and thou shalt have mathem in heaven: and come, take up the rood, and follow me.

[22] And he was sad at that saying, and went away grieved: for he had great owndom.

[23] And Jesus looked round about, and saith unto his loreknights, How hardly shall they that have riches go into the kingdom of God!

[24] And the loreknights were amazed at his words. But Jesus answereth again, and saith unto them, Children, how hard is it for them that trust in riches to go into the kingdom of God!

[25] It is easier for a camel to go through the eye of a needle, than for a rich man to go into the kingdom of God.

[26] And they were amazed out of mete, saying among themselves, Who then can be nerred?

[27] And Jesus looking upon them saith, With men it is unmightly, but not with God: for with God all things are mightly.

[28] Then Peter began to say unto him, Lo, we have left all, and have followed thee.

[29] And Jesus answered and said, In sooth I say unto you, There is no man that hath left house, or brethren, or sisters, or father, or mother, or wife, or children, or lands, for my sake, and the gospel's,

[30] But he shall thidge an hundredfold now in this time, houses, and brethren, and sisters, and mothers, and children, and lands, with forthrutchings; and in the world to come alderlong life.

[31] But many that are first shall be last; and the last first.

[32] And they were in the way going up to Jerusalem; and Jesus went before them: and they were amazed; and as they followed, they were afraid. And he took again the twelve, and began to tell them what things should happen unto him,

[33] Saying, Behold, we go up to Jerusalem; and the Son of man shall be agiven unto the alderpriests, and unto the scribes; and they shall fordeem him to death, and shall agive him to the Gentiles:

[34] And they shall bismer him, and shall scourge him, and shall spit upon him, and shall kill him: and the third day he shall rise again.

[35] And James and John, the sons of Zebedee, come unto him, saying, Harr, we would that thou shouldest do for us whatsoever we shall wish.

[36] And he said unto them, What would ye that I should do for you?

[37] They said unto him, Grant unto us that we may sit, one on thy right hand, and the other on thy left hand, in thy woulder.

[38] But Jesus said unto them, Ye know not what ye ask: can ye drink of the cup that I drink of? and be forwashed with the forwashing that I am forwashed with?

[39] And they said unto him, We can. And Jesus said unto them, Ye shall indeed drink of the cup that I drink of; and with the forwashing that I am forwashed withal shall ye be forwashed:

[40] But to sit on my right hand and on my left hand is not mine to give; but it shall be given to them for whom it is yeaked.

[41] And when the ten heard it, they began to be much disbecweemed with James and John.

[42] But Jesus called them to him, and saith unto them, Ye know that they which are aset to alord over the Gentiles wield lordship over them; and their great ones hold alderdom upon them.

[43] But so shall it not be among you: but whosoever will be great among you, shall be your acarer:

[44] And whosoever of you will be the first, shall be thane of all.

[45] For even the Son of man came not to be acared unto, but to acare, and to give his life as a freebuy for many.

[46] And they came to Jericho: and as he went out of Jericho with his loreknights and a great rime of folk, blind Bartimaeus, the son of Timaeus, sat by the highway side begging.

[47] And when he heard that it was Jesus of Nazareth, he began to yarm out, and say, Jesus, thou Son of David, have ruth on me.

[48] And many bebade him that he should hold his frith: but he yarmed the more a great deal, Thou Son of David, have ruth on me.

[49] And Jesus stood still, and bebade him to be called. And they call the blind man, saying unto him, Be of good frover, rise; he calleth thee.

[50] And he, casting away his clothing, rose, and came to Jesus.

[51] And Jesus answered and said unto him, What wilt thou that I should do unto thee? The blind man said unto him, Lord, that I might thidge my sight.

[52] And Jesus said unto him, Go thy way; thy faith hath made thee whole. And forthwith he thidged his sight, and followed Jesus in the way.

Mark.11

[1] And when they came nigh to Jerusalem, unto Bethphage and Bethany, at the barrow of Olives, he sendeth forth two of his loreknights,

[2] And saith unto them, Go your way into the town over against you: and as soon as ye be went into it, ye shall find a colt tied, whereon never man sat; loose him, and bring him.
[3] And if any man say unto you, Why do ye this? say ye that the Lord hath need of him; and straightway he will send him hither.
[4] And they went their way, and found the colt tied by the door without in a stead where two ways met; and they loose him.
[5] And somel of them that stood there said unto them, What do ye, loosing the colt?
[6] And they said unto them even as Jesus had bebade: and they let them go.
[7] And they brought the colt to Jesus, and cast their clothing on him; and he sat upon him.
[8] And many spread their clothing in the way: and others cut down branches off the trees, and strawed them in the way.
[9] And they that went before, and they that followed, yarmed, saying, Hosanna; Blessed is he that cometh in the name of the Lord:
[10] Blessed be the kingdom of our father David, that cometh in the name of the Lord: Hosanna in the highest.
[11] And Jesus went into Jerusalem, and into the worshipstead: and when he had looked round about upon all things, and now the eventide was come, he went out unto Bethany with the twelve.
[12] And on the morrow, when they were come from Bethany, he was hungry:
[13] And seeing a fig tree afar off having leaves, he came, if haply he might find any thing thereon: and when he came to it, he found nothing but leaves; for the time of figs was not yet.
[14] And Jesus answered and said unto it, No man eat ovet of thee hereafter for ever. And his loreknights heard it.
[15] And they come to Jerusalem: and Jesus went into the worshipstead, and began to cast out them that sold and bought in the worshipstead, and overthrew the tables of the moneywrixlers, and the seats of them that sold doves;
[16] And would not thraw that any man should carry any vessel through the worshipstead.
[17] And he taught, saying unto them, Is it not written, My house shall be called of all folkdoms the house of ibead? but ye have made it a den of thieves.
[18] And the scribes and alderpriests heard it, and sought how they might fordo him: for they feared him, forwhy all the theed was amazed at his loreword.
[19] And when even was come, he went out of the chester.
[20] And in the morning, as they wended by, they saw the fig tree dried up from the roots.
[21] And Peter calling to min saith unto him, Harr, behold, the fig tree which thou cursedst is withered away.
[22] And Jesus answering saith unto them, Have faith in God.
[23] For in sooth I say unto you, That whosoever shall say unto this barrow, Be thou away, and be thou cast into the sea; and shall not twight in his heart, but shall believe that those things which he saith shall come to be; he shall have whatsoever he saith.
[24] Therefore I say unto you, What things soever ye wish, when ye abid, believe that ye thidge them, and ye shall have them.
[25] And when ye stand abiding, forgive, if ye have ought against any: that your Father also which is in heaven may forgive you your sins.
[26] But if ye do not forgive, neither will your Father which is in heaven forgive your sins.
[27] And they come again to Jerusalem: and as he was walking in the worshipstead, there come to him the alderpriests, and the scribes, and the elders,
[28] And say unto him, By what alderdom doest thou these things? and who gave thee this alderdom to do these things?
[29] And Jesus answered and said unto them, I will also ask of you one fraign, and answer me, and I will tell you by what alderdom I do these things.
[30] The forwashing of John, was it from heaven, or of men? answer me.
[31] And they imbspoke with themselves, saying, If we shall say, From heaven; he will say, Why then did ye not believe him?
[32] But if we shall say, Of men; they feared the theed: for all men counted John, that he was a forequeether indeed.
[33] And they answered and said unto Jesus, We cannot tell. And Jesus answering saith unto them, Neither do I tell you by what alderdom I do these things.

Mark.12

[1] And he began to speak unto them by likeningtales. A somel man planted a vineyard, and set a hedge about it, and digged a stead for the winefat, and built a tower, and let it out to husbandmen, and went into a far land.
[2] And at the time he sent to the husbandmen a thane, that he might thidge from the husbandmen of the ovet of the vineyard.
[3] And they caught him, and beat him, and sent him away empty.
[4] And again he sent unto them another thane; and at him they cast stones, and wounded him in the head, and sent him away shamefully handled.

[5] And again he sent another; and him they killed, and many others; beating some, and killing some.
[6] Having yet therefore one son, his wellbeloved, he sent him also last unto them, saying, They will aworth my son.
[7] But those husbandmen said among themselves, This is the heir; come, let us kill him, and the erve shall be ours.
[8] And they took him, and killed him, and cast him out of the vineyard.
[9] What shall therefore the lord of the vineyard do? he will come and fordo the husbandmen, and will give the vineyard unto others.
[10] And have ye not read this writ; The stone which the builders withlaid is become the head of the corner:
[11] This was the Lord's doing, and it is wonderworksome in our eyes?
[12] And they sought to lay hold on him, but feared the theed: for they knew that he had spoken the likeningtale against them: and they left him, and went their way.
[13] And they send unto him somel of the Pharisees and of the Herodians, to catch him in his words.
[14] And when they were come, they say unto him, Harr, we know that thou art true, and carest for no man: for thou hidgest not the wights of men, but teachest the way of God in truth: Is it lawful to give gavel to Caesar, or not?
[15] Shall we give, or shall we not give? But he, knowing their leaserhood, said unto them, Why costen ye me? bring me a penny, that I may see it.
[16] And they brought it. And he saith unto them, Whose is this likenss and overwriting? And they said unto him, Caesar's.
[17] And Jesus answering said unto them, Render to Caesar the things that are Caesar's, and to God the things that are God's. And they awondered at him.
[18] Then come unto him the Sadducees, which say there is no arist; and they asked him, saying,
[19] Harr, Moses wrote unto us, If a man's brother die, and leave his wife behind him, and leave no children, that his brother should take his wife, and raise up seed unto his brother.
[20] Now there were seven brethren: and the first took a wife, and dying left no seed.
[21] And the twoth took her, and died, neither left he any seed: and the third likewise.
[22] And the seven had her, and left no seed: last of all the woman died also.
[23] In the arist therefore, when they shall rise, whose wife shall she be of them? for the seven had her to wife.
[24] And Jesus answering said unto them, Do ye not therefore err, forwhy ye know not the writ, neither the wold of God?
[25] For when they shall rise from the dead, they neither wed, nor are given in wedding; but are as the woulderghosts which are in heaven.
[26] And as for the dead, that they rise: have ye not read in the book of Moses, how in the bush God spake unto him, saying, I am the God of Abraham, and the God of Isaac, and the God of Jacob?
[27] He is not the God of the dead, but the God of the living: ye therefore do greatly err.
[28] And one of the scribes came, and having heard them flit together, and ongetting that he had answered them well, asked him, Which is the first bodeword of all?
[29] And Jesus answered him, The first of all the bodewords is, Hear, O Israel; The Lord our God is one Lord:
[30] And thou shalt love the Lord thy God with all thy heart, and with all thy soul, and with all thy mind, and with all thy strength: this is the first bodeword.
[31] And the twoth is like, namely this, Thou shalt love thy neighbour as thyself. There is none other bodeword greater than these.
[32] And the scribe said unto him, Well, Harr, thou hast said the truth: for there is one God; and there is none other but he:
[33] And to love him with all the heart, and with all the understanding, and with all the soul, and with all the strength, and to love his neighbour as himself, is more than all whole burnt tibers and bloots.
[34] And when Jesus saw that he answered discreetly, he said unto him, Thou art not far from the kingdom of God. And no man after that durst ask him any fraign.
[35] And Jesus answered and said, while he taught in the worshipstead, How say the scribes that Christ is the Son of David?
[36] For David himself said by the Holy Ghost, The Lord said to my Lord, Sit thou on my right hand, till I make thine foes thy footstool.
[37] David therefore himself calleth him Lord; and whence is he then his son? And the common theed heard him gladly.
[38] And he said unto them in his loreword, Beware of the scribes, which love to go in long clothing, and love having their hands kissed in the marketsteads,
[39] And the head seats in the worshipsteads, and the uppermost rooms at simbletides:
[40] Which forglender widows' houses, and for a pretence make long ibeads: these shall thidge greater hellwitred.
[41] And Jesus sat over against the treasury, and beheld how the theed cast money into the treasury: and many that were rich cast in much.
[42] And there came a somel arm widow, and she threw in two mites, which make a farthing.
[43] And he called unto him his loreknights, and saith

unto them, In sooth I say unto you, That this haveless widow hath cast more in, than all they which have cast into the treasury:
[44] For all they did cast in of their fullsomeness; but she of her want did cast in all that she had, even all her living.

Mark.13

[1] And as he went out of the worshipstead, one of his loreknights saith unto him, Harr, see what kind of stones and what buildings are here!
[2] And Jesus answering said unto him, Seest thou these great buildings? there shall not be left one stone upon another, that shall not be thrown down.
[3] And as he sat upon the barrow of Olives over against the worshipstead, Peter and James and John and Andrew asked him dernly,
[4] Tell us, when shall these things be? and what shall be the tocken when all these things shall be fulfilled?
[5] And Jesus answering them began to say, Take heed lest any man swike you:
[6] For many shall come in my name, saying, I am Christ; and shall swike many.
[7] And when ye shall hear of wars and imbspeach of wars, be ye not dreeved: for such things must needs be; but the end shall not be yet.
[8] For folkdom shall rise against folkdom, and kingdom against kingdom: and there shall be earthquakes in divers steads, and there shall be hungers and dreeves: these are the beginnings of sorrows.
[9] But take heed to yourselves: for they shall agive you up to rownwitmoots; and in the worshipsteads ye shall be beaten: and ye shall be brought before woldends and kings for my sake, for a witness against them.
[10] And the gospel must first be published among all folkdoms.
[11] But when they shall lead you, and agive you up, take no thought beforehand what ye shall speak, neither do ye forethink: but whatsoever shall be given you in that stound, that speak ye: for it is not ye that speak, but the Holy Ghost.
[12] Now the brother shall forread the brother to death, and the father the son; and children shall rise up against their akennends, and shall have them be put to death.
[13] And ye shall be hated of all men for my name's sake: but he that shall thole unto the end, the same shall be nerred.
[14] But when ye shall see the grir of forwastedness, spoken of by Daniel the forequeether, standing where it ought not, (let him that readeth understand,) then let them that be in Judaea flee to the barrows:

[15] And let him that is on the housetop not go down into the house, neither go therein, to take any thing out of his house:
[16] And let him that is in the field not wharve back again for to take up his clothing.
[17] But woe to them that are with child, and to them that give suck in those days!
[18] And abid ye that your flight be not in the winter.
[19] For in those days shall be brockening, such as was not from the beginning of the ishaft which God created unto this time, neither shall be.
[20] And unless that the Lord had shortened those days, no flesh should be nerred: but for the chosen's sake, whom he hath chosen, he hath shortened the days.
[21] And then if any man shall say to you, Lo, here is Christ; or, lo, he is there; believe him not:
[22] For unsooth Christs and unsooth forequeethers shall rise, and shall shew tockens and wonders, to seduce, if it were mightly, even the chosen.
[23] But take ye heed: behold, I have foretold you all things.
[24] But in those days, after that dretching, the sun shall be darkened, and the moon shall not give her light,
[25] And the stars of heaven shall fall, and the wolds that are in heaven shall be shaken.
[26] And then shall they see the Son of man coming in the clouds with great wold and woulder.
[27] And then shall he send his woulderghosts, and shall gather together his chosen from the four winds, from the uttermost part of the earth to the uttermost part of heaven.
[28] Now learn a likeningtale of the fig tree; When her branch is yet tender, and putteth forth leaves, ye know that summer is near:
[29] So ye in like kind, when ye shall see these things come to be, know that it is nigh, even at the doors.
[30] In sooth I say unto you, that this strind shall not wend, till all these things be done.
[31] Heaven and earth shall wend away: but my words shall not wend away.
[32] But of that day and that stound knoweth no man, no, not the woulderghosts which are in heaven, neither the Son, but the Father.
[33] Take ye heed, watch and abid: for ye know not when the time is.
[34] For the Son of man is as a man taking a far sith, who left his house, and gave alderdom to his thanes, and to every man his work, and bebade the porter to watch.
[35] Watch ye therefore: for ye know not when the harr of the house cometh, at even, or at midnight, or at the cockcrowing, or in the morning:

[36] Lest coming suddenly he find you sleeping.
[37] And what I say unto you I say unto all, Watch.

Mark.14

[1] After two days was the simbletide of the eastersimble, and of unleavened bread: and the alderpriests and the scribes sought how they might take him by craft, and put him to death.
[2] But they said, Not on the simbletide day, lest there be an uproar of the theed.
[3] And being in Bethany in the house of Simon the leper, as he sat at meat, there came a woman having an alabaster box of smearls of spikenard very precious; and she brake the box, and poured it on his head.
[4] And there were some that had unfairnessanger within themselves, and said, Why was this waste of the smearls made?
[5] For it might have been sold for more than three hundred pence, and have been given to the arm. And they murmured against her.
[6] And Jesus said, Let her alone; why dreeve ye her? she hath wrought a good work on me.
[7] For ye have the arm with you always, and whensoever ye will ye may do them good: but me ye have not always.
[8] She hath done what she could: she is come aforehand to asmear my body to the burying.
[9] In sooth I say unto you, Wheresoever this gospel shall be preached throughout the whole world, this also that she hath done shall be spoken of for a min of her.
[10] And Judas Iscariot, one of the twelve, went unto the alderpriests, to forread him unto them.
[11] And when they heard it, they were glad, and hoted to give him money. And he sought how he might hapfully forread him.
[12] And the first day of unleavened bread, when they killed the eastersimble, his loreknights said unto him, Where wilt thou that we go and yark that thou mayest eat the eastersimble?
[13] And he sendeth forth two of his loreknights, and saith unto them, Go ye into the chester, and there shall meet you a man bearing a pitcher of water: follow him.
[14] And wheresoever he shall go in, say ye to the goodman of the house, The Harr saith, Where is the guestroom, where I shall eat the eastersimble with my loreknights?
[15] And he will shew you a large upper room sided and yeaked: there make ready for us.
[16] And his loreknights went forth, and came into the chester, and found as he had said unto them: and they made ready the eastersimble.
[17] And in the evening he cometh with the twelve.
[18] And as they sat and did eat, Jesus said, In sooth I say unto you, One of you which eateth with me shall forread me.
[19] And they began to be sorrowful, and to say unto him one by one, Is it I? and another said, Is it I?
[20] And he answered and said unto them, It is one of the twelve, that dippeth with me in the dish.
[21] The Son of man indeed goeth, as it is written of him: but woe to that man by whom the Son of man is forread! good were it for that man if he had never been born.
[22] And as they did eat, Jesus took bread, and blessed, and brake it, and gave to them, and said, Take, eat: this is my body.
[23] And he took the cup, and when he had given thanks, he gave it to them: and they all drank of it.
[24] And he said unto them, This is my blood of the new kitheness, which is shed for many.
[25] In sooth I say unto you, I will drink no more of the ovet of the vine, until that day that I drink it new in the kingdom of God.
[26] And when they had sung an hymn, they went out into the barrow of Olives.
[27] And Jesus saith unto them, All ye shall be abellowed forwhy of me this night: for it is written, I will smite the shepherd, and the sheep shall be scattered.
[28] But after that I am risen, I will go before you into Galilee.
[29] But Peter said unto him, Although all shall be abellowed, yet will not I.
[30] And Jesus saith unto him, In sooth I say unto thee, That this day, even in this night, before the cock crow twice, thou shalt andsake me thrice.
[31] But he spake the more feelingfully, If I should die with thee, I will not andsake thee in any wise. Likewise also said they all.
[32] And they came to a stead which was named Gethsemane: and he saith to his loreknights, Sit ye here, while I shall abid.
[33] And he taketh with him Peter and James and John, and began to be sore amazed, and to be very heavy;
[34] And saith unto them, My soul is outestly sorrowful unto death: tarry ye here, and watch.
[35] And he went forward a little, and fell on the ground, and abade that, if it were acomingly, the stound might wend from him.
[36] And he said, Abba, Father, all things are mightly unto thee; take away this cup from me: nevertheless not what I will, but what thou wilt.
[37] And he cometh, and findeth them sleeping, and saith unto Peter, Simon, sleepest thou? couldest not thou watch one stound?
[38] Watch ye and abid, lest ye go into costening. The ferth truly is ready, but the flesh is weak.
[39] And again he went away, and abade, and spake

the same words.
[40] And when he edwhorve, he found them asleep again, (for their eyes were heavy,) neither wist they what to answer him.
[41] And he cometh the third time, and saith unto them, Sleep on now, and take your rest: it is enough, the stound is come; behold, the Son of man is forread into the hands of sinners.
[42] Rise up, let us go; lo, he that forreadeth me is at hand.
[43] And forthwith, while he yet spake, cometh Judas, one of the twelve, and with him a great dright with swords and staves, from the alderpriests and the scribes and the elders.
[44] And he that forread him had given them a token, saying, Whomsoever I shall kiss, that same is he; take him, and lead him away safely.
[45] And as soon as he was come, he goeth straightway to him, and saith, Harr, harr; and kissed him.
[46] And they laid their hands on him, and took him.
[47] And one of them that stood by drew a sword, and smote a thane of the high priest, and cut off his ear.
[48] And Jesus answered and said unto them, Are ye come out, as against a thief, with swords and with staves to take me?
[49] I was daily with you in the worshipstead teaching, and ye took me not: but the writ must be fulfilled.
[50] And they all forsook him, and fled.
[51] And there followed him a somel young man, having a linen cloth cast about his naked body; and the young men laid hold on him:
[52] And he left the linen cloth, and fled from them naked.
[53] And they led Jesus away to the high priest: and with him were gathered all the alderpriests and the elders and the scribes.
[54] And Peter followed him afar off, even into the thronestead of the high priest: and he sat with the thanes, and warmed himself at the fire.
[55] And the alderpriests and all the rownwitmoot sought for witness against Jesus to put him to death; and found none.
[56] For many bare unsooth witness against him, but their witness thweered not together.
[57] And there arose somel, and bare unsooth witness against him, saying,
[58] We heard him say, I will fordo this worshipstead that is made with hands, and within three days I will build another made without hands.
[59] But neither so did their witness thweer together.
[60] And the high priest stood up in the midst, and asked Jesus, saying, Answerest thou nothing? what is it which these witness against thee?
[61] But he held his frith, and answered nothing. Again the high priest asked him, and said unto him, Art thou the Christ, the Son of the Blessed?
[62] And Jesus said, I am: and ye shall see the Son of man sitting on the right hand of wold, and coming in the clouds of heaven.
[63] Then the high priest rent his clothes, and saith, What need we any further witnesses?
[64] Ye have heard the evilsaking: what think ye? And they all fordeemed him to be guilty of death.
[65] And some began to spit on him, and to cover his anlit, and to hit him, and to say unto him, Forequeethe: and the thanes did strike him with the palms of their hands.
[66] And as Peter was beneath in the thronestead, there cometh one of the maids of the high priest:
[67] And when she saw Peter warming himself, she looked upon him, and said, And thou also wast with Jesus of Nazareth.
[68] But he andsook, saying, I know not, neither understand I what thou sayest. And he went out into the porch; and the cock crew.
[69] And a maid saw him again, and began to say to them that stood by, This is one of them.
[70] And he andsook it again. And a little after, they that stood by said again to Peter, Surely thou art one of them: for thou art a Galilaean, and thy speech thweerth thereto.
[71] But he began to curse and to swear, saying, I know not this man of whom ye speak.
[72] And in that timeling the cock crew. And Peter called to mind the word that Jesus said unto him, Before the cock crow twice, thou shalt andsake me thrice. And when he thought thereon, he wept.

Mark.15

[1] And straightway in the morning the alderpriests held an upseek with the elders and scribes and the whole rownwitmoot, and bound Jesus, and bore him away, and agave him to Pilate.
[2] And Pilate asked him, Art thou the King of the Jews? And he answering said unto him, Thou sayest it.
[3] And the alderpriests wrayed him of many things: but he answered nothing.
[4] And Pilate asked him again, saying, Answerest thou nothing? behold how many things they witness against thee.
[5] But Jesus yet answered nothing; so that Pilate awondered.
[6] Now at that simbletide he alet unto them one witerner, whomsoever they wished.
[7] And there was one named Barabbas, which lay bound with them that had made uprise against him, who had done murder in the uprise.
[8] And the dright yarming aloud began to wish him to

do as he had ever done unto them.

[9] But Pilate answered them, saying, Will ye that I alet unto you the King of the Jews?

[10] For he knew that the alderpriests had given him over for ond.

[11] But the alderpriests stirred the theed, that he should rather alet Barabbas unto them.

[12] And Pilate answered and said again unto them, What will ye then that I shall do unto him whom ye call the King of the Jews?

[13] And they yarmed out again, Roodfasten him.

[14] Then Pilate said unto them, Why, what evil hath he done? And they yarmed out the more outestly, Roodfasten him.

[15] And so Pilate, willing to content the theed, alet Barabbas unto them, and agave Jesus, when he had scourged him, to be roodfastened.

[16] And the heregomes led him away into the hall, called Praetorium; and they call together the whole band.

[17] And they clothed him with purple, and platted a kinhelm of thorns, and put it about his head,

[18] And began to salute him, Hail, King of the Jews!

[19] And they smote him on the head with a reed, and did spit upon him, and bowing their knees worshipped him.

[20] And when they had bismered him, they took off the purple from him, and put his own clothes on him, and led him out to roodfasten him.

[21] And they thrack one Simon a Cyrenian, who wended by, coming out of the land, the father of Alexander and Rufus, to bear his rood.

[22] And they bring him unto the stead Golgotha, which is, being awended, The stead of a skull.

[23] And they gave him to drink wine mingled with myrrh: but he thidged it not.

[24] And when they had roodfastened him, they parted his clothing, casting lots upon them, what every man should take.

[25] And it was the third stound, and they roodfastened him.

[26] And the overwriting of his wraying was written over, THE KING OF THE JEWS.

[27] And with him they roodfasten two thieves; the one on his right hand, and the other on his left.

[28] And the writ was fulfilled, which saith, And he was arimed with the wrongdoers.

[29] And they that wended by railed on him, wagging their heads, and saying, Ah, thou that fordoest the worshipstead, and buildest it in three days,

[30] Nerr thyself, and come down from the rood.

[31] Likewise also the alderpriests bismering said among themselves with the scribes, He nerred others; himself he cannot nerr.

[32] Let Christ the King of Israel ntherastie now from the rood, that we may see and believe. And they that were roodfastened with him slighted him.

[33] And when the sixth stound was come, there was darkness over the whole land until the ninth stound.

[34] And at the ninth stound Jesus yarmed with a loud steven, saying, Eloi, Eloi, lama sabachthani? which is, being awended, My God, my God, why hast thou forsaken me?

[35] And some of them that stood by, when they heard it, said, Behold, he calleth Elias.

[36] And one ran and filled a spunge full of vinegar, and put it on a reed, and gave him to drink, saying, Let alone; let us see whether Elias will come to take him down.

[37] And Jesus yarmed with a loud steven, and gave up the ghost.

[38] And the veil of the worshipstead was rent in twain from the top to the bottom.

[39] And when the hundredman, which stood over against him, saw that he so yarmed out, and gave up the ghost, he said, Truly this man was the Son of God.

[40] There were also women looking on afar off: among whom was Mary Magdalene, and Mary the mother of James the less and of Joses, and Salome;

[41] (Who also, when he was in Galilee, followed him, and acared unto him;) and many other women which came up with him unto Jerusalem.

[42] And now when the even was come, forwhy it was the reening, that is, the day before the sabbath,

[43] Joseph of Arimathaea, and oreable counseller, which also waited for the kingdom of God, came, and went in boldly unto Pilate, and craved the body of Jesus.

[44] And Pilate awondered if he were already dead: and calling unto him the hundredman, he asked him whether he had been any while dead.

[45] And when he knew it of the hundredman, he gave the body to Joseph.

[46] And he bought fine linen, and took him down, and wrapped him in the linen, and laid him in a lichrest which was hewn out of a rock, and rolled a stone unto the door of the lichrest.

[47] And Mary Magdalene and Mary the mother of Joses beheld where he was laid.

Mark.16

[1] And when the sabbath was past, Mary Magdalene, and Mary the mother of James, and Salome, had bought sweet spices, that they might come and asmear him.

[2] And very early in the morning the first day of the week, they came unto the lichrest at the rising of the sun.

[3] And they said among themselves, Who shall roll us away the stone from the door of the lichrest?
[4] And when they looked, they saw that the stone was rolled away: for it was very great.
[5] And going into the lichrest, they saw a young man sitting on the right side, clothed in a long white clothing; and they were affrighted.
[6] And he saith unto them, Be not affrighted: Ye seek Jesus of Nazareth, which was roodfastened: he is risen; he is not here: behold the stead where they laid him.
[7] But go your way, tell his loreknights and Peter that he goeth before you into Galilee: there shall ye see him, as he said unto you.
[8] And they went out quickly, and fled from the lichrest; for they bived and were amazed: neither said they any thing to any man; for they were afraid.
[9] Now when Jesus was risen early the first day of the week, he trod up first to Mary Magdalene, out of whom he had cast seven devils.
[10] And she went and told them that had been with him, as they mourned and wept.
[11] And they, when they had heard that he was alive, and had been seen of her, believed not.
[12] After that he trod up in another form unto two of them, as they walked, and went into the land.
[13] And they went and told it unto the others: neither believed they them.
[14] Afterward he trod up unto the eleven as they sat at meat, and upbraided them with their unbelief and hardness of heart, forwhy they believed not them which had seen him after he was risen.
[15] And he said unto them, Go ye into all the world, and preach the gospel to every creature.
[16] He that believeth and is forwashed shall be nerred; but he that believeth not shall be damned.
[17] And these tockens shall follow them that believe; In my name shall they cast out devils; they shall speak with new tongues;
[18] They shall take up serpents; and if they drink any deadly thing, it shall not hurt them; they shall lay hands on the sick, and they shall recover.
[19] So then after the Lord had spoken unto them, he was thidged up into heaven, and sat on the right hand of God.
[20] And they went forth, and preached everywhere, the Lord working with them, and confirming the word with tockens following. Amen.

Bible, King James Version

Luke

Luke.1

[1] Forasmuch as many have taken in hand to set forth in order a forthspel of those things which are most surely believed among us,
[2] Even as they gave them over unto us, which from the beginning were eyewitnesses, and acarers of the word;
[3] It thenched good to me also, having had fullfremmed understanding of all things from the very first, to write unto thee in order, most great Theophilus,
[4] That thou mightest know the wiss of those things, wherein thou hast been taught.
[5] There was in the days of Herod, the king of Judaea, a somel priest named Zacharias, of the course of Abia: and his wife was of the daughters of Aaron, and her name was Elisabeth.
[6] And they were both rightsome before God, walking in all the bodewords and biddings of the Lord tealless.
[7] And they had no child, forwhy that Elisabeth was barren, and they both were now well stricken in years.
[8] And it came to be, that while he fremmed the priest's office before God in the order of his course,
[9] By to the thew of the priest's office, his lot was to burn stoor when he went into the worshipstead of the Lord.
[10] And the whole dright of the theed were abiding without at the time of stoor.
[11] And there trod up unto him a woulderghost of the Lord standing on the right side of the altar of stoor.
[12] And when Zacharias saw him, he was dreeved, and fear fell upon him.
[13] But the woulderghost said unto him, Fear not, Zacharias: for thy ibead is heard; and thy wife Elisabeth shall bear thee a son, and thou shalt call his name John.
[14] And thou shalt have mirth and gladness; and many shall aglee at his birth.
[15] For he shall be great in the sight of the Lord, and shall drink neither wine nor strong drink; and he shall be filled with the Holy Ghost, even from his mother's womb.
[16] And many of the children of Israel shall he wharve to the Lord their God.
[17] And he shall go before him in the ferth and wold of Elias, to wharve the hearts of the fathers to the children, and the unhearsome to the wisdom of the rightful; to make ready a theed yeaked for the Lord.
[18] And Zacharias said unto the woulderghost, Whereby shall I know this? for I am an old man, and my wife well stricken in years.
[19] And the woulderghost answering said unto him, I

am Gabriel, that stand in the atwist of God; and am sent to speak unto thee, and to shew thee these glad tidings.
[20] And, behold, thou shalt be dumb, and not able to speak, until the day that these things shall be fremmed, forwhy thou believest not my words, which shall be fulfilled in their time.
[21] And the theed waited for Zacharias, and awondered that he tarried so long in the worshipstead.
[22] And when he came out, he could not speak unto them: and they ongot that he had seen an aldersight in the worshipstead: for he beckoned unto them, and belived speechless.
[23] And it came to be, that, as soon as the days of his thaning were fullworked, he wote to his own house.
[24] And after those days his wife Elisabeth kenned, and hid herself five months, saying,
[25] Thus hath the Lord dealt with me in the days wherein he looked on me, to take away my edwite among men.
[26] And in the sixth month the woulderghost Gabriel was sent from God unto a chester of Galilee, named Nazareth,
[27] To a maiden betrothed to a man whose name was Joseph, of the house of David; and the maiden's name was Mary.
[28] And the woulderghost came in unto her, and said, Hail, thou that art highly favoured, the Lord is with thee: blessed art thou among women.
[29] And when she saw him, she was dreeved at his saying, and cast in her mind what kind of oretokening this should be.
[30] And the woulderghost said unto her, Fear not, Mary: for thou hast found favour with God.
[31] And, behold, thou shalt ken in thy womb, and bring forth a son, and shalt call his name JESUS.
[32] He shall be great, and shall be called the Son of the Highest: and the Lord God shall give unto him the throne of his father David:
[33] And he shall reign over the house of Jacob for ever; and of his kingdom there shall be no end.
[34] Then said Mary unto the woulderghost, How shall this be, seeing I know not a man?
[35] And the woulderghost answered and said unto her, The Holy Ghost shall come upon thee, and the wold of the Highest shall overshadow thee: therefore also that holy thing which shall be born of thee shall be called the Son of God.
[36] And, behold, thy cousin Elisabeth, she hath also kenned a son in her old age: and this is the sixth month with her, who was called barren.
[37] For with God nothing shall be unmightly.
[38] And Mary said, Behold the handmaid of the Lord; be it unto me by to thy word. And the woulderghost wote from her.

[39] And Mary arose in those days, and went into the hill land with haste, into a chester of Juda;
[40] And went into the house of Zacharias, and saluted Elisabeth.
[41] And it came to be, that, when Elisabeth heard the oretokening of Mary, the babe leaped in her womb; and Elisabeth was filled with the Holy Ghost:
[42] And she spake out with a loud steven, and said, Blessed art thou among women, and blessed is the ovet of thy womb.
[43] And whence is this to me, that the mother of my Lord should come to me?
[44] For, lo, as soon as the steven of thy oretokening sounded in mine ears, the babe leaped in my womb for mirth.
[45] And blessed is she that believed: for there shall be a fremance of those things which were told her from the Lord.
[46] And Mary said, My soul doth magnify the Lord,
[47] And my ferth hath agleed in God my Saviour.
[48] For he hath hidged the low estate of his handmaiden: for, behold, from henceforth all strinds shall call me blessed.
[49] For he that is mighty hath done to me great things; and holy is his name.
[50] And his ruth is on them that fear him from strind to strind.
[51] He hath shewed strength with his arm; he hath scattered the proud in the imagifolkdom of their hearts.
[52] He hath put down the mighty from their seats, and reamed them of low degree.
[53] He hath filled the hungry with good things; and the rich he hath sent empty away.
[54] He hath holpen his thane Israel, in min of his ruth;
[55] As he spake to our fathers, to Abraham, and to his seed for ever.
[56] And Mary abode with her about three months, and edwhorve to her own house.
[57] Now Elisabeth's full time came that she should give birth; and she brought forth a son.
[58] And her neighbours and her cousins heard how the Lord had shewed great ruth upon her; and they agleed with her.
[59] And it came to be, that on the eighth day they came to forsnithe the child; and they called him Zacharias, after the name of his father.
[60] And his mother answered and said, Not so; but he shall be called John.
[61] And they said unto her, There is none of thy kindred that is called by this name.
[62] And they made tockens to his father, how he would have him called.
[63] And he asked for a writing table, and wrote, saying, His name is John. And they awondered all.
[64] And his mouth was opened forthwith, and his

tongue loosed, and he spake, and praised God.
[65] And fear came on all that dwelt round about them: and all these sayings were noised abroad throughout all the hill land of Judaea.
[66] And all they that heard them laid them up in their hearts, saying, What kind of child shall this be! And the hand of the Lord was with him.
[67] And his father Zacharias was filled with the Holy Ghost, and forequothe, saying,
[68] Blessed be the Lord God of Israel; for he hath neased and aleesed his theed,
[69] And hath raised up an horn of aredding for us in the house of his thane David;
[70] As he spake by the mouth of his holy forequeethers, which have been since the world began:
[71] That we should be nerred from our foes, and from the hand of all that hate us;
[72] To frem the ruth hoted to our fathers, and to mun his holy oathbind;
[73] The oath which he sware to our father Abraham,
[74] That he would grant unto us, that we being agiven out of the hand of our foes might theen him without fear,
[75] In holiness and rightsomeness before him, all the days of our life.
[76] And thou, child, shalt be called the forequeether of the Highest: for thou shalt go before the anlit of the Lord to yark his ways;
[77] To give knowledge of holse unto his theed by the eftgiving of their sins,
[78] Through the tender ruth of our God; whereby the dayspring from on high hath neased us,
[79] To give light to them that sit in darkness and in the shadow of death, to guide our feet into the way of frith.
[80] And the child grew, and waxed strong in ferth, and was in the throughdryland till the day of his shewing unto Israel.

Luke.2

[1] And it came to be in those days, that there went out a decree from Caesar Augustus, that all the world should be taxed.
[2] (And this taxing was first made when Cyrenius was awieldend of Syria.)
[3] And all went to be taxed, every one into his own chester.
[4] And Joseph also went up from Galilee, out of the chester of Nazareth, into Judaea, unto the chester of David, which is called Bethlehem; (forwhy he was of the house and lineage of David:)
[5] To be taxed with Mary his betrthed wife, being great with child.

[6] And so it was, that, while they were there, the days were fullgone that she should give birth.
[7] And she brought forth her firstborn son, and wrapped him in swaddling clothes, and laid him in a manger; forwhy there was no room for them in the inn.
[8] And there were in the same land shepherds abiding in the field, keeping watch over their flock by night.
[9] And, lo, the woulderghost of the Lord came upon them, and the woulder of the Lord shone round about them: and they were sore afraid.
[10] And the woulderghost said unto them, Fear not: for, behold, I bring you good tidings of great mirth, which shall be to all theed.
[11] For unto you is born this day in the chester of David a Saviour, which is Christ the Lord.
[12] And this shall be a tocken unto you; Ye shall find the babe wrapped in swaddling clothes, lying in a manger.
[13] And suddenly there was with the woulderghost a dright of the heavenly host praising God, and saying,
[14] Woulder to God in the highest, and on earth frith, good will toward men.
[15] And it came to be, as the woulderghosts were gone away from them into heaven, the shepherds said one to another, Let us now go even unto Bethlehem, and see this thing which is come to be, which the Lord hath made known unto us.
[16] And they came with haste, and found Mary, and Joseph, and the babe lying in a manger.
[17] And when they had seen it, they made known abroad the saying which was told them bemeeting this child.
[18] And all they that heard it wondered at those things which were told them by the shepherds.
[19] But Mary kept all these things, and pondered them in her heart.
[20] And the shepherds edwhorve, woulderening and praising God for all the things that they had heard and seen, as it was told unto them.
[21] And when eight days were fullworked for the forsnithing of the child, his name was called JESUS, which was so named of the woulderghost before he was kenned in the womb.
[22] And when the days of luttering by to the law of Moses were fullworked, they brought him to Jerusalem, to bring him before the Lord;
[23] (As it is written in the law of the Lord, Every weapman that openeth the womb shall be called holy to the Lord;)
[24] And to offer a bloot by to that which is said in the law of the Lord, A pair of turtledoves, or two young pigeons.
[25] And, behold, there was a man in Jerusalem, whose name was Simeon; and the same man was upright and heartfast, waiting for the frovering of Israel: and the

Holy Ghost was upon him.

[26] And it was swettled unto him by the Holy Ghost, that he should not see death, before he had seen the Lord's Christ.

[27] And he came by the Ferth into the worshipstead: and when the akennends brought in the child Jesus, to do for him after the thew of the law,

[28] Then took he him up in his arms, and blessed God, and said,

[29] Lord, now lettest thou thy thane wite in frith, by to thy word:

[30] For mine eyes have seen thy aredding,

[31] Which thou hast yeaked before the anlit of all theed;

[32] A light to lighten the Gentiles, and the woulder of thy theed Israel.

[33] And Joseph and his mother awondered at those things which were spoken of him.

[34] And Simeon blessed them, and said unto Mary his mother, Behold, this child is set for the fall and rising again of many in Israel; and for a tocken which shall be spoken against;

[35] (Yea, a sword shall pierce through thy own soul also,) that the thoughts of many hearts may be swettled.

[36] And there was one Anna, a forequeetheress, the daughter of Phanuel, of the tribe of Aser: she was of a great age, and had lived with an husband seven years from her maidenhood;

[37] And she was a widow of about fourscore and four years, which wote not from the worshipstead, but theened God with fastings and ibeads night and day.

[38] And she coming in that instant gave thanks likewise unto the Lord, and spake of him to all them that looked for aleesedness in Jerusalem.

[39] And when they had fremmed all things by to the law of the Lord, they edwhorve into Galilee, to their own chester Nazareth.

[40] And the child grew, and waxed strong in ferth, filled with wisdom: and the grace of God was upon him.

[41] Now his akennends went to Jerusalem every year at the simbletide of the eastersimble.

[42] And when he was twelve years old, they went up to Jerusalem after the thew of the simbletide.

[43] And when they had fulfilled the days, as they edwhorve, the child Jesus tarried behind in Jerusalem; and Joseph and his mother knew not of it.

[44] But they, supposing him to have been in the togetherred, went a day's sith; and they sought him among their kinsfolk and kithsfolk.

[45] And when they found him not, they whorve back again to Jerusalem, seeking him.

[46] And it came to be, that after three days they found him in the worshipstead, sitting in the midst of the doctors, both hearing them, and asking them fraigns.

[47] And all that heard him were amazed at his understanding and answers.

[48] And when they saw him, they were amazed: and his mother said unto him, Son, why hast thou thus dealt with us? behold, thy father and I have sought thee sorrowing.

[49] And he said unto them, How is it that ye sought me? wist ye not that I must be about my Father's business?

[50] And they understood not the saying which he spake unto them.

[51] And he went down with them, and came to Nazareth, and was undertheed unto them: but his mother kept all these sayings in her heart.

[52] And Jesus waxed in wisdom and height and in rith with God and man.

Luke.3

[1] Now in the fifteenth year of the reign of Tiberius Caesar, Pontius Pilate being awieldend of Judaea, and Herod being tetrarch of Galilee, and his brother Philip tetrarch of Ituraea and of the imbstead of Trachonitis, and Lysanias the tetrarch of Abilene,

[2] Annas and Caiaphas being the high priests, the word of God came unto John the son of Zacharias in the wilderness.

[3] And he came into all the land about Jordan, preaching the forwashing of berueing for the eftgiving of sins;

[4] As it is written in the book of the words of Esaias the forequeether, saying, The steven of one yarming in the wilderness, Yark ye the way of the Lord, make his paths straight.

[5] Every valley shall be filled, and every barrow and hill shall be brought low; and the crooked shall be made straight, and the rough ways shall be made smooth;

[6] And all flesh shall see the aredding of God.

[7] Then said he to the dright that came forth to be forwashed of him, O strind of vipers, who hath warned you to flee from the wrath to come?

[8] Bring forth therefore ovets worthy of berueing, and begin not to say within yourselves, We have Abraham to our father: for I say unto you, That God is able of these stones to raise up children unto Abraham.

[9] And now also the axe is laid unto the root of the trees: every tree therefore which bringeth not forth good ovet is hewn down, and cast into the fire.

[10] And the theed asked him, saying, What shall we do then?

[11] He answereth and saith unto them, He that hath two coats, let him impart to him that hath none; and he

that hath meat, let him do likewise.

[12] Then came also tollners to be forwashed, and said unto him, Harr, what shall we do?

[13] And he said unto them, Do not go beyond the scale which is agiven you.

[14] And the heregomes likewise asked of him, saying, And what shall we do? And he said unto them, Do violence to no man, neither wray any unsoothly; and be content with your wages.

[15] And as the theed were in ween, and all men mused in their hearts of John, whether he were the Christ, or not;

[16] John answered, saying unto them all, I indeed forwash you with water; but one mightier than I cometh, the latchet of whose shoes I am not worthy to unloose: he shall forwash you with the Holy Ghost and with fire:

[17] Whose fan is in his hand, and he will throughly clean his floor, and will gather the wheat into his garner; but the chaff he will burn with fire unquenchable.

[18] And many other things in his teaching preached he unto the theed.

[19] But Herod the tetrarch, being reproved by him for Herodias his brother Philip's wife, and for all the evils which Herod had done,

[20] Added yet this above all, that he shut up John in witern.

[21] Now when all the theed were forwashed, it came to be, that Jesus also being forwashed, and abiding, the heaven was opened,

[22] And the Holy Ghost stighed down in a bodily shape like a dove upon him, and a steven came from heaven, which said, Thou art my beloved Son; in thee I am well becweemed.

[23] And Jesus himself began to be about thirty years of age, being (as was weend) the son of Joseph, which was the son of Heli,

[24] Which was the son of Matthat, which was the son of Levi, which was the son of Melchi, which was the son of Janna, which was the son of Joseph,

[25] Which was the son of Mattathias, which was the son of Amos, which was the son of Naum, which was the son of Esli, which was the son of Nagge,

[26] Which was the son of Maath, which was the son of Mattathias, which was the son of Semei, which was the son of Joseph, which was the son of Juda,

[27] Which was the son of Joanna, which was the son of Rhesa, which was the son of Zorobabel, which was the son of Salathiel, which was the son of Neri,

[28] Which was the son of Melchi, which was the son of Addi, which was the son of Cosam, which was the son of Elmodam, which was the son of Er,

[29] Which was the son of Jose, which was the son of Eliezer, which was the son of Jorim, which was the son of Matthat, which was the son of Levi,

[30] Which was the son of Simeon, which was the son of Juda, which was the son of Joseph, which was the son of Jonan, which was the son of Eliakim,

[31] Which was the son of Melea, which was the son of Menan, which was the son of Mattatha, which was the son of Nathan, which was the son of David,

[32] Which was the son of Jesse, which was the son of Obed, which was the son of Booz, which was the son of Salmon, which was the son of Naasson,

[33] Which was the son of Aminadab, which was the son of Aram, which was the son of Esrom, which was the son of Phares, which was the son of Juda,

[34] Which was the son of Jacob, which was the son of Isaac, which was the son of Abraham, which was the son of Thara, which was the son of Nachor,

[35] Which was the son of Saruch, which was the son of Ragau, which was the son of Phalec, which was the son of Heber, which was the son of Sala,

[36] Which was the son of Cainan, which was the son of Arphaxad, which was the son of Sem, which was the son of Noe, which was the son of Lamech,

[37] Which was the son of Mathusala, which was the son of Enoch, which was the son of Jared, which was the son of Maleleel, which was the son of Cainan,

[38] Which was the son of Enos, which was the son of Seth, which was the son of Adam, which was the son of God.

Luke.4

[1] And Jesus being full of the Holy Ghost edwhorve from Jordan, and was led by the Ferth into the wilderness,

[2] Being forty days costened of the devil. And in those days he did eat nothing: and when they were ended, he afterward hungered.

[3] And the devil said unto him, If thou be the Son of God, bebid this stone that it be made bread.

[4] And Jesus answered him, saying, It is written, That man shall not live by bread alone, but by every word of God.

[5] And the devil, taking him up into an high barrow, shewed unto him all the kingdoms of the world in a moment of time.

[6] And the devil said unto him, All this wold will I give thee, and the woulder of them: for that is agiven unto me; and to whomsoever I will I give it.

[7] If thou therefore wilt worship me, all shall be thine.

[8] And Jesus answered and said unto him, Get thee behind me, Hellwarden: for it is written, Thou shalt worship the Lord thy God, and him only shalt thou theen.

[9] And he brought him to Jerusalem, and set him on a

pinnacle of the worshipstead, and said unto him, If thou be the Son of God, cast thyself down from hence:
[10] For it is written, He shall give his woulderghosts care over thee, to keep thee:
[11] And in their hands they shall bear thee up, lest at any time thou dash thy foot against a stone.
[12] And Jesus answering said unto him, It is said, Thou shalt not costen the Lord thy God.
[13] And when the devil had ended all the costening, he wote from him for a time.
[14] And Jesus edwhorve in the wold of the Ferth into Galilee: and there went out a fame of him through all the imbstead.
[15] And he taught in their worshipsteads, being woulderened of all.
[16] And he came to Nazareth, where he had been brought up: and, as his thew was, he went into the worshipstead on the sabbath day, and stood up for to read.
[17] And there was given unto him the book of the forequeether Esaias. And when he had opened the book, he found the stead where it was written,
[18] The Ferth of the Lord is upon me, forwhy he hath asmeared me to preach the gospel to the arm; he hath sent me to heal the brokenhearted, to preach aleeseing to the haftlings, and edstatheling of sight to the blind, to set free them that are bruised,
[19] To preach the onfangsome year of the Lord.
[20] And he closed the book, and he gave it again to the acarer, and sat down. And the eyes of all them that were in the worshipstead were fastened on him.
[21] And he began to say unto them, This day is this writ fulfilled in your ears.
[22] And all bare him witness, and wondered at the gracious words which came out of his mouth. And they said, Is not this Joseph's son?
[23] And he said unto them, Ye will surely say unto me this proverb, Physician, heal thyself: whatsoever we have heard done in Capernaum, do also here in thy land.
[24] And he said, In sooth I say unto you, No forequeether is accepted in his own land.
[25] But I tell you of a truth, many widows were in Israel in the days of Elias, when the heaven was shut up three years and six months, when great hunger was throughout all the land;
[26] But unto none of them was Elias sent, nerr unto Sarepta, a chester of Sidon, unto a woman that was a widow.
[27] And many lepers were in Israel in the time of Eliseus the forequeether; and none of them was cleansed, saving Naaman the Syrian.
[28] And all they in the worshipstead, when they heard these things, were filled with wrath,
[29] And rose up, and thrust him out of the chester, and led him unto the brow of the hill whereon their chester was built, that they might cast him down headlong.
[30] But he wending through the midst of them went his way,
[31] And came down to Capernaum, a chester of Galilee, and taught them on the sabbath days.
[32] And they were amazed at his loreword: for his word was with wold.
[33] And in the worshipstead there was a man, which had a ferth of an unclean devil, and yarmed out with a loud steven,
[34] Saying, Let us alone; what have we to do with thee, thou Jesus of Nazareth? art thou come to fordo us? I know thee who thou art; the Holy One of God.
[35] And Jesus scolded him, saying, Hold thy frith, and come out of him. And when the devil had thrown him in the midst, he came out of him, and hurt him not.
[36] And they were all amazed, and spake among themselves, saying, What a word is this! for with alderdom and wold he bebideth the unclean ferths, and they come out.
[37] And the fame of him went out into every stead of the land round about.
[38] And he arose out of the worshipstead, and went into Simon's house. And Simon's wife's mother was taken with a great fever; and they besought him for her.
[39] And he stood over her, and scolded the fever; and it left her: and forthwith she arose and acared unto them.
[40] Now when the sun was setting, all they that had any sick with divers cothes brought them unto him; and he laid his hands on every one of them, and healed them.
[41] And devils also came out of many, yarming out, and saying, Thou art Christ the Son of God. And he rebuking them thrawed them not to speak: for they knew that he was Christ.
[42] And when it was day, he wote and went into a throughdry stead: and the theed sought him, and came unto him, and stayed him, that he should not wite from them.
[43] And he said unto them, I must preach the kingdom of God to other chesters also: for therefore am I sent.
[44] And he preached in the worshipsteads of Galilee.

Luke.5

[1] And it came to be, that, as the theed pressed upon him to hear the word of God, he stood by the lake of Gennesaret,
[2] And saw two ships standing by the lake: but the fishermen were gone out of them, and were washing their nets.

[3] And he went into one of the ships, which was Simon's, and told him to thrust out a little from the land. And he sat down, and taught the theed out of the ship.

[4] Now when he had left speaking, he said unto Simon, Launch out into the deep, and let down your nets for a draught.

[5] And Simon answering said unto him, Harr, we have toiled all the night, and have taken nothing: nevertheless at thy word I will let down the net.

[6] And when they had this done, they inclosed a great dright of fishes: and their net brake.

[7] And they beckoned unto their partners, which were in the other ship, that they should come and help them. And they came, and filled both the ships, so that they began to sink.

[8] When Simon Peter saw it, he fell down at Jesus' knees, saying, Wite from me; for I am a sinful man, O Lord.

[9] For he was amazed, and all that were with him, at the draught of the fishes which they had taken:

[10] And so was also James, and John, the sons of Zebedee, which were partners with Simon. And Jesus said unto Simon, Fear not; from henceforth thou shalt catch men.

[11] And when they had brought their ships to land, they forsook all, and followed him.

[12] And it came to be, when he was in a somel chester, behold a man full of leprosy: who seeing Jesus fell on his anlit, and besought him, saying, Lord, if thou wilt, thou canst make me clean.

[13] And he put forth his hand, and rone him, saying, I will: be thou clean. And forthwith the leprosy wote from him.

[14] And he bebade him to tell no man: but go, and shew thyself to the priest, and offer for thy cleansing, by as Moses bebade, for a witness unto them.

[15] But so much the more went there a fame abroad of him: and great drights came together to hear, and to be healed by him of their cothes.

[16] And he withdrew himself into the wilderness, and abade.

[17] And it came to be on a somel day, as he was teaching, that there were Pharisees and doctors of the law sitting by, which were come out of every town of Galilee, and Judaea, and Jerusalem: and the wold of the Lord was atbeen to heal them.

[18] And, behold, men brought in a bed a man which was taken with a palsy: and they sought means to bring him in, and to lay him before him.

[19] And when they could not find by what way they might bring him in forwhy of the dright, they went upon the housetop, and let him down through the tiling with his couch into the midst before Jesus.

[20] And when he saw their faith, he said unto him, Man, thy sins are forgiven thee.

[21] And the scribes and the Pharisees began to grounds, saying, Who is this which speaketh evilsaking? Who can forgive sins, but God alone?

[22] But when Jesus ongot their thoughts, he answering said unto them, What grounds ye in your hearts?

[23] Whether is easier, to say, Thy sins be forgiven thee; or to say, Rise up and walk?

[24] But that ye may know that the Son of man hath wold upon earth to forgive sins, (he said unto the sick of the palsy,) I say unto thee, Arise, and take up thy couch, and go into thine house.

[25] And forthwith he rose up before them, and took up that whereon he lay, and wote to his own house, woulderening God.

[26] And they were all amazed, and they woulderened God, and were filled with fear, saying, We have seen strange things to day.

[27] And after these things he went forth, and saw a tollner, named Levi, sitting at the receipt of thew: and he said unto him, Follow me.

[28] And he left all, rose up, and followed him.

[29] And Levi made him a great simbletide in his own house: and there was a great maith of tollners and of others that sat down with them.

[30] But their scribes and Pharisees murmured against his loreknights, saying, Why do ye eat and drink with tollners and sinners?

[31] And Jesus answering said unto them, They that are whole need not a physician; but they that are sick.

[32] I came not to call the rightsome, but sinners to beruenig.

[33] And they said unto him, Why do the loreknights of John fast often, and make ibeads, and likewise the loreknights of the Pharisees; but thine eat and drink?

[34] And he said unto them, Can ye make the children of the brideroom fast, while the bridegroom is with them?

[35] But the days will come, when the bridegroom shall be taken away from them, and then shall they fast in those days.

[36] And he spake also a likeningtale unto them; No man putteth a piece of a new clothing upon an old; if otherwise, then both the new maketh a rent, and the piece that was taken out of the new thweerth not with the old.

[37] And no man putteth new wine into old bottles; else the new wine will burst the bottles, and be spilled, and the bottles shall swelt.

[38] But new wine must be put into new bottles; and both are pretheened.

[39] No man also having drunk old wine straightway wisheth new: for he saith, The old is better.

Luke.6

[1] And it came to be on the twoth sabbath after the first, that he went through the corn fields; and his loreknights plucked the ears of corn, and did eat, rubbing them in their hands.
[2] And somel of the Pharisees said unto them, Why do ye that which is not lawful to do on the sabbath days?
[3] And Jesus answering them said, Have ye not read so much as this, what David did, when himself was an hungred, and they which were with him;
[4] How he went into the house of God, and did take and eat the shewbread, and gave also to them that were with him; which it is not lawful to eat but for the priests alone?
[5] And he said unto them, That the Son of man is Lord also of the sabbath.
[6] And it came to be also on another sabbath, that he went into the worshipstead and taught: and there was a man whose right hand was withered.
[7] And the scribes and Pharisees watched him, whether he would heal on the sabbath day; that they might find an wraying against him.
[8] But he knew their thoughts, and said to the man which had the withered hand, Rise up, and stand forth in the midst. And he arose and stood forth.
[9] Then said Jesus unto them, I will ask you one thing; Is it lawful on the sabbath days to do good, or to do evil? to nerr life, or to fordo it?
[10] And looking round about upon them all, he said unto the man, Stretch forth thy hand. And he did so: and his hand was edstatheled whole as the other.
[11] And they were filled with madness; and cwothe one with another what they might do to Jesus.
[12] And it came to be in those days, that he went out into a barrow to abid, and throughstood all night in ibead to God.
[13] And when it was day, he called unto him his loreknights: and of them he chose twelve, whom also he named loreknights;
[14] Simon, (whom he also named Peter,) and Andrew his brother, James and John, Philip and Bartholomew,
[15] Matthew and Thomas, James the son of Alphaeus, and Simon called Zelotes,
[16] And Judas the brother of James, and Judas Iscariot, which also was the traitor.
[17] And he came down with them, and stood in the open, and the togethred of his loreknights, and a great dright of theed out of all Judaea and Jerusalem, and from the sea coast of Tyre and Sidon, which came to hear him, and to be healed of their cothes;
[18] And they that were dretched with unclean ferths: and they were healed.
[19] And the whole dright sought to rine him: for there went thrith out of him, and healed them all.
[20] And he lifted up his eyes on his loreknights, and said, Blessed be ye arm: for yours is the kingdom of God.
[21] Blessed are ye that hunger now: for ye shall be filled. Blessed are ye that weep now: for ye shall laugh.
[22] Blessed are ye, when men shall hate you, and when they shall sunder you from their fereship, and shall threap you, and cast out your name as evil, for the Son of man's sake.
[23] Aglee ye in that day, and leap for mirth: for, behold, your edlean is great in heaven: for in the like kind did their fathers unto the forequeethers.
[24] But woe unto you that are rich! for ye have thidged your frover.
[25] Woe unto you that are full! for ye shall hunger. Woe unto you that laugh now! for ye shall mourn and weep.
[26] Woe unto you, when all men shall speak well of you! for so did their fathers to the unsooth forequeethers.
[27] But I say unto you which hear, Love your foes, do good to them which hate you,
[28] Bless them that curse you, and abid for them which slightfully use you.
[29] And unto him that smiteth thee on the one cheek offer also the other; and him that taketh away thy cloke forbid not to take thy coat also.
[30] Give to every man that asketh of thee; and of him that taketh away thy goods ask them not again.
[31] And as ye would that men should do to you, do ye also to them likewise.
[32] For if ye love them which love you, what thank have ye? for sinners also love those that love them.
[33] And if ye do good to them which do good to you, what thank have ye? for sinners also do even the same.
[34] And if ye lend to them of whom ye hope to thidge, what thank have ye? for sinners also lend to sinners, to thidge as much again.
[35] But love ye your foes, and do good, and lend, hoping for nothing again; and your edlean shall be great, and ye shall be the children of the Highest: for he is kind unto the unthankful and to the evil.
[36] Be ye therefore ruthful, as your Father also is ruthful.
[37] Deem not, and ye shall not be deemed: fordeem not, and ye shall not be fordeemed: forgive, and ye shall be forgiven:
[38] Give, and it shall be given unto you; good mete, pressed down, and shaken together, and running over, shall men give into your bosom. For with the same mete that ye mete withal it shall be meted to you again.
[39] And he spake a likeningtale unto them, Can the blind lead the blind? shall they not both fall into the ditch?

[40] The loreknight is not above his harr: but every one that is fullfremmed shall be as his harr.
[41] And why beholdest thou the mote that is in thy brother's eye, but ongetst not the beam that is in thine own eye?
[42] Either how canst thou say to thy brother, Brother, let me pull out the mote that is in thine eye, when thou thyself beholdest not the beam that is in thine own eye? Thou leaser, cast out first the beam out of thine own eye, and then shalt thou see clearly to pull out the mote that is in thy brother's eye.
[43] For a good tree bringeth not forth brosened ovet; neither doth a brosened tree bring forth good ovet.
[44] For every tree is known by his own ovet. For of thorns men do not gather figs, nor of a bramble bush gather they grapes.
[45] A good man out of the good mathem of his heart bringeth forth that which is good; and an evil man out of the evil mathem of his heart bringeth forth that which is evil: for of the fullsomeness of the heart his mouth speaketh.
[46] And why call ye me, Lord, Lord, and do not the things which I say?
[47] Whosoever cometh to me, and heareth my sayings, and doeth them, I will shew you to whom he is like:
[48] He is like a man which built an house, and digged deep, and laid the groundwall on a rock: and when the flood arose, the stream beat gramely upon that house, and could not shake it: for it was founded upon a rock.
[49] But he that heareth, and doeth not, is like a man that without a groundwall built an house upon the earth; against which the stream did beat gramely, and forthwith it fell; and the ruin of that house was great.

Luke.7

[1] Now when he had ended all his sayings in the theresomeness of the theed, he went into Capernaum.
[2] And a somel hundredman's thane, who was dear unto him, was sick, and ready to die.
[3] And when he heard of Jesus, he sent unto him the elders of the Jews, beseeching him that he would come and heal his thane.
[4] And when they came to Jesus, they besought him instantly, saying, That he was worthy for whom he should do this:
[5] For he loveth our folkdom, and he hath built us a worshipstead.
[6] Then Jesus went with them. And when he was now not far from the house, the hundredman sent friends to him, saying unto him, Lord, dreeve not thyself: for I am not worthy that thou shouldest go under my roof:
[7] Wherefore neither thought I myself worthy to come unto thee: but say in a word, and my thane shall be healed.
[8] For I also am a man set under alderdom, having under me heregomes, and I say unto one, Go, and he goeth; and to another, Come, and he cometh; and to my thane, Do this, and he doeth it.
[9] When Jesus heard these things, he awondered at him, and whorve him about, and said unto the theed that followed him, I say unto you, I have not found so great faith, no, not in Israel.
[10] And they that were sent, edwharving to the house, found the thane whole that had been sick.
[11] And it came to be the day after, that he went into a chester called Nain; and many of his loreknights went with him, and much theed.
[12] Now when he came nigh to the gate of the chester, behold, there was a dead man carried out, the only son of his mother, and she was a widow: and much theed of the chester was with her.
[13] And when the Lord saw her, he had evensorrow on her, and said unto her, Weep not.
[14] And he came and rone the bier: and they that bare him stood still. And he said, Young man, I say unto thee, Arise.
[15] And he that was dead sat up, and began to speak. And he gave him to his mother.
[16] And there came a fear on all: and they woulderened God, saying, That a great forequeether is risen up among us; and, That God hath neased his theed.
[17] And this imbspeak of him went forth throughout all Judaea, and throughout all the imbstead.
[18] And the loreknights of John shewed him of all these things.
[19] And John calling unto him two of his loreknights sent them to Jesus, saying, Art thou he that should come? or look we for another?
[20] When the men were come unto him, they said, John Forwasher hath sent us unto thee, saying, Art thou he that should come? or look we for another?
[21] And in that same stound he healed many of their cothes and smittles, and of evil ferths; and unto many that were blind he gave sight.
[22] Then Jesus answering said unto them, Go your way, and tell John what things ye have seen and heard; how that the blind see, the lame walk, the lepers are cleansed, the deaf hear, the dead are raised, to the arm the gospel is preached.
[23] And blessed is he, whosoever shall not be abellowed in me.
[24] And when the bodebearers of John were witten, he began to speak unto the theed bemeeting John, What went ye out into the wilderness for to see? A reed shaken with the wind?
[25] But what went ye out for to see? A man clothed in

soft clothing? Behold, they which are richly clothed, and live in mathem, are in kings' courts.

[26] But what went ye out for to see? A forequeether? Yea, I say unto you, and much more than a forequeether.

[27] This is he, of whom it is written, Behold, I send my bodebearer before thy anlit, which shall yark thy way before thee.

[28] For I say unto you, Among those that are born of women there is not a greater forequeether than John the Forwasher: but he that is least in the kingdom of God is greater than he.

[29] And all the theed that heard him, and the tollners, rightsomed God, being forwashed with the forwashing of John.

[30] But the Pharisees and lawyers withlaid the counsel of God against themselves, being not forwashed of him.

[31] And the Lord said, Whereunto then shall I liken the men of this strind? and to what are they like?

[32] They are like unto children sitting in the marketstead, and calling one to another, and saying, We have piped unto you, and ye have not danced; we have mourned to you, and ye have not wept.

[33] For John the Forwasher came neither eating bread nor drinking wine; and ye say, He hath a devil.

[34] The Son of man is come eating and drinking; and ye say, Behold a gluttonous man, and a winebibber, a friend of tollners and sinners!

[35] But wisdom is rightsomed of all her children.

[36] And one of the Pharisees wished him that he would eat with him. And he went into the Pharisee's house, and sat down to meat.

[37] And, behold, a woman in the chester, which was a sinner, when she knew that Jesus sat at meat in the Pharisee's house, brought an alabaster box of smearls,

[38] And stood at his feet behind him weeping, and began to wash his feet with tears, and did wipe them with the hairs of her head, and kissed his feet, and asmeared them with the smearls.

[39] Now when the Pharisee which had bidden him saw it, he spake within himself, saying, This man, if he were a forequeether, would have known who and what kind of woman this is that rineeth him: for she is a sinner.

[40] And Jesus answering said unto him, Simon, I have somewhat to say unto thee. And he saith, Harr, say on.

[41] There was a somel lender which had two owers: the one owed five hundred pence, and the other fifty.

[42] And when they had nothing to pay, he frankly forgave them both. Tell me therefore, which of them will love him most?

[43] Simon answered and said, I ween that he, to whom he forgave most. And he said unto him, Thou hast rightly deemed.

[44] And he whorve to the woman, and said unto Simon, Seest thou this woman? I went into thine house, thou gavest me no water for my feet: but she hath washed my feet with tears, and wiped them with the hairs of her head.

[45] Thou gavest me no kiss: but this woman since the time I came in hath not stopped kissing my feet.

[46] My head with oil thou didst not asmear: but this woman hath asmeared my feet with smearls.

[47] Wherefore I say unto thee, Her sins, which are many, are forgiven; for she loved much: but to whom little is forgiven, the same loveth little.

[48] And he said unto her, Thy sins are forgiven.

[49] And they that sat at meat with him began to say within themselves, Who is this that forgiveth sins also?

[50] And he said to the woman, Thy faith hath nerred thee; go in frith.

Luke.8

[1] And it came to be afterward, that he went throughout every chester and town, preaching and shewing the glad tidings of the kingdom of God: and the twelve were with him,

[2] And somel women, which had been healed of evil ferths and cothes, Mary called Magdalene, out of whom went seven devils,

[3] And Joanna the wife of Chuza Herod's steward, and Susanna, and many others, which acared unto him of their canhood.

[4] And when much theed were gathered together, and were come to him out of every chester, he spake by a likeningtale:

[5] A sower went out to sow his seed: and as he sowed, some fell by the way side; and it was trodden down, and the fowls of the air forglendered it.

[6] And some fell upon a rock; and as soon as it was sprung up, it withered away, forwhy it lacked moisture.

[7] And some fell among thorns; and the thorns sprang up with it, and choked it.

[8] And other fell on good ground, and sprang up, and bare ovet an hundredfold. And when he had said these things, he yarmed, He that hath ears to hear, let him hear.

[9] And his loreknights asked him, saying, What might this likeningtale be?

[10] And he said, Unto you it is given to know the mysteries of the kingdom of God: but to others in likeningtales; that seeing they might not see, and hearing they might not understand.

[11] Now the likeningtale is this: The seed is the word of God.

[12] Those by the way side are they that hear; then cometh the devil, and taketh away the word out of their

hearts, lest they should believe and be nerred.

[13] They on the rock are they, which, when they hear, thidge the word with mirth; and these have no root, which for a while believe, and in time of costening fall away.

[14] And that which fell among thorns are they, which, when they have heard, go forth, and are choked with cares and riches and pleasures of this life, and bring no ovet to fullfremmedness.

[15] But that on the good ground are they, which in an honest and good heart, having heard the word, keep it, and bring forth ovet with patience.

[16] No man, when he hath lighted a candle, covereth it with a vessel, or putteth it under a bed; but setteth it on a candlestick, that they which go in may see the light.

[17] For nothing is dern, that shall not be made swettle; neither any thing hid, that shall not be known and come abroad.

[18] Take heed therefore how ye hear: for whosoever hath, to him shall be given; and whosoever hath not, from him shall be taken even that which he thencheth to have.

[19] Then came to him his mother and his brethren, and could not come at him for the press.

[20] And it was told him by somel which said, Thy mother and thy brethren stand without, wishing to see thee.

[21] And he answered and said unto them, My mother and my brethren are these which hear the word of God, and do it.

[22] Now it came to be on a somel day, that he went into a ship with his loreknights: and he said unto them, Let us go over unto the other side of the lake. And they launched forth.

[23] But as they sailed he fell asleep: and there came down a storm of wind on the lake; and they were filled with water, and were in jeopardy.

[24] And they came to him, and awoke him, saying, Harr, harr, we swelt. Then he arose, and scolded the wind and the rushing of the water: and they stopped, and there was a stillness.

[25] And he said unto them, Where is your faith? And they being afraid wondered, saying one to another, What kind of man is this! for he bebideth even the winds and water, and they hearsome him.

[26] And they arrived at the land of the Gadarenes, which is over against Galilee.

[27] And when he went forth to land, there met him out of the chester a somel man, which had devils long time, and ware no clothes, neither abode in any house, but in the tombs.

[28] When he saw Jesus, he yarmed out, and fell down before him, and with a loud steven said, What have I to do with thee, Jesus, thou Son of God most high? I beseech thee, sousel me not.

[29] (For he had bebade the unclean ferth to come out of the man. For oftentimes it had caught him: and he was kept bound with chains and in fetters; and he brake the bands, and was driven of the devil into the wilderness.)

[30] And Jesus asked him, saying, What is thy name? And he said, Legion: forwhy many devils were went into him.

[31] And they besought him that he would not bebid them to go out into the deep.

[32] And there was there an herd of many swine feeding on the barrow: and they besought him that he would thraw them to go into them. And he thrawed them.

[33] Then went the devils out of the man, and went into the swine: and the herd ran violently down a steep stead into the lake, and were choked.

[34] When they that fed them saw what was done, they fled, and went and told it in the chester and in the land.

[35] Then they went out to see what was done; and came to Jesus, and found the man, out of whom the devils were witten, sitting at the feet of Jesus, clothed, and in his right mind: and they were afraid.

[36] They also which saw it told them by what means he that was throughtaken of the devils was healed.

[37] Then the whole dright of the land of the Gadarenes round about besought him to wite from them; for they were taken with great fear: and he went up into the ship, and edwhorve back again.

[38] Now the man out of whom the devils were witten besought him that he might be with him: but Jesus sent him away, saying,

[39] Edwharve to thine own house, and shew how great things God hath done unto thee. And he went his way, and published throughout the whole chester how great things Jesus had done unto him.

[40] And it came to be, that, when Jesus was edwhorve, the theed gladly thidged him: for they were all waiting for him.

[41] And, behold, there came a man named Jairus, and he was a woldend of the worshipstead: and he fell down at Jesus' feet, and besought him that he would come into his house:

[42] For he had one only daughter, about twelve years of age, and she lay a dying. But as he went the theed thronged him.

[43] And a woman having an issue of blood twelve years, which had spent all her living upon physicians, neither could be healed of any,

[44] Came behind him, and rone the border of his clothing: and forthwith her issue of blood stanched.

[45] And Jesus said, Who rone me? When all andsook, Peter and they that were with him said, Harr, the dright throng thee and press thee, and sayest thou, Who rone

me?

[46] And Jesus said, Somebody hath rinen me: for I onget that thrith is gone out of me.

[47] And when the woman saw that she was not hid, she came biving, and falling down before him, she akithed unto him before all the theed for what grounds she had rinen him and how she was healed forthwith.

[48] And he said unto her, Daughter, be of good frover: thy faith hath made thee whole; go in frith.

[49] While he yet spake, there cometh one from the woldend of the worshipstead's house, saying to him, Thy daughter is dead; dreeve not the Harr.

[50] But when Jesus heard it, he answered him, saying, Fear not: believe only, and she shall be made whole.

[51] And when he came into the house, he thrawed no man to go in, nerr Peter, and James, and John, and the father and the mother of the maiden.

[52] And all wept, and bewailed her: but he said, Weep not; she is not dead, but sleepeth.

[53] And they laughed him to scorn, knowing that she was dead.

[54] And he put them all out, and took her by the hand, and called, saying, Maid, arise.

[55] And her ferth came again, and she arose straightway: and he bebade to give her meat.

[56] And her akennends were amazed: but he bebade them that they should tell no man what was done.

Luke.9

[1] Then he called his twelve loreknights together, and gave them wold and alderdom over all devils, and to heal cothes.

[2] And he sent them to preach the kingdom of God, and to heal the sick.

[3] And he said unto them, Take nothing for your sith, neither staves, nor scrip, neither bread, neither money; neither have two coats apiece.

[4] And whatsoever house ye go into, there abide, and thence wite.

[5] And whosoever will not thidge you, when ye go out of that chester, shake off the very dust from your feet for a witness against them.

[6] And they wote, and went through the towns, preaching the gospel, and healing every where.

[7] Now Herod the tetrarch heard of all that was done by him: and he was bewildered, forwhy that it was said of some, that John was risen from the dead;

[8] And of some, that Elias had trodden up; and of others, that one of the old forequeethers was risen again.

[9] And Herod said, John have I beheaded: but who is this, of whom I hear such things? And he wished to see him.

[10] And the loreknights, when they were edwhorven, told him all that they had done. And he took them, and went aside dernly into a throughdry stead belonging to the chester called Bethsaida.

[11] And the theed, when they knew it, followed him: and he thidged them, and spake unto them of the kingdom of God, and healed them that had need of healing.

[12] And when the day began to wear away, then came the twelve, and said unto him, Send the dright away, that they may go into the towns and land round about, and lodge, and get victuals: for we are here in a throughdry stead.

[13] But he said unto them, Give ye them to eat. And they said, We have no more but five loaves and two fishes; unless we should go and buy meat for all this theed.

[14] For they were about five thousand men. And he said to his loreknights, Make them sit down by fifties in a maith.

[15] And they did so, and made them all sit down.

[16] Then he took the five loaves and the two fishes, and looking up to heaven, he blessed them, and brake, and gave to the loreknights to set before the dright.

[17] And they did eat, and were all filled: and there was taken up of breaklings that belived to them twelve baskets.

[18] And it came to be, as he was alone abiding, his loreknights were with him: and he asked them, saying, Whom say the theed that I am?

[19] They answering said, John the Forwasher; but some say, Elias; and others say, that one of the old forequeethers is risen again.

[20] He said unto them, But whom say ye that I am? Peter answering said, The Christ of God.

[21] And he straitly bebade them, and bebade them to tell no man that thing;

[22] Saying, The Son of man must thraw many things, and be withlaid of the elders and alderpriests and scribes, and be slain, and be raised the third day.

[23] And he said to them all, If any man will come after me, let him andsake himself, and take up his rood daily, and follow me.

[24] For whosoever will nerr his life shall lose it: but whosoever will lose his life for my sake, the same shall nerr it.

[25] For how is a man in shreep, if he underfang the whole world, and lose himself, or be cast away?

[26] For whosoever shall be ashamed of me and of my words, of him shall the Son of man be ashamed, when he shall come in his own woulder, and in his Father's, and of the holy woulderghosts.

[27] But I tell you of a truth, there be some standing here, which shall not taste of death, till they see the kingdom of God.

[28] And it came to be about an eight days after these sayings, he took Peter and John and James, and went up into a barrow to abid.
[29] And as he abade, the neb of his anlit was awended, and his clothing was white and glistering.
[30] And, behold, there talked with him two men, which were Moses and Elias:
[31] Who trod up in thrum, and spake of his death which he should wok full at Jerusalem.
[32] But Peter and they that were with him were heavy with sleep: and when they were awake, they saw his woulder, and the two men that stood with him.
[33] And it came to be, as they wote from him, Peter said unto Jesus, Harr, it is good for us to be here: and let us make three tields; one for thee, and one for Moses, and one for Elias: not knowing what he said.
[34] While he thus spake, there came a cloud, and overshadowed them: and they feared as they went into the cloud.
[35] And there came a steven out of the cloud, saying, This is my beloved Son: hear him.
[36] And when the steven was past, Jesus was found alone. And they kept it close, and told no man in those days any of those things which they had seen.
[37] And it came to be, that on the next day, when they were come down from the hill, much theed met him.
[38] And, behold, a man of the crowd yarmed out, saying, Harr, I beseech thee, look upon my son: for he is mine only child.
[39] And, lo, a ferth taketh him, and he suddenly yarmth out; and it teareth him that he foameth again, and bruising him hardly witeth from him.
[40] And I besought thy loreknights to cast him out; and they could not.
[41] And Jesus answering said, O faithless and woughly strind, how long shall I be with you, and thraw you? Bring thy son hither.
[42] And as he was yet a coming, the devil threw him down, and tare him. And Jesus scolded the unclean ferth, and healed the child, and gave him again to his father.
[43] And they were all amazed at the mighty wold of God. But while they wondered every one at all things which Jesus did, he said unto his loreknights,
[44] Let these sayings sink down into your ears: for the Son of man shall be given over into the hands of men.
[45] But they understood not this saying, and it was hid from them, that they freeded it not: and they feared to ask him of that saying.
[46] Then there arose a flit among them, which of them should be greatest.
[47] And Jesus, freeding the thought of their heart, took a child, and set him by him,
[48] And said unto them, Whosoever shall thidge this child in my name thidgeth me: and whosoever shall thidge me thidgeth him that sent me: for he that is least among you all, the same shall be great.
[49] And John answered and said, Harr, we saw one casting out devils in thy name; and we forbad him, forwhy he followeth not with us.
[50] And Jesus said unto him, Forbid him not: for he that is not against us is for us.
[51] And it came to be, when the time was come that he should be thidged up, he stedfastly set his anlit to go to Jerusalem,
[52] And sent bodebearers before his anlit: and they went, and went into a town of the Samaritans, to make ready for him.
[53] And they did not thidge him, forwhy his anlit was as though he would go to Jerusalem.
[54] And when his loreknights James and John saw this, they said, Lord, wilt thou that we bebid fire to come down from heaven, and consume them, even as Elias did?
[55] But he whorve, and threaped them, and said, Ye know not what kind of ferth ye are of.
[56] For the Son of man is not come to fordo men's lives, but to nerr them. And they went to another town.
[57] And it came to be, that, as they went in the way, a somel man said unto him, Lord, I will follow thee whithersoever thou goest.
[58] And Jesus said unto him, Foxes have holes, and birds of the air have nests; but the Son of man hath not where to lay his head.
[59] And he said unto another, Follow me. But he said, Lord, thraw me first to go and bury my father.
[60] Jesus said unto him, Let the dead bury their dead: but go thou and preach the kingdom of God.
[61] And another also said, Lord, I will follow thee; but let me first go bid them farewell, which are at home at my house.
[62] And Jesus said unto him, No man, having put his hand to the plough, and looking back, is fit for the kingdom of God.

Luke.10

[1] After these things the Lord aset other seventy also, and sent them two and two before his anlit into every chester and stead, whither he himself would come.
[2] Therefore said he unto them, The harvest truly is great, but the swinkers are few: abid ye therefore the Lord of the harvest, that he would send forth swinkers into his harvest.
[3] Go your ways: behold, I send you forth as lambs among wolves.
[4] Carry neither purse, nor scrip, nor shoes: and salute no man by the way.
[5] And into whatsoever house ye go, first say, Frith be

to this house.
[6] And if the son of frith be there, your frith shall rest upon it: if not, it shall wharve to you again.
[7] And in the same house belive, eating and drinking such things as they give: for the swinker is worthy of his hire. Go not from house to house.
[8] And into whatsoever chester ye go, and they thidge you, eat such things as are set before you:
[9] And heal the sick that are therein, and say unto them, The kingdom of God is come nigh unto you.
[10] But into whatsoever chester ye go, and they thidge you not, go your ways out into the streets of the same, and say,
[11] Even the very dust of your chester, which cleaveth on us, we do wipe off against you: notwithstanding be ye sure of this, that the kingdom of God is come nigh unto you.
[12] But I say unto you, that it shall be more tolerable in that day for Sodom, than for that chester.
[13] Woe unto thee, Chorazin! woe unto thee, Bethsaida! for if the mighty works had been done in Tyre and Sidon, which have been done in you, they had a great while ago berueed, sitting in sackcloth and ashes.
[14] But it shall be more tolerable for Tyre and Sidon at the deeming, than for you.
[15] And thou, Capernaum, which art reamed to heaven, shalt be thrust down to hell.
[16] He that heareth you heareth me; and he that forhoweth you forhoweth me; and he that forhoweth me forhoweth him that sent me.
[17] And the seventy edwhorve again with mirth, saying, Lord, even the devils are undertheed unto us through thy name.
[18] And he said unto them, I beheld Hellwarden as lightning fall from heaven.
[19] Behold, I give unto you wold to tread on nadders and scorpions, and over all the wold of the foe: and nothing shall by any means hurt you.
[20] Notwithstanding in this aglee not, that the ferths are undertheed unto you; but rather aglee, forwhy your names are written in heaven.
[21] In that stound Jesus agleed in ferth, and said, I thank thee, O Father, Lord of heaven and earth, that thou hast hid these things from the wise and prudent, and hast swettled them unto babes: even so, Father; for so it thenched good in thy sight.
[22] All things are given to me of my Father: and no man knoweth who the Son is, but the Father; and who the Father is, but the Son, and he to whom the Son will swettle him.
[23] And he whorve him unto his loreknights, and said dernly, Blessed are the eyes which see the things that ye see:
[24] For I tell you, that many forequeethers and kings have wished to see those things which ye see, and have not seen them; and to hear those things which ye hear, and have not heard them.
[25] And, behold, a somel lawyer stood up, and costened him, saying, Harr, what shall I do to erve alderlong life?
[26] He said unto him, What is written in the law? how readest thou?
[27] And he answering said, Thou shalt love the Lord thy God with all thy heart, and with all thy soul, and with all thy strength, and with all thy mind; and thy neighbour as thyself.
[28] And he said unto him, Thou hast answered right: this do, and thou shalt live.
[29] But he, willing to rightsome himself, said unto Jesus, And who is my neighbour?
[30] And Jesus answering said, A somel man went down from Jerusalem to Jericho, and fell among thieves, which stripped him of his clothing, and wounded him, and wote, leaving him half dead.
[31] And by chance there came down a somel priest that way: and when he saw him, he wended by on the other side.
[32] And likewise a Levite, when he was at the stead, came and looked on him, and wended by on the other side.
[33] But a somel Samaritan, as he sithed, came where he was: and when he saw him, he had evensorrow on him,
[34] And went to him, and bound up his wounds, pouring in oil and wine, and set him on his own beast, and brought him to an inn, and took care of him.
[35] And on the morrow when he wote, he took out two pence, and gave them to the host, and said unto him, Take care of him; and whatsoever thou spendest more, when I come again, I will repay thee.
[36] Which now of these three, thinkest thou, was neighbour unto him that fell among the thieves?
[37] And he said, He that shewed ruth on him. Then said Jesus unto him, Go, and do thou likewise.
[38] Now it came to be, as they went, that he went into a somel town: and a somel woman named Martha thidged him into her house.
[39] And she had a sister called Mary, which also sat at Jesus' feet, and heard his word.
[40] But Martha was cumbered about much serving, and came to him, and said, Lord, dost thou not care that my sister hath left me to theen alone? bid her therefore that she help me.
[41] And Jesus answered and said unto her, Martha, Martha, thou art careful and dreeved about many things:
[42] But one thing is needful: and Mary hath chosen that good part, which shall not be taken away from her.

Luke.11

[1] And it came to be, that, as he was abiding in a somel stead, when he stopped, one of his loreknights said unto him, Lord, teach us to abid, as John also taught his loreknights.
[2] And he said unto them, When ye abid, say, Our Father which art in heaven, Hallowed be thy name. Thy kingdom come. Thy will be done, as in heaven, so in earth.
[3] Give us day by day our daily bread.
[4] And forgive us our sins; for we also forgive every one that is sin against us. And lead us not into costening; but spare us from evil.
[5] And he said unto them, Which of you shall have a friend, and shall go unto him at midnight, and say unto him, Friend, lend me three loaves;
[6] For a friend of mine in his sith is come to me, and I have nothing to set before him?
[7] And he from within shall answer and say, Dreeve me not: the door is now shut, and my children are with me in bed; I cannot rise and give thee.
[8] I say unto you, Though he will not rise and give him, forwhy he is his friend, yet forwhy of his nagging he will rise and give him as many as he needeth.
[9] And I say unto you, Ask, and it shall be given you; seek, and ye shall find; knock, and it shall be opened unto you.
[10] For every one that asketh thidgeth; and he that seeketh findeth; and to him that knocketh it shall be opened.
[11] If a son shall ask bread of any of you that is a father, will he give him a stone? or if he ask a fish, will he for a fish give him a serpent?
[12] Or if he shall ask an egg, will he offer him a scorpion?
[13] If ye then, being evil, know how to give good gifts unto your children: how much more shall your heavenly Father give the Holy Ferth to them that ask him?
[14] And he was casting out a devil, and it was dumb. And it came to be, when the devil was gone out, the dumb spake; and the theed wondered.
[15] But some of them said, He casteth out devils through Beelzebub the woldend of the devils.
[16] And others, costening him, sought of him a tocken from heaven.
[17] But he, knowing their thoughts, said unto them, Every kingdom todealt against itself is brought to forwastedness; and a house todealt against a house falleth.
[18] If Hellwarden also be todealt against himself, how shall his kingdom stand? forwhy ye say that I cast out devils through Beelzebub.
[19] And if I by Beelzebub cast out devils, by whom do your sons cast them out? therefore shall they be your deemers.
[20] But if I with the finger of God cast out devils, no twight the kingdom of God is come upon you.
[21] When a strong man armed keepeth his thronestead, his goods are in frith:
[22] But when a stronger than he shall come upon him, and overcome him, he taketh from him all his armour wherein he trusted, and todealth his spoils.
[23] He that is not with me is against me: and he that gathereth not with me scattereth.
[24] When the unclean ferth is gone out of a man, he walketh through dry steads, seeking rest; and finding none, he saith, I will edwharve unto my house whence I came out.
[25] And when he cometh, he findeth it swept and garnished.
[26] Then goeth he, and taketh to him seven other ferths more wicked than himself; and they go in, and dwell there: and the last state of that man is worse than the first.
[27] And it came to be, as he spake these things, a somel woman of the crowd lifted up her steven, and said unto him, Blessed is the womb that bare thee, and the breasts which thou hast sucked.
[28] But he said, Yea rather, blessed are they that hear the word of God, and keep it.
[29] And when the theed were gathered thick together, he began to say, This is an evil strind: they seek a tocken; and there shall no tocken be given it, but the tocken of Jonas the forequeether.
[30] For as Jonas was a tocken unto the Ninevites, so shall also the Son of man be to this strind.
[31] The queen of the south shall rise up in the deeming with the men of this strind, and fordeem them: for she came from the utmost parts of the earth to hear the wisdom of Solomon; and, behold, a greater than Solomon is here.
[32] The men of Nineve shall rise up in the deeming with this strind, and shall fordeem it: for they berueed at the preaching of Jonas; and, behold, a greater than Jonas is here.
[33] No man, when he hath lighted a candle, putteth it in a dern stead, neither under a bushel, but on a candlestick, that they which come in may see the light.
[34] The light of the body is the eye: therefore when thine eye is single, thy whole body also is full of light; but when thine eye is evil, thy body also is full of darkness.
[35] Take heed therefore that the light which is in thee be not darkness.
[36] If thy whole body therefore be full of light, having no part dark, the whole shall be full of light, as when the bright shining of a candle doth give thee light.
[37] And as he spake, a somel Pharisee besought him

to dine with him: and he went in, and sat down to meat.

[38] And when the Pharisee saw it, he awondered that he had not first washed before dinner.

[39] And the Lord said unto him, Now do ye Pharisees make clean the outside of the cup and the platter; but your inward part is full of ravening and wickedness.

[40] Ye fools, did not he that made that which is without make that which is within also?

[41] But rather give alms of such things as ye have; and, behold, all things are clean unto you.

[42] But woe unto you, Pharisees! for ye tithe mint and rue and all kind of herbs, and wend over deeming and the love of God: these ought ye to have done, and not to leave the other undone.

[43] Woe unto you, Pharisees! for ye love the uppermost seats in the worshipsteads, and greetings in the markets.

[44] Woe unto you, scribes and Pharisees, leasers! for ye are as graves which thench not, and the men that walk over them are not aware of them.

[45] Then answered one of the lawyers, and said unto him, Harr, thus saying thou atwitest us also.

[46] And he said, Woe unto you also, ye lawyers! for ye lade men with burdens dretchful to be borne, and ye yourselves rine not the burdens with one of your fingers.

[47] Woe unto you! for ye build the lichrests of the forequeethers, and your fathers killed them.

[48] Truly ye bear witness that ye allow the deeds of your fathers: for they indeed killed them, and ye build their lichrests.

[49] Therefore also said the wisdom of God, I will send them forequeethers and loreknights, and some of them they shall slay and dretch:

[50] That the blood of all the forequeethers, which was shed from the ishaft of the world, may be tharfed of this strind;

[51] From the blood of Abel unto the blood of Zacharias, which swelted between the altar and the worshipstead: in sooth I say unto you, It shall be tharfed of this strind.

[52] Woe unto you, lawyers! for ye have taken away the key of knowledge: ye went not in yourselves, and them that were going in ye hindered.

[53] And as he said these things unto them, the scribes and the Pharisees began to thrave him gramely, and to grill him to speak of many things:

[54] Laying wait for him, and seeking to catch something out of his mouth, that they might wray him.

Luke.12

[1] In the mean time, when there were gathered together an unarimingly dright of flok, insomuch that they trode one upon another, he began to say unto his loreknights first of all, Beware ye of the leaven of the Pharisees, which is leaserhood.

[2] For there is nothing covered, that shall not be swettled; neither hid, that shall not be known.

[3] Therefore whatsoever ye have spoken in darkness shall be heard in the light; and that which ye have spoken in the ear in closets shall be proclaimed upon the housetops.

[4] And I say unto you my friends, Be not afraid of them that kill the body, and after that have no more that they can do.

[5] But I will forewarn you whom ye shall fear: Fear him, which after he hath killed hath wold to cast into hell; yea, I say unto you, Fear him.

[6] Are not five sparrows sold for two farthings, and not one of them is forgotten before God?

[7] But even the very hairs of your head are all arimed. Fear not therefore: ye are of more worth than many sparrows.

[8] Also I say unto you, Whosoever shall andet me before men, him shall the Son of man also andet before the woulderghosts of God:

[9] But he that andsaketh me before men shall be andsook before the woulderghosts of God.

[10] And whosoever shall speak a word against the Son of man, it shall be forgiven him: but unto him that evilsaketh against the Holy Ghost it shall not be forgiven.

[11] And when they bring you unto the worshipsteads, and unto awieldends, and wolds, take ye no thought how or what thing ye shall answer, or what ye shall say:

[12] For the Holy Ghost shall teach you in the same stound what ye ought to say.

[13] And one of the crowd said unto him, Harr, speak to my brother, that he todeal the erve with me.

[14] And he said unto him, Man, who made me a deemer or a todealer over you?

[15] And he said unto them, Take heed, and beware of andiness: for a man's life bestandeth not in the fullsomeness of the things which he owneth.

[16] And he spake a likeningtale unto them, saying, The ground of a somel rich man brought forth plentifully:

[17] And he thought within himself, saying, What shall I do, forwhy I have no room where to bestow my ovets?

[18] And he said, This will I do: I will pull down my barns, and build greater; and there will I bestow all my ovets and my goods.

[19] And I will say to my soul, Soul, thou hast much goods laid up for many years; take thine ease, eat,

drink, and be merry.
[20] But God said unto him, Thou fool, this night thy soul shall be needed of thee: then whose shall those things be, which thou hast fremmed?
[21] So is he that layeth up mathem for himself, and is not rich toward God.
[22] And he said unto his loreknights, Therefore I say unto you, Take no thought for your life, what ye shall eat; neither for the body, what ye shall put on.
[23] The life is more than meat, and the body is more than clothing.
[24] Hidge the ravens: for they neither sow nor reap; which neither have storehouse nor barn; and God feedeth them: how much more are ye better than the fowls?
[25] And which of you with taking thought can add to his height one cubit?
[26] If ye then be not able to do that thing which is least, why take ye thought for the rest?
[27] Hidge the lilies how they grow: they toil not, they spin not; and yet I say unto you, that Solomon in all his woulder was not arrayed like one of these.
[28] If then God so clothe the grass, which is to day in the field, and to morrow is cast into the oven; how much more will he clothe you, O ye of little faith?
[29] And seek not ye what ye shall eat, or what ye shall drink, neither be ye of twightful mind.
[30] For all these things do the folkdoms of the world seek after: and your Father knoweth that ye have need of these things.
[31] But rather seek ye the kingdom of God; and all these things shall be added unto you.
[32] Fear not, little flock; for it is your Father's good pleasure to give you the kingdom.
[33] Sell that ye have, and give alms; find yourselves bags which wax not old, a mathem in the heavens that faileth not, where no thief nighledgeth, neither moth broseneth.
[34] For where your mathem is, there will your heart be also.
[35] Let your loins be girded about, and your lights burning;
[36] And ye yourselves like unto men that wait for their lord, when he will edwharve from the wedding; that when he cometh and knocketh, they may open unto him forthwith.
[37] Blessed are those thanes, whom the lord when he cometh shall find watching: in sooth I say unto you, that he shall gird himself, and make them to sit down to meat, and will come forth and theen them.
[38] And if he shall come in the twoth watch, or come in the third watch, and find them so, blessed are those thanes.
[39] And this know, that if the goodman of the house had known what stound the thief would come, he would have watched, and not have thrawed his house to be broken through.
[40] Be ye therefore ready also: for the Son of man cometh at a stound when ye think not.
[41] Then Peter said unto him, Lord, speakest thou this likeningtale unto us, or even to all?
[42] And the Lord said, Who then is that faithful and wise steward, whom his lord shall make woldend over his household, to give them their muchthdeal of meat in due time?
[43] Blessed is that thane, whom his lord when he cometh shall find so doing.
[44] Of a truth I say unto you, that he will make him woldend over all that he hath.
[45] But and if that thane say in his heart, My lord delayeth his coming; and shall begin to beat the menthanes and maidens, and to eat and drink, and to be drunken;
[46] The lord of that thane will come in a day when he looketh not for him, and at an stound when he is not aware, and will cut him in sunder, and will aset him his muchthdeal with the unbelievers.
[47] And that thane, which knew his lord's will, and yeaked not himself, neither did by to his will, shall be beaten with many stripes.
[48] But he that knew not, and did do things worthy of stripes, shall be beaten with few stripes. For unto whomsoever much is given, of him shall be much tharfed: and to whom men have given much, of him they will ask the more.
[49] I am come to send fire on the earth; and what will I if it be already kindled?
[50] But I have a forwashing to be forwashed with; and how am I straitened till it be fullworked!
[51] Ween ye that I am come to give frith on earth? I tell you, Nay; but rather asundering:
[52] For from henceforth there shall be five in one house todealt, three against two, and two against three.
[53] The father shall be todealt against the son, and the son against the father; the mother against the daughter, and the daughter against the mother; the mother in law against her daughter in law, and the daughter in law against her mother in law.
[54] And he said also to the theed, When ye see a cloud rise out of the west, straightway ye say, There cometh a shower; and so it is.
[55] And when ye see the south wind blow, ye say, There will be heat; and it cometh to be.
[56] Ye leasers, ye can atell the anlit of the sky and of the earth; but how is it that ye do not atell this time?
[57] Yea, and why even of yourselves deem ye not what is right?
[58] When thou goest with thine foe to the awieldend, as thou art in the way, give workfastness that thou mayest be agiven from him; lest he hale thee to the

deemer, and the deemer give thee over to the lawswinkers, and the lawswinkers cast thee into witern.
[59] I tell thee, thou shalt not wite thence, till thou hast paid the very last mite.

Luke.13

[1] There were atbeen at that time some that told him of the Galilaeans, whose blood Pilate had mingled with their bloots.
[2] And Jesus answering said unto them, Ween ye that these Galilaeans were sinners above all the Galilaeans, forwhy they thrawed such things?
[3] I tell you, Nay: but, unless ye berue, ye shall all likewise swelt.
[4] Or those eighteen, upon whom the tower in Siloam fell, and slew them, think ye that they were sinners above all men that dwelt in Jerusalem?
[5] I tell you, Nay: but, unless ye berue, ye shall all likewise swelt.
[6] He spake also this likeningtale; A somel man had a fig tree planted in his vineyard; and he came and sought ovet thereon, and found none.
[7] Then said he unto the dresser of his vineyard, Behold, these three years I come seeking ovet on this fig tree, and find none: cut it down; why cumbereth it the ground?
[8] And he answering said unto him, Lord, let it alone this year also, till I shall dig about it, and dung it:
[9] And if it bear ovet, well: and if not, then after that thou shalt cut it down.
[10] And he was teaching in one of the worshipsteads on the sabbath.
[11] And, behold, there was a woman which had a ferth of cothe eighteen years, and was bowed together, and could in no wise lift up herself.
[12] And when Jesus saw her, he called her to him, and said unto her, Woman, thou art loosed from thine cothe.
[13] And he laid his hands on her: and forthwith she was made straight, and woulderened God.
[14] And the woldend of the worshipstead answered with unfairnessanger, forwhy that Jesus had healed on the sabbath day, and said unto the theed, There are six days in which men ought to work: in them therefore come and be healed, and not on the sabbath day.
[15] The Lord then answered him, and said, Thou leaser, doth not each one of you on the sabbath loose his ox or his ass from the stall, and lead him away to watering?
[16] And ought not this woman, being a daughter of Abraham, whom Hellwarden hath bound, lo, these eighteen years, be loosed from this bond on the sabbath day?
[17] And when he had said these things, all his foes were ashamed: and all the theed agleed for all the wouldersome things that were done by him.
[18] Then said he, Unto what is the kingdom of God like? and whereunto shall I resemble it?
[19] It is like a grain of mustard seed, which a man took, and cast into his worttown; and it grew, and waxed a great tree; and the fowls of the air lodged in the branches of it.
[20] And again he said, Whereunto shall I liken the kingdom of God?
[21] It is like leaven, which a woman took and hid in three metes of meal, till the whole was leavened.
[22] And he went through the chesters and towns, teaching, and sithing toward Jerusalem.
[23] Then said one unto him, Lord, are there few that be nerred? And he said unto them,
[24] Strive to go in at the strait gate: for many, I say unto you, will seek to go in, and shall not be able.
[25] When once the harr of the house is risen up, and hath shut to the door, and ye begin to stand without, and to knock at the door, saying, Lord, Lord, open unto us; and he shall answer and say unto you, I know you not whence ye are:
[26] Then shall ye begin to say, We have eaten and drunk in thy atwist, and thou hast taught in our streets.
[27] But he shall say, I tell you, I know you not whence ye are; wite from me, all ye workers of unrightdom.
[28] There shall be weeping and gnashing of teeth, when ye shall see Abraham, and Isaac, and Jacob, and all the forequeethers, in the kingdom of God, and you yourselves thrust out.
[29] And they shall come from the east, and from the west, and from the north, and from the south, and shall sit down in the kingdom of God.
[30] And, behold, there are last which shall be first, and there are first which shall be last.
[31] The same day there came somel of the Pharisees, saying unto him, Get thee out, and wite hence: for Herod will kill thee.
[32] And he said unto them, Go ye, and tell that fox, Behold, I cast out devils, and I do healdeeds to day and to morrow, and the third day I shall be fullfremmed.
[33] Nevertheless I must walk to day, and to morrow, and the day following: for it cannot be that a forequeether swelt out of Jerusalem.
[34] O Jerusalem, Jerusalem, which killest the forequeethers, and stonest them that are sent unto thee; how often would I have gathered thy children together, as a hen doth gather her brood under her wings, and ye would not!
[35] Behold, your house is left unto you desolate: and in sooth I say unto you, Ye shall not see me, until the

time come when ye shall say, Blessed is he that cometh in the name of the Lord.

Luke.14

[1] And it came to be, as he went into the house of one of the head Pharisees to eat bread on the sabbath day, that they watched him.
[2] And, behold, there was a somel man before him which had the dropsy.
[3] And Jesus answering spake unto the lawyers and Pharisees, saying, Is it lawful to heal on the sabbath day?
[4] And they held their frith. And he took him, and healed him, and let him go;
[5] And answered them, saying, Which of you shall have an ass or an ox fallen into a pit, and will not straightway pull him out on the sabbath day?
[6] And they could not answer him again to these things.
[7] And he put forth a likeningtale to those which were bidden, when he marked how they chose out the alder rooms; saying unto them,
[8] When thou art bidden of any man to a wedding, sit not down in the highest room; lest a more oreable man than thou be bidden of him;
[9] And he that bade thee and him come and say to thee, Give this man stead; and thou begin with shame to take the lowest room.
[10] But when thou art bidden, go and sit down in the lowest room; that when he that bade thee cometh, he may say unto thee, Friend, go up higher: then shalt thou have worship in the atwist of them that sit at meat with thee.
[11] For whosoever reameth himself shall be lowered; and he that lowereth himself shall be reamed.
[12] Then said he also to him that bade him, When thou makest a dinner or an evenmeal, call not thy friends, nor thy brethren, neither thy kinsmen, nor thy rich neighbours; lest they also bid thee again, and a edlean be made thee.
[13] But when thou makest a simbletide, call the arm, the crippled, the lame, the blind:
[14] And thou shalt be blessed; for they cannot edlean thee: for thou shalt be edlean at the arist of the upright.
[15] And when one of them that sat at meat with him heard these things, he said unto him, Blessed is he that shall eat bread in the kingdom of God.
[16] Then said he unto him, A somel man made a great evenmeal, and bade many:
[17] And sent his thane at evenmeal time to say to them that were bidden, Come; for all things are now ready.
[18] And they all with one mind began to make outspeak. The first said unto him, I have bought a piece of ground, and I must needs go and see it: I abid brook my unawist.
[19] And another said, I have bought five yoke of oxen, and I go to prove them: I abid thee brook my unawist.
[20] And another said, I have heamed a wife, and therefore I cannot come.
[21] So that thane came, and shewed his lord these things. Then the harr of the house being angry said to his thane, Go out quickly into the streets and lanes of the chester, and bring in hither the arm, and the crippled, and the halt, and the blind.
[22] And the thane said, Lord, it is done as thou hast bebade, and yet there is room.
[23] And the lord said unto the thane, Go out into the highways and hedges, and bid them come in, that my house may be filled.
[24] For I say unto you, That none of those men which were bidden shall taste of my evenmeal.
[25] And there went great drights with him: and he whorve, and said unto them,
[26] If any man come to me, and hate not his father, and mother, and wife, and children, and brethren, and sisters, yea, and his own life also, he cannot be my loreknight.
[27] And whosoever doth not bear his rood, and come after me, cannot be my loreknight.
[28] For which of you, intending to build a tower, sitteth not down first, and counteth the cost, whether he have enoughsome to beend it?
[29] Lest haply, after he hath laid the groundwall, and is not able to beend it, all that behold it begin to bismer him,
[30] Saying, This man began to build, and was not able to beend.
[31] Or what king, going to make war against another king, sitteth not down first, and findeth out whether he be able with ten thousand to meet him that cometh against him with twenty thousand?
[32] Or else, while the other is yet a great way off, he sendeth a handleband, and wisheth readens of frith.
[33] So likewise, whosoever he be of you that forsaketh not all that he hath, he cannot be my loreknight.
[34] Salt is good: but if the salt have lost his smack, wherewith shall it be worted?
[35] It is neither fit for the land, nor yet for the dunghill; but men cast it out. He that hath ears to hear, let him hear.

Luke.15

[1] Then drew near unto him all the tollners and sinners for to hear him.
[2] And the Pharisees and scribes murmured, saying, This man thidgeth sinners, and eateth with them.
[3] And he spake this likeningtale unto them, saying,
[4] What man of you, having an hundred sheep, if he lose one of them, doth not leave the ninety and nine in the wilderness, and go after that which is lost, until he find it?
[5] And when he hath found it, he layeth it on his shoulders, agleeing.
[6] And when he cometh home, he calleth together his friends and neighbours, saying unto them, Aglee with me; for I have found my sheep which was lost.
[7] I say unto you, that likewise mirth shall be in heaven over one sinner that berueeth, more than over ninety and nine rightful wights, which need no berueing.
[8] Either what woman having ten pieces of silver, if she lose one piece, doth not light a candle, and sweep the house, and seek earnestly till she find it?
[9] And when she hath found it, she calleth her friends and her neighbours together, saying, Aglee with me; for I have found the piece which I had lost.
[10] Likewise, I say unto you, there is mirth in the atwist of the woulderghosts of God over one sinner that berueeth.
[11] And he said, A somel man had two sons:
[12] And the younger of them said to his father, Father, give me the muchthdeal of goods that falleth to me. And he todealt unto them his living.
[13] And not many days after the younger son gathered all together, and took his sith into a far land, and there wasted his ownings with unsnotter living.
[14] And when he had spent all, there arose a mighty hunger in that land; and he began to be in want.
[15] And he went and fayed himself to a wight of that land; and he sent him into his fields to feed swine.
[16] And he would fain have filled his belly with the husks that the swine did eat: and no man gave unto him.
[17] And when he came to himself, he said, How many hired thanes of my father's have bread enough and to spare, and I swelt with hunger!
[18] I will arise and go to my father, and will say unto him, Father, I have sinned against heaven, and before thee,
[19] And am no more worthy to be called thy son: make me as one of thy hired thanes.
[20] And he arose, and came to his father. But when he was yet a great way off, his father saw him, and had evensorrow, and ran, and fell on his neck, and kissed him.
[21] And the son said unto him, Father, I have sinned against heaven, and in thy sight, and am no more worthy to be called thy son.
[22] But the father said to his thanes, Bring forth the best robe, and put it on him; and put a ring on his hand, and shoes on his feet:
[23] And bring hither the fatted calf, and kill it; and let us eat, and be merry:
[24] For this my son was dead, and is alive again; he was lost, and is found. And they began to be merry.
[25] Now his elder son was in the field: and as he came and drew nigh to the house, he heard swincingcraft and dancing.
[26] And he called one of the thanes, and asked what these things meant.
[27] And he said unto him, Thy brother is come; and thy father hath killed the fatted calf, forwhy he hath thidged him safe and sound.
[28] And he was angry, and would not go in: therefore came his father out, and intreated him.
[29] And he answering said to his father, Lo, these many years do I theen thee, neither wronged I at any time thy bodeword: and yet thou never gavest me a kid, that I might make merry with my friends:
[30] But as soon as this thy son was come, which hath forglendered thy living with harlots, thou hast killed for him the fatted calf.
[31] And he said unto him, Son, thou art ever with me, and all that I have is thine.
[32] It was meet that we should make merry, and be glad: for this thy brother was dead, and is alive again; and was lost, and is found.

Luke.16

[1] And he said also unto his loreknights, There was a somel rich man, which had a steward; and the same was wrayed unto him that he had wasted his goods.
[2] And he called him, and said unto him, How is it that I hear this of thee? give grounds of thy stewardship; for thou mayest be no longer steward.
[3] Then the steward said within himself, What shall I do? for my lord taketh away from me the stewardship: I cannot dig; to beg I am ashamed.
[4] I see what I must do, that, when I am put out of the stewardship, they may thidge me into their houses.
[5] So he called every one of his lord's owers unto him, and said unto the first, How much owest thou unto my lord?
[6] And he said, An hundred firkins of oil. And he said unto him, Take thy bill, and sit down quickly, and write fifty.
[7] Then said he to another, And how much owest thou? And he said, An hundred metes of wheat. And he said unto him, Take thy bill, and write fourscore.
[8] And the lord praised the knavish steward, forwhy

he had done wisely: for the children of this world are in their strind wiser than the children of light.

[9] And I say unto you, Make to yourselves friends of the mammon of unrightsomeness; that, when ye fail, they may thidge you into everlasting wonestows.

[10] He that is faithful in that which is least is faithful also in much: and he that is unrightful in the least is unrightful also in much.

[11] If therefore ye have not been faithful in the unrightsome mammon, who will lay to your trust the true riches?

[12] And if ye have not been faithful in that which is another man's, who shall give you that which is your own?

[13] No thane can theen two harrs: for either he will hate the one, and love the other; or else he will hold to the one, and forhow the other. Ye cannot theen God and mammon.

[14] And the Pharisees also, who were andy, heard all these things: and they scorned him.

[15] And he said unto them, Ye are they which rightsome yourselves before men; but God knoweth your hearts: for that which is highly adeared among men is worthless in the sight of God.

[16] The law and the forequeethers were until John: since that time the kingdom of God is preached, and every man presseth into it.

[17] And it is easier for heaven and earth to wend, than one tittle of the law to fail.

[18] Whosoever putteth away his wife, and eweneth another, begoeth dernlyership: and whosoever eweneth her that is put away from her husband begoeth dernlyership.

[19] There was a somel rich man, which was clothed in purple and fine linen, and fared richly every day:

[20] And there was a somel beggar named Lazarus, which was laid at his gate, full of sores,

[21] And wanting to be fed with the crumbs which fell from the rich man's table: moreover the dogs came and licked his sores.

[22] And it came to be, that the beggar died, and was carried by the woulderghosts into Abraham's bosom: the rich man also died, and was buried;

[23] And in hell he lift up his eyes, being in sousels, and seeth Abraham afar off, and Lazarus in his bosom.

[24] And he yarmed and said, Father Abraham, have ruth on me, and send Lazarus, that he may dip the tip of his finger in water, and cool my tongue; for I am souseled in this flame.

[25] But Abraham said, Son, mun that thou in thy lifetime thidgedst thy good things, and likewise Lazarus evil things: but now he is frovered, and thou art souseled.

[26] And beside all this, between us and you there is a great gulf fixed: so that they which would wend from hence to you cannot; neither can they hand to us, that would come from thence.

[27] Then he said, I abid thee therefore, father, that thou wouldest send him to my father's house:

[28] For I have five brethren; that he may bear witness unto them, lest they also come into this stead of sousel.

[29] Abraham saith unto him, They have Moses and the forequeethers; let them hear them.

[30] And he said, Nay, father Abraham: but if one went unto them from the dead, they will berue.

[31] And he said unto him, If they hear not Moses and the forequeethers, neither will they be persuaded, though one rose from the dead.

Luke.17

[1] Then said he unto the loreknights, It is unmightly but that hut be done to men's ferths: but woe unto him, through whom they come!

[2] It were better for him that a millstone were hanged about his neck, and he cast into the sea, than that he should abellow one of these little ones.

[3] Take heed to yourselves: If thy brother sin against thee, chide him; and if he berue, forgive him.

[4] And if he sin against thee seven times in a day, and seven times in a day wharve again to thee, saying, I berue; thou shalt forgive him.

[5] And the loreknights said unto the Lord, bewax our faith.

[6] And the Lord said, If ye had faith as a grain of mustard seed, ye might say unto this sycamine tree, Be thou plucked up by the root, and be thou planted in the sea; and it should hearsome you.

[7] But which of you, having a thane plowing or feeding cattle, will say unto him by and by, when he is come from the field, Go and sit down to meat?

[8] And will not rather say unto him, Make ready wherewith I may sup, and gird thyself, and theen me, till I have eaten and drunken; and afterward thou shalt eat and drink?

[9] Doth he thank that thane forwhy he did the things that were bebade him? I trow not.

[10] So likewise ye, when ye shall have done all those things which are bebade you, say, We are unnotesome thanes: we have done that which was our duty to do.

[11] And it came to be, as he went to Jerusalem, that he wended through the midst of Samaria and Galilee.

[12] And as he went into a somel town, there met him ten men that were lepers, which stood afar off:

[13] And they lifted up their stevens, and said, Jesus, Harr, have ruth on us.

[14] And when he saw them, he said unto them, Go shew yourselves unto the priests. And it came to be, that, as they went, they were cleansed.

[15] And one of them, when he saw that he was healed, whorve back, and with a loud steven woulderened God,
[16] And fell down on his anlit at his feet, giving him thanks: and he was a Samaritan.
[17] And Jesus answering said, Were there not ten cleansed? but where are the nine?
[18] There are not found that edwhorve to give woulder to God, nerr this stranger.
[19] And he said unto him, Arise, go thy way: thy faith hath made thee whole.
[20] And when he was asked by the Pharisees, when the kingdom of God should come, he answered them and said, The kingdom of God cometh not with warning:
[21] Neither shall they say, Lo here! or, lo there! for, behold, the kingdom of God is within you.
[22] And he said unto the loreknights, The days will come, when ye shall wish to see one of the days of the Son of man, and ye shall not see it.
[23] And they shall say to you, See here; or, see there: go not after them, nor follow them.
[24] For as the lightning, that lighteneth out of the one part under heaven, shineth unto the other part under heaven; so shall also the Son of man be in his day.
[25] But first must he thraw many things, and be withlaid of this strind.
[26] And as it was in the days of Noe, so shall it be also in the days of the Son of man.
[27] They did eat, they drank, they heamed wives, they were given in wedlock, until the day that Noe went into the ark, and the flood came, and fordid them all.
[28] Likewise also as it was in the days of Lot; they did eat, they drank, they bought, they sold, they planted, they builded;
[29] But the same day that Lot went out of Sodom it rained fire and brimstone from heaven, and fordid them all.
[30] Even thus shall it be in the day when the Son of man is swettled.
[31] In that day, he which shall be upon the housetop, and his stuff in the house, let him not come down to take it away: and he that is in the field, let him likewise not edwharve back.
[32] Mun Lot's wife.
[33] Whosoever shall seek to nerr his life shall lose it; and whosoever shall lose his life shall pretheen it.
[34] I tell you, in that night there shall be two men in one bed; the one shall be taken, and the other shall be left.
[35] Two women shall be grinding together; the one shall be taken, and the other left.
[36] Two men shall be in the field; the one shall be taken, and the other left.
[37] And they answered and said unto him, Where, Lord? And he said unto them, Wheresoever the body is, thither will the eagles be gathered together.

Luke.18

[1] And he spake a likeningtale unto them to this end, that men ought always to abid, and not to faint;
[2] Saying, There was in a chester a deemer, which feared not God, neither hidged man:
[3] And there was a widow in that chester; and she came unto him, saying, Bewrake me of mine adversary.
[4] And he would not for a while: but afterward he said within himself, Though I fear not God, nor hidge man;
[5] Yet forwhy this widow dreeveth me, I will bewrake her, lest by her throughstanding coming she weary me.
[6] And the Lord said, Hear what the unrightful deemer saith.
[7] And shall not God bewrake his own chosen, which yarm day and night unto him, though he bear long with them?
[8] I tell you that he will bewrake them speedily. Nevertheless when the Son of man cometh, shall he find faith on the earth?
[9] And he spake this likeningtale unto somel which trusted in themselves that they were rightsome, and forhowed others:
[10] Two men went up into the worshipstead to abid; the one a Pharisee, and the other a tollner.
[11] The Pharisee stood and abade thus with himself, God, I thank thee, that I am not as other men are, neednimmers, unupright, forliers, or even as this tollners
[12] I fast twice in the week, I give tithes of all that I own.
[13] And the tollner, standing afar off, would not lift up so much as his eyes unto heaven, but smote upon his breast, saying, God be ruthful to me a sinner.
[14] I tell you, this man went down to his house rightsomed rather than the other: for every one that reameth himself shall be lowered; and he that lowereth himself shall be reamed.
[15] And they brought unto him also infants, that he would rine them: but when his loreknights saw it, they scolded them.
[16] But Jesus called them unto him, and said, Thraw little children to come unto me, and forbid them not: for of such is the kingdom of God.
[17] In sooth I say unto you, Whosoever shall not thidge the kingdom of God as a little child shall in no wise go therein.
[18] And a somel woldend asked him, saying, Good Harr, what shall I do to erve alderlong life?
[19] And Jesus said unto him, Why callest thou me

good? none is good, nerr one, that is, God.
[20] Thou knowest the bodewords, Do not bego dernlyership, Do not kill, Do not steal, Do not bear unsooth witness, Ore thy father and thy mother.
[21] And he said, All these have I kept from my youth up.
[22] Now when Jesus heard these things, he said unto him, Yet lackest thou one thing: sell all that thou hast, and britten unto the arm, and thou shalt have mathem in heaven: and come, follow me.
[23] And when he heard this, he was very sorrowful: for he was very rich.
[24] And when Jesus saw that he was very sorrowful, he said, How hardly shall they that have riches go into the kingdom of God!
[25] For it is easier for a camel to go through a needle's eye, than for a rich man to go into the kingdom of God.
[26] And they that heard it said, Who then can be nerred?
[27] And he said, The things which are unmightly with men are mightly with God.
[28] Then Peter said, Lo, we have left all, and followed thee.
[29] And he said unto them, In sooth I say unto you, There is no man that hath left house, or akennends, or brethren, or wife, or children, for the kingdom of God's sake,
[30] Who shall not thidge manifold more in this here time, and in the world to come life everlasting.
[31] Then he took unto him the twelve, and said unto them, Behold, we go up to Jerusalem, and all things that are written by the forequeethers bemeeting the Son of man shall be fullworked.
[32] For he shall be given unto the Gentiles, and shall be bismered, and spitefully slighted, and spitted on:
[33] And they shall scourge him, and put him to death: and the third day he shall rise again.
[34] And they understood none of these things: and this saying was hid from them, neither knew they the things which were spoken.
[35] And it came to be, that as he was come nigh unto Jericho, a somel blind man sat by the way side begging:
[36] And hearing the dright wend by, he asked what it meant.
[37] And they told him, that Jesus of Nazareth wendeth by.
[38] And he yarmed, saying, Jesus, thou Son of David, have ruth on me.
[39] And they which went before threaped him, that he should hold his frith: but he yarmed so much the more, Thou Son of David, have ruth on me.
[40] And Jesus stood, and bebade him to be brought unto him: and when he was come near, he asked him,
[41] Saying, What wilt thou that I shall do unto thee?

And he said, Lord, that I may thidge my sight.
[42] And Jesus said unto him, Thidge thy sight: thy faith hath nerred thee.
[43] And forthwith he thidged his sight, and followed him, woulderening God: and all the theed, when they saw it, gave praise unto God.

Luke.19

[1] And Jesus went and wended through Jericho.
[2] And, behold, there was a man named Zacchaeus, which was the alder among the tollners, and he was rich.
[3] And he sought to see Jesus who he was; and could not for the press, forwhy he was little of height.
[4] And he ran before, and climbed up into a sycomore tree to see him: for he was to go by that way.
[5] And when Jesus came to the stead, he looked up, and saw him, and said unto him, Zacchaeus, make haste, and come down; for to day I must abide at thy house.
[6] And he made haste, and came down, and thidged him mirthfully.
[7] And when they saw it, they all murmured, saying, That he was gone to be guest with a man that is a sinner.
[8] And Zacchaeus stood, and said unto the Lord; Behold, Lord, the half of my goods I give to the arm; and if I have taken any thing from any man by unsooth wraying, I edstathel him fourfold.
[9] And Jesus said unto him, On this day is holse come to this house, forsomuch as he also is a son of Abraham.
[10] For the Son of man is come to seek and to nerr that which was lost.
[11] And as they heard these things, he added and spake a likeningtale, forwhy he was nigh to Jerusalem, and forwhy they thought that the kingdom of God should forthwith tread up.
[12] He said therefore, A somel athelman went into a far land to thidge for himself a kingdom, and to edwharve.
[13] And he called his ten thanes, and gave them ten pounds, and said unto them, Occupy till I come.
[14] But his chesterware hated him, and sent a message after him, saying, We will not have this man to reign over us.
[15] And it came to be, that when he was edwhorven having thidged the kingdom, then he bebade these thanes to be called unto him, to whom he had given the money, that he might know how much every man had agot by trading.
[16] Then came the first, saying, Lord, thy pound hath agot ten pounds.

[17] And he said unto him, Well, thou good thane: forwhy thou hast been faithful in a very little, have thou alderdom over ten chesters.
[18] And the twoth came, saying, Lord, thy pound hath agot five pounds.
[19] And he said likewise to him, Be thou also over five chesters.
[20] And another came, saying, Lord, behold, here is thy pound, which I have kept laid up in a napkin:
[21] For I feared thee, forwhy thou art a strack man: thou takest up that thou layedst not down, and reapest that thou didst not sow.
[22] And he saith unto him, Out of thine own mouth will I deem thee, thou wicked thane. Thou knewest that I was a strack man, taking up that I laid not down, and reaping that I did not sow:
[23] Wherefore then gavest not thou my money into the bank, that at my coming I might have agotten mine own with eke?
[24] And he said unto them that stood by, Take from him the pound, and give it to him that hath ten pounds.
[25] (And they said unto him, Lord, he hath ten pounds.)
[26] For I say unto you, That unto every one which hath shall be given; and from him that hath not, even that he hath shall be taken away from him.
[27] But those mine foes, which would not that I should reign over them, bring hither, and slay them before me.
[28] And when he had thus spoken, he went before, stighing up up to Jerusalem.
[29] And it came to be, when he was come nigh to Bethphage and Bethany, at the barrow called the barrow of Olives, he sent two of his loreknights,
[30] Saying, Go ye into the town over against you; in the which at your going ye shall find a colt tied, whereon yet never man sat: loose him, and bring him hither.
[31] And if any man ask you, Why do ye loose him? thus shall ye say unto him, Forwhy the Lord hath need of him.
[32] And they that were sent went their way, and found even as he had said unto them.
[33] And as they were loosing the colt, the owners thereof said unto them, Why loose ye the colt?
[34] And they said, The Lord hath need of him.
[35] And they brought him to Jesus: and they cast their clothing upon the colt, and they set Jesus thereon.
[36] And as he went, they spread their clothes in the way.
[37] And when he was come nigh, even now at the descent of the barrow of Olives, the whole dright of the loreknights began to aglee and praise God with a loud steven for all the mighty works that they had seen;
[38] Saying, Blessed be the King that cometh in the name of the Lord: frith in heaven, and thrum in the highest.
[39] And some of the Pharisees from among the dright said unto him, Harr, chide thy loreknights.
[40] And he answered and said unto them, I tell you that, if these should hold their frith, the stones would forthwith yarm out.
[41] And when he was come near, he beheld the chester, and wept over it,
[42] Saying, If thou hadst known, even thou, at least in this thy day, the things which belong unto thy frith! but now they are hid from thine eyes.
[43] For the days shall come upon thee, that thine foes shall cast a trench about thee, and imbhold thee, and keep thee in on every side,
[44] And shall lay thee even with the ground, and thy children within thee; and they shall not leave in thee one stone upon another; forwhy thou knewest not the time of thy neasing.
[45] And he went into the worshipstead, and began to cast out them that sold therein, and them that bought;
[46] Saying unto them, It is written, My house is the house of ibead: but ye have made it a den of thieves.
[47] And he taught daily in the worshipstead. But the alderpriests and the scribes and the alder of the theed sought to fordo him,
[48] And could not find what they might do: for all the theed were very attentive to hear him.

Luke.20

[1] And it came to be, that on one of those days, as he taught the theed in the worshipstead, and preached the gospel, the alderpriests and the scribes came upon him with the elders,
[2] And spake unto him, saying, Tell us, by what alderdom doest thou these things? or who is he that gave thee this alderdom?
[3] And he answered and said unto them, I will also ask you one thing; and answer me:
[4] The forwashing of John, was it from heaven, or of men?
[5] And they imbspoke with themselves, saying, If we shall say, From heaven; he will say, Why then believed ye him not?
[6] But and if we say, Of men; all the theed will stone us: for they be persuaded that John was a forequeether.
[7] And they answered, that they could not tell whence it was.
[8] And Jesus said unto them, Neither tell I you by what alderdom I do these things.
[9] Then began he to speak to the theed this likeningtale; A somel man planted a vineyard, and let it forth to husbandmen, and went into a far land for a

long time.

[10] And at the time he sent a thane to the husbandmen, that they should give him of the ovet of the vineyard: but the husbandmen beat him, and sent him away empty.

[11] And again he sent another thane: and they beat him also, and entreated him shamefully, and sent him away empty.

[12] And again he sent a third: and they wounded him also, and cast him out.

[13] Then said the lord of the vineyard, What shall I do? I will send my beloved son: it may be they will aworth him when they see him.

[14] But when the husbandmen saw him, they imbspoke among themselves, saying, This is the heir: come, let us kill him, that the erve may be ours.

[15] So they cast him out of the vineyard, and killed him. What therefore shall the lord of the vineyard do unto them?

[16] He shall come and fordo these husbandmen, and shall give the vineyard to others. And when they heard it, they said, God forbid.

[17] And he beheld them, and said, What is this then that is written, The stone which the builders withlaid, the same is become the head of the corner?

[18] Whosoever shall fall upon that stone shall be broken; but on whomsoever it shall fall, it will grind him to powder.

[19] And the alderpriests and the scribes the same stound sought to lay hands on him; and they feared the theed: for they ongot that he had spoken this likeningtale against them.

[20] And they watched him, and sent forth spies, which should feign themselves rightful men, that they might take hold of his words, that so they might give him over unto the wold and alderdom of the awieldend.

[21] And they asked him, saying, Harr, we know that thou sayest and teachest rightly, neither hidgest thou the wights of any, but teachest the way of God truly:

[22] Is it lawful for us to give gavel unto Caesar, or no?

[23] But he ongot their craftiness, and said unto them, Why costen ye me?

[24] Shew me a penny. Whose likeness and overwriting hath it? They answered and said, Caesar's.

[25] And he said unto them, Render therefore unto Caesar the things which be Caesar's, and unto God the things which be God's.

[26] And they could not take hold of his words before the theed: and they awondered at his answer, and held their frith.

[27] Then came to him somel of the Sadducees, which andsake that there is any arist; and they asked him,

[28] Saying, Harr, Moses wrote unto us, If any man's brother die, having a wife, and he die without children, that his brother should take his wife, and raise up seed unto his brother.

[29] There were therefore seven brethren: and the first took a wife, and died without children.

[30] And the twoth took her to wife, and he died childless.

[31] And the third took her; and in like kind the seven also: and they left no children, and died.

[32] Last of all the woman died also.

[33] Therefore in the arist whose wife of them is she? for seven had her to wife.

[34] And Jesus answering said unto them, The children of this world wed, and are given in wedlock:

[35] But they which shall be bethought worthy to underfang that world, and the arist from the dead, neither wed, nor are given in wedlock:

[36] Neither can they die any more: for they are sameworthed unto the woulderghosts; and are the children of God, being the children of the arist.

[37] Now that the dead are raised, even Moses shewed at the bush, when he calleth the Lord the God of Abraham, and the God of Isaac, and the God of Jacob.

[38] For he is not a God of the dead, but of the living: for all live unto him.

[39] Then somel of the scribes answering said, Harr, thou hast well said.

[40] And after that they durst not ask him any fraign at all.

[41] And he said unto them, How say they that Christ is David's son?

[42] And David himself saith in the book of Psalms, The LORD said unto my Lord, Sit thou on my right hand,

[43] Till I make thine foes thy footstool.

[44] David therefore calleth him Lord, how is he then his son?

[45] Then in the theresomeness of all the theed he said unto his loreknights,

[46] Beware of the scribes, which wish to walk in long robes, and love greetings in the markets, and the highest seats in the worshipsteads, and the alder rooms at simbletides;

[47] Which forglender widows' houses, and for a shew make long ibeads: the same shall thidge greater hellwitred.

Luke.21

[1] And he looked up, and saw the rich men casting their gifts into the treasury.

[2] And he saw also a somel arm widow casting in thither two mites.

[3] And he said, Of a truth I say unto you, that this arm widow hath cast in more than they all:

[4] For all these have of their fullsomeness cast in unto the tibers of God: but she of her penury hath cast in all the living that she had.
[5] And as some spake of the worshipstead, how it was adorned with goodly stones and gifts, he said,
[6] As for these things which ye behold, the days will come, in the which there shall not be left one stone upon another, that shall not be thrown down.
[7] And they asked him, saying, Harr, but when shall these things be? and what tocken will there be when these things shall come to be?
[8] And he said, Take heed that ye be not swoke: for many shall come in my name, saying, I am Christ; and the time draweth near: go ye not therefore after them.
[9] But when ye shall hear of wars and dwolm, be not ghasted: for these things must first come to be; but the end is not by and by.
[10] Then said he unto them, Folkdom shall rise against folkdom, and kingdom against kingdom:
[11] And great earthquakes shall be in divers steads, and hungers, and cothes; and fearful sights and great tockens shall there be from heaven.
[12] But before all these, they shall lay their hands on you, and dretch you, giving you up to the worshipsteads, and into witerns, being brought before kings and woldends for my name's sake.
[13] And it shall wharve to you for a witness.
[14] Settle it therefore in your hearts, not to throughthink before what ye shall answer:
[15] For I will give you a mouth and wisdom, which all your foes shall not be able to gainsay nor resist.
[16] And ye shall be forread both by akennends, and brethren, and kinsfolks, and friends; and some of you shall they have put to death.
[17] And ye shall be hated of all men for my name's sake.
[18] But there shall not an hair of your head swelt.
[19] In your thild own ye your souls.
[20] And when ye shall see Jerusalem imbheld with heres, then know that the forwastedness thereof is nigh.
[21] Then let them which are in Judaea flee to the barrows; and let them which are in the midst of it wite out; and let not them that are in the countries go thereinto.
[22] For these be the days of wrake, that all things which are written may be fulfilled.
[23] But woe unto them that are with child, and to them that give suck, in those days! for there shall be great swench in the land, and wrath upon this theed.
[24] And they shall fall by the edge of the sword, and shall be led away haftlings into all folkdoms: and Jerusalem shall be trodden down of the Gentiles, until the times of the Gentiles be fulfilled.
[25] And there shall be tockens in the sun, and in the moon, and in the stars; and upon the earth swench of folkdoms, with dreevedness; the sea and the waves roaring;
[26] Men's hearts failing them for fear, and for looking after those things which are coming on the earth: for the wolds of heaven shall be shaken.
[27] And then shall they see the Son of man coming in a cloud with wold and great woulder.
[28] And when these things begin to come to be, then look up, and lift up your heads; for your aleesing draweth nigh.
[29] And he spake to them a likeningtale; Behold the fig tree, and all the trees;
[30] When they now shoot forth, ye see and know of your own selves that summer is now nigh at hand.
[31] So likewise ye, when ye see these things come to be, know ye that the kingdom of God is nigh at hand.
[32] In sooth I say unto you, This strind shall not wend away, till all be fulfilled.
[33] Heaven and earth shall wend away: but my words shall not wend away.
[34] And take heed to yourselves, lest at any time your hearts be overloaded with overdoing, and drunkenness, and cares of this life, and so that day come upon you unawares.
[35] For as a snare shall it come on all them that dwell on the anlit of the whole earth.
[36] Watch ye therefore, and abid always, that ye may be bethought worthy to withfare all these things that shall come to be, and to stand before the Son of man.
[37] And in the day time he was teaching in the worshipstead; and at night he went out, and abode in the barrow that is called the barrow of Olives.
[38] And all the theed came early in the morning to him in the worshipstead, for to hear him.

Luke.22

[1] Now the simbletide of unleavened bread drew nigh, which is called the Eastersimble.
[2] And the alderpriests and scribes sought how they might kill him; for they feared the theed.
[3] Then went Hellwarden into Judas overnamed Iscariot, being of the rime of the twelve.
[4] And he went his way, and met with the alderpriests and captains, how he might forread him unto them.
[5] And they were glad, and hoted to give him money.
[6] And he hoted, and sought tideliness to forread him unto them in the untheresomeness of the dright.
[7] Then came the day of unleavened bread, when the eastersimble must be killed.
[8] And he sent Peter and John, saying, Go and yark us the eastersimble, that we may eat.
[9] And they said unto him, Where wilt thou that we

yark?

[10] And he said unto them, Behold, when ye are went into the chester, there shall a man meet you, bearing a pitcher of water; follow him into the house where he goeth in.

[11] And ye shall say unto the goodman of the house, The Harr saith unto thee, Where is the guestroom, where I shall eat the eastersimble with my loreknights?

[12] And he shall shew you a large upper room sided: there make ready.

[13] And they went, and found as he had said unto them: and they made ready the eastersimble.

[14] And when the stound was come, he sat down, and the twelve loreknights with him.

[15] And he said unto them, With wish I have wished to eat this eastersimble with you before I thraw:

[16] For I say unto you, I will not any more eat thereof, until it be fulfilled in the kingdom of God.

[17] And he took the cup, and gave thanks, and said, Take this, and todeal it among yourselves:

[18] For I say unto you, I will not drink of the ovet of the vine, until the kingdom of God shall come.

[19] And he took bread, and gave thanks, and brake it, and gave unto them, saying, This is my body which is given for you: this do in min of me.

[20] Likewise also the cup after evenmeal, saying, This cup is the new kitheness in my blood, which is shed for you.

[21] But, behold, the hand of him that forreadeth me is with me on the table.

[22] And truly the Son of man goeth, as it was determined: but woe unto that man by whom he is forread!

[23] And they began to inquire among themselves, which of them it was that should do this thing.

[24] And there was also a strife among them, which of them should be bethought the greatest.

[25] And he said unto them, The kings of the Gentiles wield lordship over them; and they that wield alderdom upon them are called rightdoers.

[26] But ye shall not be so: but he that is greatest among you, let him be as the younger; and he that is alder, as he that doth theen.

[27] For whether is greater, he that sitteth at meat, or he that theenth? is not he that sitteth at meat? but I am among you as he that theenth.

[28] Ye are they which have held fast with me in my stounds of constening.

[29] And I aset unto you a kingdom, as my Father hath aset unto me;

[30] That ye may eat and drink at my table in my kingdom, and sit on thrones judging the twelve tribes of Israel.

[31] And the Lord said, Simon, Simon, behold, Hellwarden hath wished to have you, that he may sift you as wheat:

[32] But I have abidden for thee, that thy faith fail not: and when thou art forwended, strengthen thy brethren.

[33] And he said unto him, Lord, I am ready to go with thee, both into witern, and to death.

[34] And he said, I tell thee, Peter, the cock shall not crow this day, before that thou shalt thrice andsake that thou knowest me.

[35] And he said unto them, When I sent you without purse, and scrip, and shoes, lacked ye any thing? And they said, Nothing.

[36] Then said he unto them, But now, he that hath a purse, let him take it, and likewise his scrip: and he that hath no sword, let him sell his clothing, and buy one.

[37] For I say unto you, that this that is written must yet be fullworked in me, And he was reckoned among the wrongdoers: for the things bemeeting me have an end.

[38] And they said, Lord, behold, here are two swords. And he said unto them, It is enough.

[39] And he came out, and went, as he was wont, to the barrow of Olives; and his loreknights also followed him.

[40] And when he was at the stead, he said unto them, Abid that ye go not into costening.

[41] And he was withdrawn from them about a stone's cast, and kneeled down, and abade,

[42] Saying, Father, if thou be willing, take this cup away from me: nevertheless not my will, but thine, be done.

[43] And there trod up a woulderghost unto him from heaven, strengthening him.

[44] And being in a swench he abade more earnestly: and his sweat was as it were great drops of blood falling down to the ground.

[45] And when he rose up from ibead, and was come to his loreknights, he found them sleeping for sorrow,

[46] And said unto them, Why sleep ye? rise and abid, lest ye go into costening.

[47] And while he yet spake, behold a dright, and he that was called Judas, one of the twelve, went before them, and drew near unto Jesus to kiss him.

[48] But Jesus said unto him, Judas, forreadest thou the Son of man with a kiss?

[49] When they which were about him saw what would follow, they said unto him, Lord, shall we smite with the sword?

[50] And one of them smote the thane of the high priest, and cut off his right ear.

[51] And Jesus answered and said, Thraw ye thus far. And he rone his ear, and healed him.

[52] Then Jesus said unto the alderpriests, and captains of the worshipstead, and the elders, which were come to him, Be ye come out, as against a thief, with swords

and staves?

[53] When I was daily with you in the worshipstead, ye stretched forth no hands against me: but this is your stound, and the wold of darkness.

[54] Then took they him, and led him, and brought him into the high priest's house. And Peter followed afar off.

[55] And when they had kindled a fire in the midst of the hall, and were set down together, Peter sat down among them.

[56] But a somel maid beheld him as he sat by the fire, and earnestly looked upon him, and said, This man was also with him.

[57] And he andsook him, saying, Woman, I know him not.

[58] And after a little while another saw him, and said, Thou art also of them. And Peter said, Man, I am not.

[59] And about the space of one stound after another belieffastly besoothed, saying, Of a truth this fellow also was with him: for he is a Galilaean.

[60] And Peter said, Man, I know not what thou sayest. And forthwith, while he yet spake, the cock crew.

[61] And the Lord whorve, and looked upon Peter. And Peter muned the word of the Lord, how he had said unto him, Before the cock crow, thou shalt andsake me thrice.

[62] And Peter went out, and wept bitterly.

[63] And the men that held Jesus bismered him, and smote him.

[64] And when they had blindfolded him, they struck him on the anlit, and asked him, saying, Forequeethe, who is it that smote thee?

[65] And many other things evilsakingly spake they against him.

[66] And as soon as it was day, the elders of the theed and the alderpriests and the scribes came together, and led him into their rownwitmoot, saying,

[67] Art thou the Christ? tell us. And he said unto them, If I tell you, ye will not believe:

[68] And if I also ask you, ye will not answer me, nor let me go.

[69] Hereafter shall the Son of man sit on the right hand of the wold of God.

[70] Then said they all, Art thou then the Son of God? And he said unto them, Ye say that I am.

[71] And they said, What need we any further witness? for we ourselves have heard of his own mouth.

Luke.23

[1] And the whole dright of them arose, and led him unto Pilate.

[2] And they began to wray him, saying, We found this fellow miswending the folkdom, and forbidding to give gavel to Caesar, saying that he himself is Christ a King.

[3] And Pilate asked him, saying, Art thou the King of the Jews? And he answered him and said, Thou sayest it.

[4] Then said Pilate to the alderpriests and to the theed, I find no guilt in this man.

[5] And they were the more fierce, saying, He stirreth up the theed, teaching throughout all Jewry, beginning from Galilee to this stead.

[6] When Pilate heard of Galilee, he asked whether the man were a Galilaean.

[7] And as soon as he knew that he belonged unto Herod's deemdom, he sent him to Herod, who himself also was at Jerusalem at that time.

[8] And when Herod saw Jesus, he was outestly glad: for he was wishsome to see him of a long time, forwhy he had heard many things of him; and he hoped to have seen some wonder done by him.

[9] Then he fraigned with him in many words; but he answered him nothing.

[10] And the alderpriests and scribes stood and earnestly beguilted him.

[11] And Herod with his men of war set him at nought, and bismered him, and arrayed him in a litty robe, and sent him again to Pilate.

[12] And the same day Pilate and Herod were made friends together: for before they were at scorn between themselves.

[13] And Pilate, when he had called together the alderpriests and the woldends and the theed,

[14] Said unto them, Ye have brought this man unto me, as one that miswendeth the theed: and, behold, I, having undersought him before you, have found no guilt in this man in those things whereof ye beguilt him:

[15] No, nor yet Herod: for I sent you to him; and, lo, nothing worthy of death is done unto him.

[16] I will therefore whip him, and alet him.

[17] (For of needtharf he must alet one unto them at the simbletide.)

[18] And they yarmed out all at once, saying, Away with this man, and alet unto us Barabbas:

[19] (Who for a somel mone made in the chester, and for murder, was cast into witern.)

[20] Pilate therefore, willing to alet Jesus, spake again to them.

[21] But they yarmed, saying, Roodfasten him, roodfasten him.

[22] And he said unto them the third time, Why, what evil hath he done? I have found no grounds for death in him: I will therefore whip him, and let him go.

[23] And they were forthwith with loud stevens, bebiding that he might be roodfastened. And the stevens of them and of the alderpriests swithered.

[24] And Pilate gave deemword that it should be as they called for.
[25] And he alet unto them him that for mone and murder was cast into witern, whom they had wished; but he gave Jesus over to their will.
[26] And as they led him away, they laid hold upon one Simon, a Cyrenian, coming out of the land, and on him they laid the rood, that he might bear it after Jesus.
[27] And there followed him a great togetherred of theed, and of women, which also bewailed and yawled him.
[28] But Jesus wharving unto them said, Daughters of Jerusalem, weep not for me, but weep for yourselves, and for your children.
[29] For, behold, the days are coming, in the which they shall say, Blessed are the barren, and the wombs that never bare, and the paps which never gave suck.
[30] Then shall they begin to say to the barrows, Fall on us; and to the hills, Cover us.
[31] For if they do these things in a green tree, what shall be done in the dry?
[32] And there were also two other, wrongdoers, led with him to be put to death.
[33] And when they were come to the stead, which is called Calvary, there they roodfastened him, and the wrongdoers, one on the right hand, and the other on the left.
[34] Then said Jesus, Father, forgive them; for they know not what they do. And they parted his clothing, and cast lots.
[35] And the theed stood beholding. And the woldends also with them derided him, saying, He nerred others; let him nerr himself, if he be Christ, the chosen of God.
[36] And the heregomes also bismered him, coming to him, and tiber him vinegar,
[37] And saying, If thou be the king of the Jews, nerr thyself.
[38] And a overwriting also was written over him in letters of Greek, and Latin, and Hebrew, THIS IS THE KING OF THE JEWS.
[39] And one of the wrongdoers which were hanged railed on him, saying, If thou be Christ, nerr thyself and us.
[40] But the other answering scolded him, saying, Dost not thou fear God, seeing thou art in the same fordeeming?
[41] And we indeed rightfully; for we thidge the due edlean of our deeds: but this man hath done nothing amiss.
[42] And he said unto Jesus, Lord, mun me when thou comest into thy kingdom.
[43] And Jesus said unto him, In sooth I say unto thee, To day shalt thou be with me in narxenwong.
[44] And it was about the sixth stound, and there was a darkness over all the earth until the ninth stound.
[45] And the sun was darkened, and the veil of the worshipstead was rent in the midst.
[46] And when Jesus had yarmed with a loud steven, he said, Father, into thy hands I sed forth my ferth: and having said thus, he gave up the ghost.
[47] Now when the hundredman saw what was done, he woulderened God, saying, Truly this was a rightsome man.
[48] And all the theed that came together to that sight, beholding the things which were done, smote their breasts, and edwhorve.
[49] And all his couthledgings, and the women that followed him from Galilee, stood afar off, beholding these things.
[50] And, behold, there was a man named Joseph, a redeman; and he was a good man, and a rightful:
[51] (The same had not thweered to the rownwitmoot and deed of them;) he was of Arimathaea, a chester of the Jews: who also himself waited for the kingdom of God.
[52] This man went unto Pilate, and begged the body of Jesus.
[53] And he took it down, and wrapped it in linen, and laid it in a lichrest that was hewn in stone, wherein never man before was laid.
[54] And that day was the reening, and the sabbath drew on.
[55] And the women also, which came with him from Galilee, followed after, and beheld the lichrest, and how his body was laid.
[56] And they edwhorve, and yeaked spices and smearlss; and rested the sabbath day by to the bodeword.

Luke.24

[1] Now upon the first day of the week, very early in the morning, they came unto the lichrest, bringing the spices which they had yeaked, and somel others with them.
[2] And they found the stone rolled away from the lichrest.
[3] And they went in, and found not the body of the Lord Jesus.
[4] And it came to be, as they were much bewildered thereabout, behold, two men stood by them in shining clothing:
[5] And as they were afraid, and bowed down their anlits to the earth, they said unto them, Why seek ye the living among the dead?
[6] He is not here, but is risen: mun how he spake unto you when he was yet in Galilee,
[7] Saying, The Son of man must be given over into the hands of sinful men, and be roodfastened, and the

third day rise again.
[8] And they muned his words,
[9] And edwhorve from the lichrest, and told all these things unto the eleven, and to all the rest.
[10] It was Mary Magdalene, and Joanna, and Mary the mother of James, and other women that were with them, which told these things unto the loreknights.
[11] And their words thenched to them as idle tales, and they believed them not.
[12] Then arose Peter, and ran unto the lichrest; and stooping down, he beheld the linen clothes laid by themselves, and wote, wondering in himself at that which was come to be.
[13] And, behold, two of them went that same day to a town called Emmaus, which was from Jerusalem about threescore furlongs.
[14] And they talked together of all these things which had happened.
[15] And it came to be, that, while they afered together and cwothe, Jesus himself drew near, and went with them.
[16] But their eyes were holden that they should not know him.
[17] And he said unto them, What kind of togetherspeaks are these that ye have one to another, as ye walk, and are sad?
[18] And the one of them, whose name was Cleopas, answering said unto him, Art thou only a stranger in Jerusalem, and hast not known the things which are come to be therein these days?
[19] And he said unto them, What things? And they said unto him, Bemeeting Jesus of Nazareth, which was a forequeether mighty in deed and word before God and all the theed:
[20] And how the alderpriests and our woldends gave him over to be fordeemed to death, and have roodfastened him.
[21] But we trusted that it had been he which should have aleesed Israel: and beside all this, to day is the third day since these things were done.
[22] Yea, and somel women also of our togethered made us amazed, which were early at the lichrest;
[23] And when they found not his body, they came, saying, that they had also seen an aldersight of woulderghosts, which said that he was alive.
[24] And somel of them which were with us went to the lichrest, and found it even so as the women had said: but him they saw not.
[25] Then he said unto them, O fools, and slow of heart to believe all that the forequeethers have spoken:
[26] Ought not Christ to have thrawed these things, and to go into his woulder?
[27] And beginning at Moses and all the forequeethers, he throughtold them in all the writ the things bemeeting himself.

[28] And they drew nigh unto the town, whither they went: and he made as though he would have gone further.
[29] But they constrained him, saying, Abide with us: for it is toward evening, and the day is far spent. And he went in to tarry with them.
[30] And it came to be, as he sat at meat with them, he took bread, and blessed it, and brake, and gave to them.
[31] And their eyes were opened, and they knew him; and he vanished out of their sight.
[32] And they said one to another, Did not our heart burn within us, while he talked with us by the way, and while he opened to us the writ?
[33] And they rose up the same stound, and edwhorve to Jerusalem, and found the eleven gathered together, and them that were with them,
[34] Saying, The Lord is risen indeed, and hath trodden up to Simon.
[35] And they told what things were done in the way, and how he was known of them in breaking of bread.
[36] And as they thus spake, Jesus himself stood in the midst of them, and saith unto them, Frith be unto you.
[37] But they were ghasted and affrighted, and weend that they had seen a ferth.
[38] And he said unto them, Why are ye dreeved? and why do thoughts arise in your hearts?
[39] Behold my hands and my feet, that it is I myself: handle me, and see; for a ferth hath not flesh and bones, as ye see me have.
[40] And when he had thus spoken, he shewed them his hands and his feet.
[41] And while they yet believed not for mirth, and wondered, he said unto them, Have ye here any meat?
[42] And they gave him a piece of a broiled fish, and of an honeycomb.
[43] And he took it, and did eat before them.
[44] And he said unto them, These are the words which I spake unto you, while I was yet with you, that all things must be fulfilled, which were written in the law of Moses, and in the forequeethers, and in the psalms, bemeeting me.
[45] Then opened he their understanding, that they might understand the writ,
[46] And said unto them, Thus it is written, and thus it behoved Christ to thraw, and to rise from the dead the third day:
[47] And that beruneing and eftgiving of sins should be preached in his name among all folkdoms, beginning at Jerusalem.
[48] And ye are witnesses of these things.
[49] And, behold, I send the hote of my Father upon you: but tarry ye in the chester of Jerusalem, until ye be laid on with wold from on high.
[50] And he led them out as far as to Bethany, and he

lifted up his hands, and blessed them.
[51] And it came to be, while he blessed them, he was parted from them, and carried up into heaven.
[52] And they worshipped him, and edwhorve to Jerusalem with great mirth:
[53] And were throughstandingly in the worshipstead, praising and blessing God. Amen.

Bible, King James Version

John

John.1

[1] In the beginning was the Word, and the Word was with God, and the Word was God.
[2] The same was in the beginning with God.
[3] All things were made by him; and without him was not any thing made that was made.
[4] In him was life; and the life was the light of men.
[5] And the light shineth in darkness; and the darkness understood it not.
[6] There was a man sent from God, whose name was John.
[7] The same came for a witness, to bear witness of the Light, that all men through him might believe.
[8] He was not that Light, but was sent to bear witness of that Light.
[9] That was the true Light, which lighteth every man that cometh into the world.
[10] He was in the world, and the world was made by him, and the world knew him not.
[11] He came unto his own, and his own thidged him not.
[12] But as many as thidged him, to them gave he wold to become the sons of God, even to them that believe on his name:
[13] Which were born, not of blood, nor of the will of the flesh, nor of the will of man, but of God.
[14] And the Word was made flesh, and dwelt among us, (and we beheld his woulder, the woulder as of the only begotten of the Father,) full of grace and truth.
[15] John bare witness of him, and yarmed, saying, This was he of whom I spake, He that cometh after me is forechosen before me: for he was before me.
[16] And of his fulness have all we thidged, and grace for grace.
[17] For the law was given by Moses, but grace and truth came by Jesus Christ.
[18] No man hath seen God at any time; the only begotten Son, which is in the bosom of the Father, he hath akithed him.
[19] And this is the rake of John, when the Jews sent priests and Levites from Jerusalem to ask him, Who art thou?
[20] And he andetted, and andsook not; but andetted, I am not the Christ.
[21] And they asked him, What then? Art thou Elias? And he saith, I am not. Art thou that forequeether? And he answered, No.
[22] Then said they unto him, Who art thou? that we may give an answer to them that sent us. What sayest thou of thyself?
[23] He said, I am the steven of one yarming in the wilderness, Make straight the way of the Lord, as said the forequeether Esaias.
[24] And they which were sent were of the Pharisees.
[25] And they asked him, and said unto him, Why forwashest thou then, if thou be not that Christ, nor Elias, neither that forequeether?
[26] John answered them, saying, I forwash with water: but there standeth one among you, whom ye know not;
[27] He it is, who coming after me is forechosen before me, whose shoe's latchet I am not worthy to unloose.
[28] These things were done in Bethabara beyond Jordan, where John was forwashing.
[29] The next day John seeth Jesus coming unto him, and saith, Behold the Lamb of God, which taketh away the sin of the world.
[30] This is he of whom I said, After me cometh a man which is forechosen before me: for he was before me.
[31] And I knew him not: but that he should be made swettle to Israel, therefore am I come forwashing with water.
[32] And John bare rake, saying, I saw the Ferth stighing down from heaven like a dove, and it abode upon him.
[33] And I knew him not: but he that sent me to forwash with water, the same said unto me, Upon whom thou shalt see the Ferth stighing down, and beliving on him, the same is he which forwasheth with the Holy Ghost.
[34] And I saw, and bare rake that this is the Son of God.
[35] Again the next day after John stood, and two of his loreknights;
[36] And looking upon Jesus as he walked, he saith, Behold the Lamb of God!
[37] And the two loreknights heard him speak, and they followed Jesus.
[38] Then Jesus whorve, and saw them following, and saith unto them, What seek ye? They said unto him, Rabbi, (which is to say, being awended, Harr,) where

dwellest thou?

[39] He saith unto them, Come and see. They came and saw where he dwelt, and abode with him that day: for it was about the tenth stound.

[40] One of the two which heard John speak, and followed him, was Andrew, Simon Peter's brother.

[41] He first findeth his own brother Simon, and saith unto him, We have found the Messias, which is, being awended, the Christ.

[42] And he brought him to Jesus. And when Jesus beheld him, he said, Thou art Simon the son of Jona: thou shalt be called Cephas, which is by awending, A stone.

[43] The day following Jesus would go forth into Galilee, and findeth Philip, and saith unto him, Follow me.

[44] Now Philip was of Bethsaida, the chester of Andrew and Peter.

[45] Philip findeth Nathanael, and saith unto him, We have found him, of whom Moses in the law, and the forequeethers, did write, Jesus of Nazareth, the son of Joseph.

[46] And Nathanael said unto him, Can there any good thing come out of Nazareth? Philip saith unto him, Come and see.

[47] Jesus saw Nathanael coming to him, and saith of him, Behold an Israelite indeed, in whom is no guile!

[48] Nathanael saith unto him, Whence knowest thou me? Jesus answered and said unto him, Before that Philip called thee, when thou wast under the fig tree, I saw thee.

[49] Nathanael answered and saith unto him, Rabbi, thou art the Son of God; thou art the King of Israel.

[50] Jesus answered and said unto him, Forwhy I said unto thee, I saw thee under the fig tree, believest thou? thou shalt see greater things than these.

[51] And he saith unto him, In sooth, in sooth, I say unto you, Hereafter ye shall see heaven open, and the woulderghosts of God stighing up and stighing down upon the Son of man.

John.2

[1] And the third day there was a wedding in Cana of Galilee; and the mother of Jesus was there:

[2] And both Jesus was called, and his loreknights, to the wedding.

[3] And when they wanted wine, the mother of Jesus saith unto him, They have no wine.

[4] Jesus saith unto her, Woman, what have I to do with thee? mine stound is not yet come.

[5] His mother saith unto the thanes, Whatsoever he saith unto you, do it.

[6] And there were set there six waterpots of stone, after the kind of the luttering of the Jews, inholding two or three firkins apiece.

[7] Jesus saith unto them, Fill the waterpots with water. And they filled them up to the brim.

[8] And he saith unto them, Draw out now, and bear unto the overseer of the simbletide. And they bare it.

[9] When the woldend of the simbletide had tasted the water that was made wine, and knew not whence it was: (but the thanes which drew the water knew;) the overseer of the simbletide called the bridegroom,

[10] And saith unto him, Every man at the beginning doth set forth good wine; and when men have well drunk, then that which is worse: but thou hast kept the good wine until now.

[11] This beginning of wonders did Jesus in Cana of Galilee, and swettled forth his woulder; and his loreknights believed on him.

[12] After this he went down to Capernaum, he, and his mother, and his brethren, and his loreknights: and they stood through there not many days.

[13] And the Jews' eastersimble was at hand, and Jesus went up to Jerusalem,

[14] And found in the worshipstead those that sold oxen and sheep and doves, and the wrixlers of money sitting:

[15] And when he had made a scourge of small cords, he drove them all out of the worshipstead, and the sheep, and the oxen; and poured out the wrixlers' money, and overthrew the tables;

[16] And said unto them that sold doves, Take these things hence; make not my Father's house an house of merchandise.

[17] And his loreknights muned that it was written, The zeal of thine house hath eaten me up.

[18] Then answered the Jews and said unto him, What tocken shewest thou unto us, seeing that thou doest these things?

[19] Jesus answered and said unto them, Fordo this worshipstead, and in three days I will raise it up.

[20] Then said the Jews, Forty and six years was this worshipstead in building, and wilt thou rear it up in three days?

[21] But he spake of the worshipstead of his body.

[22] When therefore he was risen from the dead, his loreknights muned that he had said this unto them; and they believed the writ, and the word which Jesus had said.

[23] Now when he was in Jerusalem at the eastersimble, in the simbletide day, many believed in his name, when they saw the wonders which he did.

[24] But Jesus did not trust them, forwhy he knew all men,

[25] And needed not that any should bear witness of man: for he knew what was in man.

John.3

[1] There was a man of the Pharisees, named Nicodemus, a woldend of the Jews:
[2] The same came to Jesus by night, and said unto him, Rabbi, we know that thou art a teacher come from God: for no man can do these wonders that thou doest, unless God be with him.
[3] Jesus answered and said unto him, In sooth, in sooth, I say unto thee, Unless a man be born again, he cannot see the kingdom of God.
[4] Nicodemus saith unto him, How can a man be born when he is old? can he go the twoth time into his mother's womb, and be born?
[5] Jesus answered, In sooth, in sooth, I say unto thee, Unless a man be born of water and of the Ferth, he cannot go into the kingdom of God.
[6] That which is born of the flesh is flesh; and that which is born of the Ferth is ferth.
[7] Awonder not that I said unto thee, Ye must be born again.
[8] The wind bloweth where it listeth, and thou hearest the sound thereof, but canst not tell whence it cometh, and whither it goeth: so is every one that is born of the Ferth.
[9] Nicodemus answered and said unto him, How can these things be?
[10] Jesus answered and said unto him, Art thou a harr of Israel, and knowest not these things?
[11] In sooth, in sooth, I say unto thee, We speak that we do know, and bear witness that we have seen; and ye thidge not our witness.
[12] If I have told you earthly things, and ye believe not, how shall ye believe, if I tell you of heavenly things?
[13] And no man hath stighed up up to heaven, but he that came down from heaven, even the Son of man which is in heaven.
[14] And as Moses lifted up the serpent in the wilderness, even so must the Son of man be lifted up:
[15] That whosoever believeth in him should not swelt, but have alderlong life.
[16] For God so loved the world, that he gave his only begotten Son, that whosoever believeth in him should not swelt, but have everlasting life.
[17] For God sent not his Son into the world to fordeem the world; but that the world through him might be nerred.
[18] He that believeth on him is not fordeemed: but he that believeth not is fordeemed already, forwhy he hath not believed in the name of the only begotten Son of God.
[19] And this is the fordeeming, that light is come into the world, and men loved darkness rather than light, forwhy their deeds were evil.
[20] For every one that doeth evil hateth the light, neither cometh to the light, lest his deeds should be reproved.
[21] But he that doeth truth cometh to the light, that his deeds may be made swettle, that they are wrought in God.
[22] After these things came Jesus and his loreknights into the land of Judaea; and there he tarried with them, and forwashed.
[23] And John also was forwashing in Aenon near to Salim, forwhy there was much water there: and they came, and were forwashed.
[24] For John was not yet cast into witern.
[25] Then there arose a fraign between some of John's loreknights and the Jews about siferening.
[26] And they came unto John, and said unto him, Rabbi, he that was with thee beyond Jordan, to whom thou barest witness, behold, the same forwashth, and all men come to him.
[27] John answered and said, A man can thidge nothing, unless it be given him from heaven.
[28] Ye yourselves bear me witness, that I said, I am not the Christ, but that I am sent before him.
[29] He that hath the bride is the bridegroom: but the friend of the bridegroom, which standeth and heareth him, agleeth greatly forwhy of the bridegroom's steven: this my mirth therefore is fulfilled.
[30] He must wax, but I must wane.
[31] He that cometh from above is above all: he that is of the earth is earthly, and speaketh of the earth: he that cometh from heaven is above all.
[32] And what he hath seen and heard, that he testifieth; and no man thidgeth his witness.
[33] He that hath thidged his witness hath set to his seal that God is true.
[34] For he whom God hath sent speaketh the words of God: for God giveth not the Ferth by measure unto him.
[35] The Father loveth the Son, and hath given all things into his hand.
[36] He that believeth on the Son hath everlasting life: and he that believeth not the Son shall not see life; but the wrath of God abideth on him.

John.4

[1] When therefore the Lord knew how the Pharisees had heard that Jesus made and forwashed more loreknights than John,
[2] (Though Jesus himself forwashed not, but his loreknights,)
[3] He left Judaea, and wote again into Galilee.
[4] And he must needs go through Samaria.
[5] Then cometh he to a chester of Samaria, which is

called Sychar, near to the parcel of ground that Jacob gave to his son Joseph.
[6] Now Jacob's well was there. Jesus therefore, being wearied with his sith, sat thus on the well: and it was about the sixth stound.
[7] There cometh a woman of Samaria to draw water: Jesus saith unto her, Give me to drink.
[8] (For his loreknights were gone away unto the chester to buy meat.)
[9] Then saith the woman of Samaria unto him, How is it that thou, being a Jew, askest drink of me, which am a woman of Samaria? for the Jews have no dealings with the Samaritans.
[10] Jesus answered and said unto her, If thou knewest the gift of God, and who it is that saith to thee, Give me to drink; thou wouldest have asked of him, and he would have given thee living water.
[11] The woman saith unto him, Sir, thou hast nothing to draw with, and the well is deep: from whence then hast thou that living water?
[12] Art thou greater than our father Jacob, which gave us the well, and drank thereof himself, and his children, and his cattle?
[13] Jesus answered and said unto her, Whosoever drinketh of this water shall thirst again:
[14] But whosoever drinketh of the water that I shall give him shall never thirst; but the water that I shall give him shall be in him a well of water springing up into everlasting life.
[15] The woman saith unto him, Sir, give me this water, that I thirst not, neither come hither to draw.
[16] Jesus saith unto her, Go, call thy husband, and come hither.
[17] The woman answered and said, I have no husband. Jesus said unto her, Thou hast well said, I have no husband:
[18] For thou hast had five husbands; and he whom thou now hast is not thy husband: in that saidst thou truly.
[19] The woman saith unto him, Sir, I onget that thou art a forequeether.
[20] Our fathers worshipped in this barrow; and ye say, that in Jerusalem is the stead where men ought to worship.
[21] Jesus saith unto her, Woman, believe me, the stound cometh, when ye shall neither in this barrow, nor yet at Jerusalem, worship the Father.
[22] Ye worship ye know not what: we know what we worship: for aredding is of the Jews.
[23] But the stound cometh, and now is, when the true worshippers shall worship the Father in ferth and in truth: for the Father seeketh such to worship him.
[24] God is a Ferth: and they that worship him must worship him in ferth and in truth.
[25] The woman saith unto him, I know that Messias cometh, which is called Christ: when he is come, he will tell us all things.
[26] Jesus saith unto her, I that speak unto thee am he.
[27] And upon this came his loreknights, and awondered that he talked with the woman: yet no man said, What seekest thou? or, Why talkest thou with her?
[28] The woman then left her waterpot, and went her way into the chester, and saith to the men,
[29] Come, see a man, which told me all things that ever I did: is not this the Christ?
[30] Then they went out of the chester, and came unto him.
[31] In the mean while his loreknights abade him, saying, Harr, eat.
[32] But he said unto them, I have meat to eat that ye know not of.
[33] Therefore said the loreknights one to another, Hath any man brought him ought to eat?
[34] Jesus saith unto them, My meat is to do the will of him that sent me, and to beend his work.
[35] Say not ye, There are yet four months, and then cometh harvest? behold, I say unto you, Lift up your eyes, and look on the fields; for they are white already to harvest.
[36] And he that reapeth thidgeth wages, and gathereth ovet unto life alderlong: that both he that soweth and he that reapeth may aglee together.
[37] And herein is that saying true, One soweth, and another reapeth.
[38] I sent you to reap that whereon ye bestowed no swink: other men swinked, and ye are went into their swinks.
[39] And many of the Samaritans of that chester believed on him for the saying of the woman, which bore witness, He told me all that ever I did.
[40] So when the Samaritans were come unto him, they besought him that he would tarry with them: and he abode there two days.
[41] And many more believed forwhy of his own word;
[42] And said unto the woman, Now we believe, not forwhy of thy saying: for we have heard him ourselves, and know that this is indeed the Christ, the Saviour of the world.
[43] Now after two days he wote thence, and went into Galilee.
[44] For Jesus himself bore witness, that a forequeether hath no ore in his own land.
[45] Then when he was come into Galilee, the Galilaeans thidged him, having seen all the things that he did at Jerusalem at the simbletide: for they also went unto the simbletide.
[46] So Jesus came again into Cana of Galilee, where he made the water wine. And there was a somel

athelman, whose son was sick at Capernaum.
[47] When he heard that Jesus was come out of Judaea into Galilee, he went unto him, and besought him that he would come down, and heal his son: for he was at the point of death.
[48] Then said Jesus unto him, Unless ye see tockens and wonders, ye will not believe.
[49] The athelman saith unto him, Sir, come down ere my child die.
[50] Jesus saith unto him, Go thy way; thy son liveth. And the man believed the word that Jesus had spoken unto him, and he went his way.
[51] And as he was now going down, his thanes met him, and told him, saying, Thy son liveth.
[52] Then inquired he of them the stound when he began to amend. And they said unto him, Yesterday at the seventh stound the fever left him.
[53] So the father knew that it was at the same stound, in the which Jesus said unto him, Thy son liveth: and himself believed, and his whole house.
[54] This is again the twoth wonder that Jesus did, when he was come out of Judaea into Galilee.

John.5

[1] After this there was a simbletide of the Jews; and Jesus went up to Jerusalem.
[2] Now there is at Jerusalem by the sheep market a pool, which is called in the Hebrew tongue Bethesda, having five porches.
[3] In these lay a great dright of impotent folk, of blind, halt, withered, waiting for the moving of the water.
[4] For a woulderghost went down at a somel time into the pool, and dreeved the water: whosoever then first after the troubling of the water stepped in was made whole of whatsoever cothe he had.
[5] And a somel man was there, which had an cothe thirty and eight years.
[6] When Jesus saw him lie, and knew that he had been now a long time in that case, he saith unto him, Wilt thou be made whole?
[7] The impotent man answered him, Sir, I have no man, when the water is dreeved, to put me into the pool: but while I am coming, another steppeth down before me.
[8] Jesus saith unto him, Rise, take up thy bed, and walk.
[9] And forthwith the man was made whole, and took up his bed, and walked: and on the same day was the sabbath.
[10] The Jews therefore said unto him that was healed, It is the sabbath day: it is not lawful for thee to carry thy bed.

[11] He answered them, He that made me whole, the same said unto me, Take up thy bed, and walk.
[12] Then asked they him, What man is that which said unto thee, Take up thy bed, and walk?
[13] And he that was healed wist not who it was: for Jesus had conveyed himself away, a dright being in that stead.
[14] Afterward Jesus findeth him in the worshipstead, and said unto him, Behold, thou art made whole: sin no more, lest a worse thing come unto thee.
[15] The man wote, and told the Jews that it was Jesus, which had made him whole.
[16] And therefore did the Jews dretch Jesus, and sought to slay him, forwhy he had done these things on the sabbath day.
[17] But Jesus answered them, My Father worketh hitherto, and I work.
[18] Therefore the Jews sought the more to kill him, forwhy he not only had broken the sabbath, but said also that God was his Father, making himself sameworth with God.
[19] Then answered Jesus and said unto them, In sooth, in sooth, I say unto you, The Son can do nothing of himself, but what he seeth the Father do: for what things soever he doeth, these also doeth the Son likewise.
[20] For the Father loveth the Son, and sheweth him all things that himself doeth: and he will shew him greater works than these, that ye may awonder.
[21] For as the Father raiseth up the dead, and quickeneth them; even so the Son quickeneth whom he will.
[22] For the Father deemeth no man, but hath handed down all deeming unto the Son:
[23] That all men should ore the Son, even as they ore the Father. He that oreth not the Son oreth not the Father which hath sent him.
[24] In sooth, in sooth, I say unto you, He that heareth my word, and believeth on him that sent me, hath everlasting life, and shall not come into fordeeming; but is wended from death unto life.
[25] In sooth, in sooth, I say unto you, The stound is coming, and now is, when the dead shall hear the steven of the Son of God: and they that hear shall live.
[26] For as the Father hath life in himself; so hath he given to the Son to have life in himself;
[27] And hath given him alderdom to fremm deeming also, forwhy he is the Son of man.
[28] Marvel not at this: for the stound is coming, in the which all that are in the graves shall hear his steven,
[29] And shall come forth; they that have done good, unto the arist of life; and they that have done evil, unto the arist of hellwitred.
[30] I can of mine own self do nothing: as I hear, I deem: and my deeming is rightful; forwhy I seek not

mine own will, but the will of the Father which hath sent me.
[31] If I bear witness of myself, my witness is not true.
[32] There is another that beareth witness of me; and I know that the witness which he witnesseth of me is true.
[33] Ye sent unto John, and he bare witness unto the truth.
[34] But I thidge not witness from man: but these things I say, that ye might be nerred.
[35] He was a burning and a shining light: and ye were willing for a time to aglee in his light.
[36] But I have greater witness than that of John: for the works which the Father hath given me to beend, the same works that I do, bear witness of me, that the Father hath sent me.
[37] And the Father himself, which hath sent me, hath borne witness of me. Ye have neither heard his steven at any time, nor seen his shape.
[38] And ye have not his word abiding in you: for whom he hath sent, him ye believe not.
[39] Search the writ; for in them ye think ye have alderlong life: and they are they which bear witness of me.
[40] And ye will not come to me, that ye might have life.
[41] I thidge not ore from men.
[42] But I know you, that ye have not the love of God in you.
[43] I am come in my Father's name, and ye thidge me not: if another shall come in his own name, him ye will thidge.
[44] How can ye believe, which thidge ore one of another, and seek not the ore that cometh from God only?
[45] Do not think that I will wray you to the Father: there is one that wrayeth you, even Moses, in whom ye trust.
[46] For had ye believed Moses, ye would have believed me: for he wrote of me.
[47] But if ye believe not his writings, how shall ye believe my words?

John.6

[1] After these things Jesus went over the sea of Galilee, which is the sea of Tiberias.
[2] And a great dright followed him, forwhy they saw his wonders which he did on them that were cothed.
[3] And Jesus went up into a barrow, and there he sat with his loreknights.
[4] And the eastersimble, a simbletide of the Jews, was nigh.
[5] When Jesus then lifted up his eyes, and saw a great crowd come unto him, he saith unto Philip, Whence shall we buy bread, that these may eat?
[6] And this he said to prove him: for he himself knew what he would do.
[7] Philip answered him, Two hundred pennyworth of bread is not enoughsome for them, that every one of them may take a little.
[8] One of his loreknights, Andrew, Simon Peter's brother, saith unto him,
[9] There is a lad here, which hath five barley loaves, and two small fishes: but what are they among so many?
[10] And Jesus said, Make the men sit down. Now there was much grass in the stead. So the men sat down, in rime about five thousand.
[11] And Jesus took the loaves; and when he had given thanks, he brittened to the loreknights, and the loreknights to them that were set down; and likewise of the fishes as much as they would.
[12] When they were filled, he said unto his loreknights, Gather up the breaklings that belive, that nothing be lost.
[13] Therefore they gathered them together, and filled twelve baskets with the breaklings of the five barley loaves, which belived over and above unto them that had eaten.
[14] Then those men, when they had seen the wonder that Jesus did, said, This is of a truth that forequeether that should come into the world.
[15] When Jesus therefore ongot that they would come and take him by force, to make him a king, he wote again into a barrow himself alone.
[16] And when even was now come, his loreknights went down unto the sea,
[17] And went into a ship, and went over the sea toward Capernaum. And it was now dark, and Jesus was not come to them.
[18] And the sea arose by grounds of a great wind that blew.
[19] So when they had rowed about five and twenty or thirty furlongs, they see Jesus walking on the sea, and drawing nigh unto the ship: and they were afraid.
[20] But he saith unto them, It is I; be not afraid.
[21] Then they willingly thidged him into the ship: and forthwith the ship was at the land whither they went.
[22] The day following, when the theed which stood on the other side of the sea saw that there was none other boat there, nerr that one whereinto his loreknights were went, and that Jesus went not with his loreknights into the boat, but that his loreknights were gone away alone;
[23] (Howbeit there came other boats from Tiberias nigh unto the stead where they did eat bread, after that the Lord had given thanks:)
[24] When the theed therefore saw that Jesus was not

there, neither his loreknights, they also took shipping, and came to Capernaum, seeking for Jesus.
[25] And when they had found him on the other side of the sea, they said unto him, Rabbi, when camest thou hither?
[26] Jesus answered them and said, In sooth, in sooth, I say unto you, Ye seek me, not forwhy ye saw the wonders, but forwhy ye did eat of the loaves, and were filled.
[27] Swink not for the meat which swelteth, but for that meat which tholeth unto everlasting life, which the Son of man shall give unto you: for him hath God the Father sealed.
[28] Then said they unto him, What shall we do, that we might work the works of God?
[29] Jesus answered and said unto them, This is the work of God, that ye believe on him whom he hath sent.
[30] They said therefore unto him, What tocken shewest thou then, that we may see, and believe thee? what dost thou work?
[31] Our fathers did eat manna in the throughdryland; as it is written, He gave them bread from heaven to eat.
[32] Then Jesus said unto them, In sooth, in sooth, I say unto you, Moses gave you not that bread from heaven; but my Father giveth you the true bread from heaven.
[33] For the bread of God is he which cometh down from heaven, and giveth life unto the world.
[34] Then said they unto him, Lord, evermore give us this bread.
[35] And Jesus said unto them, I am the bread of life: he that cometh to me shall never hunger; and he that believeth on me shall never thirst.
[36] But I said unto you, That ye also have seen me, and believe not.
[37] All that the Father giveth me shall come to me; and him that cometh to me I will in no wise cast out.
[38] For I came down from heaven, not to do mine own will, but the will of him that sent me.
[39] And this is the Father's will which hath sent me, that of all which he hath given me I should lose nothing, but should raise it up again at the last day.
[40] And this is the will of him that sent me, that every one which seeth the Son, and believeth on him, may have everlasting life: and I will raise him up at the last day.
[41] The Jews then murmured at him, forwhy he said, I am the bread which came down from heaven.
[42] And they said, Is not this Jesus, the son of Joseph, whose father and mother we know? how is it then that he saith, I came down from heaven?
[43] Jesus therefore answered and said unto them, Murmur not among yourselves.
[44] No man can come to me, unless the Father which hath sent me draw him: and I will raise him up at the last day.
[45] It is written in the forequeethers, And they shall be all taught of God. Every man therefore that hath heard, and hath learned of the Father, cometh unto me.
[46] Not that any man hath seen the Father, nerr he which is of God, he hath seen the Father.
[47] In sooth, in sooth, I say unto you, He that believeth on me hath everlasting life.
[48] I am that bread of life.
[49] Your fathers did eat manna in the wilderness, and are dead.
[50] This is the bread which cometh down from heaven, that a man may eat thereof, and not die.
[51] I am the living bread which came down from heaven: if any man eat of this bread, he shall live for ever: and the bread that I will give is my flesh, which I will give for the life of the world.
[52] The Jews therefore strove among themselves, saying, How can this man give us his flesh to eat?
[53] Then Jesus said unto them, In sooth, in sooth, I say unto you, Unless ye eat the flesh of the Son of man, and drink his blood, ye have no life in you.
[54] Whoso eateth my flesh, and drinketh my blood, hath alderlong life; and I will raise him up at the last day.
[55] For my flesh is meat indeed, and my blood is drink indeed.
[56] He that eateth my flesh, and drinketh my blood, dwelleth in me, and I in him.
[57] As the living Father hath sent me, and I live by the Father: so he that eateth me, even he shall live by me.
[58] This is that bread which came down from heaven: not as your fathers did eat manna, and are dead: he that eateth of this bread shall live for ever.
[59] These things said he in the worshipstead, as he taught in Capernaum.
[60] Many therefore of his loreknights, when they had heard this, said, This is an hard saying; who can hear it?
[61] When Jesus knew in himself that his loreknights murmured at it, he said unto them, Doth this abellow you?
[62] What and if ye shall see the Son of man astie up where he was before?
[63] It is the ferth that quickeneth; the flesh notesometh nothing: the words that I speak unto you, they are ferth, and they are life.
[64] But there are some of you that believe not. For Jesus knew from the beginning who they were that believed not, and who should forread him.
[65] And he said, Therefore said I unto you, that no man can come unto me, unless it were given unto him of my Father.
[66] From that time many of his loreknights went back,

and walked no more with him.
[67] Then said Jesus unto the twelve, Will ye also go away?
[68] Then Simon Peter answered him, Lord, to whom shall we go? thou hast the words of alderlong life.
[69] And we believe and are sure that thou art that Christ, the Son of the living God.
[70] Jesus answered them, Have not I chosen you twelve, and one of you is a devil?
[71] He spake of Judas Iscariot the son of Simon: for he it was that should forread him, being one of the twelve.

John.7

[1] After these things Jesus walked in Galilee: for he would not walk in Jewry, forwhy the Jews sought to kill him.
[2] Now the Jews' simbletide of tields was at hand.
[3] His brethren therefore said unto him, Wite hence, and go into Judaea, that thy loreknights also may see the works that thou doest.
[4] For there is no man that doeth any thing in dern, and he himself seeketh to be known openly. If thou do these things, shew thyself to the world.
[5] For neither did his brethren believe in him.
[6] Then Jesus said unto them, My time is not yet come: but your time is alway ready.
[7] The world cannot hate you; but me it hateth, forwhy I bear witness of it, that the works thereof are evil.
[8] Go ye up unto this simbletide: I go not up yet unto this simbletide; for my time is not yet full come.
[9] When he had said these words unto them, he abode still in Galilee.
[10] But when his brethren were gone up, then went he also up unto the simbletide, not openly, but as it were in dern.
[11] Then the Jews sought him at the simbletide, and said, Where is he?
[12] And there was much murmuring among the theed bemeeting him: for some said, He is a good man: others said, Nay; but he swiketh the theed.
[13] Howbeit no man spake openly of him for fear of the Jews.
[14] Now about the midst of the simbletide Jesus went up into the worshipstead, and taught.
[15] And the Jews awondered, saying, How knoweth this man letters, having never learned?
[16] Jesus answered them, and said, My loreword is not mine, but his that sent me.
[17] If any man will do his will, he shall know of the loreword, whether it be of God, or whether I speak of myself.
[18] He that speaketh of himself seeketh his own woulder: but he that seeketh his woulder that sent him, the same is true, and no unrightsomeness is in him.
[19] Did not Moses give you the law, and yet none of you keepeth the law? Why go ye about to kill me?
[20] The theed answered and said, Thou hast a devil: who goeth about to kill thee?
[21] Jesus answered and said unto them, I have done one work, and ye all marvel.
[22] Moses therefore gave unto you forsnithing; (not forwhy it is of Moses, but of the fathers;) and ye on the sabbath day forsnithe a man.
[23] If a man on the sabbath day thidge forsnithing, that the law of Moses should not be broken; are ye angry at me, forwhy I have made a man every whit whole on the sabbath day?
[24] Deem not by to the outsee, but deem rightsome deeming.
[25] Then said some of them of Jerusalem, Is not this he, whom they seek to kill?
[26] But, lo, he speaketh boldly, and they say nothing unto him. Do the woldends know indeed that this is the very Christ?
[27] Howbeit we know this man whence he is: but when Christ cometh, no man knoweth whence he is.
[28] Then yarmed Jesus in the worshipstead as he taught, saying, Ye both know me, and ye know whence I am: and I am not come of myself, but he that sent me is true, whom ye know not.
[29] But I know him: for I am from him, and he hath sent me.
[30] Then they sought to take him: but no man laid hands on him, forwhy his stound was not yet come.
[31] And many of the theed believed on him, and said, When Christ cometh, will he do more wonders than these which this man hath done?
[32] The Pharisees heard that the theed murmured such things bemeeting him; and the Pharisees and the alderpriests sent lawswinkerss to take him.
[33] Then said Jesus unto them, Yet a little while am I with you, and then I go unto him that sent me.
[34] Ye shall seek me, and shall not find me: and where I am, thither ye cannot come.
[35] Then said the Jews among themselves, Whither will he go, that we shall not find him? will he go unto the scattered among the Gentiles, and teach the Gentiles?
[36] What kind of saying is this that he said, Ye shall seek me, and shall not find me: and where I am, thither ye cannot come?
[37] In the last day, that great day of the simbletide, Jesus stood and yarmed, saying, If any man thirst, let him come unto me, and drink.
[38] He that believeth on me, as the writ hath said, out of his belly shall flow eas of living water.

[39] (But this spake he of the Ferth, which they that believe on him should thidge: for the Holy Ghost was not yet given; forwhy that Jesus was not yet woulderened.)
[40] Many of the theed therefore, when they heard this saying, said, Of a truth this is the Forequeether.
[41] Others said, This is the Christ. But some said, Shall Christ come out of Galilee?
[42] Hath not the writ said, That Christ cometh of the seed of David, and out of the town of Bethlehem, where David was?
[43] So there was idole among the theed forwhy of him.
[44] And some of them would have taken him; but no man laid hands on him.
[45] Then came the lawswinkerss to the alderpriests and Pharisees; and they said unto them, Why have ye not brought him?
[46] The lawswinkerss answered, Never man spake like this man.
[47] Then answered them the Pharisees, Are ye also swoke?
[48] Have any of the woldends or of the Pharisees believed on him?
[49] But this theed who knoweth not the law are cursed.
[50] Nicodemus saith unto them, (he that came to Jesus by night, being one of them,)
[51] Doth our law deem any man, before it hear him, and know what he doeth?
[52] They answered and said unto him, Art thou also of Galilee? Search, and look: for out of Galilee ariseth no forequeether.
[53] And every man went unto his own house.

John.8

[1] Jesus went unto the barrow of Olives.
[2] And early in the morning he came again into the worshipstead, and all the theed came unto him; and he sat down, and taught them.
[3] And the scribes and Pharisees brought unto him a woman taken in dernlyership; and when they had set her in the midst,
[4] They say unto him, Harr, this woman was taken in dernlyership, in the very act.
[5] Now Moses in the law bebade us, that such should be stoned: but what sayest thou?
[6] This they said, costening him, that they might have to wray him. But Jesus stooped down, and with his finger wrote on the ground, as though he heard them not.
[7] So when they stood through asking him, he lifted up himself, and said unto them, He that is without sin among you, let him first cast a stone at her.
[8] And again he stooped down, and wrote on the ground.
[9] And they which heard it, being convicted by their own conscience, went out one by one, beginning at the eldest, even unto the last: and Jesus was left alone, and the woman standing in the midst.
[10] When Jesus had lifted up himself, and saw none but the woman, he said unto her, Woman, where are those thine wrayrs? hath no man fordeemed thee?
[11] She said, No man, Lord. And Jesus said unto her, Neither do I fordeem thee: go, and sin no more.
[12] Then spake Jesus again unto them, saying, I am the light of the world: he that followeth me shall not walk in darkness, but shall have the light of life.
[13] The Pharisees therefore said unto him, Thou bearest rake of thyself; thy rake is not true.
[14] Jesus answered and said unto them, Though I bear rake of myself, yet my rake is true: for I know whence I came, and whither I go; but ye cannot tell whence I come, and whither I go.
[15] Ye deem after the flesh; I deem no man.
[16] And yet if I deem, my deeming is true: for I am not alone, but I and the Father that sent me.
[17] It is also written in your law, that the witness of two men is true.
[18] I am one that bear witness of myself, and the Father that sent me beareth witness of me.
[19] Then said they unto him, Where is thy Father? Jesus answered, Ye neither know me, nor my Father: if ye had known me, ye should have known my Father also.
[20] These words spake Jesus in the treasury, as he taught in the worshipstead: and no man laid hands on him; for his stound was not yet come.
[21] Then said Jesus again unto them, I go my way, and ye shall seek me, and shall die in your sins: whither I go, ye cannot come.
[22] Then said the Jews, Will he kill himself? forwhy he saith, Whither I go, ye cannot come.
[23] And he said unto them, Ye are from beneath; I am from above: ye are of this world; I am not of this world.
[24] I said therefore unto you, that ye shall die in your sins: for if ye believe not that I am he, ye shall die in your sins.
[25] Then said they unto him, Who art thou? And Jesus saith unto them, Even the same that I said unto you from the beginning.
[26] I have many things to say and to deem of you: but he that sent me is true; and I speak to the world those things which I have heard of him.
[27] They understood not that he spake to them of the Father.
[28] Then said Jesus unto them, When ye have lifted

up the Son of man, then shall ye know that I am he, and that I do nothing of myself; but as my Father hath taught me, I speak these things.

[29] And he that sent me is with me: the Father hath not left me alone; for I do always those things that becweem him.

[30] As he spake these words, many believed on him.

[31] Then said Jesus to those Jews which believed on him, If ye stand through in my word, then are ye my loreknights indeed;

[32] And ye shall know the truth, and the truth shall make you free.

[33] They answered him, We be Abraham's seed, and were never in bondage to any man: how sayest thou, Ye shall be made free?

[34] Jesus answered them, In sooth, in sooth, I say unto you, Whosoever begoeth sin is the thane of sin.

[35] And the thane abideth not in the house for ever: but the Son abideth ever.

[36] If the Son therefore shall make you free, ye shall be free indeed.

[37] I know that ye are Abraham's seed; but ye seek to kill me, forwhy my word hath no stead in you.

[38] I speak that which I have seen with my Father: and ye do that which ye have seen with your father.

[39] They answered and said unto him, Abraham is our father. Jesus saith unto them, If ye were Abraham's children, ye would do the works of Abraham.

[40] But now ye seek to kill me, a man that hath told you the truth, which I have heard of God: this did not Abraham.

[41] Ye do the deeds of your father. Then said they to him, We be not born of dernlyership; we have one Father, even God.

[42] Jesus said unto them, If God were your Father, ye would love me: for I wote forth and came from God; neither came I of myself, but he sent me.

[43] Why do ye not understand my speech? even forwhy ye cannot hear my word.

[44] Ye are of your father the devil, and the lusts of your father ye will do. He was a murderer from the beginning, and abode not in the truth, forwhy there is no truth in him. When he speaketh a lie, he speaketh of his own: for he is a liar, and the father of it.

[45] And forwhy I tell you the truth, ye believe me not.

[46] Which of you throughguilteth me of sin? And if I say the truth, why do ye not believe me?

[47] He that is of God heareth God's words: ye therefore hear them not, forwhy ye are not of God.

[48] Then answered the Jews, and said unto him, Say we not well that thou art a Samaritan, and hast a devil?

[49] Jesus answered, I have not a devil; but I ore my Father, and ye do unworth me.

[50] And I seek not mine own woulder: there is one that seeketh and deemeth.

[51] In sooth, in sooth, I say unto you, If a man keep my saying, he shall never see death.

[52] Then said the Jews unto him, Now we know that thou hast a devil. Abraham is dead, and the forequeethers; and thou sayest, If a man keep my saying, he shall never taste of death.

[53] Art thou greater than our father Abraham, which is dead? and the forequeethers are dead: whom makest thou thyself?

[54] Jesus answered, If I ore myself, my ore is nothing: it is my Father that oreth me; of whom ye say, that he is your God:

[55] Yet ye have not known him; but I know him: and if I should say, I know him not, I shall be a liar like unto you: but I know him, and keep his saying.

[56] Your father Abraham agleed to see my day: and he saw it, and was glad.

[57] Then said the Jews unto him, Thou art not yet fifty years old, and hast thou seen Abraham?

[58] Jesus said unto them, In sooth, in sooth, I say unto you, Before Abraham was, I am.

[59] Then took they up stones to cast at him: but Jesus hid himself, and went out of the worshipstead, going through the midst of them, and so wended by.

John.9

[1] And as Jesus wended by, he saw a man which was blind from his birth.

[2] And his loreknights asked him, saying, Harr, who did sin, this man, or his akennends, that he was born blind?

[3] Jesus answered, Neither hath this man sinned, nor his akennends: but that the works of God should be made swettle in him.

[4] I must work the works of him that sent me, while it is day: the night cometh, when no man can work.

[5] As long as I am in the world, I am the light of the world.

[6] When he had thus spoken, he spat on the ground, and made clay of the spittle, and he asmeared the eyes of the blind man with the clay,

[7] And said unto him, Go, wash in the pool of Siloam, (which is by awending, Sent.) He went his way therefore, and washed, and came seeing.

[8] The neighbours therefore, and they which before had seen him that he was blind, said, Is not this he that sat and begged?

[9] Some said, This is he: others said, He is like him: but he said, I am he.

[10] Therefore said they unto him, How were thine eyes opened?

[11] He answered and said, A man that is called Jesus made clay, and asmeared mine eyes, and said unto me,

Go to the pool of Siloam, and wash: and I went and washed, and I thidged sight.

[12] Then said they unto him, Where is he? He said, I know not.

[13] They brought to the Pharisees him that aforetime was blind.

[14] And it was the sabbath day when Jesus made the clay, and opened his eyes.

[15] Then again the Pharisees also asked him how he had thidged his sight. He said unto them, He put clay upon mine eyes, and I washed, and do see.

[16] Therefore said some of the Pharisees, This man is not of God, forwhy he keepeth not the sabbath day. Others said, How can a man that is a sinner do such wonders? And there was a idole among them.

[17] They say unto the blind man again, What sayest thou of him, that he hath opened thine eyes? He said, He is a forequeether.

[18] But the Jews did not believe bemeeting him, that he had been blind, and thidged his sight, until they called the akennends of him that had thidged his sight.

[19] And they asked them, saying, Is this your son, who ye say was born blind? how then doth he now see?

[20] His akennends answered them and said, We know that this is our son, and that he was born blind:

[21] But by what means he now seeth, we know not; or who hath opened his eyes, we know not: he is of age; ask him: he shall speak for himself.

[22] These words spake his akennends, forwhy they feared the Jews: for the Jews had thweered already, that if any man did andet that he was Christ, he should be put out of the worshipstead.

[23] Therefore said his akennends, He is of age; ask him.

[24] Then again called they the man that was blind, and said unto him, Give God the praise: we know that this man is a sinner.

[25] He answered and said, Whether he be a sinner or no, I know not: one thing I know, that, whereas I was blind, now I see.

[26] Then said they to him again, What did he to thee? how opened he thine eyes?

[27] He answered them, I have told you already, and ye did not hear: wherefore would ye hear it again? will ye also be his loreknights?

[28] Then they scorned him, and said, Thou art his loreknight; but we are Moses' loreknights.

[29] We know that God spake unto Moses: as for this fellow, we know not from whence he is.

[30] The man answered and said unto them, Why herein is a wonderworksome thing, that ye know not from whence he is, and yet he hath opened mine eyes.

[31] Now we know that God heareth not sinners: but if any man be a worshipper of God, and doeth his will, him he heareth.

[32] Since the world began was it not heard that any man opened the eyes of one that was born blind.

[33] If this man were not of God, he could do nothing.

[34] They answered and said unto him, Thou wast altogether born in sins, and dost thou teach us? And they cast him out.

[35] Jesus heard that they had cast him out; and when he had found him, he said unto him, Dost thou believe on the Son of God?

[36] He answered and said, Who is he, Lord, that I might believe on him?

[37] And Jesus said unto him, Thou hast both seen him, and it is he that talketh with thee.

[38] And he said, Lord, I believe. And he worshipped him.

[39] And Jesus said, For deeming I am come into this world, that they which see not might see; and that they which see might be made blind.

[40] And some of the Pharisees which were with him heard these words, and said unto him, Are we blind also?

[41] Jesus said unto them, If ye were blind, ye should have no sin: but now ye say, We see; therefore your sin beliveth.

John.10

[1] In sooth, in sooth, I say unto you, He that goeth not by the door into the sheepfold, but climbeth up some other way, the same is a thief and a robber.

[2] But he that goeth in by the door is the shepherd of the sheep.

[3] To him the porter openeth; and the sheep hear his steven: and he calleth his own sheep by name, and leadeth them out.

[4] And when he putteth forth his own sheep, he goeth before them, and the sheep follow him: for they know his steven.

[5] And a stranger will they not follow, but will flee from him: for they know not the steven of strangers.

[6] This likeningtale spake Jesus unto them: but they understood not what things they were which he spake unto them.

[7] Then said Jesus unto them again, In sooth, in sooth, I say unto you, I am the door of the sheep.

[8] All that ever came before me are thieves and robbers: but the sheep did not hear them.

[9] I am the door: by me if any man go in, he shall be nerred, and shall go in and out, and find pasture.

[10] The thief cometh not, but for to steal, and to kill, and to fordo: I am come that they might have life, and that they might have it more fullsomely.

[11] I am the good shepherd: the good shepherd giveth

his life for the sheep.
[12] But he that is an hireling, and not the shepherd, whose own the sheep are not, seeth the wolf coming, and leaveth the sheep, and fleeth: and the wolf catcheth them, and scattereth the sheep.
[13] The hireling fleeth, forwhy he is an hireling, and careth not for the sheep.
[14] I am the good shepherd, and know my sheep, and am known of mine.
[15] As the Father knoweth me, even so know I the Father: and I lay down my life for the sheep.
[16] And other sheep I have, which are not of this fold: them also I must bring, and they shall hear my steven; and there shall be one fold, and one shepherd.
[17] Therefore doth my Father love me, forwhy I lay down my life, that I might take it again.
[18] No man taketh it from me, but I lay it down of myself. I have wold to lay it down, and I have wold to take it again. This bodeword have I thidged of my Father.
[19] There was a idole therefore again among the Jews for these sayings.
[20] And many of them said, He hath a devil, and is mad; why hear ye him?
[21] Others said, These are not the words of him that hath a devil. Can a devil open the eyes of the blind?
[22] And it was at Jerusalem the simbletide of the thithergiving, and it was winter.
[23] And Jesus walked in the worshipstead in Solomon's porch.
[24] Then came the Jews round about him, and said unto him, How long dost thou make us to twight? If thou be the Christ, tell us forthrightly.
[25] Jesus answered them, I told you, and ye believed not: the works that I do in my Father's name, they bear witness of me.
[26] But ye believe not, forwhy ye are not of my sheep, as I said unto you.
[27] My sheep hear my steven, and I know them, and they follow me:
[28] And I give unto them alderlong life; and they shall never swelt, neither shall any man pluck them out of my hand.
[29] My Father, which gave them me, is greater than all; and no man is able to pluck them out of my Father's hand.
[30] I and my Father are one.
[31] Then the Jews took up stones again to stone him.
[32] Jesus answered them, Many good works have I shewed you from my Father; for which of those works do ye stone me?
[33] The Jews answered him, saying, For a good work we stone thee not; but for evilsaking; and forwhy that thou, being a man, makest thyself God.
[34] Jesus answered them, Is it not written in your law, I said, Ye are gods?
[35] If he called them gods, unto whom the word of God came, and the writ cannot be broken;
[36] Say ye of him, whom the Father hath hallowed, and sent into the world, Thou evilsakest; forwhy I said, I am the Son of God?
[37] If I do not the works of my Father, believe me not.
[38] But if I do, though ye believe not me, believe the works: that ye may know, and believe, that the Father is in me, and I in him.
[39] Therefore they sought again to take him: but he withfared out of their hand,
[40] And went away again beyond Jordan into the stead where John at first forwashed; and there he abode.
[41] And many came unto him, and said, John did no wonder: but all things that John spake of this man were true.
[42] And many believed on him there.

John.11

[1] Now a somel man was sick, named Lazarus, of Bethany, the town of Mary and her sister Martha.
[2] (It was that Mary which asmeared the Lord with smearls, and wiped his feet with her hair, whose brother Lazarus was sick.)
[3] Therefore his sisters sent unto him, saying, Lord, behold, he whom thou lovest is sick.
[4] When Jesus heard that, he said, This sickness is not unto death, but for the woulder of God, that the Son of God might be woulderened thereby.
[5] Now Jesus loved Martha, and her sister, and Lazarus.
[6] When he had heard therefore that he was sick, he abode two days still in the same stead where he was.
[7] Then after that saith he to his loreknights, Let us go into Judaea again.
[8] His loreknights say unto him, Harr, the Jews of late sought to stone thee; and goest thou thither again?
[9] Jesus answered, Are there not twelve stounds in the day? If any man walk in the day, he stumbleth not, forwhy he seeth the light of this world.
[10] But if a man walk in the night, he stumbleth, forwhy there is no light in him.
[11] These things said he: and after that he saith unto them, Our friend Lazarus sleepeth; but I go, that I may awake him out of sleep.
[12] Then said his loreknights, Lord, if he sleep, he shall do well.
[13] Howbeit Jesus spake of his death: but they thought that he had spoken of taking of rest in sleep.
[14] Then said Jesus unto them forthrightly, Lazarus is dead.

[15] And I am glad for your sakes that I was not there, to the goal that ye may believe; nevertheless let us go unto him.
[16] Then said Thomas, which is called Didymus, unto his fellowloreknights, Let us also go, that we may die with him.
[17] Then when Jesus came, he found that he had lain in the grave four days already.
[18] Now Bethany was nigh unto Jerusalem, about fifteen furlongs off:
[19] And many of the Jews came to Martha and Mary, to frover them bemeeting their brother.
[20] Then Martha, as soon as she heard that Jesus was coming, went and met him: but Mary sat still in the house.
[21] Then said Martha unto Jesus, Lord, if thou hadst been here, my brother had not died.
[22] But I know, that even now, whatsoever thou wilt ask of God, God will give it thee.
[23] Jesus saith unto her, Thy brother shall rise again.
[24] Martha saith unto him, I know that he shall rise again in the arist at the last day.
[25] Jesus said unto her, I am the arist, and the life: he that believeth in me, though he were dead, yet shall he live:
[26] And whosoever liveth and believeth in me shall never die. Believest thou this?
[27] She saith unto him, Yea, Lord: I believe that thou art the Christ, the Son of God, which should come into the world.
[28] And when she had so said, she went her way, and called Mary her sister dernly, saying, The Harr is come, and calleth for thee.
[29] As soon as she heard that, she arose quickly, and came unto him.
[30] Now Jesus was not yet come into the town, but was in that stead where Martha met him.
[31] The Jews then which were with her in the house, and frovered her, when they saw Mary, that she rose up hastily and went out, followed her, saying, She goeth unto the grave to weep there.
[32] Then when Mary was come where Jesus was, and saw him, she fell down at his feet, saying unto him, Lord, if thou hadst been here, my brother had not died.
[33] When Jesus therefore saw her weeping, and the Jews also weeping which came with her, he groaned in the ferth, and was dreeved,
[34] And said, Where have ye laid him? They said unto him, Lord, come and see.
[35] Jesus wept.
[36] Then said the Jews, Behold how he loved him!
[37] And some of them said, Could not this man, which opened the eyes of the blind, have brought about that even this man should not have died?
[38] Jesus therefore again groaning in himself cometh to the grave. It was a cave, and a stone lay upon it.
[39] Jesus said, Take ye away the stone. Martha, the sister of him that was dead, saith unto him, Lord, by this time he stinketh: for he hath been dead four days.
[40] Jesus saith unto her, Said I not unto thee, that, if thou wouldest believe, thou shouldest see the woulder of God?
[41] Then they took away the stone from the stead where the dead was laid. And Jesus lifted up his eyes, and said, Father, I thank thee that thou hast heard me.
[42] And I knew that thou hearest me always: but forwhy of the theed which stand by I said it, that they may believe that thou hast sent me.
[43] And when he thus had spoken, he yarmed with a loud steven, Lazarus, come forth.
[44] And he that was dead came forth, bound hand and foot with graveclothes: and his anlit was bound about with a napkin. Jesus saith unto them, Loose him, and let him go.
[45] Then many of the Jews which came to Mary, and had seen the things which Jesus did, believed on him.
[46] But some of them went their ways to the Pharisees, and told them what things Jesus had done.
[47] Then gathered the alderpriests and the Pharisees a rownwitmoot, and said, What do we? for this man doeth many wonders.
[48] If we let him thus alone, all men will believe on him: and the Romans shall come and take away both our stead and folkdom.
[49] And one of them, named Caiaphas, being the high priest that same year, said unto them, Ye know nothing at all,
[50] Nor bethink that it is tharfly for us, that one man should die for the theed, and that the whole folkdom swelt not.
[51] And this spake he not of himself: but being high priest that year, he forequothe that Jesus should die for that folkdom;
[52] And not for that folkdom only, but that also he should gather together in one the children of God that were scattered abroad.
[53] Then from that day forth they took thoughting together for to put him to death.
[54] Jesus therefore walked no more openly among the Jews; but went thence unto a land near to the wilderness, into a chester called Ephraim, and there throughstoodwith his loreknights.
[55] And the Jews' eastersimble was nigh at hand: and many went out of the land up to Jerusalem before the eastersimble, to cleanse themselves.
[56] Then sought they for Jesus, and spake among themselves, as they stood in the worshipstead, What think ye, that he will not come to the simbletide?
[57] Now both the alderpriests and the Pharisees had

given a bodeword, that, if any man knew where he were, he should shew it, that they might take him.

John.12

[1] Then Jesus six days before the eastersimble came to Bethany, where Lazarus was which had been dead, whom he raised from the dead.
[2] There they made him a evenmeal; and Martha theened: but Lazarus was one of them that sat at the table with him.
[3] Then took Mary a pound of smearls of spikenard, very costly, and asmeared the feet of Jesus, and wiped his feet with her hair: and the house was filled with the odour of the smearls.
[4] Then saith one of his loreknights, Judas Iscariot, Simon's son, which should forread him,
[5] Why was not this smearls sold for three hundred pence, and given to the arm?
[6] This he said, not that he cared for the arm; but forwhy he was a thief, and had the bag, and bare what was put therein.
[7] Then said Jesus, Let her alone: against the day of my burying hath she kept this.
[8] For the arm always ye have with you; but me ye have not always.
[9] Much theed of the Jews therefore knew that he was there: and they came not for Jesus' sake only, but that they might see Lazarus also, whom he had raised from the dead.
[10] But the alderpriests consulted that they might put Lazarus also to death;
[11] Forwhy that by grounds of him many of the Jews went away, and believed on Jesus.
[12] On the next day much theed that were come to the simbletide, when they heard that Jesus was coming to Jerusalem,
[13] Took branches of palm trees, and went forth to meet him, and yarmed, Hosanna: Blessed is the King of Israel that cometh in the name of the Lord.
[14] And Jesus, when he had found a young ass, sat thereon; as it is written,
[15] Fear not, daughter of Sion: behold, thy King cometh, sitting on an ass's colt.
[16] These things understood not his loreknights at the first: but when Jesus was woulderened, then muned they that these things were written of him, and that they had done these things unto him.
[17] The theed therefore that was with him when he called Lazarus out of his grave, and raised him from the dead, bare rake.
[18] For this whyth the theed also met him, for that they heard that he had done this wonder.
[19] The Pharisees therefore said among themselves, Onget ye how ye swither nothing? behold, the world is gone after him.
[20] And there were somel Greeks among them that came up to worship at the simbletide:
[21] The same came therefore to Philip, which was of Bethsaida of Galilee, and wished him, saying, Sir, we would see Jesus.
[22] Philip cometh and telleth Andrew: and again Andrew and Philip tell Jesus.
[23] And Jesus answered them, saying, The stound is come, that the Son of man should be woulderened.
[24] In sooth, in sooth, I say unto you, Unless a corn of wheat fall into the ground and die, it abideth alone: but if it die, it bringeth forth much ovet.
[25] He that loveth his life shall lose it; and he that hateth his life in this world shall keep it unto life alderlong.
[26] If any man theen me, let him follow me; and where I am, there shall also my thane be: if any man theen me, him will my Father ore.
[27] Now is my soul dreeved; and what shall I say? Father, nerr me from this stound: but for this whyth came I unto this stound.
[28] Father, woulderen thy name. Then came there a steven from heaven, saying, I have both woulderened it, and will woulderen it again.
[29] The theed therefore, that stood by, and heard it, said that it thundered: others said, A woulderghost spake to him.
[30] Jesus answered and said, This steven came not forwhy of me, but for your sakes.
[31] Now is the deeming of this world: now shall the atheling of this world be cast out.
[32] And I, if I be lifted up from the earth, will draw all men unto me.
[33] This he said, ameaning what death he should die.
[34] The theed answered him, We have heard out of the law that Christ abideth for ever: and how sayest thou, The Son of man must be lifted up? who is this Son of man?
[35] Then Jesus said unto them, Yet a little while is the light with you. Walk while ye have the light, lest darkness come upon you: for he that walketh in darkness knoweth not whither he goeth.
[36] While ye have light, believe in the light, that ye may be the children of light. These things spake Jesus, and wote, and did hide himself from them.
[37] But though he had done so many wonders before them, yet they believed not on him:
[38] That the saying of Esaias the forequeether might be fulfilled, which he spake, Lord, who hath believed our report? and to whom hath the arm of the Lord been swettled?
[39] Therefore they could not believe, forwhy that Esaias said again,

[40] He hath blinded their eyes, and hardened their heart; that they should not see with their eyes, nor understand with their heart, and be forwended, and I should heal them.
[41] These things said Esaias, when he saw his woulder, and spake of him.
[42] Nevertheless among the alder woldends also many believed on him; but forwhy of the Pharisees they did not andet him, lest they should be put out of the worshipstead:
[43] For they loved the praise of men more than the praise of God.
[44] Jesus yarmed and said, He that believeth on me, believeth not on me, but on him that sent me.
[45] And he that seeth me seeth him that sent me.
[46] I am come a light into the world, that whosoever believeth on me should not abide in darkness.
[47] And if any man hear my words, and believe not, I deem him not: for I came not to deem the world, but to nerr the world.
[48] He that withlayeth me, and thidgeth not my words, hath one that deemeth him: the word that I have spoken, the same shall deem him in the last day.
[49] For I have not spoken of myself; but the Father which sent me, he gave me a bodeword, what I should say, and what I should speak.
[50] And I know that his bodeword is life everlasting: whatsoever I speak therefore, even as the Father said unto me, so I speak.

John.13

[1] Now before the simbletide of the eastersimble, when Jesus knew that his stound was come that he should wite out of this world unto the Father, having loved his own which were in the world, he loved them unto the end.
[2] And evenmeal being ended, the devil having now put into the heart of Judas Iscariot, Simon's son, to forread him;
[3] Jesus knowing that the Father had given all things into his hands, and that he was come from God, and went to God;
[4] He riseth from evenmeal, and laid aside his clothing; and took a towel, and girded himself.
[5] After that he poureth water into a bason, and began to wash the loreknights' feet, and to wipe them with the towel wherewith he was girded.
[6] Then cometh he to Simon Peter: and Peter saith unto him, Lord, dost thou wash my feet?
[7] Jesus answered and said unto him, What I do thou knowest not now; but thou shalt know hereafter.
[8] Peter saith unto him, Thou shalt never wash my feet. Jesus answered him, If I wash thee not, thou hast no part with me.
[9] Simon Peter saith unto him, Lord, not my feet only, but also my hands and my head.
[10] Jesus saith to him, He that is washed needeth not nerr to wash his feet, but is clean every whit: and ye are clean, but not all.
[11] For he knew who should forread him; therefore said he, Ye are not all clean.
[12] So after he had washed their feet, and had taken his clothing, and was set down again, he said unto them, Know ye what I have done to you?
[13] Ye call me Harr and Lord: and ye say well; for so I am.
[14] If I then, your Lord and Harr, have washed your feet; ye also ought to wash one another's feet.
[15] For I have given you a bisen, that ye should do as I have done to you.
[16] In sooth, in sooth, I say unto you, The thane is not greater than his lord; neither he that is sent greater than he that sent him.
[17] If ye know these things, happy are ye if ye do them.
[18] I speak not of you all: I know whom I have chosen: but that the writ may be fulfilled, He that eateth bread with me hath lifted up his heel against me.
[19] Now I tell you before it come, that, when it is come to be, ye may believe that I am he.
[20] In sooth, in sooth, I say unto you, He that thidgeth whomsoever I send thidgeth me; and he that thidgeth me thidgeth him that sent me.
[21] When Jesus had thus said, he was dreeved in ferth, and bore witness, and said, In sooth, in sooth, I say unto you, that one of you shall forread me.
[22] Then the loreknights looked one on another, twighting of whom he spake.
[23] Now there was leaning on Jesus' bosom one of his loreknights, whom Jesus loved.
[24] Simon Peter therefore beckoned to him, that he should ask who it should be of whom he spake.
[25] He then lying on Jesus' breast saith unto him, Lord, who is it?
[26] Jesus answered, He it is, to whom I shall give a sop, when I have dipped it. And when he had dipped the sop, he gave it to Judas Iscariot, the son of Simon.
[27] And after the sop Hellwarden went into him. Then said Jesus unto him, That thou doest, do quickly.
[28] Now no man at the table knew for what ithank he spake this unto him.
[29] For some of them thought, forwhy Judas had the bag, that Jesus had said unto him, Buy those things that we have need of against the simbletide; or, that he should give something to the arm.
[30] He then having thidged the sop went forthwith out: and it was night.
[31] Therefore, when he was gone out, Jesus said, Now

is the Son of man woulderened, and God is woulderened in him.

[32] If God be woulderened in him, God shall also woulderen him in himself, and shall straightway woulderen him.

[33] Little children, yet a little while I am with you. Ye shall seek me: and as I said unto the Jews, Whither I go, ye cannot come; so now I say to you.

[34] A new bodeword I give unto you, That ye love one another; as I have loved you, that ye also love one another.

[35] By this shall all men know that ye are my loreknights, if ye have love one to another.

[36] Simon Peter said unto him, Lord, whither goest thou? Jesus answered him, Whither I go, thou canst not follow me now; but thou shalt follow me afterwards.

[37] Peter said unto him, Lord, why cannot I follow thee now? I will lay down my life for thy sake.

[38] Jesus answered him, Wilt thou lay down thy life for my sake? In sooth, in sooth, I say unto thee, The cock shall not crow, till thou hast andsook me thrice.

John.14

[1] Let not your heart be dreeved: ye believe in God, believe also in me.

[2] In my Father's house are many mansions: if it were not so, I would have told you. I go to yark a stead for you.

[3] And if I go and yark a stead for you, I will come again, and thidge you unto myself; that where I am, there ye may be also.

[4] And whither I go ye know, and the way ye know.

[5] Thomas saith unto him, Lord, we know not whither thou goest; and how can we know the way?

[6] Jesus saith unto him, I am the way, the truth, and the life: no man cometh unto the Father, but by me.

[7] If ye had known me, ye should have known my Father also: and from henceforth ye know him, and have seen him.

[8] Philip saith unto him, Lord, shew us the Father, and it sufficeth us.

[9] Jesus saith unto him, Have I been so long time with you, and yet hast thou not known me, Philip? he that hath seen me hath seen the Father; and how sayest thou then, Shew us the Father?

[10] Believest thou not that I am in the Father, and the Father in me? the words that I speak unto you I speak not of myself: but the Father that dwelleth in me, he doeth the works.

[11] Believe me that I am in the Father, and the Father in me: or else believe me for the very works' sake.

[12] In sooth, in sooth, I say unto you, He that believeth on me, the works that I do shall he do also; and greater works than these shall he do; forwhy I go unto my Father.

[13] And whatsoever ye shall ask in my name, that will I do, that the Father may be woulderened in the Son.

[14] If ye shall ask any thing in my name, I will do it.

[15] If ye love me, keep my bodewords.

[16] And I will abid the Father, and he shall give you another Froverer, that he may abide with you for ever;

[17] Even the Ferth of truth; whom the world cannot thidge, forwhy it seeth him not, neither knoweth him: but ye know him; for he dwelleth with you, and shall be in you.

[18] I will not leave you froverless: I will come to you.

[19] Yet a little while, and the world seeth me no more; but ye see me: forwhy I live, ye shall live also.

[20] At that day ye shall know that I am in my Father, and ye in me, and I in you.

[21] He that hath my bodewords, and keepeth them, he it is that loveth me: and he that loveth me shall be loved of my Father, and I will love him, and will swettle myself to him.

[22] Judas saith unto him, not Iscariot, Lord, how is it that thou wilt swettle thyself unto us, and not unto the world?

[23] Jesus answered and said unto him, If a man love me, he will keep my words: and my Father will love him, and we will come unto him, and make our abode with him.

[24] He that loveth me not keepeth not my sayings: and the word which ye hear is not mine, but the Father's which sent me.

[25] These things have I spoken unto you, being yet atbeen with you.

[26] But the Froverer, which is the Holy Ghost, whom the Father will send in my name, he shall teach you all things, and bring all things to your min, whatsoever I have said unto you.

[27] Frith I leave with you, my frith I give unto you: not as the world giveth, give I unto you. Let not your heart be dreeved, neither let it be afraid.

[28] Ye have heard how I said unto you, I go away, and come again unto you. If ye loved me, ye would aglee, forwhy I said, I go unto the Father: for my Father is greater than I.

[29] And now I have told you before it come to be, that, when it is come to be, ye might believe.

[30] Hereafter I will not talk much with you: for the atheling of this world cometh, and hath nothing in me.

[31] But that the world may know that I love the Father; and as the Father gave me bodeword, even so I do. Arise, let us go hence.

John.15

[1] I am the true vine, and my Father is the husbandman.
[2] Every branch in me that beareth not ovet he taketh away: and every branch that beareth ovet, he cut it of, that it may bring forth more ovet.
[3] Now ye are clean through the word which I have spoken unto you.
[4] Abide in me, and I in you. As the branch cannot bear ovet of itself, unless it abide in the vine; no more can ye, unless ye abide in me.
[5] I am the vine, ye are the branches: He that abideth in me, and I in him, the same bringeth forth much ovet: for without me ye can do nothing.
[6] If a man abide not in me, he is cast forth as a branch, and is withered; and men gather them, and cast them into the fire, and they are burned.
[7] If ye abide in me, and my words abide in you, ye shall ask what ye will, and it shall be done unto you.
[8] Herein is my Father woulderened, that ye bear much ovet; so shall ye be my loreknights.
[9] As the Father hath loved me, so have I loved you: throughstand ye in my love.
[10] If ye keep my bodewords, ye shall abide in my love; even as I have kept my Father's bodewords, and abide in his love.
[11] These things have I spoken unto you, that my mirth might belive in you, and that your mirth might be full.
[12] This is my bodeword, That ye love one another, as I have loved you.
[13] Greater love hath no man than this, that a man lay down his life for his friends.
[14] Ye are my friends, if ye do whatsoever I bebid you.
[15] Henceforth I call you not thanes; for the thane knoweth not what his lord doeth: but I have called you friends; for all things that I have heard of my Father I have made known unto you.
[16] Ye have not chosen me, but I have chosen you, and hoded you, that ye should go and bring forth ovet, and that your ovet should belive: that whatsoever ye shall ask of the Father in my name, he may give it you.
[17] These things I bebid you, that ye love one another.
[18] If the world hate you, ye know that it hated me before it hated you.
[19] If ye were of the world, the world would love his own: but forwhy ye are not of the world, but I have chosen you out of the world, therefore the world hateth you.
[20] Mun the word that I said unto you, The thane is not greater than his lord. If they have dretched me, they will also dretch you; if they have kept my saying, they will keep yours also.
[21] But all these things will they do unto you for my name's sake, forwhy they know not him that sent me.
[22] If I had not come and spoken unto them, they had not had sin: but now they have no cloke for their sin.
[23] He that hateth me hateth my Father also.
[24] If I had not done among them the works which none other man did, they had not had sin: but now have they both seen and hated both me and my Father.
[25] But this cometh to be, that the word might be fulfilled that is written in their law, They hated me without grounds.
[26] But when the Froverer is come, whom I will send unto you from the Father, even the Ferth of truth, which cometh out from the Father, he shall bear witness of me:
[27] And ye also shall bear witness, forwhy ye have been with me from the beginning.

John.16

[1] These things have I spoken unto you, that ye should not be abellowed.
[2] They shall put you out of the worshipsteads: yea, the time cometh, that whosoever killeth you will think that he doeth God service.
[3] And these things will they do unto you, forwhy they have not known the Father, nor me.
[4] But these things have I told you, that when the time shall come, ye may mun that I told you of them. And these things I said not unto you at the beginning, forwhy I was with you.
[5] But now I go my way to him that sent me; and none of you asketh me, Whither goest thou?
[6] But forwhy I have said these things unto you, sorrow hath filled your heart.
[7] Nevertheless I tell you the truth; It is tharfly for you that I go away: for if I go not away, the Froverer will not come unto you; but if I wite, I will send him unto you.
[8] And when he is come, he will reprove the world of sin, and of rightsomeness, and of deeming:
[9] Of sin, forwhy they believe not on me;
[10] Of rightsomeness, forwhy I go to my Father, and ye see me no more;
[11] Of deeming, forwhy the atheling of this world is deemed.
[12] I have yet many things to say unto you, but ye cannot bear them now.
[13] Howbeit when he, the Ferth of truth, is come, he will guide you into all truth: for he shall not speak of himself; but whatsoever he shall hear, that shall he speak: and he will shew you things to come.
[14] He shall woulderen me: for he shall thidge of mine, and shall shew it unto you.
[15] All things that the Father hath are mine: therefore said I, that he shall take of mine, and shall shew it unto

you.

[16] A little while, and ye shall not see me: and again, a little while, and ye shall see me, forwhy I go to the Father.

[17] Then said some of his loreknights among themselves, What is this that he saith unto us, A little while, and ye shall not see me: and again, a little while, and ye shall see me: and, Forwhy I go to the Father?

[18] They said therefore, What is this that he saith, A little while? we cannot tell what he saith.

[19] Now Jesus knew that they were whishsome to ask him, and said unto them, Do ye inquire among yourselves of that I said, A little while, and ye shall not see me: and again, a little while, and ye shall see me?

[20] In sooth, in sooth, I say unto you, That ye shall weep and cwithe, but the world shall aglee: and ye shall be sorrowful, but your sorrow shall be whorve into mirth.

[21] A woman when she is in birthswink hath sorrow, forwhy her stound is come: but as soon as she is birthed off of the child, she muneth no more the arveth, for mirth that a man is born into the world.

[22] And ye now therefore have sorrow: but I will see you again, and your heart shall aglee, and your mirth no man taketh from you.

[23] And in that day ye shall ask me nothing. In sooth, in sooth, I say unto you, Whatsoever ye shall ask the Father in my name, he will give it you.

[24] Hitherto have ye asked nothing in my name: ask, and ye shall thidge, that your mirth may be full.

[25] These things have I spoken unto you in byspells: but the time cometh, when I shall no more speak unto you in byspells, but I shall shew you openly of the Father.

[26] At that day ye shall ask in my name: and I say not unto you, that I will abid the Father for you:

[27] For the Father himself loveth you, forwhy ye have loved me, and have believed that I came out from God.

[28] I came forth from the Father, and am come into the world: again, I leave the world, and go to the Father.

[29] His loreknights said unto him, Lo, now speakest thou openly, and speakest no likeningtale.

[30] Now are we sure that thou knowest all things, and needest not that any man should ask thee: by this we believe that thou camest forth from God.

[31] Jesus answered them, Do ye now believe?

[32] Behold, the stound cometh, yea, is now come, that ye shall be scattered, every man to his own, and shall leave me alone: and yet I am not alone, forwhy the Father is with me.

[33] These things I have spoken unto you, that in me ye might have frith. In the world ye shall have dretching: but be of good cheer; I have overcome the world.

John.17

[1] These words spake Jesus, and lifted up his eyes to heaven, and said, Father, the stound is come; woulderen thy Son, that thy Son also may woulderen thee:

[2] As thou hast given him wold over all flesh, that he should give alderlong life to as many as thou hast given him.

[3] And this is life alderlong, that they might know thee the only true God, and Jesus Christ, whom thou hast sent.

[4] I have woulderened thee on the earth: I have beended the work which thou gavest me to do.

[5] And now, O Father, woulderen thou me with thine own self with the woulder which I had with thee before the world was.

[6] I have swettled thy name unto the men which thou gavest me out of the world: thine they were, and thou gavest them me; and they have kept thy word.

[7] Now they have known that all things whatsoever thou hast given me are of thee.

[8] For I have given unto them the words which thou gavest me; and they have thidged them, and have known surely that I came out from thee, and they have believed that thou didst send me.

[9] I abid for them: I abid not for the world, but for them which thou hast given me; for they are thine.

[10] And all mine are thine, and thine are mine; and I am woulderened in them.

[11] And now I am no more in the world, but these are in the world, and I come to thee. Holy Father, keep through thine own name those whom thou hast given me, that they may be one, as we are.

[12] While I was with them in the world, I kept them in thy name: those that thou gavest me I have kept, and none of them is lost, but the son of evil; that the writ might be fulfilled.

[13] And now come I to thee; and these things I speak in the world, that they might have my mirth fulfilled in themselves.

[14] I have given them thy word; and the world hath hated them, forwhy they are not of the world, even as I am not of the world.

[15] I abid not that thou shouldest take them out of the world, but that thou shouldest keep them from the evil.

[16] They are not of the world, even as I am not of the world.

[17] Hallow them through thy truth: thy word is truth.

[18] As thou hast sent me into the world, even so have I also sent them into the world.

[19] And for their sakes I hallow myself, that they also might be hallowed through the truth.

[20] Neither abid I for these alone, but for them also which shall believe on me through their word;
[21] That they all may be one; as thou, Father, art in me, and I in thee, that they also may be one in us: that the world may believe that thou hast sent me.
[22] And the woulder which thou gavest me I have given them; that they may be one, even as we are one:
[23] I in them, and thou in me, that they may be made fullfremmed in one; and that the world may know that thou hast sent me, and hast loved them, as thou hast loved me.
[24] Father, I will that they also, whom thou hast given me, be with me where I am; that they may behold my woulder, which thou hast given me: for thou lovedst me before the statheling of the world.
[25] O rightsome Father, the world hath not known thee: but I have known thee, and these have known that thou hast sent me.
[26] And I have akithed unto them thy name, and will akithe it: that the love wherewith thou hast loved me may be in them, and I in them.

John.18

[1] When Jesus had spoken these words, he went forth with his loreknights over the brook Cedron, where was a worttown, into the which he went, and his loreknights.
[2] And Judas also, which forread him, knew the stead: for Jesus ofttimes woned thither with his loreknights.
[3] Judas then, having thidged a band of men and lawswinkerss from the alderpriests and Pharisees, cometh thither with lanterns and torches and weapons.
[4] Jesus therefore, knowing all things that should come upon him, went forth, and said unto them, Whom seek ye?
[5] They answered him, Jesus of Nazareth. Jesus saith unto them, I am he. And Judas also, which forread him, stood with them.
[6] As soon then as he had said unto them, I am he, they went backward, and fell to the ground.
[7] Then asked he them again, Whom seek ye? And they said, Jesus of Nazareth.
[8] Jesus answered, I have told you that I am he: if therefore ye seek me, let these go their way:
[9] That the saying might be fulfilled, which he spake, Of them which thou gavest me have I lost none.
[10] Then Simon Peter having a sword drew it, and smote the high priest's thane, and cut off his right ear. The thane's name was Malchus.
[11] Then said Jesus unto Peter, Put up thy sword into the sheath: the cup which my Father hath given me, shall I not drink it?
[12] Then the band and the captain and lawswinkerss of the Jews took Jesus, and bound him,
[13] And led him away to Annas first; for he was father in law to Caiaphas, which was the high priest that same year.
[14] Now Caiaphas was he, which gave rede to the Jews, that it was tharfly that one man should die for the theed.
[15] And Simon Peter followed Jesus, and so did another loreknight: that loreknight was known unto the high priest, and went in with Jesus into the thronestead of the high priest.
[16] But Peter stood at the door without. Then went out that other loreknight, which was known unto the high priest, and spake unto her that kept the door, and brought in Peter.
[17] Then saith the damsel that kept the door unto Peter, Art not thou also one of this man's loreknights? He saith, I am not.
[18] And the thanes and lawswinkerss stood there, who had made a fire of coals; for it was cold: and they warmed themselves: and Peter stood with them, and warmed himself.
[19] The high priest then asked Jesus of his loreknights, and of his loreword.
[20] Jesus answered him, I spake openly to the world; I ever taught in the worshipstead, and in the worshipstead, whither the Jews always go; and in dern have I said nothing.
[21] Why askest thou me? ask them which heard me, what I have said unto them: behold, they know what I said.
[22] And when he had thus spoken, one of the lawswinkerss which stood by struck Jesus with the palm of his hand, saying, Answerest thou the high priest so?
[23] Jesus answered him, If I have spoken evil, bear witness of the evil: but if well, why smitest thou me?
[24] Now Annas had sent him bound unto Caiaphas the high priest.
[25] And Simon Peter stood and warmed himself. They said therefore unto him, Art not thou also one of his loreknights? He andsook it, and said, I am not.
[26] One of the thanes of the high priest, being his kinsman whose ear Peter cut off, saith, Did not I see thee in the worttown with him?
[27] Peter then andsook again: and forthwith the cock crew.
[28] Then led they Jesus from Caiaphas unto the hall of deeming: and it was early; and they themselves went not into the deeminghall, lest they should be brosened; but that they might eat the eastersimble.
[29] Pilate then went out unto them, and said, What wraught bring ye against this man?
[30] They answered and said unto him, If he were not a wrongdoer, we would not have given him up unto thee.

[31] Then said Pilate unto them, Take ye him, and deem him by to your law. The Jews therefore said unto him, It is not lawful for us to put any man to death:
[32] That the saying of Jesus might be fulfilled, which he spake, ameaning what death he should die.
[33] Then Pilate went into the deeminghall again, and called Jesus, and said unto him, Art thou the King of the Jews?
[34] Jesus answered him, Sayest thou this thing of thyself, or did others tell it thee of me?
[35] Pilate answered, Am I a Jew? Thine own folkdom and the alderpriests have gave thee over unto me: what hast thou done?
[36] Jesus answered, My kingdom is not of this world: if my kingdom were of this world, then would my thanes fight, that I should not be given over to the Jews: but now is my kingdom not from hence.
[37] Pilate therefore said unto him, Art thou a king then? Jesus answered, Thou sayest that I am a king. To this end was I born, and for this cause came I into the world, that I should bear witness unto the truth. Every one that is of the truth heareth my steven.
[38] Pilate saith unto him, What is truth? And when he had said this, he went out again unto the Jews, and saith unto them, I find in him no guilt at all.
[39] But ye have a thew, that I should alet unto you one at the eastersimble: will ye therefore that I alet unto you the King of the Jews?
[40] Then yarmed they all again, saying, Not this man, but Barabbas. Now Barabbas was a robber.

John.19

[1] Then Pilate therefore took Jesus, and scourged him.
[2] And the heregomes platted a kinhelm of thorns, and put it on his head, and they put on him a purple robe,
[3] And said, Hail, King of the Jews! and they smote him with their hands.
[4] Pilate therefore went forth again, and saith unto them, Behold, I bring him forth to you, that ye may know that I find no guilt in him.
[5] Then came Jesus forth, wearing the kinhelm of thorns, and the purple robe. And Pilate saith unto them, Behold the man!
[6] When the alderpriests therefore and lawswinkerss saw him, they yarmed out, saying, Roodfasten him, roodfasten him. Pilate saith unto them, Take ye him, and roodfasten him: for I find no guilt in him.
[7] The Jews answered him, We have a law, and by our law he ought to die, forwhy he made himself the Son of God.
[8] When Pilate therefore heard that saying, he was the more afraid;
[9] And went again into the deeming hall, and saith unto Jesus, Whence art thou? But Jesus gave him no answer.
[10] Then saith Pilate unto him, Speakest thou not unto me? knowest thou not that I have wold to roodfasten thee, and have wold to alet thee?
[11] Jesus answered, Thou couldest have no wold at all against me, unless it were given thee from above: therefore he that gave me over unto thee hath the greater sin.
[12] And from thenceforth Pilate sought to alet him: but the Jews yarmed out, saying, If thou let this man go, thou art not Caesar's friend: whosoever maketh himself a king speaketh against Caesar.
[13] When Pilate therefore heard that saying, he brought Jesus forth, and sat down in the deemingseat in a stead that is called the Steening, but in the Hebrew, Gabbatha.
[14] And it was the reening of the eastersimble, and about the sixth stound: and he saith unto the Jews, Behold your King!
[15] But they yarmed out, Away with him, away with him, roodfasten him. Pilate saith unto them, Shall I roodfasten your King? The alderpriest answered, We have no king but Caesar.
[16] Then gave he him therefore unto them to be roodfastened. And they took Jesus, and led him away.
[17] And he bearing his rood went forth into a stead called the stead of a skull, which is called in the Hebrew Golgotha:
[18] Where they roodfastened him, and two other with him, on either side one, and Jesus in the midst.
[19] And Pilate wrote a title, and put it on the rood. And the writing was, JESUS OF NAZARETH THE KING OF THE JEWS.
[20] This title then read many of the Jews: for the stead where Jesus was roodfastened was nigh to the chester: and it was written in Hebrew, and Greek, and Latin.
[21] Then said the alderpriests of the Jews to Pilate, Write not, The King of the Jews; but that he said, I am King of the Jews.
[22] Pilate answered, What I have written I have written.
[23] Then the heregomes, when they had roodfastened Jesus, took his clothing, and made four parts, to every heregome a part; and also his coat: now the coat was without seam, woven from the top throughout.
[24] They said therefore among themselves, Let us not rend it, but cast lots for it, whose it shall be: that the writ might be fulfilled, which saith, They parted my clothing among them, and for my vesture they did cast lots. These things therefore the heregomes did.
[25] Now there stood by the rood of Jesus his mother, and his mother's sister, Mary the wife of Cleophas, and Mary Magdalene.
[26] When Jesus therefore saw his mother, and the

loreknight standing by, whom he loved, he saith unto his mother, Woman, behold thy son!
[27] Then saith he to the loreknight, Behold thy mother! And from that stound that loreknight took her unto his own home.
[28] After this, Jesus knowing that all things were now fullworked, that the writ might be fulfilled, saith, I thirst.
[29] Now there was set a vessel full of vinegar: and they filled a spunge with vinegar, and put it upon hyssop, and put it to his mouth.
[30] When Jesus therefore had thidged the vinegar, he said, It is beended: and he bowed his head, and gave up the ghost.
[31] The Jews therefore, forwhy it was the reening, that the bodies should not belive upon the rood on the sabbath day, (for that sabbath day was an high day,) besought Pilate that their legs might be broken, and that they might be taken away.
[32] Then came the heregomes, and brake the legs of the first, and of the other which was roodfastened with him.
[33] But when they came to Jesus, and saw that he was dead already, they brake not his legs:
[34] But one of the heregomes with a spear pierced his side, and forthwith came there out blood and water.
[35] And he that saw it bare rake, and his rake is true: and he knoweth that he saith true, that ye might believe.
[36] For these things were done, that the writ should be fulfilled, A bone of him shall not be broken.
[37] And again another writ saith, They shall look on him whom they pierced.
[38] And after this Joseph of Arimathaea, being a loreknight of Jesus, but dernly for fear of the Jews, besought Pilate that he might take away the body of Jesus: and Pilate gave him leave. He came therefore, and took the body of Jesus.
[39] And there came also Nicodemus, which at the first came to Jesus by night, and brought a mixture of myrrh and aloes, about an hundred pound weight.
[40] Then took they the body of Jesus, and wound it in linen clothes with the spices, as the kind of the Jews is to bury.
[41] Now in the stead where he was roodfastened there was a worttown; and in the worttown a new lichrest, wherein was never man yet laid.
[42] There laid they Jesus therefore forwhy of the Jews' reening day; for the lichrest was nigh at hand.

John.20

[1] The first day of the week cometh Mary Magdalene early, when it was yet dark, unto the lichrest, and seeth the stone taken away from the lichrest.
[2] Then she runneth, and cometh to Simon Peter, and to the other loreknight, whom Jesus loved, and saith unto them, They have taken away the Lord out of the lichrest, and we know not where they have laid him.
[3] Peter therefore went forth, and that other loreknight, and came to the lichrest.
[4] So they ran both together: and the other loreknight did outrun Peter, and came first to the lichrest.
[5] And he stooping down, and looking in, saw the linen clothes lying; yet went he not in.
[6] Then cometh Simon Peter following him, and went into the lichrest, and seeth the linen clothes lie,
[7] And the napkin, that was about his head, not lying with the linen clothes, but wrapped together in a stead by itself.
[8] Then went in also that other loreknight, which came first to the lichrest, and he saw, and believed.
[9] For as yet they knew not the writ, that he must rise again from the dead.
[10] Then the loreknights went away again unto their own home.
[11] But Mary stood without at the lichrest weeping: and as she wept, she stooped down, and looked into the lichrest,
[12] And seeth two woulderghosts in white sitting, the one at the head, and the other at the feet, where the body of Jesus had lain.
[13] And they say unto her, Woman, why weepest thou? She saith unto them, Forwhy they have taken away my Lord, and I know not where they have laid him.
[14] And when she had thus said, she whorve herself back, and saw Jesus standing, and knew not that it was Jesus.
[15] Jesus saith unto her, Woman, why weepest thou? whom seekest thou? She, supposing him to be the worttowner, saith unto him, Sir, if thou have borne him hence, tell me where thou hast laid him, and I will take him away.
[16] Jesus saith unto her, Mary. She whorve herself, and saith unto him, Rabboni; which is to say, Harr.
[17] Jesus saith unto her, Rine me not; for I am not yet stighed up to my Father: but go to my brethren, and say unto them, I astie unto my Father, and your Father; and to my God, and your God.
[18] Mary Magdalene came and told the loreknights that she had seen the Lord, and that he had spoken these things unto her.
[19] Then the same day at evening, being the first day of the week, when the doors were shut where the loreknights were gathered for fear of the Jews, came Jesus and stood in the midst, and saith unto them, Frith be unto you.
[20] And when he had so said, he shewed unto them

his hands and his side. Then were the loreknights glad, when they saw the Lord.

[21] Then said Jesus to them again, Frith be unto you: as my Father hath sent me, even so send I you.

[22] And when he had said this, he breathed on them, and saith unto them, Thidge ye the Holy Ghost:

[23] Whose soever sins ye forgive, they are forgiven unto them; and whose soever sins ye akeep, they are akept.

[24] But Thomas, one of the twelve, called Didymus, was not with them when Jesus came.

[25] The other loreknights therefore said unto him, We have seen the Lord. But he said unto them, Unless I shall see in his hands the print of the nails, and put my finger into the print of the nails, and thrust my hand into his side, I will not believe.

[26] And after eight days again his loreknights were within, and Thomas with them: then came Jesus, the doors being shut, and stood in the midst, and said, Frith be unto you.

[27] Then saith he to Thomas, reach hither thy finger, and behold my hands; and reach hither thy hand, and thrust it into my side: and be not faithless, but believing.

[28] And Thomas answered and said unto him, My Lord and my God.

[29] Jesus saith unto him, Thomas, forwhy thou hast seen me, thou hast believed: blessed are they that have not seen, and yet have believed.

[30] And many other tockens truly did Jesus in the atwist of his loreknights, which are not written in this book:

[31] But these are written, that ye might believe that Jesus is the Christ, the Son of God; and that believing ye might have life through his name.

John.21

[1] After these things Jesus shewed himself again to the loreknights at the sea of Tiberias; and on this wise shewed he himself.

[2] There were together Simon Peter, and Thomas called Didymus, and Nathanael of Cana in Galilee, and the sons of Zebedee, and two other of his loreknights.

[3] Simon Peter saith unto them, I go a fishing. They say unto him, We also go with thee. They went forth, and went into a ship forthwith; and that night they caught nothing.

[4] But when the morning was now come, Jesus stood on the shore: but the loreknights knew not that it was Jesus.

[5] Then Jesus saith unto them, Children, have ye any meat? They answered him, No.

[6] And he said unto them, Cast the net on the right side of the ship, and ye shall find. They cast therefore, and now they were not able to draw it for the dright of fishes.

[7] Therefore that loreknight whom Jesus loved saith unto Peter, It is the Lord. Now when Simon Peter heard that it was the Lord, he girt his fisher's coat unto him, (for he was naked,) and did cast himself into the sea.

[8] And the other loreknights came in a little ship; (for they were not far from land, but as it were two hundred cubits,) dragging the net with fishes.

[9] As soon then as they were come to land, they saw a fire of coals there, and fish laid thereon, and bread.

[10] Jesus saith unto them, Bring of the fish which ye have now caught.

[11] Simon Peter went up, and drew the net to land full of great fishes, and hundred and fifty and three: and for all there were so many, yet was not the net broken.

[12] Jesus saith unto them, Come and dine. And none of the loreknights durst ask him, Who art thou? knowing that it was the Lord.

[13] Jesus then cometh, and taketh bread, and giveth them, and fish likewise.

[14] This is now the third time that Jesus shewed himself to his loreknights, after that he was risen from the dead.

[15] So when they had dined, Jesus saith to Simon Peter, Simon, son of Jonas, lovest thou me more than these? He saith unto him, Yea, Lord; thou knowest that I love thee. He saith unto him, Feed my lambs.

[16] He saith to him again the twoth time, Simon, son of Jonas, lovest thou me? He saith unto him, Yea, Lord; thou knowest that I love thee. He saith unto him, Feed my sheep.

[17] He saith unto him the third time, Simon, son of Jonas, lovest thou me? Peter was grieved forwhy he said unto him the third time, Lovest thou me? And he said unto him, Lord, thou knowest all things; thou knowest that I love thee. Jesus saith unto him, Feed my sheep.

[18] In sooth, in sooth, I say unto thee, When thou wast young, thou girdedst thyself, and walkedst whither thou wouldest: but when thou shalt be old, thou shalt stretch forth thy hands, and another shall gird thee, and carry thee whither thou wouldest not.

[19] This spake he, ameaning by what death he should woulderen God. And when he had spoken this, he saith unto him, Follow me.

[20] Then Peter, wharving about, seeth the loreknight whom Jesus loved following; which also leaned on his breast at evenmeal, and said, Lord, which is he that forreadeth thee?

[21] Peter seeing him saith to Jesus, Lord, and what shall this man do?

[22] Jesus saith unto him, If I will that he tarry till I

come, what is that to thee? follow thou me.

[23] Then went this saying abroad among the brethren, that that loreknight should not die: yet Jesus said not unto him, He shall not die; but, If I will that he tarry till I come, what is that to thee?

[24] This is the loreknight which bears witness of these things, and wrote these things: and we know that his witness is true.

[25] And there are also many other things which Jesus did, the which, if they should be written every one, I ween that even the world itself could not inhold the books that should be written. Amen.

Wordbook

aban	"to summon, to proclaim"
abare	"to lay bare; to disclose"
abear	"to bear or behave"
abearing	"bearing; behavior"
abearingly	"bearable"
abeat	"to beat"
abid	"to ask for; to pray for"
abite	"to bite in pieces"
ablan	past tense of *ablin*
ablast	"to blast upon"
ablin	"to cease, to leave off; to desist"
ablinningness	"cessation"
ablend	"to make blind"
ablind	"to grow blind"
ablow	"to blow up"
ablun or ablunen	past participle of *ablin*
abow	"to bow, to bend"
abraid	"to move quickly, to spring up, to awake"
aburst	"to burst out"
abusy	"to busy, to occupy"
abusying	"occupation"
abuy	"to pay for; to atone for"
acarve	"to cut off"
accurse	"to put a curse on"
achen	strong past participle of *ache* (like shaken)
acknow	"to acknowledge"
acome	"to come to; to endure"
acomingly	"tolerable; possible"
acomingliness	"possiblity"
acraft	"to devise"
acrechurl	"a rustic, ploughman, farmer"
acreman	"a farmer"
acremeal	"acre by acre; by acres"
acretining	"an acre's fencing or enclosure"
acresplot	"an acre"
acunning	"experience, trial"
adaw	"to dawn; to awake"
aday	"at day"
adays	"at day"
addle	"mud, dirt, filthy place"
addleseath	"sewer, sink"
adead	"to deaden"
adeal	"to deal out, to divide"
adeave	"to deafen"
adelve	"to delve"
adight	"to ordain, to dispose"
ado	"to do away"
adown	"down; downwards"
adread	"to dread"
adreadingly	"terrible"
adreeze	"to fall to pieces, to decline, to vanish, to fail"
adrive	"to drive away"
adrorn	past participle of *adreeze*
adroze	past tense of *adreeze*
adumb	"to become dumb"
afall	"to fall down"
afand	"to prove"
afandingly	"proveable"
afasten	"to make firm"
afastlo	"certainly!"
afear	"to frighten"
afeed	"to feed"
afile	"to make foul, to befoul"
afleam	"to put to flight"
afleshness	"incarnation"
afore	"before"
aforn	"before"
afoul	"to become foul"
Africanish	"African"
afright	"to be frightened"
aft	"from behind"
aftercomer	"later comer"
afterdeal	"disadvantage"
aftereld	"advanced age"
afterend	"latter end"
afterfollow	"follow after"
afterfollower	"follower"
afterfollowingness	"succession"
aftmost	"last, hindmost"
aftward	"behind"
againchar	"return"
againcome	"return"
againflowing	"flowing back and forth"
againfold	"to fold or roll back"
againrising	"resurrection"
againward	"going back"
againwardly	"adversative"
agame	"in jest"
aghast	"to terrify"
agin	"to begin"

aginningly	"inchoative"	alderly	"chief, authoritative"
agive	"to give up or back"	aldermost	"most of all"
ago	"to go away"	aldernext	"next of all"
agone	"gone away; ago"	aldership	"seniority, headship"
agrief	"in grief"	alderthane	"chief thane"
agrise	"to be afraid"	alderwisest	"wisest of all"
agrisen	past participle of *agrise*	alderworst	"worst of all"
agrose	past tense of *agrise*	aleam	"to illumine"
aguilt	"to be in fault"	aleave	"to allow"
aheight	"aloft"	alecleave	"ale-cellar"
ahigh	"on high"	aleese	"to release or redeem"
aise	"awe; terror"	aleesend	"releaser, redeemer"
aise	"to frighten"	aleesedness	"release, redemption"
aiseful	"fearful"	aleeseness	"release, redemption"
aisely	"terrible"	aleesing	"release, redemption"
aising	"terror"	alength	"at full length; lengthwise"
aith	"harrow"	alight	"to enlighten"
aith	"to harrow"	alighting	"illumination"
aither	"harrower"	alikeness	"image; statue"
aiwhat	"anything"	alimp	"to happen"
aiwhere	"everywhere"	allbeliefly	"universally believed; catholic"
aiwhence	"from all parts, everywhere"	allgodweb	"allsilk-cloth"
aiwhich	"each, every"	allgodwebben	"allsilken"
aiwhither	"in all direction"	allkin	"of every kind"
aiwho	"each one, everyone"	allkind	"of every kind"
aiwhose	"altogether, in every way, entirely"	allmight	"omnipotence"
aken	"to bring forth"	alls	"entirely"
aakennend	"parent"	allskins	"of every kind"
akenning	"birth"	allutterly	"entirely"
akenningly	"native"	allwoldend	"allruling-one; God"
akithe	"to show or reveal; to declare"	ally	"of all, universal; catholic"
alame	"to grow lame"	amar	"to mar"
alder	"chief; life, age"	ambight	"service; servant"
alder-	"of all"	ambightthane	"servant"
alderapostle	"chief apostle"	amorrow	"in the morning"
alderbane	"life-destroyer"	andet	"to confess"
alderbest	"best of all"	anether	"to lower; to humiliate"
alderbishop	"archbishop"	anew	"to renew"
alderbold	"palace, mansion"	anfang	"acceptance"
alderborough	"metropolis"	anget	"intellect"
aldercare	"great sorrow"	angetful	"intelligent"
alderdevil	"archdevil"	angetness	"understanding"
alderdom	"power, authority"	angin	"beginning"
alderfairest	"fairest of all"	angmoodness	"sorrow"
alderfirst	"first of all"	angsome	"hard"
alderfrea	"lord, chief"	angsomeness	"hardship, anxiety"
alderlast	"last of all"	anight	"at night"
alderleast	"least of all"	anlit	"face"
alderless	"lordless; lifeless"	anon	"at once"
alderliefest	"dearest of all"	anonrights	"immediatly"
alderliness	"authority"	anseen	"face"
alderlong	"lifelong, eternal"	anward	"present"

anwardness	"presence"	arveth	"difficulty"
appleber	"applebearing"	arvethfind	"difficult to find"
appled	"round like an apple"	arvethheld	"difficult to hold"
applehoard	"stock of apples"	arvethtell	"difficult to count"
applekin	"kind of apple"	arvethwin	"difficult to win"
appletown	"pomarium"	asake	"to deny, to renounce"
aqueal	"to die, to perish"	asear	"to grow sear"
aqueath	"to say or speak out; to resound"	aseek	"to seek out"
aquell	"to kill"	aseekingly	"seekable"
aquench	"to quench"	asench	"to make sink"
aquern	"squirrel"	aset	"to set, to appoint"
aquetch	"to make move or shake; to move or shake"	ashame	"to feel shame"
aquick	"to quicken, to become alive"	ashbore	"spearbearer"
aquine	"to diminish"	ashearingly	"disjunctive"
aquinen	past participle of *aquine*	ashort	"to become short"
aquink	"to vanish, to be extinguished or eclipsed"	ashun	"to shun"
aquone	past tense of *aquine*	asilk	"to slacken"
Arabish	"Arabian"	asink	"to sink down"
ard	"region"	asker	"questioner; plaintiff"
ard	"to dwell"	aslake	"to become slack"
ardfast	"settled, abiding"	aslakingly	"remissive"
ardingly	"habitable"	aspring	"to spring up"
ardingstow	"dwelling-place"	astel	"bookmark"
aread	"to stipulate; to interpret"	astell	"to set, to establish"
areadness	"stipulation"	astench	"to annoy with stench"
arear	"to rear up"	astie	"to go; to ascend" (other spelling *asty, astigh*)
ared	"to save"	astien	past participle of *astie*
aredding	"salvation"	astir	"to stir up"
aright	"rightly"	astirring	"motion"
arime	"to count"	astoe	past tense of *astie*
arine	"to touch"	astretch	"to stretch out"
arinen	past participle of *arine*	asty	"to go; to ascend" (other spelling *astie*)
arist	"resurrection"	astying	"ascension"
aristhight	"hope of resurrection"	asunder	"to seperate"
arm	"poor"	asundering	"division"
armbye	"bracelet"	aswelt	"to faint, to die"
armedder	"brachial vein"	aswike	"to abandon, to betray, to decieve"
armgreat	"as thick as an arm"	atbe	"to be present"
armheart	"tender-hearted"	atbraid	"to take away"
armheartness	"compassion"	atbraidingly	"ablative"
arming	"poor person; wretch"	ateke	"addition"
armshank	"armbone"	atell	"to tell, to narrate"
armstrong	"strong of arm"	atend	"to set on fire; to kindle"
armswith	"strong of arm"	atew	"to reveal"
armth	"poverty"	atewingly	"indicative"
arn	"building" (other spelling *ern*)	atewness	"revelation"
arood	"on the rood"	atfang	"to seize at"
arone	past tense of *arine*	atflee	"to flee away"
arow	"in a row"	atfore	"before"
arseling or arselings	"backwards"	atgather	"together"
arsetharm	"the lower bowel"	athel	"noble"
arsethirl	"arse-passage; anus"	athel	"to dignify, to honour"

athelkind	"nobleborn"	aweed	"to rave, to be mad"
athelkindness	"nobleness"	aweigh	"to bear up"
atheling	"prince"	awield	"to govern"
Athenish	"Athenian"	awend	"to turn; to change; to translate"
athester	"to become dark"	awendingly	"changeable"
athind	"behind"	awendingliness	"changeableness"
athink	"to displease"	awhape	"to strike, to confound"
athirst	"to suffer from thirst"	awhaped	"amazed"
athold	"to retain"	awheen	"to vex"
athreet	"to tire"	awoo	"to woo"
athrism	"to suffocate"	awork	"at work"
atight	"to entice"	awough	"crookedly"
atire	"to become exhausted"	awrite	"to write down"
atiringly	"exhaustable"	awrothe	"to become wroth"
atlout	"to hide oneself"	axle	"shoulder"
atnext	"at last"	axlecloth	"scapular"
atreach	"to reach at; to snatch away"	axlispann	"place where the two beams of a cross intersect"
atread	"to advise"	axlistall	"shoulder-companion"
atright	"right at hand"		
atrights	"almost, nearly"	backling or backlings	"backwards"
atrin	"touch"	backslittle	"backbiting"
atrine	"to touch at"	backtharm	"rectum"
atrinen	past participle of *atrine*	backtharms	"entrails"
atrone	past tense of *atrine*	baft	"behind"
atsake	"to to deny, to renounce"	bain	"both"
atsparn	strong past tense of *atspurn*	bairn	"child"
atspornen	strong past participle of *atspurn*	bairneak	"pregnant"
atspring	"to spring up"	bairnhood	"childhood"
atspurn	"to dash the foot against"	bairnteam	"offspring, brood of children"
atstand	"to stand at hand"	bakemeat	"pie; baked food"
atstart	"to start away"	baken	strong past participle of bake (like shaken)
atter	"poison'	bakern	"bakery"
atter	"to poison"	balecraft	"baleful art"
atterber	"poisionous"	balefight	"deadly fight"
attercop	"spider"	baleless	"harmless"
attercraft	"skill of poisoning"	balespel	"baleful discourse"
atterly	"poisonous"	ball	strong past tense of bell
attern	"poisonous"	ballock	"testicle"
attery	"poisonous"	ballockcod	"scrotum"
attle	"terrible"	barker	"watchdog"
atwain	"in two; asunder"	barm	"lap; bosom"
atween	"between"	barmcloth	"apron"
atwist	"presence"	barn	strong past tense of burn
atwite	"to reproach"	barnet	"a burning; arson"
atwitten	past participle of *atwite*	barrow	"to protect"
atwixt	"betwixt, among"	barrow	"hill; mound; burial mound"
atwo	"in two"	barst	strong past tense of burst (other spelling brast)
atwote	past tense of *atwite*	basten	"of bast"
aught	"anything"	batharn	"bathhouse"
awaycome	"to come away"	bathvat	"bathtub"
awaygo	"to go away"	baxter	"(female) baker"
awayward	"going away"	bead	"prayer"

beadhouse	"house of prayer"	beem	"trumpet"
beadman	"worshipper"	beemother	"queen-bee"
beadred	"prayer; intercession"	been	"prayer; request"
beanbellies	"beanpods"	beenripe	"service to a landowner at harvest time"
beanen	"of beans"	beership	"feast"
beankin	"a kind of bean"	beentide	"prayer-time"
bearend	"bearing-one; bearer"	beet	"boast"
bearfell	"bearskin"	beet	"to amend"
bearling	"young bear"	beeting	"amendment"
beathe	"to warm"	beetingness	"amendment"
bebathe	"to bathe, to wash"	beetly	"boastful"
bebiddingly	"imperative"	beetness	"reparation"
bebled	"covered in blood"	be-ew	"to join in marriage; to marry"
bebleed	"to cover with blood"	befang	"to envelope"
bebloody	"to make bloody"	befast	"to fasten; to establish; to entrust to"
bebode	"commandment"	befasten	"to fasten; to establish; to entrust to"
bebodeday	"aset day"	befathom	"to surround"
bebodered	"command, authority"	befold	"to envelope"
beburiedness	"burial"	befoot	"to cut off one's feet"
bebury	"to bury"	beforecome	"to come before"
beburying	"burial"	beforegird	"to gird before"
bechar	"to mislead"	beforego	"to go before"
becheap	"to bargain; to sell; to buy"	beforegoer	"forerunner"
bechide	"to chide about"	beforeknow	"to foreknow"
bechirm	"to scream at"	beforerunner	"forerunner"
beckoningly	"indicative; allegorical"	beforesee	"to foresee"
becleam	"to plaster over with"	beforesend	"to send before"
beclip	"to embrace"	beforeset	"to set before"
bedbolster	"bolster, pillow"	beforespeaker	"spokesman"
bedbower	"bedchamber"	beforespeaking	"preface"
bedark	"to darken"	beforestretch	"to hold out"
bedaw	"to dawn upon"	beforewalling	"the outwork"
bedelve	"to dig about"	beforewarn	"to warn before"
bedern	"to conceal"	befrine	"to question, to learn"
bedfere	"bedfellow"	begale	"to sing incantations over"
bedidder	"to delude"	begang	"a going about"
bedight	"to adorn"	bego	"to go about something; to surround"
bedit	"to shut"	begone	"surrounded"
bedolven	"buried"	begrave	"to bury"
bedreaf	"bedclothes"	begrow	"to grow around"
bedrench	"to soak"	begster	"(female) beggar"
bedship	"cohabitation"	behang	"to hang around"
bedthane	"bedservant"	behem	"to hem around"
beeast	"to the east of"	behence	"on this side of"
beeastnorth	"to the northeast of"	behest	"a promise; a command"
beeastsouth	"to the southeast of"	behest	"to promise"
beech	"books"	behew	"to chop"
beechen	"of beech"	behide	"to conceal"
beed	"table"	behie	"to make haste"
beedarn	"table-room"	beholden	past participle of behold
beedreaf	"tablecloth"	beholdend	"beholder"
beedvat	"table-cup"	beholdness	"observation"

behorrow	"to defile"	berueness	"comiseration"
behote	"promise"	besee	"to see upon"
behote	"to promise"	beseen	"seen; appearing; clad"
behoteland	"promised land"	besench	"to submerge"
behoter	"promiser"	beshine	"to shine upon"
behow	"to observe clearly"	beshite	"to befoul with excrement"
behue	"to dissimilate"	beshitten	past participle of beshite
beknow	"to known about; to acknowledge"	beshote	past tense of beshote
beknowing	"knowledge"	beshrew	"to put a curse upon"
beknowledge	"to acknowledge"	besmite	"to defile"
belaugh	"to laugh at"	besmoke	"to blacken with smoke"
belew	"to betray"	besoken	"request"
belewing	"betrayal"	besouth	"to the south of"
beliefiest	"lack of belief"	bespringe	"besprinkle"
beliefly	"credible"	bestalk	"to move stealthly"
beliefsome	"faithful"	bestand	"to stand by"
belight	"to illumine"	besweat	"to cover with sweat"
belike	"probably; perhaps"	beswicken	past participle of beswike
belimb	"to dismember"	beswike	"to deceive"
belimp	"event"	beswiker	"deceiver"
belimp	"to befall; to appertain to"	beswiking	"deception"
belirt	"to deceive"	beswoke	past tense of beswike
belive	"livelihood, means of living"	bet	"better"
belive	"to remain"	bethinking	"meditation"
belive	"quickly"	betiding	"occurance"
bell	"to bellow"	betield	"to cover"
bellringster	"(female) bellringer"	betimber	"to construct"
belode	"to excuse"	betime	"to happen"
beloding	"apology"	betimes	"at a good time"
belodingly	"apologetic"	betine	"to hedge in"
belook	"to behold"	betining	"conclusion"
belove	"to love, to delight in"	betread	"to tread over"
bemaze	"to confuse"	betrend	"to encircle"
bemoan	"a complaint"	betwixt	"between; among"
bemole	"to soil, to sully with moles/spots"	betwixtsend	"to send between"
bemong	"among"	bewall	"to surround with a wall"
ben	"wound"	bewallow	"to wallow about"
benake	"to lay bare"	bewed	"to betroth"
benim	"to take away; to deprive of"	beweddingly	"relating to marriage"
benorth	"to the north of"	beweep	"bewail"
bent	"grassy slope"	beweepingly	"lamentable"
bepeach	"to deceive"	bewend	"to turn away or around"
berain	"to rain upon"	bewest	"to the west of"
bere	"barley"	bewield	"to wholly control oneself"
berecroft	"barley-field"	bewimple	"to cover with a wimple"
bereleap	"a basket for barley"	bewind	"to envelope"
beren	"of barley"	bewindle	"hedge, border"
beride	"to ride around; to overtake"	bewist	"being, living"
berine	"to touch"	bewray	"to reveal, to accuse"
berise	"to befit, to become"	bield	"boldness; a shelter"
bern	"man"	bigh	"a bend; corner; curve"
berue	"to repent, to comiserate"	bigh	"to bend"

bighingly	"flexible"	boardcloth	"tablecloth"
bight	"a bend"	boardfellow	"companion"
bin	"within"	boardknife	"tableknife"
bine	"cultivated; inhabited"	boardless	"without a table"
bir	"to pertain to"	boardwall	"phalanx"
birl	"cupbearer"	bode	"messenger"
birl	"to act as cupbearer; to pour out drink"	bode	"command; message"
birthbold	"ancestral mansion"	bodeship	"command"
birther	"child-bearing"	bodeword	"commandment-word"
birththinen	"midwife"	boding	"announcement; preaching"
birthtide	"nativity"	bodingday	"Annunciation day"
bisen	"example"	bold	"house"
bismer	"disgrace"	bolder	"prince"
bismer	"to mock"	boldhood	"boldness"
bisson	"blind"	book	strong past tense of bake (like shook)
bitmeal	"bit by bit"	bookcraft	"book-learning"
bive	"to tremble"	bookcrafty	"booklearned"
blackhorn	"inkhorn"	booker	"scholar, scribe, writer"
blan	past tense of blin	bookfodder	"bookcase"
blead	"a blast; an inspiration"	bookhouse	"library"
bleat	"wretched"	bookspel	"tale in a book"
blee	"colour"	bookstaff	"letter"
bleeboard	"coloured board"	bootday	"day of atonement"
bleefow	"variagated"	booten	"to make or become better"
bleesteening	"tessellated pavement"	bootener	"healer"
blessedhood	"blessedness"	bootening	"amendment"
blicken	past participle of blike	bon	"cup"
blike	"to shine"	bondhood	"servitude"
blin	"cessation"	bondship	"condition of a bondman"
blin	"to cease"	bonen	"made of bone"
blindfell	"to strike blind"	bork	strong past tense of bark
blinness	"cessation"	borken	strong past participle of bark
blissfulhood	"blissfulness"	boroughfolk	"townfolk"
blissingly	"exulting"	boroughknave	"townlad"
blissy	"joyful"	boroughman	"townsman"
blitheheart	"happy"	boroughmoot	"townmeeting"
blithemood	"of cheerful mood"	boroughreeve	"townreeve"
bloke	past participle of blike	boroughtown	"fortified town"
blooddollow	"bloody wound"	boroughwall	"townwall"
blooded	"stained with blood"	boroughware	"borough-citizens"
blooden	"of blood"	borsten	strong past participle of burst
bloodfow	"blood-stained"	bosomy	"sinuous"
bloodiron	"lancet, fleam"	bote	strong past tense of bite (like wrote)
bloodsax	"lancet"	boughtling	"one ransomed"
bloodwite	"fine for blood shedding"	boul	"bracelet; necklace; brooch"
bloodwreaker	"avenger of blood"	bour	"freeholder of the lowest class, peasant, farmer"
bloot	"sacrifice"	bout	"without"
blooter	"sacrificer"	bove	"above"
blootmonth	"November"	bow	"to dwell; to inhabit"
blow	"to blossom"	bowerknight	"chamberlain"
blowingly	"blooming"	bowerthane	"page; chamberlain"
blun or blunen	past participle of blin	bowfodder	"case for the bow"

brake	a past tense of break.	bye	"ring"
brant	"steep"	bylive	"life-nourishment"
brast	strong past tense of burst (other spelling barst)	byname	"pronoun"
breadleap	"breadbasket"	byspell	"proverb"
breastthank	"mind"	byspellbook	"book of proverbs"
breem	"wouldersome"	bytale	"parable"
breem	"to glorify"	bywist	"sustenance"
breird	"to incite"	byword	"proverb; adverb"
breirdness	"incitement"	cale	"to be or become cold"
brem	"to roar"	calen	past participle of cale
bremming	"roaring"	camp	"battle"
brerd	"brim"	camp	"to strive, to fight"
brerdful	"brimful"	campalder	"commander"
brewern	"brew-house"	campdom	"military service, warfare"
bridegift	"giving in marriage"	camphood	"warfare"
brideleeth	"epithalamium"	campifere	"fellow soldier"
bridesong	"epithalamium"	camply	"military"
bridething	"nuptials"	campred	"war, warfare"
bridgeboot	"repairing or restoration of a bridge"	campstead	"battlefield"
bridgeward	"bridgekeeper"	can	"cognizance"
bridlethongs	"reins"	candlebore	"acolyte"
brim	"sea"	candlesnittles	"candlesnuffers"
brimfowl	"seabird"	char	"a turn"
Britland	"Britain"	char	"to turn"
britten	"to distribute"	cheap	"to bargain, to buy or sell"
brittening	"distribution"	cheaping	"act of buying, market"
brittlehood	"frailty"	cheapingbooth	"marketbooth"
brokebacked	"hunchback"	cheapingtown	"markettown"
brokefooted	"broken footed"	cheast	"strife"
brokelegged	"broken legged"	cheastful	"contentious"
brokeshanked	"broken legged"	cheeseleap	"cheesebasket"
brookingly	"serviceable"	cheesestitch	"peice of cheese"
brord	"point"	cheesewright	"cheesemaker"
brosen	"to crumble; to decay"	chessil	"gravel"
broseningly	"corruptable"	chessilber	"gravelly"
brotherred	"fellowship"	chessilly	"gravelly"
brothersib	"kinship of brothers"	chester	"fort; city"
brotherson	"brother's son"	chesterware	"citizens"
brow	strong past tense of brew	chide	"strife"
brown	strong past participle of brew	chidester	"(female) a scold"
bud	"beetle"	chigh	"to call"
burien	"burying-place; grave"	chigher	"one that calls"
burielsong	"dirge"	chighing	"a calling"
burl	"trunk"	chighingly	"vocative"
burn	"stream; spring"	child	"to bring forth (children)"
burnen	strong past participle of burn	childly	"child-like"
burst	"calamity"	childyoung	"youthful"
bursty	"broken"	childyouth	"childhood"
burthen	"burden"	chillicle	"icicle"
busihood	"busy condition"	chine	"to crack"
busiship	"business"	chinen	past participle of chine
busy	"labour; occupation"	chining	"gaping; open"

chirm	"outcry"	cost	"option; choice, quality, manner"
chone	past tense of chine	cost	"to tempt"
churchboot	"repair of church"	costen	"to try, to tempt"
churchgang	"churchgoing"	costening	"temptation"
churchgrith	"church-peace"	costing	"temptation"
churchhood	"an order or role of the church"	cothe	"disease; sickness"
churchreaf	"robbery of churches"	cothey	"diseased"
churchsoken	"congregation"	couth	"known"
churchthane	"minister of a church"	couthledge	"to make known"
churchthaning	"churchservice"	couthledging	"aquaintance"
churchware	"congregation"	couthly	"familiar"
churchweed	"church-vestament"	couthman	"aquaintance"
churchyearn	"eager to go to church"	couthname	"surname"
churlborn	"lowborn"	couthness	"familiarity; knowledge"
clamb	strong past tense of climb (other spelling clomb)	couthred	"familiarity"
clayen	"made of clay"	covegods	"household gods"
cleam	"to smear"	cowmig	"cow urine"
cleanheart	"pure in heart"	cradlebairn	"child in a cradle"
cleanship	"purity"	craftful	"crafty"
cleep	"to call"	craftly	"technical"
cleeping	"a calling; a crying"	craftspeech	"technical speech"
cleepingly	"vocalic; vocative"	crew	strong past tense of crow
clin	"to resound"	cram	past tense of crim (like swam)
clip	"to embrace"	crang	past tense of cring (like sang)
clipping	"act of embracing"	crim	"to cram"
clipple	"vocalic"	cring	"to fall in defeat"
cliver	"claw"	croft	"field"
cloam	"mud; paste; mortar"	crope	strong past tense of creep
clomb	strong past tense of climb (other spelling clamb)	cropen	strong past participle of creep
clomben	strong past participle of climb (other spelling clumben)	crown	strong past participle of crow
cloudy	"rocky"	crum	past participle of crim (like swum)
clumben	strong past participle of climb (other spelling clomben)	crump	"crooked"
coaf	"eager"	crung	past participle of cring (like sung)
coafship	"eagerness"	cumble	"banner"
coalmouse	"titmouse"	cursedhood	"cursedness"
coalswart	"coal-black"	dalk	"bracelet, brooch, pin"
cod	"bag; a husk or pod; the scrotum"	dalve	strong past tense of delve
coker	"quiver"	dare	"injury"
come	"a comer, a stranger"	darf	"bold"
comelihood	"comeliness"	darfship	"boldness"
comeling	"stranger"	darkful	"teneberous"
comelithe	"hospitable"	darkhood	"obscurity"
cool	past tense of cale	darkling	"in the dark"
corn	"chosen"	darve	"to labour" (other spelling derve)
cornness	"choice; election"	daven	"to befit"
cornship	"election"	daw	"to dawn"
cornhouse	"granary"	dawing	"dawn"
corther	"troop"	daws	"days"
corve	strong past tense of carve	daygang	"a day's going"
corvel	"to mince"	daymeal	"horologue"
corven	strong past participle of carve	daymealspile	"gnomon of a dial"
cosp	"fetter; bond"	dayred	"day-break; dawn"

dayrim	"the edge of dawn"	dighter	"disposer, guider"
daytide	"daytime"	dishthane	"table servant"
daywork	"work of a day"	dism	"vapour"
daywhomly	"daily"	dit	"to shut"
daywist	"food, meal"	dith	"fuel; tinder"
dead	"to become or make dead"	dizzidom	"folly"
dealend	"divider; participator, partner"	dizziship	"folly"
dealmeal	"part by part"	doleland	"land under joint ownership"
dealnimmend	"sharer, participator"	dollow	"wound"
dealnimming	"participation"	dollow	"to wound"
dean	"valley"	dollowboot	"compensation for wound"
dearworth	"precious"	dollowsalve	"salve for a wound"
deathshildy	"worthy of death"	dolven	strong past participle of delve
deathshildiness	"worthiness of death"	dook	"bastard"
deedbeet	"to make amends for"	dookinchel	"little bastard"
deedbeeter	"a penitent"	doombook	"code of laws"
deedboot	"atonement, repetence"	doomer	"judge"
deedkeen	"keen with deeds"	doomern	"judgement-house; court"
deedly	"active"	doomfast	"just"
deem	"judge"	doomhouse	"judgement-house; court"
deemend	"judge"	doomly	"of judgement"
deemer	"judge"	doomsettle	"judgement-seat"
deeming	"judgement"	doomsman	"judge"
deemster	"(female) judge; dempster"	doomstool	"judgement seat"
deepthankle	"deeply contemplative"	doorthane	"door-servant"
deeren	"of deer"	doorthinen	"female door-servant"
deerfellen	"made of fells (skins)"	doorward	"doorkeeper"
deernet	"hunting-net"	dorve	past tense of darve
deeve	"befitting"	dorven	past participle of darve
deeveness	"agreeableness"	doughtihood	"bravery"
delf	"excavation"	douth	"nobles"
delver	"excavater"	douthking	"prince"
dem	"injury"	douthknight	"retainer"
derf	"hard work"	douthman	"retainer"
derfsome	"troublesome"	down	"mountain or hill"
dern	"hidden"	downelf	"mountainelf"
dern	"to keep secret"	downlandish	"mountainous"
dernlie	"to fornicate"	downly	"of a mountain"
dernship	"privity"	downshraff	"mountaincave"
dernwrit	"apocryphal writing"	drake	"dragon"
derve	"to labour" (other spelling darve)	drape	past tense of dreep (other spelling drope)
devilhood	"nature of the devil"	drast	"dregs"
devilcraft	"witchcraft"	drasty	"full of dregs; crude; filthy"
devilsick	"possessed by devil(s)"	draught	"lifestyle"
devilyield	"devilworship; idoltry"	draughten	"to behave"
dey	"(woman) breadmaker"	dreadless	"fearless"
didder	"to delude"	dready	"timid"
diddering	"delusion"	dreamcraft	"skill at music"
dight	"to arrange"	dreamly	"joyous"
dight	"arrangement"	dreamreader	"interpreter of dreams"
dightend	"disposer, guider"	drear	"blood"
dightener	"steward, dispensater"	drear	"dreary"

drearfow	"bloodstained"	dun	"to darken; to become dun"
drearied	"saddened"	durstledge	"to dare"
drearihood	"sorrow"	durstledge	"courage; daring"
drearileer	"dreary-faced"	dursty	"daring"
drearimood	"dreary-mooded"	durstiness	"boldness"
dree	"to lead a life"	dusk	"to darken"
dreeledge	"to put in order; regulate"	duskness	"darkness"
dreep	"to slay"	dwale	"sleeping-potion"
dreeve	"to disturb"	dwease	"stupid"
dreevedness	"disturbance; confusion"	dwild	"error"
dreeveness	"disturbance; confusion"	dwildafterfollowing	"heresy"
dreever	"disturber"	dwildman	"heretic"
dreeze	"to fall"	dwimmer	"phantom; ghost; illusion"
dreezingly	"perishable"	dwimmercraft	"magic art"
drench	"a drink; a potion"	dwimmerlock	"magic play"
drenchcup	"drinking-cup"	dwimmerly	"illusory"
drenchflood	"deluge"	dwine	"to dwindle"
dret	"to consume"	dwinen	past participle of dwine
dretch	"to vex"	dwone	past tense of dwine
dretchedness	"hardship"	dwole	"error; heresy"
dretching	"tribulation"	dwoleman	"a person that is in the wrong; heretic"
dright	"multitude; retinue, host"	dwolesome	"erroneous; heretic; misleading"
drighten	"lord"	dwoling	"delusion"
drightfare	"retinue"	dwolm	"chaos"
drightfolk	"dependants"	dwoly	"foolish"
drightful	"wouldersome"	dyester	"(female) one who dyes"
drightly	"lordly, noble"	ea	"water; river"
drightman	"vassal"	eabridge	"bridge over a river"
drightness	"majesty"	eafrog	"waterfrog"
drightship	"lordship"	eal	"to burn"
drite	"to defecate"	ealy	"of a river"
dritten	past participle of drite	eam	"uncle"
droof	"dirty"	earcleansend	"the little finger"
droove	"to trouble"	earfinger	"the little finger"
droovy	"troubled"	earpreen	"earring"
drope	past tense of dreep (other spelling drape)	earthapple	"cucumber"
dropen	past participle of dreep	earthchine	"cleft in the earth"
dropfow	"covered in drops"	earthcraft	"geometry"
dropmeal	"drop by drop"	earthdin	"earthquake"
drorn	past participle of dreeze	earthfast	"fixed in the earth"
drornly	"perishable"	earthhouse	"cave-dwelling"
drote	past tense of drite	earthirl	"ear-passage"
drough	"to dry up"	earthivy	"ground-ivy"
droze	past tense of dreeze (like froze)	earthkenned	"earth-born"
drunken	"to be drunk; to get drunk"	earthkind	"earthly"
drunkenhood	"drunkenness"	earthrich	"earthly kingdom""
drunkenlew	"habitually drunk"	earthshraff	"earth-cave"
drunkenship	"drunkenness"	earthstirring	"earthquake"
drunkensome	"given to drink"	earthtilth	"agriculture"
dullship	"folly"	earthware	"earthdwellers"
dullwillen	"rash"	earthwassom	"earthfruit"
dullyelp	"dull boast"	eason	"slave"

Eastermonth	"April"	edquick	"to requicken, to revive"
Eastersimble	"Passover"	edquid	"relation, narrative"
eastright	"due east"	edshaft	"a new creation"
eastsouthlong	"from east to south"	edsight	"a relooking, respect"
eath	"easy"	edspelling	"recapitulation"
eathbeet	"easy to amend"	edstathel	"to reestablish"
eathfall	"easy to overcome"	edwend	"to return"
eathfeel	"easily felt"	edwhirft	"a change back, a reverse"
eathfind	"easy to find""	edwite	"reproach"
eathlear	"easy to teach"	edwite	"to reproach"
eathleech	"easy to cure"	edyield	"reypayment"
eathly	"easy"	edyield	"to repay"
eathmeed	"to humble"	edyieldend	"remunerator"
eathmeed	"humbleness"	edyoung	"being or becoming young again"
eathmood	"humble"	eft	"again"
eathmoodness	"humbleness"	eftarise	"to arise again"
eathmoody	"humble"	eftarist	"resurrection"
eathness	"easiness"	eftboot	"restoration to health"
eathseen	"easily seen"	eftcome	"to return"
eathwin	"easy to win"	eftflow	"to flow back"
eathyearn	"easy to please"	eftgiveness	"remission"
eatly	"eatable"	eftlooking	"a relooking; respect"
eaves	"to clip the edges"	eftnewing	"restoration"
eech	"eternal"	eftsit	"to reside"
eechly	"eternal"	eftsoon	"soon again"
eechness	"eternity"	eftsoons	"soon again"
ed	"riches"	eighthurned	"eight-cornered"
edchigh	"to recall"	eke	"also"
edder	"enclosure"	eke	"addition"
edder	"artery"	ekename	"nickname"
eddersax	"lancet"	eld	"(old) age"
eddish	"park; enclosed pasture"	eld	"to delay, to put off"
eddishhen	"quail"	elding	"delay, tarrying"
eddishward	"park-keeper"	eldingly	"dilatory"
eddiness	"happiness"	elderfather	"grandfather"
eddy	"happy"	eldern	"elderly"
edgelings	"on the edge"	elflock	"hair matted together as if by elves"
edgift	"restitution"	elland	"foreign land"
edgin	"to begin again"	ellandish	"foreign"
edgrowing	"a growing again"	ellen	"courage"
edhue	"to reshape"	ellenning	"encouragement"
edken	"to reconcieve"	eller	"elsewhere"
edlean	"reward"	elhued	"changed in colour"
edlean	"to reward"	elrordy	"of strange speech"
edleanend	"rewarder"	eltheed	"foreign nation"
edleaning	"recompense"	eltheedy	"foreign"
edledge	"to repeat"	emforth	"according"
ednew	"edstatheled"	emmet	"ant"
ednew	"to edstathel"	empt	"leisure"
ednewend	"edstathelr"	emptwhile	"leisure"
ednewing	"restoration"	endbeird	"to put in order; arrange"
edquick	"regenerate, edstatheled to life"	endbeirdness	"order; succession"

endday	"deathday"	evenlearner	"fellow student"
endly	"final"	evenledge	"to be like; to imitate"
endnext	"extreme; final; last"	evenledger	"imitator"
Engle	"the Angles"	evenledgester	"(female) imitator"
enow	"enough"	evenledging	"imitation; copying"
ent	"giant"	evenlief	"equally dear"
entish	"giantish"	evenlike	"an equal"
ere	"before"	evenling	"consort, fellow"
ereday	"early day, morn, dawn"	evenlock	"evening-sacrifice"
eredays	"early days; former days"	evenlong	"equally long"
eredeed	"former deed"	evenly	"of the evening"
erelong	"beforelong; soon"	evenmighty	"equally mighty"
eremornly	"of early morning"	evennight	"equinox"
erer	"earlier, sooner"	evenold	"contemporary"
erewakle	"early awake"	evenrord	"evening-meal; supper"
erewhile	"some time ago"	evenrord	"to sup"
ern	"eagle"	evensorrow	"commiserate"
ern	"building" (other spelling arn)	evensorrowing	"commiseration"
ernkin	"the kin of eagles"	eventhane	"fellow servant"
errandfast	"bound on an errand"	eventide	"evening-time"
errandrake	"messenger"	evenworth	"equivelant"
erst	"earliest, first"	evenwright	"fellow worker"
erstwhile	"former"	ever	"boar"
erstwhile	"formerly"	everfern	"a kind of fern; polypody"
erve	"to inherit"	evil	"to inflict evil; to become evil"
erve	"inheritance; cattle"	evilbearend	"bringer of evil"
ervebeech	"will, testament"	evildeed	"an evil deed"
ervedole	"division of an inheritance"	evilful	"full of evil; malicious"
erveflit	"dispute about inheritance"	evilling	"injury"
ervehand	"natural successor"	evilkind	"of evil origin or quality"
erveland	"inherited land"	evilly	"evil-like"
erveward	"heir"	evilsake	"to blaspheme"
erveward	"to inherit"	evilsaking	"blasphemy"
ervewardness	"heritage"	evilwilling	"malicious"
ervewardwriter	"will-writer"	evilwillingness	"malice"
ervewrit	"will, testament"	evilyearnness	"eagerness for evil; malice"
ethel	"homeland"	evore	"heir"
ethem	"air, breath"	evest	"envy"
ettle	"voracious"	evesty	"envious"
evenbliss	"to rejoice equally"	ew	"law; marriage; scripture"
evenchristian	"fellow christian"	ew	"to show"
evencome	"to come together"	ewbeech	"lawbooks"
eveneech	"co-eternal"	ewbebode	"commandment of law"
evenfeal	"just as much"	ewbreach	"dernlyership; breach of marriage"
evenfrever	"to console"	ewcraft	"skill with law"
evengloam	"evening-twilight"	ewcrafty	"skilled with law"
evengloaming	"evening-twilight"	ewen	"to marry"
evengood	"equally good"	ewening	"wedlock"
evenhigh	"equally high"	ewfast	"righteous"
evenholy	"equally holy"	ewfastness	"righteousness; religion"
evenhood	"equality"	ewish	"offence"
evenknight	"fellow knight"	ewishly	"offensive"

ewishbearend	"middle-finger" (literally "offence-bearing (one)")	faxed	"hairy; longhaired (of a comet)"
ewly	"legal, lawful"	faxfalling	"shedding of hair, mange"
ewt	"newt"	faxfang	"pulling of hair"
eyedoor	"window"	faxhoar	"hoary-haired"
eyehurn	"corner of the eye"	faxneedle	"hairneedle, crisping pin"
eyering	"eyesocket; pupil"	faxnet	"hairnet"
eyeseen	"visible to the eye"	faxpreen	"hairpin"
eyethirl	"window"	faxwound	"wound under the hair"
eyne	"eyes"	fay	"to join"
fack	"interval; space between"	fay	"a joining"
fackful	"broad; spacious"	fayedness	"conjunction"
fad	"orderly"	faying	"conjunction"
fade	"to arrange"	feal	"many; much; very"
fading	"arrangement"	fealfold	"manifold"
fadly	"fit, suitable"	fealfold	"to multiply"
fain	"glad"	feallief	"very dear"
fain	"gladly; willingly"	fealspreckle	"very loquacious"
fainhood	"gladness"	fealspreckleness	"hyper-loquacity"
fainness	"gladness"	fealsinny	"very sinful"
fair	"to make or become fair"	fearings	"suddenly; unexpectedly"
fairhood	"beauty"	fearlock	"fear"
fairship	"beauty"	fearly	"dangerous, dreadful; strange"
fallingly	"unstable"	fearly	"a wonder"
fand	"to try"	fearly	"to wonder"
fand	"experiment"	fearspel	"dreadful discourse"
fander	"tester"	feathern	"made of feathers"
fanding	"investigation"	featherhame	"plumage"
fang	"to seize, to catch"	feddle	"feeding"
farecart	"cart for sending outside a manor"	feebehote	"promise of money"
fareld	"way; faring; journey"	feeboot	"money-compensation"
faren or farn	strong past participle of fare	feeyearn	"eager for money"
farforth	"to such an extent"	feedness	"nourishment"
farkind	"foreign"	feeless	"without money"
farkith	"distant land"	feelless	"without feeling; dead"
farland	"distant land"	feelness	"sensation"
farsib	"distantly related"	feeshaft	"destitute"
fass	"fringe, border"	feeshaftness	"poverty"
fasten	"fortress"	feeth	"locomotion"
fastmood	"firm in mind"	feethhere	"infantry"
fastread	"firm in council"	feething	"walking motion"
fastreadness	"constancy"	feethkemp	"footsoldier"
fastship	"firmness"	feethman	"pedestrian; footsoldier"
fathood	"fatness"	feethspeedy	speedy of foot"
fattish	"fat, plump"	feewite	"penalty for coining false money"
fathern	"of a father; paternal"	feeze	"to drive away"
fathernknossel	"father's kin"	feld	strong past tense of fold (like held)
fathernkin	"father's kin"	fellen	"of fells (skins)"
fathernhalf	"father's half"	fellow	"to be fellow with"
fatherethel	"father-homeland"	fellowred	"fellowship"
fatherqueller	"slayer of a father"	fellowship	"to associate with"
fax	"hair"	fenny	"marshy"
faxcloth	"hair-cloth"	fere	"to go, to travel"

fere	"companion"	flard	"nonsense"
fereledge	"to associate with"	flard	"to be foolish"
ferely	"associated"	flarder	"trifler"
fereship	"companionship"	fleam	"a fleeing"
ferered	"companionship"	fleamer	"banisher"
ferk	"to assist; to bring; to convey"	fleed	"in flood; overflowing"
fettle	"to bind, to fit; to make ready"	fleety	"fleet"
fey	"fated"	fleshhame	"body"
feydom	"the state of being fated"	fleshhamed	"incarnate"
feyship	"slaughter"	fleshhewer	"butcher"
fie	"to hate"	flet	"floor"
fieldhouse	"tent"	flew	strong past tense of flow
fieldswam	"field-fungus or toadstool"	flinten	"of flint"
fieldish	"belonging to the country"	flintsax	"flintknife"
fiendly	"hostile"	flit	"dispute"
fiendred	"emnity"	flitcraft	"skill of disputing; dialectics; logic"
fiendship	"hostility"	flitcraftly	"of disputing; logical""
feird	"national militia"	flite	"to dispute"
feird	"to go on military expedition"	fliter	"disputer"
feirdfare	"a going to war"	fliting	"contention"
feirdly	"martial"	flitten	past participle of flite
feirdleeth	"warsong"	floatly	"nautical; naval"
feirdwite	"fine in lieu of military service"	floatman	"sailor, pirate"
fether	"to load with a fother"	floatship	"ship; bark"
fickle	"to deceive, to flatter"	flockmeal	"in flocks or crowds"
fickling	"flattery"	flone	"arrow"
fiftyday	"pentecost"	flooden	"of a flood"
fightingstead	"battleground"	floodly	"of or belong to a flood"
fightling	"fighter"	flook	"to clap"
fightlock	"fighting"	flote	past tense of flite
fightwite	"penalty for fighting"	flowl	"fleet"
fillingly	"expletive; capable of completion"	flown	strong past participle of flow
filst	"help"	flykin	"a kind or race of flies"
filst	"to help"	flyrift	"fly-curtain"
filthhood	"dirtiness"	foor	strong past tense of fare
findle	"invention"	foor	"journey; path"
findy	"capable"	foothot	"hastily"
fine	"pile"	fnad	"fringe, border, hem"
fingerling	"thimble"	fnast	"breath"
fint	"consequence"	fnast	"to breathe"
firen	"crime"	foal	"to bring forth a foal"
firen	"of fire"	fodder	"case, sheath"
firren	"made of fir"	foeship	"enmity"
firmth	"harbouring, entertainment"	foken	"deceit"
fisheth	"the act of fishing"	fokendeed	"crime"
fishleap	"fishbasket"	fokenful	"deceitful"
fit	"part of a song or poem"	fokenless	"deceitless"
fivebeech	"pentateuch"	fokenly	"deceitful"
fivel	"sea monster"	fold	"earth"
fix	"female fox"	folden	strong past participle of fold
fixen	"of a female fox"	folkking	"king of the people"
fixenhide	"she-fox's skin"	folkly	"public, popular, common"

folkred	"people"	foreboding	"prophecy"
followingly	"that should be followed"	forebody	"chest"
followsome	"obsequious"	forebreast	"chest"
followster	"(female) follower"	foreby	"nearby"
foor	"journey"	forechoose	"to choose in preference"
foor	strong past tense of fare	forecome	"to come before"
foorbed	"portable bed; litter"	foredeed	"previous or former deed"
foorbook	"itinerary"	foredoor	"vestibule"
foormeal	"meal for a journey"	forefax	"forelocks"
footcosp	"fetter"	foreglew	"foreknowing; prudent"
footcosp	"to fetter"	forekindred	"progeny"
footcoth	"foot disease"	forekithe	"to make known beforehand"
footfollower	"follower on foot"	foreld	"very old age"
footlame	"lame in the foot"	forequeether	"prophet"
footlast	"footprint"	forequid	"foretelling, prophecy"
footmeal	"foot by foot; step by step"	forequidder	"foreteller"
footsettle	"footstool"	forelook	"to look before"
footshamble	"footstool"	forelooker	"provider"
footshank	"foreleg"	forename	"pronomen"
footspore	"footprint"	forenight	"early part of night"
footswath	"footprint"	forerunnel	"forerunner"
footthweal	"washing of the feat"	foresaidness	"preface"
footwelm	"instep, sole of the foot"	foresaw	"preface"
forbind	"to bind up"	foresend	"to send before"
forbite	"to bite in pieces"	foreseenness	"foresight; providence"
forblack	"very black"	foreset	"to set before; to propose"
forbleed	"to bleed to exhaustion"	foresetness	"proposition; preposition"
forblow	"to blow to pieces"	foreshow	"to foresee; to preordain; to provide with"
forbode	"prohibition"	foreshowing	"contemplation, foresight, providence"
forbow	"to bend from, to refrain from; to avoid"	foresit	"to preside over"
forbreak	"to break to pieces"	forespeaker	"advocate"
forbrit	"to break in pieces"	forespeech	"advocacy; excuse; preface"
forbritten	"to break in pieces"	forestep	"to precede"
forcarve	"to carve to pieces"	forestight	"to foreordain"
forcleave	"to cleave in pieces"	foreteeth	"front teeth"
forcling	"to wither"	forethank	"forethought"
forcouth	"wicked; infamous"	forethankful	"forethoughtful"
fordeem	"to condemn"	forethankle	"prudent"
fordeemedly	"condemnable"	forethankleness	"prudence"
fordit	"to obstruct; to block up"	forething	"to intercede"
fordo	"to destroy"	forethinger	"interceder"
fordreeve	"to perturb"	forethingred	"intercession"
fordull	"to become dull"	forethink	"to premeditate"
fordwilm	"to confound"	forewall	"rampart, bulwark"
fordwine	"to fade away"	forewise	"foreknowing"
forebe	"to be over; to rule over"	forewit	"to foreknow"
forebeacon	"portent; fortoken"	forewit	"foreknowledge"
forebirth	"previous birth"	forewitter	"foreknower"
forebisen	"example, parable"	forewitting	"foreknowledge"
forebisen	"to exemplify"	forewittingly	"foreknowing"
forebisening	"parable"	forewitty	"foreknowing"
forebode	"prophecy"		

foreyard	"court"	forlost	"utterly lost"
foreyed	"proverb"	forloze	past tense of forleeze
forfang	"capture; seizure"	formany	"very many"
forfare	"to fare ill; to perish"	formeal	"negotiation; agreement"
forgettle	"forgetful"	formelt	"to melt away"
forgift	"forgiveness"	formfather	"formost father"
forgivenly	"forgiveable"	fornigh	'very nigh, nearly, almost"
forgivester	"(female) forgiver"	fornim	"to take away; to deprive of"
forglender	"to devour"	foroft	"very often"
forgnaw	"to eat up"	forold	"to grow old; to decay"
forgnide	"to grind together"	forout	"without"
forgnidden	"contrite"	forpear	"to turn away; to pervert; to spoil"
forgniddenness	"tribulation"	forqueath	"to speak ill of"
forgrind	"to grind down; to ruin"	forread	"to betray; to deceive"
forhard	"very hard"	forsay	"to accuse falsely; to slander"
forharry	"to harry"	forsee	"to neglect; to despise"
forharrying	"destruction"	forseenly	"despicable"
forhave	"to restrain"	forseenness	"neglect"
forhaved	"continent; abstemious"	forseethe	"to boil away"
forhavedness	"restraint"	forsench	"to submerge"
forheal	"to conceal; to protect"	forshame	"to put to shame"
forhealer	"protector"	forshape	"to change shape; to transform"
forhealing	"cover, shelter, protection"	forshapen	"transformed"
forheed	"to neglect"	forshrench	"to supplant, to overcome, to vanquish"
forhew	"to hew in pieces"	forshrink	"to shrink, to wither"
forhide	"to hide"	forshut	"to exclude; to prevent"
forhoar	"to grow hoary"	forsit	"to neglect; to block"
forhold	"to forsake"	forsmite	"to smite to pieces"
forhote	"to renounce; to forswear"	forsooth	"in truth"
forhow	"to neglect; to condemn; to despise"	forspeak	"to speak amiss"
forhowedly	"contemptuous"	forspend	"to squander; to exhaust"
forhowedness	"contempt"	forspenning	"enticement"
forhowingly	"contemptible"	forspenster	"procuress"
foridle	"to become idle"	forstand	"to defend"
forlainess	"prostitution"	forstrong	"very strong"
forlead	"to mislead"	forswart	"to blacken"
forlear	"to seduce"	forsweal	"to burn up"
forleese	"to lose; to abandon" (other spelling forleeze)	forswelt	"to faint, to die"
forleesing	"loss"	forswie	"to pass over in silence"
forleeze	"to lose; to abandon" (other spelling forleese)	forsworkenly	"dark"
forlet	"to abandon"	forsworkenness	"darkenning"
forletten	strong past participle of forlet	forswornness	"perjury"
forlie	"to commit adultry; to fornicate"	fortend	"to burn away"
forlier	"dernlyership, fornication"	forth	"to promote, to push forth"
forlier	"one that commits dernlyership or fornication"	forthbear	"to bear forth"
forlier	"to commite dernlyership or fornication"	forthblow	"to blow forth"
forlierwife	"prostitute"	forthbring	"to bring forth"
forlittle	"very little"	forthcleep	"to call forth"
forlive	"to degenerate"	forthcome	"a coming forth"
forlore	"destruction"	forthdeed	"advantage"
forlorn	past participle of forleese / forleeze	forthdo	"to puth forth"
forlose	past tense of forleese (other spelling forloze)	forthfare	"to depart; to die"

forthfare	"departure; death"	forwhy	"why; wherefore"
forthflow	"to flow forth"	forwork	"to do wrong"
forthfoor	"departure; death"	forworth	"to perish; to deteriorate"
forthgang	"a going forth"	forwound	"to wound"
forthglide	"to glide forth or away"	forwray	"to accuse"
forthgo	"to go forth"	forwreak	"to drive forth; to expel"
forthhold	"to hold forth"	foryeam	"to neglect"
forthink	"to repent; to mistrust; to despise"	foryelp	'to boast"
forthinking	"repentance"	foryield	"to pay for; to requite; to reward"
forthkithe	"to announce forth"	fough	"joining; joint"
forthlast	"to persevere in; to accomplish"	foulhood	"foulness"
forthlead	"to lead forth"	foulsome	"foul"
forthleap	"to leap forth"	fouse	"eager"
forthlook	"to look forth"	fow	"to differ in colour"
forthlout	"to fall forth"	fow	"variegated"
forthmost	"foremost"	fowing	"variety of colour"
forthnim	"to seize"	fowlflight	"flight of birds"
forthreach	"to reach forth"	fowlkin	"race or species of bird"
forthrest	"to afflict; to oppress"	fowlwhate	"auger"
forthrestness	"tribulation"	fother	"carriageload; a load"
forthright	"straightaway"	foxing	"fox-like craftiness"
forthring	"to oppress"	frain	"question"
forthrism	"to choke; to suffocate; to strangle"	fraining	"question"
forthshaft	"creature; created thing"	fraked	"vile"
forthshow	"to show forth"	frank	"lance; javelin"
forthsith	"a going forth; departure"	fravel	"cunning"
forthspel	"declaration"	fravelness	"shrewdness"
forthspownness	"prosperity"	fray	"hearsay"
forthstep	"to advance forth"	frea	"lord"
forthward	"inclined forwards; forward"	freary	"freezing; chilly; cold in sadness"
forthwardness	"progress"	freed	"peace"
forthwax	"to wax forth"	freed	"to perceive; to experience"
forthway	"journey; departure"	freedingly	"perceptible"
forwend	"to convert"	freelock	"voluntary offering"
forthy	"for that; therefore; consequently"	freename	"surname"
forthyeet	"to pour forth"	freeship	"liberty"
forthild	"to endure with patience"	freet	"freedom"
forthilm	"to shut in; to envelope"	frelse	"to free; to celebrate"
fortight	"to seduce"	frelse	"freedom"
fortighting	"seduction"	frem	"to perform"
fortread	"to tread"	fremful	"useful"
fortrow	"to be presumptuous"	fremming	"purpose"
fortrowedness	"presumption"	fremsome	"beneficient"
fortrowing	"presumption"	fremsomeness	"beneficience"
forwand	"to be reluctant"	frettle	"greedy, gluttonous"
forwarp	"to throw away or off"	frever	"to console; to comfort"
forwax	"to grow excessively"	frickle	"appetite"
forweary	"very weary"	frickle	"to desire"
forweary	"to make weary"	friendhold	"amiable"
forweird	"destruction"	friendlathe	"friendly invitation"
forwell	"very well"	friendlest	"want of friends"
forwept	"exhausted with weeping"	friendlihood	"friendliness"

friendlithe	"kind to one's friends"	fromspelling	"original story"
friendlore	"friendly counsel"	fromstool	"first or principle seat; paternal home"
friendman	"friend"	fromth	"origin, beginning" (other spelling frimth)
friendred	"friendship"	fromthly	"premeval; primitive; first"
friendsome	"friendly"	fromtide	"beginning"
friendspeed	"abundance of friends"	fromward	"about to depart"
friendspeedy	"rich in friends"	fromwards	"away from"
fright	"to be afraid"	fromwassom	"firstfruits"
fright	"afraid"	fromwright	"creator"
frightihood	"timidness"	frorn	"frozen"
frightmood	"timid"	frose	"to find out by inquiry"
frightness	"fear, terror"	frosing	"a questioning"
frighty	"timid"	frosttime	"winter"
frimdy	"curious"	frover	"comfort"
frimth	"origin, beginning" (other spelling fromth)	froverbook	"book of consolation"
frine	"to ask, to learn by asking"	froverghost	"consoling spirit; Holy Ghost; Comforter"
frist	"space of time, term, respite"	froverly	"comforting"
frist	"to respite, to delay"	froverword	"comforting word"
frith	"peace"	frow	"woman"
frithbreach	"breach of peace"	fullathel	"very noble"
frithe	"to make peace"	fullbeet	"to make full ammends"
frithhouse	"peacehouse; sanctuary"	fullblithe	"very blithe"
frithless	"peaceless"	fullbright	"very bright"
frithly	"peaceful"	fullbring	"to complete"
frithoath	"oath of peace"	fullclean	"very clean"
frithsoken	"asylum"	fullcouth	"wellknown"
frithsome	"peaceful"	fulldeed	"perfection"
frithsome	"to make peaceful"	fulldo	"to do fully; to complete"
frithstow	"peace-place; refuge; sanctuary"	fulldown	"flat down, completly down"
frithtoken	"sign of peace"	fullend	"to end fully"
frithwear	"treaty of peace"	fullfair	"very fair"
frithweb	"peaceweaver"	fullfatted	"very fattened"
frithyard	"peaceyard; asylum"	fullflee	"to flee fully"
frood	"old"	fullfremmed	"perfect"
from	"original"	fullfremmedness	"perfection"
fromado	"to do away from"	fullgo	"to accomplish; to carry out"
frombairn	"firstchild"	fullgood	"very good"
frombigh	"a bending away; backsliding"	fullgrow	"to grow fully"
frombirdling	"young man"	fullhoar	"very hoar"
frombring	"to bring from"	fullhood	"fullness"
fromchar	"to turn from"	fulllast	"to help"
frome	"beginning"	fullmain	"full power"
fromeld	"early age"	fullmake	"to make fully, to accomplish"
fromfare	"departure"	fullnigh	"very nigh"
fromgive	"perogative"	fulloft	"very often"
fromgore	"leader; patriarch"	fullsome	"plentious"
fromkenned	"firstborn"	fullsomehood	"abundance"
fromly	"original"	fullsomeness	"abundance"
fromshaft	"original creation"	fullthungen	"fullgrown"
fromshapen	"first-created"	fulltimber	"to build fully"
fromshild	"orignal sin"	fulltrow	"to trow fully"
fromsith	"departure"	fullwax	"to grow fully"

fullwaxen	"fullgrown"	gavelred	"tribute, rent"
fullwealy	"very wealthy"	gavelreeve	"tax-gatherer"
fullweary	"very weary"	geal	"to hinder; to delay"
fullwork	"to work fully; to complete""	geason	"destitute"
fully	"full; universal; catholic"	geat	"goats"
fulth	"fullness"	geatbucks	"he-goats"
fultum	"help"	geaten	"of goat" (other spelling goaten)
fultum	"to help; to support"	gemkin	"a kind of gems"
furn	"ancient"	gemwright	"jeweller"
furndays	"days of yore"	ghast	"terror"
furnness	"antiquity"	ghast	"to terrify"
furnwrit	"old writing"	ghastful	"terrified"
furnyear	"previous year"	ghostdom	"spirituality"
furtherover	"moreover"	ghosted	"endowed with a spirit"
gad	"society; fellowship"	ghostholy	"holy in spirit"
gade	"comrade, companion"	ghostkind	"spiritual"
gadling	"companion"	gidden	"goddess"
gainchar	"turning again"	giftleeth	"epithalamium"
gaincome	"a return"	gin	"to begin"
gaingiving	"a giving back"	ginning	"beginning"
gainsaw	"a gainsaying"	girdlestead	"waist"
gainstand	"to withstand"	give	"a giving; grace"
gainstanding	"opposition"	givekisty	"liberal in giving"
gainturn	"counterturn"	givel	"liberal"
galder	"incantation"	givelness	"liberality"
galdercraft	"art of incantation"	giveness	"grace"
galderleeth	"incantation"	gladder	"gladdener"
gale	"to sing"	gladding	"rejoicing"
gale	"singing"	gladmood	"cheerful"
galen	past participle of gale	gladship	"pleasure"
galer	"wizard, snakecharmer, enchanter"	gladsome	"pleasant'
gallock	"comfrey, gall-apple"	glassvat	"glass vessel"
gang	"to go"	gleebeam	"harp"
gang	"a going"	gleecraft	"music"
gangday	"a rogation day"	gleed	"ember, glowing coal"
gangdays	"the rogation days"	gleedream	"joy of music"
ganger	"a goer"	gleedred	"red like hot coals"
ganghouse	"privy"	gleedshovel	"fire-shovel"
gangthirl	"hole of a privy"	gleedy	"glowing"
gangtown	"latrine"	gleemaiden	"female musician"
gangweek	"rogation week"	gleeman	"minstrel"
garlicmonger	"garlic dealer"	glew	strong past tense of glow (like blew)
garsedge	"ocean"	glew	"wise"
garsom	"jewel; costly gift"	glewship	"wisdom"
gatheringly	"collective"	glidden	strong past participle of glide (like ridden)
gatherwist	"companionship"	glidder	"slippery"
gavel	"tribute"	glind	"hedge; fence"
gavelbere	"barley paid as rent"	glinge	"ornament"
gavelfish	"fish paid as rent"	glinge	"to adorn"
gavelfree	"tax-free"	gliss	"to shine"
gavelock	"a spear or dart"	glist	"to shine"
gavelly	"fiscal"	glister	"glitter; sparkle"

glister	"to shine"	gospelly	"evangelical"
glitten	"to glitter"	gospelwright	"evangelist"
glittening	"glittering"	gossipred	"sponsorial obligation"
glode	strong past tense of glide (like rode)	goundy	"full of sores"
glown	strong past participle of glow (like blown)	gouth	"war"
gnawn	strong past participle of gnaw (like drawn)	gouthcraft	"war-craft"
gneath	"niggardly"	gouthvane	"war-banner"
gneathness	"frugality"	gouthhere	"war-army"
gnew	strong past tense of gnaw (like drew)	gouthleeth	"war-song or poem"
gnidden	past participle of gnide	gouthspel	"tidings of war"
gnide	"to rub"	graft	"carved thing"
gnode	past tense of gnide	grame	"rage"
gnorn	"sad"	grame	"to vex, to anger"
goatbuck	"he-goat"	grameful	"irritating"
goaten	"of goat"	grammaticcraft	"grammar"
godbairn	"godchild"	grassearth	"pasturage in return for ploughing labour"
godfright	"godfearing"	gravesax	"graving-knife"
godfright	"fear of god"	gread	"to shout"
godfrightihood	"piety"	greading	"clamour"
godfulhood	"divinity"	great	"to make or become great"
godkind	"divine"	greaten	"to become pregnant"
godkind	"divinity"	greatwombed	"bigbellied'
godkindhood	"divinity"	gred	"lap, bosom"
godkindness	"divinity"	greenhood	"greenness"
godness	"deity"	greet	"to cry, to lament"
godweb	"purple-cloth"	grill	"to provoke"
godwebben	"of purple-cloth "	grimness	"ferocity"
godwebwright	"weaver of purple"	grin	"snare"
goldbeaten	"adorned with beaten gold"	grin	"to catch in a snare"
goldenfax	"golden-haired"	grindle	"bar; bolt"
goldfellen	"of gilded leather"	gripe	"to seize; to grip"
goldfow	"gold-covered"	grippen	strong past participle of gripe
gole	"wantoness"	gripple	"eager to seize"
goleful	"wanton"	grir	"horror"
golehood	"luxury"	gristbite	"to gnash the teeth"
goleness	"lasciviousness"	gristbote	"gnashing of the teeth"
goleship	"excessiveness"	grith	"truce, peace"
goly	"wanton"	grithbreach	"breach of peace"
gome	"man"	grithe	"to make truce"
gomekin	"the human race"	grithfulness	"peacefulness"
gomekist	"virtue"	groat	"particle"
good	"to become or make good"	grope	strong past tense of gripe
goodful	"very good"	gropingly	"tangible"
goodhood	"goodness"	groundling or groundlings	"completly to the ground"
goodless	"evil"	groundstalwart	"strong, powerful"
goodlihood	"excellence"	groundstathel	"to establish firmly"
goodship	"kindness, goodness"	groundstone	"foundation-stone"
gool	past tense of gale	groundwall	"foundation"
gooseherd	"goosekeeper"	groundwall	"to found; to establish"
gore	"spear"	groundy	"profound, radical, solid"
gospel	"to preach the gospel"	guestarn	"guest-chamber"
gospelboding	"gospel-preaching"	guestlithe	"hospitable"

guestlitheness	"hospitality"	handrail	"napkin or towel"
guilter	"one who incurs guilt"	handrin	"hand-touch"
haft	"bond or fetter; captive; captivity"	handimake	"companion"
haft	"to bind or fetter; to take take captive"	handishaft	"handiwork"
haftdom	"captivity"	handistall	"companion"
haften	"to take captive"	handiwield	"power"
haftening	"confinement"	handiwin	"hand-struggle; work"
haftling	"prisoner"	handiwrit	"handwriting; autograph"
haftneed	"custody; imprisonment"	handsax	"dirk; dagger"
haftneed	"to take captive"	handstaff	"walking stick"
haftneedling	"captive"	handstoke	"cuff, sleave"
haftneedness	"captivity"	handtame	"submissive"
hairen	"of hair"	handthane	"retainer; servant"
hairlock	"lock of hair"	handthweal	"handwashing"
hairmeal	"a hair's breadth"	handwhile	"instant"
hale	"hero"	handwrist	"the wrist"
haleth	"hero"	handwrought	"handmade"
halfcleamed	"halfplastered"	hane	"cock"
halfcleeping	"semi-vowel"	hanecreed	"cockcrow"
halfhounding	"cynocephalus"	hardheart	"hard at heart"
halfling or halflings	"in half"	hardheartness	"hardness of heart"
halfold	"half-grown"	hardiship	"bravery"
halfquick	"half-alive; half-dead"	hardmood	"brave, hardspirited"
halfsinwalt	"semi-circular"	hardmoodness	"obstinancy"
halftrindle	"hemisphere"	hardread	"firm, constant"
halfwood	"halfmad"	hardsealth	"unfortune"
halidom	"holiness; holy thing"	harkener	"listener"
halk	"corner; hiding-place; cavity"	harmdeed	"harmful action"
hallern	"hall-building"	harmly	"harmful"
hallreaf	"wall-tapestry"	harmqueath	"to speak evil of; to revile"
hallthane	"hall-officer"	harmquid	"to calumnate"
hally	"palatial"	harmquiddle	"slanderous"
halp	strong past tense of help	harmquiddle	"to slander"
halse	"neck"	harmstaff	"harm"
halse	"to entreat; to embrace"	harpnail	"plectrum"
halsebea	"neck-ring; collar; necklace"	harpsong	"hymn"
halseleather	"reins"	harpster	"(female) harper"
halsemeen	"necklace"	harpsway	"sound of the harp"
halsegound	"neck-tumor"	harr	"master"
halsing	"embrace"	harten	"of a hart"
halsingly	"entreatable"	harvestly	"of harvest; autumnal"
halter	"one who is lame"	harvestmonth	"September"
ham	"piece of pasture land"	hately	"hostile"
hame	"covering"	hatesome	"hateful"
handdeed	"exploit"	hattle	"hostile"
handfast	"handfastened"	have	"a having"
handfasten	"to join hands for a pledge; to betroth"	haveless	"poor"
handfastening	"joining hands to confirm a pledge"	havelest	"poverty"
handgrith	"security"	havel	"head"
handhaving	"having in one's own hand"	haven	strong past participle of heave (other spelling hoven)
handling or handlings	"by hand; hand to hand"	haven	"a having"
handpriest	"domestic chaplain"	havenless	"poor"

havenlest	"poverty"	heartsoreness	"grief"
having	"behaviour"	heartcothe	"heart-disease"
havingly	"habile"	hearthbaken	"baked on the hearth"
haw	"yard"	hearthfast	"settled in a home"
haw	"fruit of the hawthorn"	heartthew	"disposition of the heart"
hawkkin	"species of hawk"	heathendom	"heathenism"
hazelen	"of hazel"	heathenness	"heathenism"
headbone	"skull"	heathenship	"heathenism"
headbye	"crown"	heathenyield	"idoltry; an idol"
headchurch	"cathedral"	heave	"weight, burden"
headedder	"cephalic vein"	heavenbow	"rainbow"
headling	"an equal"	heavendew	"dew of heaven"
headly	"capital"	heavenkind	"heavenly"
headmain	"cardinal virtue"	heavenrich	"heaven's kingdom"
headmight	"chief power"	heavensettle	"heaven's throne"
headpan	"skull"	heavenware	"heaven-dwellers"
headrich	"empire"	heavied	"made heavy"
headsin	"capital sin"	heavimood	"oppressive in mood"
headstead	"chief place"	heavy	"to make heavy"
headswime	"dizziness in the head"	heddern	"storehouse"
headthew	"capital virtue"	heeve	"to lament"
headwright	"chief workman"	heevingday	"mourningday"
heaf	"lamentation"	heevingtide	"time of mourning"
heafly	"grievious"	hellen	"belonging to hell"
heafsong	"dirge"	hellhaftling	"prisoner of hell"
heal	"to conceal, to cover, to hide" (used as a strong verb)	hellsousel	"helltorment"
heal	"to conceal, to cover, to hide" (not as a strong verb)	hellstow	"place of hell"
heal	"health"	helltray	"hell-torment"
healend	"healing one, savior; Christ"	helltintray	"hell-torment"
healingly	"wholesome"	hellware	"helldwellers"
healness	"health"	hellwight	"devil"
healster	"(female) savior"	hellwite	"hell-punishment"
healwater	"holy water"	helly	"of hell; hell-like"
heam	"to marry"	helmward	"pilot"
heamed	"cohabitation; marriage"	helpingly	"helpable"
heamedchurl	"married man"	helster	"hiding-place; darkness, concealment"
heamedlock	"coition"	helster	"to hide, to conceal"
heamedship	"cohabitation; marriage"	helstery	"shadowy"
heamedthing	"coition; cohabitation; marriage"	hencesith	"departure; death"
heamedwife	"married wife"	hend	"at hand; gracious"
hean	"lowly"	hend	"to take by the hand, to seize"
heanly	"lowly; poor; abject"	hendship	"graciousness"
heapmeal	"heap by heap"	hendspeech	"gentleness of speech"
hearingly	"audible"	hendy	"gracious, courteous, clever"
hearkening	"hearing; power of hearing"	henheart	"chicken-hearted"
hearness	"hearing; respect; obedience"	hent	"to pursue; to seize"
hearsome	"obedient"	henter	"thief"
hearsome	"to obey"	herdbelly	"shepherd's bag"
hearsomeness	"obedience"	herdbook	"pastoral book"
heart	"to encourage"	herdly	"pastoral"
hearting	"encouragement"	herdness	"custody; care; watch"
heartsick	"sick in the heart"	herdred	"custody; care; keeping"

here	"army"	hindberry	"raspberry"
hereabove	"above this"	hindbrier	"raspberry bush"
hereagainst	"contrariwise"	hinder	"after"
herebefore	"before this"	hindercraft	"deceitful craft"
herecome	"a coming here; arrival; advent"	hinderful	"deceitful"
herefang	"spoil, plunder"	hinderling	"wretch"
heregang	"march of an army"	hindership	"wickedness"
heregome	"soldier"	hinderword	"deceitful word or speech"
herehouth	"booty; plunder"	hindforth	"backward"
hereinamong	"at this point; among this"	hindward	"backward"
herekemp	"soldier"	hiphalt	"lame in the hip"
herely	"martial"	hipple	"little heap"
hereof	"of this"	hipplemeal	"little heap by little heap"
herereaf	"war-plunder"	hipsax	"hipknife"
herereasow	"commander"	hirst	"to fry"
hereright	"right at this point"	hisp	"to mock, to reproach"
hererink	"warrior"	hispful	"contumelious"
hereshroud	"war-clothing"	hispingly	"abominable"
heretoeke	"besides"	hith	"advantage, gain"
heretow	"army-leader"	hithe	"to plunder"
herry	"to praise"	hithercome	"advent"
herryingly	"laudable"	hoar	"to become hoar"
hewt	"a hewing"	hoardern	"treasurhouse"
hidingcloth	"veil, curtain"	hoardcleave	"treasure-chamber"
hiddle	"secret"	hoardcove	"treasure-chamber"
hie	"haste"	hoarder	"treasurer"
hie	"to hasten"	hoardhouse	"treasury"
hie	"hastey"	hoardvat	"treasure-receptacle"
hield	"protection, loyalty"	hoardweal	"hoarded wealth"
hield	"a slope"	hoaring	"hoariness"
hield	"to incline"	hoarsehood	"hoarseness"
hieldred	"fidelity"	hode	"condition; holy order"
highangel	"archangel"	hode	"to ordain"
highcraft	"high skill"	hoding	"ordaining; consecration"
highfather	"patriarch"	hodingday	"ordaining-day"
highhood	"altitude"	hoff	"house"
highliness	"sublimity"	hoker	"derision"
highlith	"high hill or cliff"	hoker	"to mock, to scoff"
highlorrew	"head teacher"	hokerer	"mocker"
highman	"man of rank"	hokerful	"scornful"
highmight	"high authority"	hokering	"derision"
highmood	"excellent"	hokerlaughter	"laughter of scorn"
highsettle	"exalted seat"	hokerleeth	"song or poem of mockery"
highship	"lofty dignity"	hokerword	"scornful speech"
hight	past tense of hote; "is called, is named"	hold	"loyal"
hight	"to rejoice"	holdfast	"safe"
hight	"hope, joy"	holdoath	"oath of friendship or allegiance"
hightful	"hopeful"	holdred	"loyal service"
highthane	"chief officer"	holdship	"loyalty"
highwit	"high councillor"	hole	"to hollow out"
hild	"war"	hole	strong past tense of heal (like stole)
hilk	"hoarfrost"	holen	strong past participle of heal (like stolen)

holiern	"holy building"	hotheartness	"fury"
holidom	"holiness; holy thing"	houghsinew	"sinew of the heel"
holidomhouse	"sacrarium"	hounden	"of hounds; canine"
holihood	"sanctity"	houndfly	"dogfly"
holimonth	"September"	houndly	"of hounds; canine"
holinight	"holy night"	housebreach	"house-breaking"
holirift	"holy covering; veil"	housecop	"house-top"
holiship	"sanctity"	housefolk	"family"
holiware	"saints"	houseinchel	"little house"
holm	"sea"	housered	"household"
holmen	"of the holm tree"	houseship	"household, race"
holpen	strong past participle of help	housestead	"place of a house"
holse	"salvation"	housewifeship	"house management"
holthane	"woodcock"	housewist	"home"
homecome	"homecoming"	houth	"plunder"
homecouth	"familiar"	houve	"head-covering"
homefast	"settled in a house"	houve	"to put a covering on the head"
homehold	"domestic"	hove	strong past tense of heave
homesith	"return home"	hoven	strong past participle of heave (other spelling haven)
homesith	"to return home"	hover	"hump"
homesoken	"house-breaking"	hovered	"humpbacked"
homestall	"homestead"	how	"care"
hooknebbed	"hooknosed"	howful	"careful"
hool	"calumny"	howgates	"in what manner"
hopster	"(female) dancer"	howship	"prudence"
hore	"filth"	huing	"appearance, likeness; form"
horey	"filthy"	huingly	"metaphorical"
hornbore	"horn-bearer"	huekind	"familiar"
hornen	"made of horn"	hueledge	"to form; to shape; to fashion"
horrow	"filth"	huered	"family"
horrow	"to spit, to defile"	hund	"hundred"
horrowed	"filthy"	hundeightieth	"eightieth"
horsebier	"horselitter"	hundeighty	"eighty"
horsecart	"chariot"	hundeleventieth	"hundred and tenth"
horscherd	"horsekeeper"	hundeleventy	"hundred and ten"
horschere	"mounted army"	hundfold	"hundredfold"
horseknave	"horsegroom"	hundninetieth	"ninetieth"
horseknight	"groom"	hundninety	"ninety"
horsely	"like a horse"	hundredman	"centurion"
horsemonger	"horsedealer"	hundseventieth	"seventieth"
horsern	"stable"	hundseventy	"seventy"
horsethane	"groom"	hundtentieth	"hundredth"
horsewain	"chariot"	hundtenty	"hundred"
horsewhale	"walrus"	hundtentifold	"hundredfold"
hosp	"reproach"	hundtwelftieth	"hundred and twentieth"
hosply	"reproach-like; insulting"	hundtwelfty	"hundred and twenty"
hospword	"abusive speech"	hungerbitten	"starving"
hote	"to command; to promise; to call or to be called"	hungerer	"hungry person"
hote	"promise"	hungerlew	"starving"
hoten	past participle of hote	hungerstorven	"perished with hunger"
hotheart	"furious"	hungeryear	"famine-year"
hotheart	"to be or become furious"	hunteth	"hunting or what is caught by hunting"

huntethfare	"hunting expedition"	imblic	"to lie around something"
hure	"at least"	imblook	"to look around"
hurn	"corner"	imblote	"to contemplate"
hurst	"ornament"	imbloting	"contemplation"
hye	"thought, mind"	imbring	"to make a ring around something"
hyecraft	"power of mind"	imbrun	"a running around; a revolution; circuit"
hyeless	"thoughtless, rash"	imbsee	"to look around"
ibead	"prayer"	imbset	"to set around; to beset; to encompass"
ibeaten	"beaten"	imbshine	"to shine around or upon"
ibour	"freeholder of the lowest class, peasant, farmer"	imbshow	"to look around"
ichoose	"to choose"	imbshowing	"a looking around"
ickle	"icicle" (other spelling icle)	imbshride	"to clothe"
iclad	"clad"	imbsit	"to sit around; to surround; to besiege"
icle	"icicle"	imbsniddenness	"circumcision"
iclept	"called"	imbsnithe	"circumcise"
iclestone	"hailstone"	imbspeak	"to speak about"
icly	"icy; icicly"	imbspeech	"conversation, comment, criticism"
iddish	"household stuff; possessions"	imbstand	"to stand around, to surround"
idlehend	"idle-handed"	imbstandend	"one standing around"
idleyield	"vain worship, idoltry"	imbthank	"thought, reflection"
idole	"division"	imbthink	"to consider"
ifay	"joining, joint; composition; diagram"	imbthring	"to crowd around"
ifere	"companion"	imbtine	"to hedge around, to surround"
ifere	"together"	imbtrim	"to surround with fortification"
ikind	"nature"	imbout	"around, about"
ikind	"natural"	imbwax	"to grow around; to surround"
iknow	"to know"	imbwend	"to turn around"
ilike	"alike"	imbwharve	"to turn around"
imb	"around, about"	imbwhirft	"rotation, revolution, orbit"
imbard	"to dwell around"	imbwind	"to wind around"
imbbighness	"a bending around; circuit"	imean	"common"
imbbraid	"to upbraid"	imong	"mixture"
imbbraid	"a reproach"	imoot	"meeting, assembly"
imbcarve	"to circumcise"	inabear	"to bring in"
imbchar	"a turning about"	inard	"to dwell in"
imbchar	"to turn about; to make a circuit"	inbequeath	"to inculcate"
imbclip	"to embrace"	inbesting	"to penetrate; to sting in"
imbclipping	"embracing"	inblow	"to inspire"
imbcome	"assembly, convention"	inbring	"to bring in"
imbdelf	"a digging around"	incleave	"inner chamber"
imbfare	"circuit"	incothe	"internal disease"
imbfare	"to travel around"	increeping	"thrusting or creeping in"
imbfastness	"enclosure"	indelve	"to dig in"
imbfathom	"to embrace"	indrink	"to imbibe"
imbgang	"a going about; circumference"	infare	"entrance"
imbgird	"to gird around, to encircle, to surround"	infare	"to enter"
imbgo	"to go around, to surround"	infleshness	"incarnation"
imbhave	"to surround, to include, to contain"	inflock	"to flock in"
imbheedy	"careful"	infollowing	"consequence"
imbheediness	"carefulness"	ingang	"entrance"
imbhow	"consideration"	ingoing	"entrance"
imbhow	"to be anxious about"	ink	"question; scruple"

inkind	"inward"	kemb	"to comb"
inkindness	"inwardness"	kemp	"warrior"
inknight	"indoor servant"	kempster	"(female) comber; flax-comber, woolcomber"
inlandish	"native"	kempster	"(female) warrior"
inlathe	"to invite"	ken	"to conceive, to bring forth"
inlead	"to introduce"	akennend	"parent"
inlet	"to let in"	kenning	"bringing forth, birth"
inlight	"to illuminate"	kenningly	"genital"
inly	"internal"	kenningstow	"birthplace"
inmid	"in the middle (of)"	kenningtide	"time of bringing forth"
innim	"to take in"	kenster	"mother"
innoth	"womb"	Kentings	"Kentish men"
inrush	"inroad"	Kentland	"Kent"
insend	"to send in"	Kentrich	"kingdom of Kent"
instep	"entrance"	Kentware	"inhabitants of Kent"
instep	"to enter"	keybore	"key-bearer"
inwend	"to enter"	keyherd	"keykeeper"
inwit	"evil"	kie	"cows"
inwitful	"wicked"	kife	"tub"
inwith	"within"	kin	"royal, kingly"
inwitstaff	"wickedness"	kinard	"royal land"
inwone	"to inhabit"	kinbairn	"royal child"
inwrap	"to wrap in"	kinbench	"royal bench"
inwrite	"to inscribe"	kinborn	"royally born"
irord	"voice, language, speech; food, meal, feast"	kinborough	"royal city"
ishaft	"creation"	kind	"nature"
ished	"seperation, distinction, understanding"	kindbook	"Book of Genesis"
ishie	"pair of shoes"	kindhood	"kindness"
isith	"companion"	kindom	"kingly rule, realm"
itale	"number, reckoning"	kindship	"kindness"
ithank	"thought; intention; gratitude"	kindle	"offspring, brood"
ithewed	"mannered"	kine	"cows"
ithoft	"comrade, mate, follower"	kinghood	"kingship"
ithoft	"to join, to unite, to associate"	kingrich	"kingdom"
ithoftred	"fellowship"	kinhelm	"crown"
ithoftship	"fellowship"	kinhelm	"to crown"
iwhat	"each thing"	kinhome	"royal manor"
iwhence	"from every quarter"	kinhood	"kingly state or dignity"
iwhere	"everywhere"	kinland	"royal land"
iwhether	"both, either, each"	kinlord	"royal lord"
iwhich	"each"	kinly	"kingly, royal"
iwhither	"in every direction, everywither"	kinmark	"royal mark"
iwho	"each one, everyone"	kinmeed	"royal meed"
iwis	"certainly"	kinreaf	"royal robe"
iwold	"rule, control"	kinrich	"rule, sovereignty"
iwork	"workmanship"	kinright	"royal prerogative"
iwrit	"a writing"	kinring	"royal ring"
keel	"to cool"	kinseat	"royal seat"
keeling	"cooling"	kinsettle	"throne; capital city"
keelness	"coolness"	kinship	"royalty, majesty, kingly power"
keen	"brave"	kinstool	"throne, royal place"
keenship	"bravery"	kintheed	"royal nation"

kinyard	"sceptre"	last	"to load; to burden"
kinyield	"king's compensation"	lateread	"slow; deliberate"
kipe	"vessel, basket"	latesome	"tardy"
kirten	"comely, elegant"	lathe	"to invite"
kirtenledge	"to beautify, to make elegant; to make sweet"	lather	"inviter"
kist	"free choice; moral excellence; character"	lathing	"invitation"
kistiness	"liberality; goodness"	lattew	"leader"
kisty	"charitable; virtuous"	lattewdom	"leadership"
kith	"one's country, native land; one's friends or relatives"	laughterly	"ridiculous"
kithe	"to make known"	leadingly	"ductile"
kitheness	"testament"	leam	"to shine"
kithey	"knowing, familiar"	leam	"ray of light"
kittle	"to tickle"	lean	"reward"
kittling	"tickling"	leanse	"to make lean"
knape	"boy" (other spelling knave)	leap	"basket"
knavebairn	"male child"	leapgate	"a low gate"
knavechild	"male child"	lear	"to teach"
kneat	"to argue"	leared	"learned"
kneating	"dispute"	learedmen	"the learned men, the clergy"
kneemay	"kinsman"	learningchild	"student"
kneewrist	"kneejoint"	learningcraft	"the art of learning"
knidden	past participle of knide	learningknight	"disciple"
knide	"to beat"	learningmaiden	"discipless"
knifewarper	"knifethrower"	learningman	"learner"
knightbairn	"male child"	learster	"(female) instructor"
knightchild	"male child"	lease	"devoid (of)"
knightship	"knighthood"	lease	"to lie"
knightweed	"attire of a knight"	leaser	"hypocrite"
kniss	"to dash"	leasespel	"false discourse"
knode	past tense of knide	leasingmonger	"liar"
knode	"to attribute to"	leasow	"pasture"
knordledge	"to be diligent, to study"	leasow	"to feed"
knoss	"collision"	leathercod	"leatherbag"
knossel	"race, kin"	leatherwright	"leatherworker"
knownness	"knowledge"	leaved	"covered with leaves"
knowledging	"acknowledging"	leaveful	"allowable"
lair	"to lay low"	leech	"physician"
lairstow	"sepulcher"	leech	"to heal, to act as a leech"
lairwite	"a fine for lying with a bondwoman"	leechbook	"book of prescription; a physician's book"
laker	"to deride"	leechchest	"medicine chest"
lakering	"derision"	leechcraft	"art of healing"
lamp	past tense of limp	leechcrafty	"skilled at healing"
landbook	"written grant of land"	leechdom	"medicament; remedy"
landfolk	"natives; country folk"	leechen	"to heal, to act as a leech"
landgavel	"land-tax"	leechening	"healing"
landhere	"land-army"	leechfinger	"the fourth finger"
landish	"native"	leechhouse	"hospital"
landman	"country-man; native"	leechsax	"lancet"
landore	"landed property"	leed	"man; people; nation"
landway	"path"	leedbishop	"diocesan
lap	"lobe"	leedbishopric	"jurisdiction of a diocesan"
last	"a load; a burden"	leeden	"latin; any foreign tongue; warbling of birds""

leedenware	"latin people; Romans"	lichleoth	"dirge"
leedfeird	"folk-army"	lichly	"relating to the dead"
leedish	"national"	lichman	"pall-bearer"
leedkemp	"warrior"	lichrest	"sepulchre; tomb; hearse"
leedking	"king of the people"	lichsong	"dirge"
leedly	"native, national"	lichstow	"place of burial"
leedquid	"national speech"	lichthaning	"obsequies; funeral"
leedred	"country, region"	lichwieling	"necromancy"
leedshame	"disgrace of the people"	lickster	"(female) licker"
leedship	"nation, people"	lid	"ship, vessel"
leedspel	"national discourse"	lidded	"having a lid"
leedswike	"betrayer of the people"	lide	"a loud noise"
leedthew	"popular usage"	lide	"to make a noise; to be loud"
leedthue	"servant of the people"	lide	"to cover"
leen	"transitory"	lidey	"garrulous"
leer	"cheek"	liding	"a noise"
leerbone	"cheekbone"	lidfast	"fastened by a lid"
leerbolster	"pillow"	lidman	"seafarer"
leese	"to loosen; to redeem"	lidward	"shipmaster"
leesing	"deliverance"	lief	"dear"
leeth	"poem"	liefsome	"precious"
leethcraft	"poetry"	liefspel	"pleasant discourse"
leethly	"poem-like"	liespel	"false discourse"
leethwright	"poet"	liether	"noise, sound, voice"
leighter	"vice"	liether	"to sound, to speak, to sing"
leighterful	"vicious"	lietherer	"rhetorician"
lem	"to cause to sound"	lieword	"lying word"
leman	"darling"	liewright	"liar"
lentenly	"of spring, vernal"	lifeday	"lifetime"
lessing	"diminution"	lifefack	"lifetime"
let	"to hinder"	lifefast	"living"
letch	"to water; to irrigate; to moisten"	lifefast	"to endow with life"
letless	"without hinderance"	lifefasten	"to endow with life"
letten	strong past participle of let	lifeholy	"holy of life"
letter	"hinderer"	lifeholiness	"holiness of life"
letting	"impediment"	lifelest	"loss of life; death"
lew	"shelter"	lifeload	"course of life"
lew	"warm"	lifesith	"lifetime"
lew	"to betray"	lifeward	"guardian of life"
lew	strong past tense of low	lifeway	"way of life"
lewfinger	"forefinger"	lifeweal	"life-wealth"
lib	"drug"	lifewhile	"lifetime"
liblock	"occult art; use of drugs for magic"	lifewin	"life-joy"
libster	"sorceress"	lift	"air"
lich	"body, corpse"	liften	"of the air"
lichbisening	"imitation"	lifty	"airy; aerial"
lichet	"to feign"	lightbearend	"lucifer"
lichetter	"deciever, hypocrite"	lighthood	"levity"
lichhame	"body"	lightless	"dark"
lichhame	"to clothe with flesh"	lightship	"swiftness, levity"
lichhameless	"incorporeal"	lightvat	"lantern"
lichhamely	"bodily"	likingly	"agreeable"

likeworth	"pleasing"	lixing	"brightness"
limblame	"crippled"	loam	"clay; earth"
limblew	"injury to a limb"	loath	"annoyance, injury" (other spelling loth)
limbmeal	"limb by limb"	loathelihood	"loathesomeness"
limbnaked	"stark naked"	loathless	"innocent, inoffensive"
limbsick	"sick in the limbs"	loathlessness	"innocence"
limbweary	"weary in the limbs"	loathspel	"loathsome discourse"
limbwhole	"sound of limb"	lob	"spider"
limefine	"lime-heap"	locked	"hairy"
limp	"occurance"	lockfax	"hair"
limp	"to happen"	lockiwind	"hair"
limpful	"fitting; convenient"	lockstone	"stone locking or closing an entrance"
limpledge	"to unite; to connect"	lode	"to exculpate"
limply	"fitting; suitable"	lode	"coarse, journey"
link	"ridge"	lodeman	"leader"
lin	"a sound or noise"	lodeship	"leadership"
lin	"to make a noise"	loding	"exculpation"
lind	"lime-tree; linden; shield of wood"	lodingly	"excusable"
linden	"made of linden wood"	loke	"gift"
line	"flax"	loke	"to give a gift or sacrafice"
linenrail	"linen-cloth"	lokely	"sacraficial"
lire	"flesh"	Londenish	"of London"
lise	"sound, fame"	longmood	"patient"
liss	"grace; alleviation"	longmoodness	"patience"
liss	"to ease, to relieve"	loom	"frequent"
list	"(impers.) to please"	loomledge	"to frequent; to be frequent"
list	"to listen"	loomledging	"frequency"
list	"hearing"	loomliness	"frequency"
list	"skill"	losingly	"ready to lose"
listy	"skillful"	looth	"troop"
lite	"little"	loother	"robber"
litewhoon	"little, very few"	lorddom	"lordship"
lith	"cliff"	lordhield	"loyalty to a lord"
lith	"limb"	lording	"lord, master"
lithbigh	"flexible"	lordship	"to rule over"
lithcraft	"agility"	lordsoken	"act of seeking protection of a lord"
lithe	"to go"	lordswike	"betrayer to his lord"
lither	"sling; slinging pouch"	lordswiking	"betrayal of one's lord"
lither	"to hurl with a sling"	lorebisen	"instructive example"
lither	"wicked"	lorebook	"book countaining instruction"
litherhood	"wickedness"	lorecraft	"skill of knowledge/learning"
litherly	"of a sling"	loredom	"teaching"
lithinchel	"little-limb"	lorefather	"teacher, doctor"
lithweak	"weak in the limbs"	lorehouse	"school"
lithy	"flexible"	loreknight	"disciple"
little	"to lessen"	lorelest	"lack of lore"
littlemood	"pusilanimous"	lorely	"of or conductive to learning"
littling	"child"	loresmith	"teacher"
littling	"a lessening"	loresome	"teachable"
litty	"beautiful"	lorespel	"instructive discourse"
liven	"sustenance"	lorethane	"teacher"
lix	"to shine"	lorrew	"teacher"

lorrewdom	"teacherdom"	make	"mate, spouse, match"
lorrewly	"teacher-like"	makeless	"without a mate"
lote	"fraud"	malt	strong past tense of melt
loth	"annoyance, injury" (other spelling loath)	manber	"producing men"
lotland	"allotted land"	manboot	"fine paid to lord of a slain man"
loud	"sound, noise"	manifold	"to multiply"
loudclipple	"loud"	manifoldness	"multiplicity"
lout	"to bend, to stoop, to bow"	manish	"humanish"
lout	"to lie hid, to hide, to lurk"	manish	"mankind"
loveday	"day for friendly reconciliation"	manishly	"human, humane"
lovelock	"amorous play"	manishliness	"humanity; human nature; incarnation"
lovend	"lover"	manisiths	"often"
lovered	"love, the state of love"	manitew	"skillful"
lovesome	"loving"	manitewness	"dexterity"
lovesomeness	"pleasantness"	mankin	"the race of man"
lovetear	"tear of love"	mankist	"human virtue"
lovetoken	"token of love"	manless	"uninhabited by men"
loveworthy	"worthy of love"	manlike	"effigy"
lovingly	"lovable"	manqualm	"mortality, pestilence, destruction"
lown	strong past participle of low	manqueller	"murderer"
lox	"lynx"	manquild	"mortality, pestilence"
lump	past participle of limp	manred	"dependance, homage, tribute"
lunger	"soon; forthwith"	manrime	"number of man"
lustber	"desirable"	manship	"humanity, courtesy"
lustberness	"enjoyment"	manthew	"manly habit or virtue"
lustful	"to rejoice; to enjoy"	manthwear	"gentle, humane"
lustfulling	"desire"	manworth	'the worth of a man"
lustihood	"lustiness"	manworthing	"adoration of humans"
lustsome	"pleasant"	mare	"nightmare, goblin, incubus"
lustyearnness	"concupiscence"	marshware	"inhabitants of marshes"
lutter	"pure"	martyring	"passion"
lutter	"to purify"	martyrrake	"martyrology"
madhood	"madness"	mass	"to celebrate mass"
madship	"madness"	masser	"one who celebrates mass"
maff	"to go astray"	masslock	"mass-offering"
maidenchild	"female child"	massrail	"vestment for mass"
maidenly	"maiden-like"	massreaf	"mass-vestments"
maidenman	"maiden-person; maiden"	massthane	"minister of mass"
main	"might"	massthaning	"service of mass"
main	"to gain strength"	masswhile	"time of celebrating mass"
maincorther	"mighty troop"	mast	"to feed with mast"
maincraft	"mighty craft"	masten	"mast; pasture for swine"
mainfast	"vigorous"	mastenred	"right of feeding swine in mastpastures"
mainful	"powerful"	mastentree	"tree yielding mast"
mainheap	"mighty group of people"	mastling	"brass; brazen vessel; mixture of anything"
mainhorse	"powerful horse"	mastlingsmith	"brass-worker"
mainless	"powerless"	masty	"overfed with mast"
mainlest	"lack of strength"	mathe	"maggot"
mainstrong	"powerfully strong"	mathel	"to speak", to harangue"
mainthrim	"majesty"	matheller	"speaker"
maith	"family, tribe, group; province, country"	mathelern	"council-house"
maithred	"relationship"	mathelfrith	"security at public assemblies"

mathelly	"talkative"	meathful	"humane"
mathelstead	"place of assembly"	meathing	"measuring"
mathelword	"address, speech"	meathless	"immoderate; rapacious"
mathom	"treasure"	meathly	"moderate"
mathomchest	"treasurechest"	meatkin	"kind of food"
mathomcleave	"treasurechamber"	meatlest	"want of food; starvation"
mathomhoard	"treasurehoard"	meatsax	"meatknife"
mathomhouse	"treasurehouse"	meatship	"feeding, meal, provision of food"
may	"a maiden"	meatstick	"meat-utensil"
may	"kinsman"	meatswam	"edible mushroom"
mayboot	"compensation paid to the relatives of a murdered man"	medelmichel	"moderate-sized"
maychild	"young kinsman"	medtrum	"weak"
mayheamed	"incest"	medtrumness	"weakness"
mayless	"without relatives"	meech	"sword"
mayly	"belonging to relative(s)"	meed	"reward"
maymoot	"meeting of kinsmen"	meed	"to reward"
maymurder	"murder of a relative"	meedful	"meritorious"
mayrake	"generation; genealogy"	meethe	"tired, worn"
mayred	"kinship; relationship"	meethe	"to grow weary"
mayshire	"a division/district containing family members"	meetheness	"fatigue"
maysib	"relationship; affection among relatives"	meethey	"tired"
maywrit	"genealogy"	meen	"necklace"
mead	"meadow"	mennen	"handmaiden"
meadern	"meadhall"	mere	"sea"
meadbench	"bench in meadhall"	mereboat	"seaboat"
meadgreen	"green as a meadow"	meredeer	"sea-animal"
meadland	"meadowland"	merefish	"seafish"
meadshench	"meadcup"	mereflood	"body of water; deluge"
meadwong	"field where the meadhall stood"	meregroat	"pearl"
meal	"phlegm; mucus"	mereground	"the bottom of sea or lake"
mealsettle	"a seat at a table"	meremennen	"mermaid"
mealtide	"mealtime"	merenadder	"seasnake"
meanly	"common"	mereswine	"porpoise, dolphin"
meanness	"communion, fellowship"	merry	"to make merry"
meanship	"community"	mete	"measuring, moderation"
meansome	"to impart; to partake; to participate"	mete	"to measure"
meansomeness	"fellowship; participation"	mete	"(impers.) to dream"
meansoming	"fellowship; participation"	metefast	"moderate"
mear	"to declare, to glorify"	metefastness	"moderation"
mear	"famous"	metekind	"metrical"
mearly	"famous"	meteledge	"to moderate"
mearness	"famousness"	meterwright	"metrician; poet"
mearth	"glory"	meting	"dream"
mearse	"to make or become famouse"	metely	"moderate"
mearsing	"fame; celebration"	meteyard	"measuring stick"
meatern	"meathouse"	mew	strong past tense of mow
meatboard	"table"	michel	"great, much, large" (other spelling muchel)
meatcleave	"foodcloset"	michel	"to become great; to make great"
meatgavel	"payment in food"	micheling	"becoming great"
meatkisty	"hospitable"	michelmood	"magnanimous"
meath	"measure; honour"	michelness	"greatness, magnificence"
meathe	"to honour"	middaily	"meridian"

middenard	"the middle-world of men; earth"	misbisen	"to set a bad example"
middenarden	"earthly"	misborn	"misbehaved"
middenardly	"earthly"	mischar	"to pervert"
middleard	"the world of men"	misdeem	"misjudge"
middleedder	"median vein"	misdo	"to do wrong; to ill-treat""
middlen	"middle, center, midst"	misendbierd	"to arrange amiss"
middling	"middle, midst"	misfall	"to turn out ill"
middling or middlings	"to a moderate extent"	misfall	"mischance"
middness	"middle"	misfang	"to take amiss"
midder	"more in the middle"	misfare	"to go wrong"
midfast	"middle of a fast"	misgo	"to go wrong"
midlying	"lying together"	mishold	"to hold amiss; to neglect"
midmorn	"middle of the morn"	misholdsomeness	"neglectfulness"
midside	"middle of the side"	mislear	"to teach amiss"
midspeaking	"interlocution"	mislike	"(impers.) to displease"
midthole	"to sympathise"	mislimp	"to befall amiss"
midtholing	"compassion"	mislimp	"misfortune"
midthrowing	"compassion"	mislive	"to live amiss"
midwist	"presence; society"	mislived	"wicked"
midwoning	"living with someone"	mislore	"ill teaching"
midwright	"cooperator"	misly	"various"
mield	"to announce; to reveal"	mismake	"to make amiss"
mig	"urine"	misspow	"to fare amiss"
mightful	"powerful"	misqueath	"to speak ill"
mightihood	"mightiness"	misqueem	"to displease"
mightly	"possible"	missay	"to say amiss"
mild	"to become mild"	misspeech	"slander"
mildheart	"merciful"	misthee	"to degenerate"
mildheartness	"mercy, compassion"	misthink	"(impers.) to be mistaken"
mildhood	"mildness"	mistide	"to turn out ill"
mildship	"mildness"	mistight	"to lead astray"
mileway	"time taken to walk a mile" (c. 20 mins.)	mistightingly	"dehortative"
milken	"of milk"	mistihood	"mystery"
milklithe	"soft as milk"	mistruth	"unbelief, misbelief"
milksop	"a feeble fellow"	miswax	"to grow improperly"
milksucking	"suckling"	miswend	"to pervert"
milkvat	"milk-container"	miswone	"evil habit"
milt	"spleen"	miswork	"misdeed"
miltcothe	"spleendisease"	misyeem	"to neglect"
miltster	"harlot"	mithe	"to hide"
min	"memory"	mixen	"dungheap"
mindday	"anniversary; commemoration day"	mo	"more"
mindworth	"worth minding"	moe	"bad; wanton"
mindy	"mindful"	moely	"wanton"
minge	"to mix; to associate with"	moeness	"wantonness"
mingedness	"mixture; sexual intercourse"	molsen	"to moulder; to decay"
minging	"mixture"	molten	strong past participle of melt
minken	"female monk"	mon	"mindful"
mint	"to intend"	mon	"to be mindful"
mirthless	"sad"	mone	"evil deed; crime"
misbelief	"suspician"	monedeed	"evil deed"
misbelieved	"infidel"	moneful	"evil"

monely	"evil"	morntidely	"matutinal"
moncoath	"false oath"	mornwhile	"morning"
moneshild	"crime"	morrowmeal	"morning meal"
moneswear	"to forswear"	morrowtide	"morrow"
monesworn	"perjured"	morth	"death"
moneword	"wicked word"	morthdeed	"murder"
monework	"crime"	morthwright	"murderer"
monewright	"worker of evil"	motherbairn	"mother's child"
mong	"mix, mixture"	motherborough	"metropolis"
monger	"dealer, merchant"	mothern	"of mothers, maternal"
moning	"rememberance"	mothernkin	"mather's kin"
monk	"to make a monk"	mothernmay	"maternal kinsman"
monkbehote	"monastic vow"	motherriff	"mother's womb"
monkchild	"child meant for monastic life"	mound	"protection"
monklife	"monastic life"	mound	"to protect"
monkreaf	"monastic garb"	moundbierd	"to protect"
monkthew	"monastic custom"	moundbierdness	"protection"
monnight	"night corresponding to monday"	moundbore	"protector"
monthboot	"penance for a month"	moundbreach	"breach of protection"
monthsick	"menstruous"	moundcraft	"strength of protecting"
moodcare	"sorrow, grief, anxiety"	mousedun	"grayish brown like a mouse"
moodcraft	"intellegence"	mousefall	"mousetrap"
moodcrafty	"intellegent"	mousehaired	"dunhaired"
moodlest	"lack of spirit"	mouthcothe	"mouthdisease"
moodseave	"heart, spirit"	mouthfree	"free to speak"
moodthwear	"meek"	mouthroof	"palate"
moodful	"proud"	mown	strong past participle of mow
moody	"to be proud"	muchel	"great, much, large" (other spelling michel)
moonly	"lunar"	muchel	"to magnify"
moonshilling	"moonshaped ornament; coin worn as ornament"	muchel	"magnitude"
moonsick	"lunatic"	muchelhood	"greatness"
mootern	"courthouse"	muchelness	"greatness"
mootbell	"bell for summoning moot"	muleherd	"keeper of mules"
mooter	"public speaker; disputer; pleader"	mun	"remember"
moothall	"assembly hall"	nadder	"snake"
moothouse	"meeting-house"	nadderfow	"spotted like a snake"
mooting	"conversation"	nadderkin	"a family of snakes"
mootman	"orator"	naft	"a state of not having"
mootstead	"meeting-place"	nafty	"poor"
mootstead	"meeting-place"	nailsax	"knife to cut nails"
moard	"reward; pay"	nake	"boat"
more	"parsnip, carrot; root, stump"	nake	"to make naked"
more	"to root"	naked	"to make naked"
more	"to increase, to augment"	nakedhood	"nakedness"
morngive	"gift on the morn after marriage"	nalls	"not at all"
morninggive	"morning gift"	name	strong past tense of nim (like came)
mornlight	"dawn"	namechighing	"calling by name"
mornlong	"lasting a morning"	namecouth	"wellknown"
mornly	"matutinal"	namecouthhood	"renown"
mornspel	"news published at morn"	namemeal	"name by name"
mornstar	"morning-star"	nany	"not any"
morntide	"morningtime"	narrowneed	"urgent need"

narrowtharf	"urgent need"	nethergo	"to descend"
narxenwong	"paradise"	nethering	"humilation"
narxenwongly	"of paradise"	netheringly	"deserving to be lowered"
nast	"collision"	nethersty	"a descent"
nast	"to contend with"	netherstying	"a descent"
natheless	"nevertheless"	nethertorving	"a throwing down"
naught	"useless"	newbaken	"newly baked"
naughtship	"worthlessness"	newcome	"newly come"
nave	"to have not"	newkenned	"newly born"
navegore	"auger"	newleared	"newly learned"
naw	"bent down"	newling or newlings	"newly"
ne	"not; neither, nor"	newslicked	"freshly smoothed"
nease	"to visit"	newsodden	"newly boiled"
neasing	"access; visit"	nicker	"watersprite"
neat	"a bovine animal; cattle"	nie	"to bow oneself"
neaten	"small animal"	nif	"not if"
neaten	"kind of small animal"	nift	"neice"
neatenly	"animal-like"	nigh	"near, close"
neatherd	"cowherd"	nigh	"nearly; almost"
neathward	"lower"	nighbowing	"neighbour"
neave	"nephew"	nighchester	"nearby town"
neb	"face; nose"	nighfriend	"close friend"
nebcorn	"pimple"	nighhand	"near at hand"
neblit	"face"	nighledge	"to approach"
nebsalve	"face powder"	nighledge	"approach"
nebshaft	"face"	nighledging	"approach"
nee	"corpse"	nighman	"neighbouring man"
neefowl	"bird of prey"	nighmay	"close relation"
neebed	"corpsebed"	nighsib	"close relationship"
needbehovely	"necessary"	nighsib	"closely related"
needhood	"condition of needing"	nightbutterfly	"beetle or moth of the night"
needling	"slave"	nightheed	"neighbouring nation"
neednim	"to take by force"	nightide	"a time that is near"
needs	"of necessity"	nightown	"nearby town"
needtharf	"necessity"	nights	"by night"
needtharfness	"necessity"	nightspel	"charm said at night"
needwise	"needful"	nightthester	"nightdarkness"
needwiseness	"needfulness"	nightward	"nightly guardian"
needwright	"involuntary agent"	nightwhile	"space of a night'
neep	"turnip"	nighwist	"neighbourhood; nearness; cohabitation"
neighbourred	"vicinity"	nighwood	"nearby wood"
nere	"were not"	nill	"will not"
nes	"not yes"	nilling	"refusing"
nesh	"soft"	nim	"to take"
nesh	"to make or become soft"	nimming	"action of taking"
neshhood	"tenderness"	nimth	"unless; except"
nether	"to lower; to depress; to bring down"	nip	"darkness"
netherastie	"to descend"	nipful	"darkful"
netherdeal	"lower part"	nipe	"to darken"
netheredge	"lower edge"	nis	"is not"
netherfloor	"lower floor"	nit	"to wit not"
nethergang	"descent"	nit	"useful"

nite	"to thrust; to knock; to collide"	onemood	"unanimous"
nittle	"addicted to thrusting (of an ox)"	oneread	"resolute"
nitness	"usefulness"	onereadness	"unanimity"
nitworth	"useful"	onestretches	"at one stretch"
nitworthness	"utility"	onewield	"monarchy"
nith	"strife; envy; hostility"	onewill	"willful, obstinant"
nithcraft	"malice"	onewillness	"willfulness, obstinancy"
nithful	"envious; hostile"	oor	"beginning"
nithship	"wickedness"	openarse	"meddler"
nithing	"wretch"	openheaded	"bareheaded"
nivel	"brow"	ord	"point"
nivelcrump	"inclined"	ore	"honour"
noll	"top; crown of the head; the head"	ore	"to honour"
nome	strong past participle of nim (other spelling numb)	orefast	"dignified"
noonmeat	"noontime repast"	oreful	"respectful"
noonsench	"luncheon, noondrinking"	oreld	"great age"
nooth	"boldness"	oreless	"dishonourable"
nop	"to pluck"	orestaff	"kindness"
northdeal	"northern part"	oreworth	"venerable"
northeasthurn	"northeast-corner"	oreye	"invisible"
northhurn	"northern corner"	orf	"cattle, livestock"
northright	"due north"	orfkin	"cattle"
note	"utility"	orfqualm	"cattle-plague"
note	"to make use of, enjoy"	orgle	"pride"
noteful	"useful"	orgleword	"arrogant wording"
notesome	"profitable"	orgley	"ignomious"
noteyearn	"industrious"	orlay	"fate"
nould	"would not"	ormeet	"immense"
nowe	"not to owe"	ormeetness	"immensity"
nowhence	"from now where"	ormood	"despondent, despairing"
nowhither	"nowhere"	ormoodness	"desparation"
nowwhilom	"nowadays"	orold	"very old"
nuel	"abysmal"	orped	"keen, brave"
nuelness	"abyss"	orpedship	"bravery"
numb or num	strong past participle of nim (other spelling nome)	orsorrow	"without sorrow"
o	"ever"	orsorrowness	"sorrowlessness"
oad	"pile"	orsoul	"lifeless"
oakholt	"an oak wood"	ort	"contest"
oft	"often"	orth	"breath"
oftsith	"frequent"	orth	"to breathe"
oldspel	"old saying"	orthank	"intellgence"
oldyedding	"old saying"	orthankship	"mechanical art"
ole	"fire, burning"	ortrow	"despairing"
olfend	"camel"	ortrow	"to despair; to doubt; to suspect"
oll	"contumely"	ortstow	"contest-place"
ond	"envy"	orween	"hopeless, despairing"
oned	"united"	orween	"to despair"
onefold	"simple"	orwie	"not fighting, unwarlike"
onefoldness	"simplicity"	orworth	"shame, dishonour"
onehood	"unity"	otherwhile	"occasionally"
onehorn	"unicorn"	ottern	"of otter skin"
onekin	"only"	ourlandish	"of our land"

outdrive	"to drive out"	overhearness	"neglect; disobedience"
outdo	"to do out, to put out"	overhie	"overtake"
outethem	"to breathe out"	overhope	"overconfidence"
outfare	"to fare out"	overhow	"to contemn, to despise"
outfare	"exit"	overhow	"contempt"
outflow	"to flow out"	overlive	"to survive"
outgang	"a going out, exist, departure"	overlight	"to light upon"
outgangle	"fond of going out"	overmete	"excessive; immoderate"
outgo	"to go out"	overmichel	"overmuch"
outhalf	"outer side"	overmood	"pride"
outland	"foreign land"	overmood	"proud"
outlead	"to lead out"	overmoodness	"pride"
outnim	"to take out"	overmoody	"proud; arrogant"
outrider	"rider out"	overmore	"besides, moreover"
outrun	"a running out"	overnoon	"afternoon"
outshoot	"to shoot out"	oversee	"to look upon"
outshove	"to shove out"	oversealy	"on the other side of the sea"
outslide	"to slide out"	oversilver	"to cover with silver"
outstead	"foreign place"	overspeak	"to speak about"
outstraught	"outstretched"	overspeech	"talkativeness"
outwith	"on the outside, out of, beyond"	oversprecklness	"talkativeness"
ove	"above"	overswithster	"female victor"
ovemost	"abovemost"	overstie	"to climb over"
ovenbaken	"baked in an oven"	overswithe	"to overpower"
over	"upper"	overswithe	"overmuch"
overbe	"to be over; to rule"	overthatch	"to cover over"
overbide	"to outlast; to survive"	overthwart	"across"
overbridge	"to bridge over"	overtield	"to furnish with an awning"
overchar	"to cross over"	overtrow	"to over-confide"
overcliff	"overhanging cliff"	overwake	"to watch over"
overclothe	"to cover"	overwax	"to overgrow"
overcomer	"conquerer"	overween	"presumption"
overdeed	"exaggeration, intemperance"	overwhere	"everywhere"
overeak	"surplus; remainder; addition"	overwork	"superstructure"
overeat	"gluttony"	overwrit	"superscription"
overest	"uppermost"	overwry	"to cover over"
overettle	"gluttonous"	ovet	"fruit"
overfall	"to fall over"	ovost	"haste"
overfare	"a passing over"	owhat	"anything"
overfare	"to pass over"	owhen	"whenever, any or every time"
overfill	"sufeit; excess"	owhence	"from any whence"
overflowness	"superfluity"	owhere	"anywhere"
overfold	"to fold over"	owhither	"in any direction"
overfly	"to fly over"	owho	"anyone"
overfrorn	"frozen over"	owning	"possession"
overgang	"to go over"	owningly	"possessive"
overglide	"to glide over"	oxland	"land workable by one ox
overglinged	"overadorned"	pad	"toad"
overget	"to forget; to get over"	paddock	"frog or toad"
overgo	"to go over"	peach	"to deceive"
overharr	"overlord"	peasekin	"a kind of pease"
overheal	"to cover over"	pennyale	"poor ale (at a penny per gallon)

perilous	"dangerous"	quoning	"lamentation"
pight	"pitched"	quoth	past tense of queath (other spellings quath, quod)
piningstool	"stool of punishment"	rad	"quick"
pintle	"penis"	rade	"to be quick"
plail	"playful"	radmood	"hastey"
plat	"to strike, to break; to throw down flat"	radness	"quickness"
playster	"(female) athlete, player"	rail	"to clothe"
playstead	"playground"	rail	"clothing"
playstow	"playground"	railchest	"clothing-chest"
plee	"danger"	railhouse	"house for clothing; vestry"
pleely	"dangerous"	railthane	"keeper of clothing"
plightly	"dangerous"	railward	"keeper of clothing"
poke	"bag"	rake	"throat"
poundmeal	"pound by pound"	rake	"explanation, account"
prat	"trick"	rakent	"chain, fetter"
prickmeal	"point by point"	rakentie	"chain"
psalmwright	"psalmist"	rakentie	"to chain"
puck	"goblin"	ramson	"onion, garlic"
quale	"murder"	rand	"margin, border; boss of shield; shield itself"
qualmhouse	"house of torture or execution"	randbea	"boss of shield"
qualmstow	"place of execution"	randhavend	"shield bearer"
quartern	"prison"	randwie	"shieldwarrior"
quath	past tense of queath (other spellings quoth, quod)	rane	"whale" (other spelling rone)
queal	"to die"	ravenkin	"a kin of ravens"
queath	"to say"	rawness	"rawness"
queathword	"promise"	reaf	"plunder"
queem	"to gratify"	reaflock	"robbery"
queem	"pleasant"	ream	"noise"
queemness	"pleasure"	read	"advice" (other spelling rede)
qued	"filth"	readbore	"adviser"
quedhood	"badness"	readen	"condition"
quedly	"bad"	readenwrit	"written agreement"
quedness	"badness"	readfast	"resolute"
quedship	"evil"	readfastness	"resoluteness"
queller	"killer"	readful	"wise"
quelm	"to torment'	readgive	"counsellor"
quetch	"to shake, to twitch"	readingshamble	"reading stool"
quickbeam	"quicken tree"	readless	"illadvised"
quickbeamen	"of quicken tree"	readly	"advisable"
quicklock	"a living sacrifice"	readman	"counsellor"
quicksousel	"hell; torment"	readsman	"counsellor"
quicktree	"quicken tree"	readster	"(female) reader"
quid	"to talk, to say"	readwise	"wise in counsel"
quid	"saying"	reaflock	"robbery"
quild	"destruction; slaughter"	reather	"breast, bosom"
quith	"belly; womb"	reaver	"robber"
quiver	"brisk, lively"	recken	"ready"
quod	past tense of queath (other spellings quath, quoth)	recklest	"carelessness"
quole	past tense of queal (like stole)	redd	"to free from"
quolen	past participle of queal (like stolen)	redding	"freeing, salvation"
quone	"to lament"	rede	"advice"
quoney	"sad"		

reeden	"made of reed"	rime	"to count"
reen	"to arrange"	rimebook	"calendar"
rend	"to tear"	rimecraft	"arithmetic"
rep	"to touch"	rimecrafty	"skilled with numbers"
repping	"sense of touch"	rimer	"calculator"
reer	"to move, to shake"	rimple	"wrinkle"
reermouse	"bat"	rin	"contact"
reerness	"disturbance"	rindle	"runnel, runner"
reethe	"fierce"	rine	"to touch"
reethemood	"fierce-hearted"	ringnet	"ringmail"
reetheness	"fierceness"	ringiwindle	"sphere"
reeth	"victory"	rink	"man"
reeve	"to roof"	risen	"fit, meet"
reeveship	"reeve's office"	rith	"fever"
reezingly	"perishable"	rith	"rivulet, stream"
rem	"to hinder"	rither/rother	"bovine-beast"
remming	"hinderance"	ritherherd	"neatherd"
resp	"stripping, spoilation"	rithern	"of cattle, bovine"
rew	strong past tense of row	rock	"overgarment, rochet"
rich	"kingdom"	rodder	"heavens"
richdom	"kingly rule; wealth"	rodderly	"heavenly"
rid	"rider"	Romeleed	"men of Rome"
ridder	"sieve"	Romerich	"empire of Rome"
ridder	"to sift"	Rometheed	"Romans"
ridgebone	"backbone, spine"	Romeware	"the inhabitants of Rome"
ridgemarrow	"spinal marrow"	rone	"whale"
rief	"scabby, leperous"	roneroad *	"whaleroad; the sea"
riff	"belly, womb"	rood	"the cross"
rift	"veil; curtain"	roodbore	"crossbearer"
rightdoing	"doing what is right"	roodfasten	"to crucify"
rightdom	"right judgement"	roodpine	"pain of the cross"
rightend	"director, leader""	roodtoken	"sign of the cross"
righter	"director, leader"	roofwright	"roofmaker"
rightfasten	"duly ordained fast"	roomgivel	"liberal"
rightfastenday	"duly ordained fasting day"	roomgivelness	"liberality"
rightfastentide	"duly ordained time of fasting"	roomhanded	"liberal"
rightfathernkin	"direct paternal line"	roomheart	"largehearted, generous"
rightheamed	"lawful wedlock"	roomheartness	"liberality"
righting	"direction; guidance"	roommood	"liberal"
rightledge	"to make right"	roommoodness	"liberality"
rightlorddom	"lawful authority""	roomness	"breadth, abundance"
rightmothernkin	'direct maternal line"	roop	"clamour"
rights	"rightly, straightly"	roop	"to shout"
rightspel	"rightful discourse"	root	"glad"
rightthue	"lawful slave"	rootfast	"strongly rooted or established"
righttide	"proper time"	rootness	"gladness"
rightwere	"lawful husband"	rootfast	"firmly established"
rightwife	"lawful wife"	ropeincel	"small rope"
rightwise	"righteous"	rord	"voice; food"
rightwise	"to make righteous"	rord	"to speak; to feed"
rightwisehood	"righteousness"	rordday	"feast-day"
rime	"number"	rording	"refection"

rordinghouse	"refectory"	Saxish	"of the Saxons"
rordingtide	"mealtime"	Saxland	"land of the Saxons"
rorn	"fallen"	Saxleed	"the Saxon people"
rosen	"made of roses"	Saxtheed	"the Saxon nation"
rosered	"red as a rose"	sayend	"saying one, a sayer"
roughship	"roughness"	schoolfere	"school fellow"
roun	"mystery" (other spelling rown)	Scotleed	"Scottish people"
roun	"to whisper"	Scottheed	"Scottish nation"
rouse	"earth"	scurved	"scabby"
rown	"mystery"	scythed	"armed with a scythe"
rown	"to whisper"	seachessil	"seasand"
rown	strong past participle of row	seafoor	"sea-journey"
rowncrafty	"skilled in mysteries"	seaground	"seabottom"
rowner	"whisperer, talebearer"	seahalf	"seaside"
rownly	"mystical"	sealeeth	"sea-song"
rownstaff	"runic letter"	sealth	"prosperity"
rownwit	"counseller"	sealy	"of the sea, marine"
rud	"red colour; blush"	seanake	"seaship"
rud	"to become ruddy"	searim	"seashore"
ruddock	"robin"	seasith	"seavoyage"
rue	"sorrow, penitence"	seastar	"guiding star (for sailors)"
rue	"sad, sorrowful"	seath	"pit"
rueness	"penitance, contrition"	seatrail	"covering for a seat"
ruey	"sorrowful"	scave	"spirit"
ruth	"mercy"	sedge	"man"
ryen	"made of rye"	seech	"to seek"
sack	"srife, contest"	seedfowl	"bird living on seeds"
sackful	"quarrelsome"	seedkin	"kind of seed"
sackless	"innocent"	seedleap	"seedbasket"
sain	"to make the sign of the cross on; to bless"	seedly	"seminal"
sain	"saying, story, legend"	seel	"hall"
sake	"to struggle"	seel	"good"
salten	strong past participle of salt	seely	"happy; silly"
saltmere	"saltpond"	seen	"eyesight"
saltseath	"saltpit, saltspring"	seethe	"to affirm" (related to sooth)
samed	"together"	seethend	"affirming one, affirmer"
samen	"together"	seething	"affirmation, proof"
samen	"to gather, to congregate"	selcouth	"unusual; strange; wonderful"
samening	"meeting"	selcouth	"to make strange or wonderful"
sand	"a sending; mission; message" (other spelling sond)	seld	"seldom"
sare	"skill"	seldcome	"infrequent coming"
sarecraft	"artifice"	seldly	"rare, strange, wonderous" (other spelling selly)
sarecrafty	"skillful"	seldseen	"seldom seen, rare"
sarely	"artistic"	selfdeemer	"a monk living subject only to his own rules"
sarethank	"sagicity, skill"	selfdom	"independence"
sarethankle	"shrewd, wise"	selfly	"spontaneous, voluntary"
sarewrench	"skillful trick"	selfquale	"suicide"
sark	"shirt"	selfwill	"one's own will"
saught	"to conciliate"	selfwills	"voluntarily"
sax	"knife; dagger"	sellen	"gift"
Sax	"saxon (plural); a saxon"	sellend	"selling one, a seller, giver"
saxben	"knife wound"	sellingly	"sellable"

selly	"rare, strange, wonderous" (other spelling seldly)	shildful	"sinful, guilty"
selt	strong past tense of salt	shildless	"guiltless"
sench	"to make sink"	shildwite	"fine for a crime"
sengreen	"always green"	shildy	"guilty"
sengreen	"houseleek"	shilken	"female servant"
setness	"composition; constitution; statute"	shill	"to seperate"
settle	"seat"	shillingrime	"count of shillings"
settlegang	"a setting or sinking"	shime	"splendour"
sew	"sap, juice; pottage"	shime	"to shine"
sew	strong past tense of sow	shin	"phantom/illusion"
shab	"scab"	shincraft	"sorcery"
shabbed	"scabbed"	shinhue	"spectre, illusion"
shalk	"servant"	shinlock	"magic"
shamble	"stool, bench"	shinly	"spectral"
shamefast	"modest"	shinner	"magician"
shamelest	"shamelessness"	shipcraft	"shipbuilding"
shamelimb	"private part"	shipfare	"voyage"
shamely	"shameful"	shipfarend	"shipfaring one, a sailor"
shand	"shame"	shipfierd	"naval expedition"
shandly	"shameful"	shipfultom	"naval aid"
shandword	"shameful wording"	shipgome	"sailor"
shanklire	"calf of the leg"	shiphere	"naval force"
shapen	strong past participle of shape	shipinchel	"little ship"
shapend	"the shaping one, God"	shiplast	"shipload"
shapenness	"creation, formation"	shiplithend	"shipgoing one, sailor"
sharn	"dung"	shiplord	"lord of the ship"
sharnbud	"dungbeetle"	shiply	"naval"
sharnweevil	"dungbeetle"	shipper	"sailor"
sharpthankle	"quickwitted"	shipwise	"in the manner of a ship"
sharve	"to cut off"	shirt	"to shorten, to run short"
sharving	"scraping"	shite	"to defecate"
shat	"property"	shitten	past participle of shite
sheafmeal	"sheaf by sheaf"	shode	"top of head"
shean	"to break, to wrench open"	shoer	"shoemaker"
shed	"distinction"	shoethane	"shoecleaner"
shedly	"reasonable"	shoewright	"shoemaker"
shedwise	"rational"	shold	"thin, shallow"
shedwiseness	"discrimination"	shoop	strong past tense of shape (like shook)
sheen	"beautiful"	shope	"poet"
sheeply	"of a sheep"	shopecraft	"poetry"
shench	"drink"	shopeleeth	"poem"
shend	"to shame"	shopely	"poetic"
shendful	ignominious"	shoperord	"poetic language"
shendle	"reproach"	shotepast tense of shite	
shendlock	"ignominy"	shoulderrail	"cap"
shendship	"disgrace"	shower	"one that shows"
shent	"disgrace"	showern	"show-house"
shide	"slip of wood"	showingstow	"a place for showing"
shieldend	"shielding one, protector"	shraff	"cave"
shieldwright	"shieldmaker"	shram	past tense of shrim (like swam)
shill	"to seperate"	shreep	"advantage"
shild	"offence"	shreep	"suitable, fit"

shrench	"to make shrink"	sinhueship	"permanant tie, marriage"
shrewdhood	"wickedness"	sink	"treasure"
shrid	"vehicle, chariot"	sinkroden	"adorned in treasures"
shridden	past participle of shrithe	sinlust	"lust to sin"
shride	"to clothe" (cf. shroud)	sinnight	"endless night"
shridwain	"chariot"	sinnights	"in endless night; night after night"
shriftbook	"book of penances, or on penance"	sinny	"guilty"
shriftfather	"confessor"	sinred	"marriage"
shrim	"to shrink"	sinship	"marriage"
shrit	"hermaphrodite"	sinshiply	"conjugal"
shrithe	"to glide, to move"	sinsorrow	"perpetual sorrow"
shrithe	past tense of shrithe	sintrindle	"circular, globular"
shrum	past participle of shrim (like swum)	sinwalt	"round, globular"
shuck	"demon"	sinwalt	"roundness, globularity"
shucken	"devilish"	sisterbairn	"sister's child, nephew"
shymood	"timid"	sisterson	"sister's son, nephew"
sib	"peace; relationship"	sitch	"small stream"
sibkiss	"kiss of peace"	sith	"journey"
sibly	"of peace, peaceable"	sith	"since"
sibman	"relative"	sith	"comrade, companion"
sibness	"peace, kindred"	sithbook	"itinerary"
sibred	"affinity, relationship"	sithe	"to journey"
sibsome	"peacable, friendly"	sithvat	"journey"
sibsome	"to reconcile, to be reconciled"	siver	"clean, sober"
sibsoming	"peace-making"	siverly	"clean, sober"
sibyearnness	"pacific disposition"	sixedge	"sixsided"
sickle	"to become sick"	sixfeet	"of six poetic feet"
sid	"custom"	sixhurned	"having six angles"
sid	"to arrange, to set right"	slade	"valley, glade"
side	"silk"	slay	"slaughter"
side	"wide, ample"	sleepern	"dormitory"
sideling or sidelings	"sideways"	sleepber	"soporific, sleepbearing"
siden	"silken"	sleeple	"somnolent, lethargic"
sideworm	silkworm"	sleepleness	somnolence, lethargy"
sidful	"decorous"	sleeplest	"sleeplessness"
sie	"victory"	slidder	"slippery"
siebeacon	"victory-beacon"	slidder	"to slip, to slide"
siefast	"victorious"	slidderness	"slipperiness"
siefastness	"victoriousness"	slinkend	"reptile"
siely	"victorious"	slipshoe	"slipper"
siespeed	"victory-success"	slite	"to slit"
sietoken	"victory-token"	slithe	"savage"
sietiber	"victory-offering or sacrafice"	slitten	past participle of slite
silvervat	"silver vessel"	slitten	"schismatic, heretic"
simble	"festival, feast"	slittle	"biting, pungent"
simbleday	"feastday"	sloat	"morsel"
simblely	"festive"	sloethorn	"blackthorn"
simbletide	"feasttime"	sloom	"slumber"
sinboot	"penance"	slote	past tense of slite
sinfow	"sinstained"	smack	"taste"
singingly	"that may be sung"	smake	"to flatter"
sinhuen	"married couple"	smalltharms	"small intestines"

smear	"ointment, fat, grease, lard, tallow, suet"	snottership	"reasonableness"
smeargavel	"tax on unguents"	snovel	"mucus"
smearls	"ointment"	sod	a strong past tense of seethe (other spelling sothe)
smearmongster	"butter woman"	sode	"snare, cord, halter"
smearsalve	"unguent"	sodden	past participle of seethe
smeartharm	"entrail"	soken	"inquiry"
smeat	"pure"	somedeal	"somewhat"
smeatgold	"pure gold"	sond	"a sending; mission; message" (other spelling sand)
smeatgolden	"of pure gold"	soom	"arbitration"
smeath	"meditation"	soot	"sweet" (other spelling swoot)
smeddum	"flour"	sooth	"truth"
smeddumen	"of flour"	soothfast	"true, trustworthy"
smeeth	"smooth"	soothfastness	"trueness, trustworthiness"
smeeth	"to make smooth, to soften"	soothhood	"truth"
smelting	"amber"	soothquid	"true saying or speech; proverb"
smicker	"elegant"	sooths	"verily"
smilt	"mild, peaceable, calm"	soothsain	"true statement"
smiltness	"traquility, peace"	soothsaw	"true saying"
smit	"smudge, smut, blot; pollution"	soothsay	" to say the truth"
smit	"to befoul"	soothspel	"true discourse"
smithcraft	"manual art"	sorecloth	"bandage"
smolt	"peaceful"	sorespel	"sorrowful discourse"
smore	"to strangle, to choke, to suffocate"	sorrimood	"dejected"
smort	strong past tense of smart	sorrowlest	"freedom from sorrow; security"
smorten	strong past participle of smart	sorrowly	"miserable"
smow	"to creep"	sorrowstaff	"sorrow"
smowingly	"creeping"	sot	"foolish"
snead	"to cut"	sothe	strong past tense of seethe (other spelling sod)
snead	"piece, morsel"	sothood	"folly"
sneadinghouse	"cook's shop"	sothough	"however, yet, nevertheless"
sneadingsheep	"sheep for slaughter"	sothoughwhether	"however"
sneadmeal	"slice by slice, bit by bit"	sotship	"folly"
snell	"smart, swift"	soulbearend	"a human"
snellness	"agility"	souled	"having a soul"
snellship	"swiftness"	soulkind	"spiritual"
snelly	"smart, ready, bold"	soundful	"to be sound, to prosper"
snicken	past participle of snike	soureyed	"blear-eyed"
snid	"slice"	sousel	"torment"
snidden	past participle of snithe	souselquale	"painful death"
snike	"to sneak"	souselstead	"place of torment"
snite	"to blow the nose"	sowhatso	"whatsoever"
snithe	"to cut"	sowhether	"whichever"
snithing	"incision"	sown	strong past participle of sow
sniting	"blowing of nose"	spake	a past tense of speak
snitter	"wisdom"	span	past tense of spin
snittercraft	"wisdom"	spane	"suggestion"
snoke	past tense of snike	spane	"to draw on, to allure"
snore	"daughter in law"	spane	"a teat"
snothe	past tense of snithe	spaner	"seducer, enticer"
snotter	"prudent"	sparn	strong past tense of spurn
snotterly	"philosophic, wise"	spattle	"to spit out"
snotterness	"wisdom"	spattle	"spittle"

spearhalf	"male line of descent"	stathelfasten	"to make firm, to establish"
spearhand	"male line of descent"	statheling	"foundation"
speckfow	"covered in specks"	stave	"to give dictation"
speechern	"place for speaking"	steadfasthood	"steadfastness"
speedy	"lucky, prosperous"	steadfastship	"steadfastness"
spellbode	"messenger"	steadless	"unsteady"
spellbook	"book of sermons"	stean	"jug"
spelling	"speech, conversation"	stear	"story, history"
spewel	"emetic"	stearwriter	"historian"
spield	"ember, torch"	steelen	"of steel, hard as steel"
spindlehalf	"female line of descent"	steen	"to stone; to adorn with precious stones"
spir	"to track"	steenen	"of stone"
splot	"spot"	steening	"stoning"
splotted	"spotted"	steer	"control; steering"
splotty	"spotty"	steerend	"steerer; director"
spong	"clasp"	steerless	"uncontrolled"
spow	"to succeed, to thrive"	steersettle	"steerman's seat"
sprank	"a shoot"	stell	"to place"
spreckle	"loquacious"	stenchber	"stinking"
spreckleness	"loquacity"	stepbairn	"stepchild; orphan"
sprind	"vigorous, strong"	stepmeal	"step by step"
springe	"to make spring"	stere	"to burn incense"
spurnen	strong past participle of spurn	stering	"incense"
sputh	"vomitting, vomit"	sternhood	"severity"
staffcraft	"grammar"	steven	"voice"
staffcrafty	"lettered"	steven	"to institute; to arrange; to regulate"
staffifay	"syllable"	stickle	"steep; piercing; difficult"
staffkist	"letters, learning from books"	stie	"to go, to ascend"
staffleared	"instructed, learned"	stien	past participle of stie
stafflearner	"student"	stier	"climber" (other spelling styer)
stafflither	"a sling, a 'balista'"	stiffhood	"stiffness"
staffly	"literary, literal"	stight	"to direct; to arrange"
staffplay	"literary game"	stightend	"director"
staffrow	"row of letters, alphabet"	stighter	"director"
staffwise	"lettered, learned"	stighting	"direction"
staffwriter	"grammarian"	stillhood	"quietude"
staith or staithe	"shore, riverbank, landing place" (other spelling stath)	stirness	"power of motion"
stale	"place"	stirringly	"mobile"
stale	"a stealing; stolen article"	stith	"stiff"
stapen	strong past participle of step (other spelling stopen)	stithe	"to become stiff"
stark	"to become stark"	stithmood	"firm in mood"
starkblind	"starkly blind"	stithness	"strictness"
starshower	"one that shows the stars; astronomer"	stive	"to become stiff"
startwhile	"moment"	stoe	past tense of stie
starwiel	"astrology"	stonebath	"vapour-bath from water poured on heated stones"
starwieler	"astrologer"	stonebow	"arbalist"
starwieling	"astrology"	stonechessil	"sand"
starwise	"learned in the stars"	stonecloud	"rock"
stath	"shore, riverbank, landing place" (other spelling staithe)	stonedead	"dead as stone"
stathel	"to found or establish"	stonedelf	"stone-quarry"
stathel	"foundation"	stonefow	"stone paven"
stathelfast	"steadfast"	stoneinchel	"little stone"

stonekin	"a kind of stones"	sunderworthing	"special honour"
stonelink	"a stoney ridge"	suneven	"evening corresponding to sunday"
stonelith	"rocky cliff"	sungangs	"moving with the sun"
stonen	"of stone"	sunly	"solar, of the sun"
stoneshraff	"stone-cave"	sunmorn	"morning corresponding with sunday"
stonestill	"still as stone"	sunnight	"night corresponding with sunday"
stonewright	"stone-mason"	sunshime	"sunshine"
stonevat	"stone vessel"	sunstead	"solstice"
stoop	strong past tense of step	swack	"flavour, taste"
stoor	"incense"	swail	"sky"
stoorvat	"censer"	swair	"mother-in-law"
stopen	strong past participle of step (other spelling stapen)	swall	past tense of swell
storve	strong past tense of starve	swallowend	"whirlpool, abyss; a glutton, drunkard"
storven	strong past participle of starve	swallower	"a glutton"
stound	"moment"	swalt	past tense of swelt
stoundmeal	"moment by moment, time after time"	swam	"fungus"
stoven	"treetrunk"	swanger	"heavy, inert"
stowly	"local"	swangerness	"sloth, laziness"
strack	"strict"	swanroad	"swan's road, the sea"
strackness	"strictness"	swank	past tense of swink
strail	"arrow"	swanker	"slender"
strail	"to shoot an arrow"	sward	"rind, skin"
strailbore	"archer"	sware	"to answer"
streamroad	"course of a stream"	swark	"to grow dark"
strind	"generation"	swarking	"darkness"
strith	"strife"	swart	"black; dark"
stroud	"to ravage, to spoil, to plunder"	swart	"to become swart"
strouder	"plunderer"	swarve	"to polish"
strounding	"robbery; spoilation"	swather	"to sleep, to dream, to swoon"
stun	"din, crash, whirlwind"	swathledge	"to search out, to visit"
stunt	"stupid"	sway	"sound"
stuntness	"stupidity"	sway	"to make a noise"
sty	"to go, to ascend" (other spelling stic)	swaycraft	"music-craft"
styer	"climber" (other spelling stier)	swaying	"sound"
suchness	"quality, nature"	swayingly	"vocal, vowel"
summerledge	"to draw on towards summer"	sweal	"to burn"
summerly	"of summer"	swealth	"burning"
sunder	"asunder, apart"	swearingly	"jurative, used in swearing"
sunderblee	"diverse colour"	swease	"sweet"
sundercraft	"special power"	sweather	"to retire, to vanish, to decrease"
sunderfreedom	"privilege"	swevil	"sulphur"
sunderhallow	"Pharisee"	swevilthrosm	"sulphurous smoke"
sunderlipes	"seperately, specially"	sweem	"trifler"
sundermeal	"seperately"	sweer	"sad, heavy"
sunderland	"private property"	sweered	"sad, weighed down"
sunderliness	"specialness"	sweerly	"sad"
sunderlings	"seperately"	sweermood	"sad"
sunderly	"singular, special, private"	sweerness	"sadness, heaviness, sluggishness"
sunderright	"special right"	sweetheed	"The Swedish nation"
sunderrown	"private counsel"	sweft	"sleep"
sunderspeech	"private conversation"	swelm	"pain"
sunderstow	"special or seperate place"	swelt	"to die"

swench	"to vex"	swipperness	"cunningness"
swench	"trouble, toil"	swirebea	"neckband, necklace, collar, torque"
swether	"so + whether, whichever, whosoever"	swirecloth	"neckcloth"
swettle	"distinct, clear, manifest"	swire	"neck"
swettle	"to show, to reveal, to make clear; to become clear"	swirerakentie	"neckchain"
swettling	"manifestation, clarification; Epiphany"	swirerood	"cross worn on the neck"
swettlingday	"Ephiphany"	swith	"strong"
sweve	"to sleep (strong verb); to put to sleep"	swithe	"very"
sweven	"dream"	swithe	"to strengthen"
sweven	"to dream"	swither	"right (hand, side, etc)"
swevener	"dreamer"	swither	"to avail, to become strong, to prevail"
swevenrake	"interpretation of a dream"	swithly	"intense, severe"
swickcraft	"treachery"	swithmighty	"very mighty"
swick	"deceiver"	swithmood	"stout-hearted"
swick	"deceit"	swithsnell	"very swift"
swickdom	"deception"	swithstrong	"very strong"
swickful	"deceptive"	swive	"to copulate with"
swickhood	"treachery"	swiven	strong past participle of swive
swickle	"deceitful"	swoll	"heat"
swicklehood	"deception"	swolten	past participle of swelt
swicklness	"deception"	swone	"swineherd"
swie	"silence"	swonereeve	"swineherd, officer set over the depasturing of swine"
swie	"to be or become silent"	swoneright	"law as to swineherds"
swiedays	"days of silence"	swonken	past participle of swink (other spelling swunken)
swiemass	"silent mass"	swoot	"sweet"
swieness	"silence"	swordbore	"swordbearer"
swienight	"night of silence"	swordbrother	"comrade in arms"
swietime	"time of silence"	swork	past tense of swark
swieught	"dawn of the days of silence"	sworken	past participle of swark
swifthood	"savoury food"	swort	"to breathe hard, to pant"
swiftship	"swiftness"	sworting	"hard breathing, panting"
swike	"to deceive"	swortingly	"short-winded"
swikend	"deceiver"	sworve	past tense of swarve
swiking	"deception"	sworven	past participle of swarve
swime	"vertigo"	swove	strong past tense of swive
swimmingly	"able to swim"	swunken	past participle of swink (other spelling swonken)
swince	"to sound melodious, to make a melody"	swying	"silence"
swincing	"melody"	talewise	"wise in tales"
swincingcraft	"music"	talt	"unsteady"
swind	"to vanish, to pine away, to languish"	talt	"to totter"
swinen	"of swine"	talter	"to totter"
swinely	"swineish"	tamehood	"tameness"
swingle	"whip, scourge"	tavel	"dice, game with dice"
swink	"toil"	tavel	"to gamble"
swink	"to toil"	tavelboard	"gameboard"
swinkdays	"days of tribulation"	taveller	"gambler"
swinker	"labourer"	tavelstone	"gambling stone, die"
swinkful	"toilsome"	teal	"well, fit, proper"
swinkless	"without toil"	teal	"(to) blame"
swinkly	"laborous"	teal	"blame, reproach"
swip	"whip, scourge"	tealend	"slanderer, backbiter"
swipper	"cunning"		

tealless	"blameless"	theedenless	"lordless"
tealworth	"blameworthy"	theedhere	"national army"
teamful	"fruitful"	theedish	"speech, language"
teanel	"wicker basket"	theedish	"gentile"
tearileer	"with tearful cheek"	theedking	"monarch"
teen	"to injure, to vex"	theedland	"inhabited land; district"
teen	"injury"	theedledge	"to adhere to"
teenless	"free from suffering"	theedly	"national, social"
teenred	"abuse, wrong, injury"	theedness	"joining"
teenword	"reproach"	theedom	"prosperity"
tenbebode	"decalogue"	theedred	"fellowship"
tenwinter	"ten winters old"	theedship	"nation"
thack	"roof"	theet	"torrent, fountain, cataract, waterfall"
thaff	"agreeing to"	thelm	"noose"
thane	"to serve, to minister, to wait on"	thench	"seem"
thaneborn	"wellborn"	thereanent	"alongside that"
thanelaw	"rights of a thane"	therebin	"therein"
thanely	"noble, brave, loyal"	therefore	"before that"
thanered	"service, duty"	theremid	"therewith"
thaneright	"right of a thane"	therenext	"next to that"
thaneship	"service, duty; maniliness; valour"	thereout	"outside, without"
thanesome	"obedient"	thereover	"over and above that"
thaning	"service, ministry"	thererights	"thereupon, forthwith"
thaningbook	"book for divine service"	theretoeak	"besides, in addition to that"
thank	"thought"	theretogains	"on the contrary, in opposition, in exchange for"
thankle	"thoughtful"	thereimb	"thereabout"
thanklemood	"thoughtful"	thester	"darkness"
thankworth	"worthy of thanks"	thester	"to darken"
tharf	"need"	thesterful	"dark"
tharf	"unfermented bread"	thesterfulness	"darkness"
tharfless	"without cause or need"	thew	"custom, virtue, moral, manner"
tharfly	"needed"	thew	"to bring up well"
tharl	"vigorous"	thew	"servant, slave" (other spelling thue)
tharlmood	"severe"	thewed	"wellmannered, moral"
tharlwise	"strict"	thewfast	"virtuous"
tharlwiseness	"strictness"	thewfastness	"virtuousness; obedience; discipline"
tharm	"entrail; bowel"	thewful	"moral"
tharve	"to starve, be in need"	thewless	"illmannered"
tharve	"needy"	thewly	"customary, decent, moral"
tharve	"a poor man"	thickfold	"dense"
thave	"supporter"	thickfold	'to make dense"
thave	"to allow"	thickle	"corpulant"
thaving	"permission"	thie	"to take food or drink; to receive; to beg"
theal	"plank"	thiefman	"thief"
theal	"to lay with planks"	thiefyield	"payment for theft"
thealbridge	"bridge of planks"	thien	"a receiving or taking of food"
thee	"to prosper"	thiften	"handmaid"
thee	"you (accusative and dative singular)	thighsax	"hipsword, hipdagger, hipknife"
theed	"people"	thighshank	"thighbone"
theed	"to join; to associate with; to attach; to subject to"	thild	"patience"
theeden	"chief, lord"	thild	"to be patient"
theedenhold	"loyal to one's lord"	thildmood	"patient"

thildmoodness	"patience"	thrall	"serf"
thildy	"patient"	thralldom	"servitude"
thill	"orator"	thrallhood	"servitude"
thillcraft	"elocution, rhetoric"	thrallright	"a serf's right"
thind	"to swell"	thrallship	"servitude"
thind	"a swelling"	thrang	past tense of thring
thine	"your (singular)"	thrave	"to urge, compel, reprove"
thinen	"maid-servant; midwife"	threap	"to reprove"
thing	"to intercede for"	threedaily	"lasting three days"
thinging	"advocacy, intercession"	threehund	"three hundred"
thingred	"intercession"	threehood	"trinity"
thingstow	"meeting place"	threehurn(-ed)	"three cornered"
thingth	"intercession"	threefeet	"three footed"
thinhood	"thinness"	Threemilch	"May"
thirl	"to perforate, to pierce"	Threemilchmonth	"May"
thirl	"perforation"	threeness	"trinity"
thirtywinter	"thirty years old"	threewinter	"three years old"
thitherin	"therein"	threshel	"flail"
thitherwards	"therewards"	threst	"to writhe"
thitheryond	"thither"	threstness	"trouble, pain"
thivel	"shrub, bush"	thrilly	"woven with three threads"
thoe	"clay"	thrim	"multitude"
thoft	"comrade"	thrimfeird	"troop"
thoft	"to join, to associate with"	thrimsettle	"throne"
thoftred	"fellowship"	thring	"to crowd"
thoftship	"fellowship"	thrism	"to press, to oppress, to stifle"
thole	"to endure"	thrist	"daring"
tholemood	"forbearing"	thrist	"to dare, to presume"
tholemoodness	"forbearance"	thristledge	"to dare, to presume"
tholing	"passion, patience"	thristledging	"daring, presumption"
thone	"moist"	thristness	"boldness"
thornen	"of thorns, thorny"	throatbowl	"larynx"
thornhog	"hedgehog"	throck	"table"
thornthivel	"thorn bush"	thraw	"to suffer"
thorp	"farm"	thraw	"sufferer, martyr"
thost	"dung"	thrawerhood	"martyrdom"
thother	"ball"	thrawing	"suffering, passion"
thotter	"to cry, to wail"	thrawinghood	"martyrdom"
thottering	"groaning, wailing"	thrawingreading	"reading about martyrs; martyrology"
thou	"you (nominative singular)"	thrawingtide	"time of suffering"
thought	"to consider; to counsel; to deliberate"	throsm	"smoke"
thoughter	"counsellor"	throsmy	"smokey"
thoughting	"counsel"	throughbitter	"very bitter"
thoughtingly	"deliberative"	throughblow	"to blow through; to inspire"
thoughwhether	yet, moreover, however, nevertheless	throughbore	"to bore through"
thound	past tense of thind (like found)	throughbreak	"to break through"
thound or thounden	past participle of thind	throughbring	"to bring through"
thousandly	"of a thousand"	throughbright	"very bright; transparant; radiant"
thousandman	"captain of a thousand"	throughcleanse	"to cleanse thoroughly"
thousandmeal	"in thousands"	throughcreep	"to creep"
thrack	"force"	throughdelve	"to delve through"
thrake	"force"	throughdive	"to dive through"

throughdree	"to work through; to accomplish"	thweer	"united"
throughdrench	"to drench thoroughly; to saturate"	thweering	"consent"
throughdrive	"to drive or push through, to penetrate"	thweerly	"agreeing, harmonious"
througheat	"to eat through"	thweerness	"agreement, peace"
throughfare	"to fare through"	thwine	"to grow"
throughfly	"to fly through"	thwite	"to cut, to whittle"
throughgleed	"to heat through"	thy	"your (singular)"
throughgo	"to go through, to penetrate"	tial	"pulling-rope, rein"
throughheal	"to heal thoroughly"	tiber	"sacrafice"
throughheavy	"very heavy"	tidder	"to produce, to beget" (related to tudder)
throughholy	"very holy"	tidder	"to become feeble; to decay"
throughleared	"very learned"	tidder	"weak"
throughlearn	"to learn thoroughly"	tidderly	"weak"
throughloath	"very loath"	tidderness	"frailty"
throughlook	"to look through"	tid	"learned, skilled"
throughsee	"to see through"	tide	"to betide"
throughseek	"to seek through"	tideful	"seasonable"
throughseen	"transparent"	tideliness	"opportunity, fit time"
throughshildy	"very guilty"	tidely	"timely, temporal"
throughshine	"to shine through"	tidewriter	"chronicler"
throughshoot	"to shoot through, to pierce"	tield	"tent; pavilion; tabernacle"
throughshrithe	"to go through"	tieldworthing	"feast of tabernacles"
throughspeedy	"very rich"	tieldwright	"tentmaker"
throughsting	"to sting or pierce through"	tiend	"accuser"
throughstand	"to stand through; to continue"	tight	"to draw, to incite, to attract; to instruct"
throughstrong	"very strong"	tighter	"inciter"
throughswim	"to swim through"	tighting	"incitement"
throught	"exertion"	tightingly	"persuading, horatory"
throughthirl	"to pierce through"	tilefow	"tile-adorned"
throughty	"persistant"	tilen	"made of tile"
throughwhite	"very white"	tilewright	"tile-maker"
throughwone	"to abide continuously, to continue; to persevere"	till	"good"
throughwoneness	"perseverence"	timber	"to build"
throughwoning	"perseverence"	timbering	"building"
throughwoningly	"constant, continuous"	tine	"to enclose"
throw	"period"	tinen	"made of tin"
throwmeal	"at times, sometimes"	tintray	"torment"
thrung	past participle of thring	tintraying	"torment"
thrutch	"to crush"	tintrayly	"full of torment"
thue	"servant, slave"	tintraystow	"place of torment"
thueborn	"born in servitude"	tintraythane	"tormenter, torturer, executioner"
thuedom	"slavery, servitude"	tobarst	strong past tense of toburst (other spelling tobrast)
thueman	"serf"	tobeat	"to beat severely"
thuen	"female slave"	tobite	"to bite to pieces"
thuet	"service, ministry, servitude"	toblow	" to blow in pieces; to blow harshly; to inflate"
thuetly	"of a slave, servile"	toborsten	strong past participle of toburst
thunderdent	"thunderclap"	tobraid	"to tear in pieces"
thungen	"excellent"	tobreak	"to break in pieces"
thungenness	"excellence; growth; maturity"	tobrast	strong past tense of toburst (other spelling tobarst)
thurse	"giant"	tobruise	"to bruise in pieces"
thursnight	"night corresponding with 'thursday' "	toburst	"to burst apart; to cause to burst apart"
thweer	"to agree"	tocarve	"to cut to pieces, to cut away"

tochew	"to bite to pieces"	tonim	"to seperate, to take away"
tochine	"to split open"	toom	"empty, unoccupied, free from"
tochurchward	"toward church"	toom	"easy, leisure"
tocleave	"to cleave asunder, to split"	toothgar	"toothpick"
tocome	"arrival"	toqueath	"to forbid"
tocome	"to come, to arrive"	torend	"to rend apart"
todeal	"to divide"	torn	"anger"
todealingly	"seperable"	tornly	"angry"
todealtness	"division"	tornmood	"angry"
todeem	"to judge"	tornword	"offensive wording"
todin	"to strike with a sounding blow"	torun	"a running together; a concourse"
todo	"to apply, to add"	torve	"to throw"
todole	"division; a dividing point"	torving	"a throwing, a casting (of stones)"
todraw	"to draw asunder"	tosame	"together"
todrive	"to drive out or apart"	tosend	"to send to"
toeak	"besides, moreover"	toshake	"to shake in pieces"
tofare	"to go asunder"	toshean	"to break in pieces"
tofall	"to fall down"	toshed	"distinction, difference"
tofall	"descent"	toshed	"to distinguish, to seperate"
tofeeze	"to drive away, to rout"	toshoot	"to shoot or spring apart, to disperse"
toflow	"to flow down or apart"	toshove	"to shove apart"
toflowedness	"flowing, flux"	tosie	"to wear out, to be threadbare"
toflowness	"flowing, flux"	toslay	"to strike in pieces"
toforlettenness	"intermission"	toslip	"to slip away"
tofly	"to fly apart"	toslite	"to tear asunder"
tofore	"before"	toslive	"to split"
toft	"homestead"	toslittenness	"laceration"
togetherward	"towards one and other"	tosnithe	"to cut asunder"
togains or togainst	"towards"	tosooth	"in sooth, in truth, forsooth"
togo	"to go to or into"	tosow	"to scatter, to strew"
togang	"access"	tospeech	"speech to another; conversation"
togives	"freely, gratis"	tospread	"to spread out"
togrind	"to grind to pieces"	tospring	"to spring apart"
tohack	"to hack to pieces"	tosunder	"to sunder"
tohew	"to hew in pieces"	toswell	"to swell"
tokenbearend	"standard-bearer"	totear	"to tear in pieces"
toknow	'to acknowledge or understand"	tothane	"to attend upon"
toknownness	"understanding"	tothind	"to swell or puff up"
toleese	"to dissolve, to loosen"	tothoundeness	"the state of being puffed up"
toleesedness	"loosening, dissolution"	tothoundenly	"arrogant"
toleesingly	"destructive"	totorve	"to throw away"
tolie	"to lie or extend in difference directions"	totweem	"to seperate"
tolimbed	"to dismembered"	totweemedness	"seperation"
tollsettle	"place of toll or custom"	towardly	"in the future"
tollshamble	"seat of custom, treasury"	towardness	"time to come, the future"
tomarred	"defiled"	towarp	"to cast down, to destroy"
tomorn	"tomorrow"	towarpingly	"destructable"
tomids or tomidst	"amidst, among"	towend	"to overturn or overthrow"
toname	"surname"	towither	"against"
tone	"twig, rod, branch; rod of divination"	towcraft	"spinning"
tonesh	"to soften"	towly	"belonging to thread"
tonighledge	"to approach"	toworpenness	"subversion, destruction"

township	"population of a town"	tweem	"divide in two"
townsoken	"legal jurisdication over a town"	tween	"to doubt"
towrite	to write down, to describe"	tweening	"doubt"
towrithe	"to distort"	tweeningly	"doubtful"
towrittenness	"a writing down, a description"	twibeet	"subject to double compensation"
toyear	"this year"	twibill	"two-edged axe"
toyeet	"to pour away"	twibrown	"twice brewed"
tray	"misfortune"	twidaily	"lasting two days"
tray	"to trouble, to vex"	twifold	"to double"
treekin	"species of tree"	twifoldness	"duplicity"
treen	"of tree"	twilly	"doubly woven, of double threads"
treeworm	"cankerworm, caterpiller"	twinen	"of twine"
treewright	"woodworker, carpenter"	twinter	"two years old"
trim	"small piece, short length"	twiread	"uncertain"
trimming	"a confirmation, a strengthening"	twireadness	disagreement"
trimness	"firmness, strength"	twisel	"confluence, junction"
trimth	"strength, support, staff, prop"	twisel	"to fork, to divide in two"
trimmend	"supporter"	twispeech	"double speech; deceit; equivocation"
trindle	"sphere"	tye	"a drawing together, pulling, tug; a draught of water"
trindled	"rounded"	ug	"fear"
trindleness	"circuit, surrounding space"	ught	"early dawn"
trode	"a path"	ughten	"early dawn"
trome	"legion"	ughtly	"matutinal"
trouse	"brushwood (for fuel)"	ughtsong	"morning song"
trouth	"trumpeter; buffoon, actor""	ughttide	"early dawn"
trouthhorn	"trumpet, clarion"	ugsome	"fearful"
Troyish	"Trojan"	un	"to grant, to allow"
truefast	"faithful"	un	"favour, approval, permission"
trueless	"faithless"	unafightingly	"unfightable, inevitable"
truered	"fidelity"	unafilledly	"unfillable"
trueship	"fidelity"	unafillingly	"unfillable"
trum	"strong, firm, healthy"	unafounden	"undiscovered"
trum	"to grow strong"	unaleaved	"not allowed"
trumness	"soundness, health; confirmation"	unaleavingly	"not allowable"
tuck	"to disturb, to ill-treat, to torment"	unameten	"unmeasured"
tudder	"offspring"	unarimed	"unnumbered"
tudderfast	"fertile"	unarimedly	"innumerable"
tudderful	"prolific"	unarimingly	"innumerable"
tuesnight	"night corresponding with 'tuesday' "	unasayingly	"unspeakable"
tumb	"to tumble, leap, dance"	unastirringly	"immovable"
tumber	"tumbler, dancer, player"	unasunderedly	"inseperable"
tungle	"star"	unatamedly	"untameable"
tungleber	"bearing stars"	untiringly	"undefatiguable"
tunglecraft	"astronomy"	unathel	"ignoble"
tunglen	"of stars"	unathel	"to degrade"
tungler	"astrologer"	unathelborn	"not of noble birth"
turdweevil	"dungbeetle"	unathelness	"ignobility"
tweave	"to seperate from, to deprive of"	unatspornen	"not hindered"
twee	"doubt"	unawemmed	"spotless"
twee	"to doubt"	unawemmedness	"incorruption"
tweeingly	"doubtful"	unawendingly	"unchangeable"
tweely	"doubtful, ambiguous"	unawent	"unchanged"

unawently	"unchangeable"	underlout	"to submit"
unbearingly	"unbearable"	undermeal	"morning meal"
unbearingness	"barrenness"	un-dern	"unhidden"
unbeburied	"unburied"	undern	"morning (from 9 a.m. to noon); the third hour"
unbeeted	"uncompensated"	underneathmost	"lowest of all"
unbeflitten	"undisputed"	undernim	"to take in, to understand"
unbehoof	"disadvantage"	undernmeal	"morning time; morning meal" (other spelling under)
unbelievedly	"incredible"	undernmeat	"morning meal, breakfast"
unbelievely	"incredible"	underput	"to put under"
unbereavingly	"unbereavable"	undernrord	"breakfast"
unbesaken	"undisputed"	underntide	"third hour (9 a.m.), morning time; tierce"
unbesmitten	"undefiled"	undersark	"undershirt"
unbewedded	"unbetrothed; unmarried"	underseek	"to examine"
unbighed	"unbent"	underset	"to set under"
unbighingly	"inflexible"	undertheed	"subjects"
unblessing	"curse"	undertheed	"subjected"
unbliss	"unhappiness"	undertheed	"to subjoin, to add; to subjugate, to subject"
unbliss	"to make unhappy"	undertheedingly	"subjunctive"
unblithe	"unhappy"	undertheedness	"subjection, submission"
unbold	"timid"	underthue	"subject, slave"
unbroad	"narrow"	undertonguethrum	"tongue ligament"
unbrosening	"incorrutibility"	underwed	"a deposit, pledge"
unbroseningly	"incorruptible"	underwroot	"to root up"
unbuxom	"disobedient"	underyoke	"to subjugate"
unbuxomhood	"disobedience"	undolven	"untilled, undug"
unbuxomness	"disobedient"	undoom	"unjust judgement, injustice"
uncleamed	"unsmeared"	undreeved	"undisturbed"
uncleanse	"to unpurify"	undrunken	"sober"
uncleansed	"unpurified"	undursty	"timid"
uncomelithe	"inhospitable"	unealed	"unburnt"
uncunning	"ignorance"	uneared	"unploughed; uncultivated"
undavenly	"improper"	uneath	"not easy"
undeadliness	"immortality"	uneathness	"difficulty"
undeadly	"immortal"	unendingly	"infinitive, infinite"
undealt	"undivided"	unfain	"unglad"
undear	"unprecious"	unfanded	"untried"
undeed	"wicked deed"	unfar	"not far"
undeep	"shallow"	unfast	"unfastened"
undeepthankle	"shallow, silly"	unfastread	"inconstant"
underback	"backward, back, behind"	unfastreadness	"inconstancy"
underbear	"to support"	unfax	"without hair"
underbegin	"to undertake"	unforbowingly	"unavoidable"
underbow	"to submit (to)"	unforburnt	"unburnt"
undercram	"to stuff or fill underneath"	unforcouth	"reputable"
undercreep	"to be secretly grasped; to penetrate, to undermine"	unforhavedness	"incontinence"
underdelve	"to dig under, to undermine"	unforletten	"unabandoned"
underdo	"to put under"	unforrottedly	"incorruptible"
underfang	"to seize, to receive"	unforrottingly	"incorruptible"
underflow	"to flow under"	unforspornen	"not hindered"
undergang	"to undergo"	unforswied	"not passed over in silence"
underget	"to understand"	unforwandedly	"unhesitatingly"
undergin	"to begin, to undertake"	unforyolden	"unrequited"

unfoulingly	"incorruptible"	unlength	"brevity"
unfrained	"unasked"	unlichhamely	"incorporeal"
unframe	"disadvantage"	unlib	"poisonous drug, poison; witchcraft"
unfriend	"hostile person"	unlibwright	"worker of spells and poison; wizard"
unfriendship	"hostility"	unlief	"undear"
unfrith	"breach of peace"	unlimp	"mishap"
unfrood	"inexperienced"	unlimply	"unfortunate, inconvenient"
unfullfremmed	"imperfect"	unlittle	"not small, much, great, very large"
unfullfremmedness	"imperfection"	unlitty	"unsightly, deformed"
unfullfremming	"imperfection"	unlore	"bad doctrine or learning"
unfullwrought	"imperfect"	unlust	"evil desire"
unfurn	"not long ago"	unman	"monster; wicked man"
unglew	"unwise"	unmany	"not many"
unglewness	"unwiseness, folly"	unmear	"inwouldersome"
unglewship	"unwiseness, folly"	unmeathly	"excessive"
ungripingly	"incomprehensible"	unmeet	"excessive, immense"
unguestlithe	"inhospitable"	unmeetness	"excessiveness, immensity"
unhair	"to deprive of hair"	unmichel	"little"
unharmyearn	"inoffensive"	unmight	"inability, weakness"
unhattle	"unhostile, peaceable"	unmightly	"impossible"
unhealingly	"incurable"	unmildheart	"merciless"
unhealth	"illhealth; sickness"	unmindling or unmindlings	"unawares, unexpectedly"
unhearness	"hardness of hearing"	unmindy	"unmindful"
unhearsome	"disobedient"	unminged	"unmixed"
unhearsomeness	"disobedience"	unmirth	"sadness"
unheamed	"unmarried"	unmood	"depression"
unhearsome	"disobediant"	unneeding or unneedings	"without compulsion, willingly"
unhearsomeness	"disobedience"	unnigh	"not near, far away"
unhemmed	"unrestrained"	unnit	"useless"
unhend	"remote; discourteous"	unnitly	"useless"
unhendness	"remoteness"	unnitness	"uselessness"
unhent	"uncaught"	unnitworth	"unprofitable"
unhide	"to uncover, to make public"	unore	"dishonour"
uhightly	"without joy"	unore	"to dishonour"
unhode	"to unfrock, to divest of holy orders"	unorely	"dishonourable"
unhold	"disloyal"	unoreworth	"to dishonour"
unholdsome	"unchaste"	unoreworthly	"dishonourable"
unholdsomeness	"incontinence, unchastity"	unoreworthness	"dishonour"
unhope	"despair"	unovercome	"unsubdued"
unhoten	"unpromised, unbidden"	unoverswithingly	"unconquerable"
unimbfangenly	"incomprehensible"	unoverwon	"unconquered"
unimbwently	"unalterable"	unoverwrien	"not covered"
unkindly	"unnatural"	unown	"not one's own"
unkist	"mistake, vice, crime; stinginess"	unpleely	"not dangerous"
unkisty	"mean, stingy"	unqueem	"not pleasing"
unkith	"ignorance; foreign country"	unread	"folly"
unlaw	"injustice"	unreadfast	"unreliable"
unleared	"unlearned"	unreadly	"thoughtless"
unlearedly	"unteachable"	unrect	"to make sad"
unlearedness	"unlearnedness"	unrich	"poor"
unlease	"not false, true"	unrightcraving	"unright claim"
unleesingly	"inextricable"		

unrightcust	"vice"	unspeed	"want, poverty"
unrightdeed	"unrightdoing"	unspeedy	"poor"
unrightdom	"iniquity"	unstaffwise	"illiterate"
unrightful	"unjust"	unstathelfast	"unstable"
unrightheam	"to fornicate, to commit dernlyership"	unstathelfastness	"instability"
unrightheamed	"fornication, dernlyership"	unstathiness	"instability"
unrightheamed	"adulterous"	unstathy	"unstable"
unrightheamer	"fornicator, adulterer"	unstill	"to disturb"
unrightly	"unrighteous"	unstillness	"agitation"
unrightwife	"unlawful consort, mistress"	unstirringly	"immoveable"
unrightwright	"wrongdoer"	unswickle	"trustworthy"
unrime	"countless number, a great multitude"	unswith	"not strong"
unrimely	"countless"	unteal	"unwell"
unroot	"sad"	unteal	"blameless"
unroot	"to become sad"	unteally	"blameless"
unrootness	"sadness"	unteeming	"barren"
unrough	"smooth"	untellingly	"indescribable"
unsaught	"discord, disagreement"	unthank	"ingratitude; evil thought"
unsealth	"unhappiness"	unthankle	"ungrateful"
unseen	"invisible"	unthankworth	"ungrateful"
unseldom	"not seldom, frequent"	untharf	"damage, harm"
unshamefast	"impudent, shameless"	untharfs	"without cause"
unshamey	"unashamed"	unthew	"vice"
unshamely	"shameless"	unthewfast	"illmannered"
unshapen	"uncreated"	unthewful	"unmannerful"
unshedly	"unreasonable"	unthild	"impatience"
unshedwise	"unintelligent"	unthildy	"impatient"
unshedwiseness	"indiscretion"	untholingly	"intolerable"
unshild	"innocence"	untholemoodness	"impatience"
unshildy	"unguilty"	unthroughshootingly	"impenetrable"
unshoe	"to take the shoes off"	unthweer	"to disagree"
unshride	"to unclothe"	unthweer	"disagreeing, quarrelsome"
unsib	"unpeace"	unthweerly	"inharmonious"
unsib	"not related, not peaceful"	unthweerness	"discord"
unsibsome	"unpeaceful"	untidder	"firm"
unsibsomeness	"unpeacefulness"	untidely	"unseasonable"
unsid	"vice"	untime	"unseasonableness, wrong time"
unsicfast	"unvictorious"	untined	"unfenced"
unsilly	"unhappy"	untiringly	"inexhaustable"
unsinny	"guiltless"	untobroken	"unbroken"
unsith	"unfortunate journey, misfortune"	untocloven	"uncloven"
unsiver	"impure"	untodeally	"inseperable"
unslitten	"not torn"	untodealness	"undividedness"
unsmeary	"ungreasy"	untodealt	"undivided"
unsmeeth	"rough"	untodealtly	"inseperable"
unsmeethness	"roughness"	untodealtness	"undividedness"
unsodden	"uncooked"	untoshaken	"unshaken"
unsoom	"disagreement"	untoslitten	"untorn"
unsooth	"false"	untotweemed	"undivided"
unsooth	"falsehood"	untoworpenly	"inviolable"
unsoothfast	"untruthful, unjust"	untrimth	"weakness"
unsoothfastness	"injustice"	untruefast	"unfaithful"

untrum	"infirm"	uparisenness	"resurrection"
untrum	"to be infirm or sick"	uparising	"resurrection"
untrumhood	"infirm state"	upaspring	"to spring up"
untrumness	"weakness"	upastie	"to ascend"
untweeingly	"indubitable"	upastienness	"ascent"
untweely	"undoubted"	upastiennesstide	"Ascension-tide"
untwofold	"not double, without duplicity"	upastying	"ascension"
unwarely	"unwary"	upawend	"to turn upward, to raise"
unwares	"unexpectedly"	upcome	"to come up"
unwareship	"ignorance, folly"	upcome	"rising, origin, source"
unwassombearingly	"sterile"	upfleering	"upper floor of a house"
unwassombearingness	"unfruitfulness"	upfloor	"upper chamber or story, garret"
unwassomber	"unfruitful"	upfly	"to fly up"
unwassomberness	"unfruifulness"	upgang	"a rising, sunrise, ascent"
unwaxen	"immature"	upgo	"to go up"
unweather	"bad weather"	upheaping	"accumulation"
unweeded	"unclad"	uphigh	"uplifted, tall, high"
unweened	"unexpected"	uphold	"a support"
unweeningly	"incalculable"	uphouse	"upper room"
unweenly	"unpromising, hopeless"	uplade	"to draw up"
unwemmed	"unblemished"	uplandish	"from the uplands; rural, rustic"
unwill	"displeasure"	uplong	"upright, erect"
unwills	"unwillingly"	uply	"upper, lofty"
unwinsome	"unpleasant"	upping	"manifestation, accumulation"
unwintered	"immature"	uprist	"resurrection, rising"
unwit	"witless person; folly, madness"	upspring	"a springing up"
unwitened	"unpunished"	upstie	"to ascend"
unwitfastness	"madness"	upstie	"ascent"
unwitful	"unwise"		
unwitherward	"friendly"	waden	strong past participle of wade
unwithmetenly	"incomparably"	waft	"spectacle"
unwitly	"foolish"	wainer	"wagoner"
unwittle	"ignorant"	wainwright	"cartwright"
unwitty	"ignorant"	waken	"wakefulness; watch; vigil"
unwit	"witless person"	waker	"vigilant"
unwierd	"misfortune"	wakle	"vigilant"
unwone	"bad habit"	wale	"slaughter"
unwoningly	"uninhabitable"	wale	"stranger, foreigner, Welshman"
unwonely	"unusual, strange"	walekemp	"mighty warrior"
unworship	"dishonour"	walegrim	"fierce"
unworth	"to dishonour"	walerue	"cruel"
unwrithe	"to untwist"	walerueness	"cruelty"
unyare	"unready"	waleslaught	"slaughter"
unyearnful	"indifferent, slothful"	walestow	"place of slaughter"
unyore	"not long ago"	walhawk	"foreign hawk"
up	"to bring out, to disclose, to reveal"	walken	a strong past participle of walk
upablow	"to blow up"	Walkin	"men of Wales, Britons"
upahang	"to hang up"	wall	"to be agitated or rage; to bubble or boil"
upahavenness	"exultation"	wallen	past participle of wall
upaheave	"to lift up"	wallfasten	"walled place, rampart, fortification, fortress"
uparear	"to rear up"	walling	"bubbling, raging"
uparise	"to rise up"	walllime	"cement, mortar"

wallwright	"mason"	waterly	"aquatic"
walmore	"parsnip, carrot"	waternadder	"watersnake"
Waltheed	"Welsh nation"	watersheet	"watertowel"
wan	"to become wan"	watershench	"draught of water"
wanbelief	"want of faith"	watership	"sheet of waters, waters; conduit"
wance	"to become less"	watersick	"dropsickle"
wand	"to hesitate"	watersickness	"dropsy"
wand	"hesitation"	watertheet	"conduit, floodgate, torrent, cataract"
wandwarp	"mole (animal)"	watervat	"vessel for water"
wane	"deficiency"	waterweedleness	"dearth of water"
wanfax	"dark-haired"	waw	"to move, shake, swing, totter"
wanfow	"dark hued"	wawing	"moving, shaking"
wang	"cheek; jaw"	wayferend	"wayfarer" (cf. fere "to go, to travel")
wanger	"pillow"	wayfoor	"travel, journey"
wangtooth	"molar, grinder"	wayless	"out of the way; without a road"
wanhavel	"needy"	wayreaf	"highway robbery"
wanhavelness	"want, hunger"	waywitter	"guide"
wanheal	"to weaken"	waxen	strong past participle of wax
wanhealth	"poor health"	waxing	"growth, increase"
wanhope	"despair"	waxness	"increase"
waningly	"diminutive"	wead	"alter"
wankle	"unstable"	weadboot	"fine for injuring a priest, which was applied in supp
wanshape	"deformity"	weadhearth	"alter-hearth"
wanspeed	"poverty"	weadsheet	"alter-cloth"
wanspeedy	"poor"	weadstall	"place of alter"
wantonhood	"wantonness"	weadthane	"alterattendant, priest"
wantruth	"incredulity"	weadthaning	"alter-service"
wanwhole	"unsound"	weally	"rich, prosperous"
wanwit	"folly"	weally	"to be prosperous"
waple	"to bubble"	wealsome	"prosperous"
wardman	"watchman, guard"	weapman	"male, man"
wardsield	"guardhouse"	weaponbore	"weaponbearer"
ware	"the inhabitants of a place"	weaponhouse	"armoury"
wareledge	"to warn"	weaponwie	"weaponed warrior"
warely	"careful"	weaponed	"male"
wareship	"prudence"	weaponedbairn	"male child"
warn	"reluctance"	weaponedhand	"the male line"
warper	"thrower, caster"	weaponedhood	"the male sex"
warr	"callosity"	weaponedkin	"the male sex"
warry	"warty, knotty"	weaponedman	"male, man"
warth	strong past tense of worth	weaponedwifester	"hermaphrodite"
washern	"washing place"	wear	"fidelity"
washster	"(female) washer"	wearihood	"weariness"
wassom	"growth, fruit"	wearn	"to pine away"
wassom	"to grow, to bear fruit"	weary	"to make weary"
wassomber	"fruitful; fruitbearing"	weasand	"windpipe"
wassomberness	"fruitfulness"	weavels	"covering, mantle, cloak, clothing"
wassombearing	"fertile"	weaver	"unstable, wavering, wandering; flickering, expiring'
wassombearingness	"fertility"	weaverhouse	"ampitheatre"
wassomless	"fruitless"	weaverly	"theatrical"
waterbreath	"vapour"	weaverness	"show, pomp, pageant"
waterlest	"want of water"	weaverseen	"spectacle, sight, show, display"

weaverstow	"theatre"	wemmend	"adulterer, fornicator"
weaveryearness	"eagerness for sightseeing"	wemming	"defilement"
webbe	"weaver"	wenchel	"child"
webbeam	"weaver's beam"	wender	"translator, interpreter"
webly	"pertaining to weaver"	Wendle	"Vandals"
webster	"(female) weaver"	Wendlesea	"Mediterranean Sea"
webwright	"fuller"	were	"man"
wed	"pledge"	wereborrow	"pledge for the payment of his 'wereyield' "
wedbrother	"pledged brother"	werehood	"male sex, manhood"
wedfast	"to pledge"	wereless	"without a husband"
wedlow	"pledge-breaker"	werely	"male, masculine, manly"
Wednesnight	"night corresponding to Wednesday"	weremete	"man's measure, stature"
weed	"apparel"	wereyield	"compensation, value of a man's life"
weed	"to clothe"	wereyieldthief	"thief who might be redeemed by payment of the wer"
weed	"madness"	westhalf	"west side"
weed	"to become mad"	westlong	"extending westwards"
weedhound	"mad dog"	westmarch	"western boundary"
weedle	"poverty"	westnorthlong	"extending northwestwards"
weedle	"poor, destitute"	westrich	"western kingdom"
weedle	"to be poor"	westrights	"due west"
weedleness	"poverty"	wew	past tense of wow
weedling	"poor person"	wex	strong past tense of wax (other spelling wox)
weedly	"poor"	whalf	"concave"
Weedmonth	"August"	wham	"corner"
weekmeal	"week by week"	whamstone	"cornerstone"
weekwork	"work for a week by a tenant"	wharft	"revolution, circuit" (other spelling whirft)
weel	"whirlpool"	warth	"shore"
ween	"expectation"	wharve	"to turn" (used as a strong verb)
weepingly	"deplorable"	wharve	"to turn" (not as a strong verb)
weird	"fate"	whate	"omen; chance; luck"
Weirds	"The Fates"	whate	"augur"
weirdstaff	"decree of fate"	whating	"augury"
weirdwriter	"historian, chronicler"	whatship	"vigour"
weld	past tense of wold (like held)	whelkred	"shellfish red"
welk	a strong past tense of walk	whelve	"to bend over, to cover"
well	past tense of wall	whichness	"quality"
welldeed	"good deed"	whilefack	"a while's space"
welldo	"to do well"	whilend	"transitory" (other spelling whilewend)
welldoneness	"welldoing, kindness"	whilestitch	"interval"
weller	"lip"	whilewend	"transitory" (other spelling whilend)
wellfremming	"good deed, benefit"	whilewendly	"transitory"
welllike	"to please well"	whilom	"at times; at a past time; once"
welllikeworth	"wellpleasing"	whinen	strong past participle of whine
wellliving	"living well"	whirft	"revolution, circuit" (other spelling wharft)
wellwhere	"everywhere"	whiteleek	"onion"
wellwhich	"each, any, nearly every"	whitelocked	"blondehaired"
wellwilling	"wellwishing"	whitester	"(female) bleacher"
wellwillingness	"benevolence"	whone	past tense of whine (like shone)
wellworkend	"wellworker"	whoon	"little, few"
welm	"a welling, boiling"	whoon	"a little, a trifle"
wem	"to defile, to besmirch, to currupt"	whoonly	"little, small"
wemmedness	"defilement"	whorve	strong past tense of wharve

whorven	strong past participle of wharve
whyth	"reason, grounds"
wickedhood	"wickedness"
widecouth	"widely known"
widemear	"widely celebrated"
widemearse	"to spread abroad, to divulge; to celebrate"
widemearsing	"proclamation"
widesea	"open sea, ocean"
wideyill	"widespread"
wideyillness	"amplitude, spaciousness"
widge	"horse"
widowshroud	"widow's dress"
wie	"war"
wie	"to make war"
wiecraft	"warcraft"
wield	"power, control"
wiely	"war-like"
wiend	"warrior"
wifechild	"female child"
wifefast	"bound to a wife"
wifefax	"woman's hair"
wifefriend	"female friend"
wifehalf	"woman's (i.e mother's) side"
wifehand	"female inheritor, female side"
wifehood	"womanhood"
wifekin	"womankind, female sex"
wifelest	"lack of women"
wifelock	"cohabitation, fornication"
wiferail	"woman's clothing"
wifeshroud	"woman's clothing"
wifething	"marriage, cohabitation, nuptials"
wilddeer	"wild beast" (other spelling wilder)
wilder	"wild beast"
wilderkin	"a race of wild beasts"
wilderly	"savage"
wildern	"like or of wild beasts"
wildern	"a wild place; the wilderness"
wildsome	"wild"
willgame	"pleasant sport"
willingly	"desirable"
wills	"willingly, voluntarily"
willshrift	"voluntary confession"
willsith	"desired journey"
willsome	"desirable"
willsomeness	"desireableness"
willspel	"good tidings"
willy	"willing"
win	"joy"
win	"friend"
win	"toil, labour, hardship"
windedder	"windpipe"
windle	"basket"
windshovel	"fan"
windswingle	"fan"
wineberry	"whortleberry; grape"
winebough	"vineshoot, vine"
winely	"vine-like; wine-like"
winern	"tavern; wine-room"
wineshench	"draught of wine"
winetread	"wine-press"
winetree	"vine"
winewring	"wine-press"
winevat	"wine-vessel"
wineyard	"vine-yard"
wink	"a sleep, a nap"
winlust	"sensual pleasure"
winly	"pleasant"
winship	"friendship"
winsome	"to rejoice; to be winsome"
winsomely	"pleasant"
winsomeness	"pleasantness"
winster	"left"
winster	"left hand"
wintered	"grown up"
winterledge	"to grow winter"
winterly	"wintery"
wintersettle	"winter quarters"
winterstall	"winter resort"
wintertiber	"winter offering or sacrafice"
wintertide	"wintertime"
wiretree	"myrtle"
wiretreen	"of myrtle"
wisehood	"wisdom"
wiseword	"to be wise in speech"
wishingly	"desirable"
wiss	"certainty"
wiss	"to direct"
wissend	"director"
wissing	"instruction"
wist	"being; existance; wellbeing"
wistledge	"to feast"
wit	"we two"
witchdom	"witchcraft"
witching	"enchantment"
witchingdom	"witchcraft"
wite	"to impute; to blame or reproach"
wite	"to go; to depart"
wite	"punishment"
witehouse	"punishment-house"
witelest	"freedom from punishment"
witen	"to punish"
witener	"punisher"
witening	"punishment"
witeningstow	"place of punishment"

witered	"punishment"	withlead	"to lead away"
witern	"prison"	withmete	"to compare with or liken to"
witethue	"man reduced to slavery by law"	withmetenness	"comparision"
witeworth	"punishable"	withmeting	"comparison"
witfast	"strong-witted"	withmetingly	"comparative"
withaft	"behind"	withneath	"beneath"
withbraid	"to withhold, to restrain, to withstand"	withove	"above"
withchoose	"to reject"	withqueath	"to speak against, to contradict"
withcleep	"to call back, to recall"	withsake	"to forsake; to renounce; to strive against"
witheast	"eastwards"	withsaking	"renunciation"
wither	"against; contrary; hostile"	withsakingly	"used in negations"
wither	"to oppose, to resist"	withsaw	"contradiction"
wither	"adversity, resistance"	withsay	"to contradict"
witherchar	"to turn against"	withsaying	"contradiction"
withercore	"adversary, rebel, apostate, sinner"	withset	"to withstand; to set against"
withercorn	"rejected, reprobate, outcast"	withsetness	"opposition"
witherdeed	"hostile deed"	withsit	"to resist"
witherfight	"hostile fight"	withslay	"to oppose, to bring to naught"
witherful	"hostile"	withspeak	"to contradict, to gainsay"
witherfulness	"hostility"	withspurn	"to hit against"
withergame	"contest"	withwest	"to the west of"
witherghost	"hostile spirit"	withwin	"to fight against, to oppose"
witherlean	"requital"	withyond	"beyond"
witherlean	"to lean against"	witlest	"lack of wit, folly"
witherling	"adversary"	witship	"evidence, knowledge"
witherling	"one that is withered"	witten	past participle of wite
withermood	"contrary-minded"	witting	"knowledgeable"
witherquid	"contradiction"	wittle	"wise, knowing"
witherqueddle	"contradicting"	wittleness	"wisdom"
witherqueddleness	"contradiction"	witword	"testimony, testament"
witherread	"contrary, opposed"	wively	"womanly"
witherreadness	"opposition, adversity"	wo	"woe"
witherrights	"opposite"	woaden	"of woad, bluish purple"
withersack	"oposition; apostasy"	wode	"senseless" (other spelling wood)
withersake	"adversary, apostate"	wodeheartness	"madness"
withersake	"to renounce, to become an apostate"	wodehood	"fury, madness"
withersaking	"apostasy"	wodely	"foolish, mad, furious"
witherside	"opposite side"	wodeship	"insanity"
witherspeakend	"a contradicter"	wodesick	"mad"
witherstall	"resistance"	woeday	"day of woe"
witherstand	"to stand against"	woely	"woeful, sorrowful"
withertheed	"hostile people"	woemeet	"passion, anger"
withertrode	"retreat"	woemood	"angry"
witherward	"contrary"	woemoodness	"anger"
witherwardness	"opposition, hostility"	woesith	"time of woe"
witherwin	"contest"	woespel	"woeful discourse"
withfight	"to fight against"	woeword	"sentence of woe"
withfightend	"adversary"	woff	"to rave"
withfore	"before"	woffing	"raving, madness"
withgo	"to go against"	woke	"to become weak"
withhave	"to oppose or resist"	woke	"weak"
withhind	"behind"	wokely	"weakly"

wokemood	"weak-minded"	woodward	"forest keeper"
wokeness	"weakness"	wooerly	"amorous"
wokeship	"weakness"	wool	"pestilence"
woker	"increase"	woolbearing	"pestilential"
wold	"forest"	woom	"noise, tumult"
wold	"power, dominion, realm"	woop	"weeping"
wold	"to rule, to control, to possess"	wooply	"tearful, sad"
wolden	past participle of wold	woopstow	"place of mourning"
wolden	"subject (to); easily controlled"	woopy	"sad, lamenting"
woldend	"possessor, ruler"	wooth	"sound; song"
woldleather	"rein, bridle"	woothbore	"poet"
wolds	"of one's own accord, voluntarily"	woothcraft	"art of speech or song"
wolfen	"wolfish"	woothsong	"song"
wolfshead	"outlaw"	worden	strong past participle of worth (other spelling worthe
wonderblithe	"wonderfully blithe"	wordfast	"true to one's word"
wondercraft	"miraculoous power"	wordful	"talkative"
wondercrafty	"wonderfully crafty"	wordglew	"wise with words"
wonderdeed	"wonderful deed"	wordlock	"speech"
wonderfeal	"very many"	wordsnotter	"eloquent, wise in words"
wondergood	"wonderfully good"	wordsower	"rhetorician"
wondergreat	"wonderfully great"	workcraft	"mechanics"
wonderhigh	"wonderfully high"	workly	"pertaining to work"
wonderkeen	"wonderfully keen"	workreeve	"foreman, overseer"
wonderledge	"to make wonderful, to magnify"	workstone	"hewn stone"
wonderlong	"wonderfully long"	workworth	"fit for work"
wonderly	"wonderful"	worldbusying	"worldly business"
wondermichel	"wonderfully great"	worldcare	"worldly care"
wonderstrong	"wonderfully strong"	worldcraft	"worldly art"
wonderthing	"a wonderful thing"	worldcrafty	"skilled in worldly art"
wonderwork	"miracle"	worlddom	"worldly judgement"
wone	"to dwell; to inhabit; to be wont to"	worldfrith	"worldpeace"
wone	"habit"	worldhood	"secular condition"
wonely	"usual, customary"	worldkind	"worldly, secular"
woneness	"dwelling"	worldlove	"love of this world"
woning	"act of dwelling, living; a dwelling"	worldlust	"worldly lust"
woningstow	"a place of dwelling"	worldman	"man of the world"
wood	strong past tense of wade	worldought	"worldly property"
wood	"mad" (other spelling wode)	worldred	"way of the world"
wood	"to cut wood"	worldrich	"worldly kingdom"
woodbarnet	"burning of wood"	worldsake	'worldly strife"
woodber	"woodbearing"	worldship	"wordly matter"
wooder	"woodman, woodcarrier"	worldsnotter	"worldwise"
woodbuck	"wild buck, wild goat"	worldspeed	"worldly wealth"
woodfasten	"place protected by woods"	worldthing	"worldly affair"
woodfine	"pile of wood"	worldweal	"worldly wealth"
woodhewer	"woodcutter"	worldweally	"rich in worldly wealth"
woodholt	"forest, wood"	worldwin	"wordly joy"
woodhoncy	"wild honey; forest honey"	worldwitty	"worldly wise"
woodleasow	"woodpasture"	wormgalder	"charm against snakes"
woollock	"a lock of wool"	wormgaler	"snakecharmer"
woodly	"woody, wooded, wild"	wormkin	"a kind of snakes"
woodrim	"border of a wood"	worn	"multitude"

wort	"herb, vegetable, plant, spice"	wove	"to be amazed"
wort	"to season, to spice, to perfume"	wow	"to blow"
wortbed	"bed of herbs"	wown	past participle of wown
wortbreath	"fragrance"	wox	strong past tense of wax (other spelling wex)
wortdrench	"herbal drink, medicine"	wrake	"revenge"
wortkin	"a species of plant"	wrake	strong past tense of wreak (other spelling wroke)
wortkindred	"the vegetable world"	wrathe	"prop, help, support, maintenance"
worth	"to become" (strong verb)	wraught	"accusation"
worth	"to honour"	wraught	"accusation"
worthen	strong past tense of worth	wraxle	"to wrestle"
worther	"worshipper"	wraxler	"wrestler"
worthfulhood	"preciousness"	wray	"to accuse"
worthingday	"day of worship"	wrayer	"accuser"
worthingstow	"place of worship, the Tabernacle"	wraying	"accusation"
worthmind	"dignity, honour"	wrayster	"(female) accuser"
worthyearn	"eager for honour"	wreed	"bandage"
worting	"a preparation of herbs"	wreethe	"to make wroth; to get wroth"
wortmong	"mixture of herbs"	wreethe	"to support, to sustain, to uphold"
worttown	"garden"	wrench	"wile, trick"
wortrum	"root"	wrenchful	"wiley, deceitful"
wortrum	"to take root"	wrength	"wrongness; distortion; depravity"
wortvat	"scentbottle"	wrest	"strong"
wortward	"gardener"	wrestly	"pertaining to wrestling"
wote	past tense of wite	wretchdom	"misery"
woth	"journey"	wretchedhood	"misery"
wough	"wall"	wretchhood	"misery"
wough	"crookedness, error"	wrid	"shoot, plant, bush"
wough	"crooked"	wride	"to grow, to thrive, to flourish"
woughdeed	"wrong deed"	wriels	"a covering"
woughdom	"unjust judgement"	wrienness	"a covering"
woughfooted	"having deformed feet"	writhe	"a twist"
woughful	"wicked"	writhen	a strong past participle of writhe
woughgod	"false god"	writingfeather	"pen"
woughhanded	"having maimed hands"	writingiron	"writing instrument, style, pen"
woughheamed	"fornication, dernlyership"	writred	"written condition"
woughheamer	"fornicator, adulterer"	writrown	"letter, document"
woughly	"perverse"	writsax	"pen"
woughness	"crookedness"	wrixle	"to change, to barter, to exchange"
woughrail	"tapestry"	wrixle	"turn, change, exchange"
woughrift	"tapestry, veil, curtain"	wroke	strong past tense of wreak (other spelling wrake)
woughthilling	"wainscotting"	wroken	strong past participle of wreak
woulder	"glory"	wrongwise	"unjust"
woulder	"to glorify"	wrongwiseness	"iniquity"
woulderbea	"crown of glory"	wroot	"to root up"
woulderbea	"to crown"	wroot	"snout, elephant's trunk"
woulderfast	"wouldersome"	wrothe	a strong past tense of writhe
woulderful	"wouldersome"	wry	"to cover"
woulderful	"to glorify"	wry	"cover"
woulderghost	"angel"	yare	"ready"
woulderspeedy	"wouldersome"	yare	"to make ready"
wounden	"wound, twisted"	yarethankle	"ready-witted"
woundenfax	"with twisted hair or mane"	yarewittle	"wise"

yaring	"preparation"	yomer	"sad"
yark	"to prepare"	yondfare	"to traverse over or through"
yarking	"preparation"	yondflow	"to flow over or through"
yarm	"to cry out"	yondshine	"to shine over or through"
yarm	"an outcry"	yondthink	"to think over or through"
ye	"you (nominative plural)"	yonover	"thither"
ye	"and"	yoredays	"days of yore"
yeam	"care"	youngerdom	"discipleship"
yeam	"to care for"	youngership	"discipleship"
yeaming	'care"	younghood	"youth"
yeamless	"careless"	youngledge	"to pass one's youth; to grow up"
yeamlessship	"negligence"	youthhood	"adolescence"
yeamlest	"carelessness"		
yearfack	"space of a year"		
yearl	"to dress"		
yearl	"a dress"		
yearlongs	"for a year"		
yearmeal	"year by year"		
yearmind	"yearly comemoration"		
yearn	"eager"		
yearningly	"desirable"		
yearright	"yearly duty"		
yearrime	"number of years"		
yeartale	"number of years"		
yearwhomly	"yearly"		
yeat	"to say 'yea', to grant"		
yed	"to say or sing"		
yed	"saying or song"		
yedding	"saying or song"		
yeen	"yet, now"		
yeep	"extensive"		
yeeply	"clever"		
yeepness	"cleverness"		
yeepship	"cleverness"		
yelp	"a boast"		
yelp	"to boast"		
yelper	"boaster"		
yelping	"boasting"		
yer	"to sound, chatter"		
yex	"a hiccup"		
yex	"to hiccup"		
yieldwite	"a fine"		
yiss	"to be greedy, to covet"		
yisser	"miser; coveter"		
yissing	"avarice, coveting"		
yissingly	"insatiable"		
yode	"went"		
yold	strong past tense of yield		
yolden	strong past participle of yield		
yolster	"matter, pus"		
yolstery	"secreting"		
yomer	"to be sad"		